FLIGHT LIEUTENANT
THOMAS 'TOMMY' ROSE DFC

FLIGHT LIEUTENANT
THOMAS 'TOMMY' ROSE DFC
Fighter Ace, Record Breaker, Chief Test Pilot –
His Remarkable Life in the Air

SARAH CHAMBERS

AIR WORLD

FLIGHT LIEUTENANT THOMAS 'TOMMY' ROSE DFC
Fighter Ace, Record Breaker, Chief Test Pilot – His Remarkable Life in the Air

First published in Great Britain in 2022 by Air World Books,
an imprint of Pen & Sword Books Ltd, Yorkshire – Philadelphia

Copyright © Sarah Chambers, 2022

ISBN: 978 1 52678 382 0

The right of Sarah Chambers to be identified as the Author of this work has been asserted by her in accordance with the Copyright, Designs and Patents Act 1988.
A CIP catalogue record for this book is available from the British Library
All rights reserved.

No part of this book may be reproduced or transmitted in any form or by any means, electronic or mechanical including photocopying, recording or by any information storage and retrieval system, without permission from the Publisher in writing.

Typeset by SJmagic DESIGN SERVICES, India.
Printed and bound in the UK by CPI Group (UK) Ltd.

Pen & Sword Books Ltd incorporates the imprints of Pen & Sword Archaeology, Air World Books, Atlas, Aviation, Battleground, Discovery, Family History, History, Maritime, Military, Naval, Politics, Social History, Transport, True Crime, Claymore Press, Frontline Books, Praetorian Press, Seaforth Publishing and White Owl

For a complete list of Pen & Sword titles please contact:

PEN & SWORD BOOKS LTD
47 Church Street, Barnsley, South Yorkshire, S70 2AS, UK.
E-mail: enquiries@pen-and-sword.co.uk
Website: www.pen-and-sword.co.uk

Or

PEN AND SWORD BOOKS,
1950 Lawrence Roadd, Havertown, PA 19083, USA
E-mail: Uspen-and-sword@casematepublishers.com
Website: www.penandswordbooks.com

Contents

Foreword vi
Acknowledgements viii
Introduction x

Chapter 1	The Early Years.. 1	
Chapter 2	Tommy joins the Royal Navy 7	
Chapter 3	The Royal Flying Corps 1917–1918 29	
Chapter 4	The Royal Air Force 1918–1926 52	
Chapter 5	Anglo American Oil Company January 1927 – February 1928 ... 66	
Chapter 6	Midland Aero Club Castle Bromwich February 1928 – June 1929 72	
Chapter 7	Anglo American Oil Aeronautical Division 81	
Chapter 8	1931 Tommy Rose's first attempt on the Cape Town record 100	
Chapter 9	Isle of Man Air Service May 1932 – October 1932 115	
Chapter 10	Sywell September 1933 – December 1934 130	
Chapter 11	Phillips and Powis, 1 January 1935 – June 1936, Seagers Gin, July 1936 – August 1938 150	
Chapter 12	Tommy Rose and the King's Cup Air Races 182	
Chapter 13	World Air Speed Record UK to Cape Town and back January – May 1936 194	
Chapter 14	1936 – The Schlesinger Race 213	
Chapter 15	Phillips and Powis (Reading) Ltd September 1938 December 1939 234	
Chapter 16	Chief Test Pilot Phillips and Powis Aircraft Ltd....................... 249	
Chapter 17	Universal Flying Services, Fairoaks.. 274	
Chapter 18	The Alderney Years 1949–1968... 290	

Epilogue 310
Bibliography 311
Index 313

Foreword

Where do you start to write the biography of Thomas 'Tommy' Rose, a man you never knew, or, for that matter had never even heard of, until 2014?

When John Toogood, my father, died in 2014, Mark Toogood, son of Tommy's sister Mary, (who had married into the Toogood family) came to John's funeral and, after a long conversation and reminiscing about the family, as one does at these sombre events, we talked about flying, as my husband Brian has a Private Pilot's licence and I have had emergency training (on the theory of what goes up has to come down safely when there are only two of you in the cockpit).

Prior to this, we thought we were the only pilots in the family as I had thought that the whole Toogood/Rose family were only interested in sailing and golf – how wrong could I have been!

How do I, Tommy's great niece, begin to unravel the life of someone who was reported in the press as a pilot of outstanding performance and a pioneer of private flying? He had apparently been so full of life, spirit and drive, a person with a lovable personality, charming, modest, unassuming, with an incredible memory, marked individuality and genial comradeship. All of a sudden I felt that I just had to research Tommy Rose to find out more.

How do you begin to tell the story of a man you never knew and his life in the air? When I started, I was uncertain as to how much information would still be available fifty years after his death. But, with the help of the computer, memories of people who knew him, newspaper archives, *Flight International* archives (now, unfortunately, no longer available online) and some wonderful contacts, I was ready to put pen to paper!

It is said that some people leave footsteps in time and thankfully Tommy Rose has turned out to be one of them. There are several Pathe newsreels and brief recorded radio and other interviews, together with just a few written statements of Tommy over the years, including a short history of him written by Bert Clarke, the son of the ninth employee of Phillips & Powis Aircraft (Reading) Ltd, at Woodley, Berkshire (who, in 1943 changed its name to Miles Aircraft Ltd) and historian of Woodley Aerodrome but, although Bert had the run of Woodley Aerodrome as a boy, he never worked for the firm.

Bert later became a great friend of Peter Amos, the Miles Aircraft enthusiast and historian, who soon became very interested in what I was proposing, and that was to write the biography of Tommy Rose. With his help I was to learn about his life in the First World War in the Royal Navy, later transferring to the Royal Flying Corps and the Royal Air Force, before entering civil aviation, and soon I began to piece together the life and times of this outstanding aviator.

FOREWORD

As I was getting into the story, I had an incredible stroke of luck. George Burton, a friend of Peter's, was selling some Miles Aircraft magazines on Ebay and the person he sold them to just happened to mention, in conversation, that he was William Hale, Tommy Rose's grandson!

Until then I had no idea that Tommy even had a grandson and so, after Peter had given me this fantastic news, I immediately contacted William, and then went to visit the family.

William has a sister, Anna, and I also met Tommy's daughter, Elizabeth (by his first wife), who was also still alive and well then and in her nineties. However, sadly, she has since died, but it was wonderful to have been given, by luck, or fate, the opportunity to make physical contact with a genuine part of my family, something I could never have imagined when I started my quest.

William very kindly helped me piece together some of Tommy's early history and also provided some excellent family photographs of Tommy and his daughter.

Prior to this, on a visit to Alderney, I met up with Ray Parkin the last owner of the Grand Hotel on Alderney, who put me in contact with Diana (Didi) Hill and her brother Nigel Gaudion, now in their sixties, who were Tommy's godchildren on Alderney. Nigel has several important trophies that Tommy won over the years, together with some original aviation sketches, paintings, photographs and scrapbooks, which I now have copies of, as they give a wonderful insight into this great man.

I hope the reader finds this biography of Flight Lieutenant/Major Thomas 'Tommy' Rose DFC as interesting to read as it was for me to write while I was researching it.

Tommy Rose was indeed a remarkable character and one that had led a very full and interesting life.

I really wished that I had had the opportunity to have sat down and talked to him about his life and his flying career.

Sarah Chambers
August 2021

Acknowledgements

I would like to thank the many people and organisations who have contributed information used in this book. Their names appear either in the text, or the list below. I offer my sincere apologies to anyone I have inadvertently omitted.

Peter Amos for his support, advice and collaboration with writing this Biography.

Brian Chambers, for his support, patience, help and understanding during my many years of research and writing this Biography.

George Burton for accidentally finding surviving members of Tommy Rose's family!

Bert Clarke, Woodley Historian, via Peter Amos; Julian Temple, Consultant, Historian/Industrial Archaeologist and Author; Barton Stacey History Group for their brief history of the Rose family in Barton Stacey; British Newspaper Archive, whose collection of historic newspapers help me source information on Tommy's life and the Rose/Lott family.

Phillips and Powis Aircraft Ltd and Miles Aircraft Ltd archives (via Peter Amos);

Josh Spoor for his lifelong interest in Tommy Rose.

Peter Bugge, Archivist, Guild of Air Pilots and Air Navigators, for the information on Tommy joining GAPAN; Dirk Buytaert, Secretary of the Royal Antwerp Aviation Club, who confirmed Tommy's trip to Antwerp and provided further photographs of the event.

Gill Clarke, Churcher's College Archivist, for Tommy's school record; Isobel Long, Coutts Bank Assistant Archivist, for Tommy's bank application and subsequent employment records; Sarah Christian, Library and Archives Assistant, Manx National Archive, for access to the online Manx newspaper collection.

Martyn Chorlton, Author for historical information on First World War RFC airfields.

Ben Dunnell, editor of *Aeroplane* magazine; Andrew Dawrant, The Royal Aero Club Trust archives.

Malcolm Fillmore Chairman of Air-Britain (Historians) Ltd, for his help with aviation magazine archives.

ACKNOWLEDGEMENTS

Aviation Safety Network, for historical information of aircraft Tommy Rose flew; Nigel Gaudion, Tommy's godson, for help with copying Tommy's scrap books, photographic collection, personal paintings, sketches and trophies once owned by Tommy and his wife Billie.

Harry Toogood, Mary Rose's son and one of Tommy's nephews for early family photographs; William Hale, Tommy's grandson, for the chance to meet him (thanks to George Burton) and for sharing the Rose family archive.

The late Margaret Loderer, a friend of Tommy Rose in Alderney.

Paul Hopff, Vice Chairman Royal Antwerp Aviation Club; The Hampshire Genealogical Society; Diana (Didi) Hill, Tommy's goddaughter; Karen Hill, Alderney Museum Administrator,

Marisa Jefferson, Reference Intern, Dolph Briscoe Centre for American History; The University of Texas at Austin, for information on Anglo American Oil.

Michael G. Jones for his help with Tommy Rose at Fairoaks; Roger Kimbell, friend and source of some interesting information used in this Biography; David Moore, Historic Gosport UK, regarding First World War motorcycle despatch riders and Royal Naval archive.

Bath Rugby Club archive; Museum of Rugby, Twickenham, for help with Tommy's rugby years; Richmond Rugby Club.

RAF Museum Hendon, for access to their archive and confirmation of when Tommy left the RAF; RAF Disclosures Cranwell, for Tommy's service records.

Joanne Turner, Aviation Secretary, The Royal Aero Club; The Royal Aero Club Trust, Andrew Dawrant, assistant keeper of archives; Terry Mace, A Fleeting Peace, web site.

The late Ray Parkin, Tommy's friend/employer and owner of the Grand Hotel Alderney; Colin Partridge for his help with research material; Ben Brown, Sywell Museum, Northampton; Chris and Mavis Parker, Sywell, for historic photographs of Tommy Rose and Sywell Aerodrome.

Surrey History Centre, Woking; Jim Scott, Scott family Archive; Richard Smout, Isle of Wight Heritage Service Manager, for his information on Supermarine; John Oliver.

John Tayleur, Alderney, for photographs of Tommy in Alderney and as a States Member; Gill Trousdale, Secretary to the President of Alderney.

Derek Wands for his unstinting help with any questions that needed solving or clarification; Air Vice-Marshal Andrew White, RAF retired, for his help in researching the RAF archives and advice

Introduction

Thomas 'Tommy' Rose had a modest start in life, born in Hampshire to tenant farmers, the eldest of five children, he was apparently destined for the rural life. However, he commenced his working life with the Inland Revenue and later progressed to Coutts Bank on the Strand.

On the outbreak of the First World War he enlisted in the Royal Navy, as a dispatch rider, assigned to the newly formed Armoured Car Section, which was inspired by Lieutenant Commander Charles Samson. Tommy saw active service in Belgium, SW Africa and East Africa during the early stages of the war, being mentioned in dispatches by General J.C. Smuts in 1916.

Tommy Rose transferred into the fledgling Royal Flying Corps in 1917, where he learnt to fly on the Maurice Farman Shorthorn MF.11, but then went on to become a First World War Fighter Ace. He was awarded the DFC in 1918 for his courageous and outstanding flying, and his commanding officer at the time stated that he possessed a marked degree of real offensive spirit and set a notable example to other pilots in his squadron by his utter disregard of personal danger. Tommy was shot down several times, each time he was not wearing a parachute, as they were still being developed, but he showed a remarkable degree of control of his aircraft to be able to get down safely without an injury.

He transferred to the RAF when it was formed on 1 April 1918 and served in India until returning home to serve as an instructor and fighter pilot until October 1926.

After leaving the RAF he flew flying boats and an air yacht amphibian for a wealthy private owner. He was a pioneer of private flying and helped to install the UK's first fuel pump at Brooklands. He then became Sales Manager for Phillips and Powis Aircraft Ltd, Reading, and later Chief Flying Instructor at several flying schools. He was also the winner of major air races and holder of long-distance records.

In those days, long-distance records were set to be broken but, in the 1930s Tommy took the Imperial Airways route through East Africa, to set up a new world record to the Cape, beating Amy Mollison (nee Johnson), who took the shorter course down the west coast.

Yet today, little is known of this outstanding pilot, who was a true trailblazer of his time in the early part of the twentieth century. With only his maps, visual field references, and the most basic of navigational equipment, Tommy Rose achieved the most amazing feats of aviation and was considered to be one of the finest pilots of his era.

Tommy Rose was appointed Chief Test Pilot for Phillip & Powis Aircraft Ltd at Woodley (whose name was changed to Miles Aircraft Ltd in 1943), in November 1939,

INTRODUCTION

upon the tragic demise of Bill Skinner through a brain haemorrhage He then test flew all Miles monoplane elementary and advanced training aircraft, target towers, and other experimental Miles aircraft, until his retirement in January 1946.

His final pilot's logbook, fortunately the only one to have survived, shows that Tommy had, by mid-1949, when he finally retired from flying, flown over 11,200 hours. This grand total was helped by the incredible number of aircraft he test flew during the Second World War.

A truly action-packed flying life.

Tommy Rose later became General Manager of Universal Flying Services Ltd at Fairoaks Aerodrome in Surrey, and he then finally retired to Alderney in the Channel Islands to manage a hotel.

Peter Amos
18 August 2021

Chapter 1

The Early Years

It is over 127 years ago since Thomas 'Tommy' Rose was born into a very different world to the one we know today, with Queen Victoria still on the throne ruling the Empire, an expanding industrialised world, with steam powered cotton mills, which enabled Victorian Britain to produce half the worlds' supply of cotton cloth. Coal mining expanded to meet the rapid demand for steam power. There was an upsurge in railway construction, to move the coal and subsequent rise of manufactured goods to cities and ports. Ship building moved forward at a rapid pace too and, by the end of the 1880s eighty per cent of England's population lived in cities leaving twenty per cent of the population employed on the land.

Tommy Rose was born on 27 January 1895 in the village of Chilbolton, with its thatched whitewashed cottages and chocolate box rural charm, near Stockbridge, Hampshire, into a large close-knit family of farmers, with very little parochial mechanisation, no electricity and with street gas lighting still in its infancy, little or no sanitation except for outside toilets, 'privy middens'.

Tommy Rose was born into a family of three generations of farmers and was the first child born to John Rose (1869-1929) and Annie Constance Rose (nee Turley 1870-1911), The Turley's were also a farming family from Hope Bagot Shropshire. John and his wife were lodging at Durnford's Farm, Chilbolton, where John's brother William was a tenant farmer and Bailiff, while his wife Charlotte was the Post Mistress of Chilbolton Post Office.

In the middle of 1895 John moved first to Bordean farm for a year, then Basing Home Farm, Froxfield, sometime towards the end of 1896, and remained there until 1929.

Thomas Rose, Tommy Rose's grandfather (who he was named after), moved his family of six children from Garsington, Warwickshire, by the 1881 census they had settled at Newton House Farm, Newton Stacey, Hampshire, just over three miles away from his brother William at Chilbolton. Thomas Rose, took over Bordean Farm, Petersfield, Hampshire, from John when he moved to Basing Farm in 1896. Thomas senior was a tenant farmer working for the Estates Manager Joseph Gale, for the Nicholson family, farming 680 acres, employing twenty-six agricultural labourers and six boys, he was also the local farm Bailiff, until his death in 1899. Lavinia, his wife, moved to be near her son William in 1901 and lived at the Laurels, Chilbolton, until her death in 1905. Lavinia hosted the wedding of her son William to Charlotte Fairbrother, eldest daughter of John Fairbrother, another farmer's daughter, from Great Rollright, near Chipping Norton, Oxfordshire in 1899 and it is at William's farm where Tommy Rose was born in 1895.

FLIGHT LIEUTENANT THOMAS 'TOMMY' ROSE DFC

In 1897 John and Annie added to their family when John Rose arrived, followed by William Rose in 1899, Frederick Rose in 1902, and last, but not least, Mary Rose in 1907, my great-aunt.

By the 1901 census the family had moved from Chilbolton to Home Farm, Basing Park, Privett, in the Parish of Froxfield, Hampshire, just over twenty miles away from where his father, Thomas, had farmed. Basing Park is situated in an area now deemed to be one of outstanding natural beauty and is in a conservation area. Once owned by William Nicholson who, in 1863, bought the estate of Basing Park in Privett, the area at the time consisted of the big house, a small chapel and scattered farms. He proceeded to use his fortune and enormous energy to benefit the estate. William built the new church of Holy Trinity, whose spire at 180ft is the tallest of any parish church in Hampshire, he built a vicarage and school next to the church, where Tommy Rose and his siblings attended, and some workers cottages. He landscaped a park of 400 acres and added a cricket pitch.

By the end of the nineteenth century the estate covered most of Privett and the neighbouring Froxfield. When William Nicholson died in 1909, the estate passed to his son William Graham Nicholson, who later served as MP for Petersfield.

William Nicholson's wealth was derived from gin, as he owned Nicholson London Dry Gin, a distillery in Clerkenwell, London. William was also a gifted player of cricket, who, in 1864, advanced Marylebone Cricket Club £18,333 6s 8d for the purchase of Lord's cricket ground. Out of respect for such benevolence it is believed they changed the club colours from blue to deep red and yolk yellow, the colours of Nicholson London Dry Gin. The stripe is so distinctive and known around the world as the 'bacon and eggs'.

However, it was not just the MCC that flourishes from the colours of Nicholson Gin as, inside the church there is subtle reference to the Nicholson colours, and it was here each of the Rose family were Christened, and where several of the Rose family are buried.

William was also an active member of the Governors for Privett School, and by all accounts was a very kind benefactor to all those living on his estate, and this of course included the Rose family.

It was in this agricultural bucolic environment with none of the modern amenities we expect today that Tommy Rose and his family grew up. It was accepted back in those days that village children would help with the harvest, milking, and other jobs around the farm, at harvest times the poorer children were often marked absent in school register.

The School Years

Tommy Rose and his siblings first attended Privett village school, where they all received a basic primary education. Tom, as he was then known, received a school prize for what would be called today 'creative writing' as reported in the *Hampshire Chronicle* 25 November 1905, and he left Privett school in July 1907.

Tommy Rose then went to Churchers College, Petersfield, Hampshire, between 30 October 1907 and April 1911, where he was described as a 'boarder' in the

THE EARLY YEARS

Tommy Rose's birth certificate.

1910 census, one of just 108 boys, sixty of whom were boarders. The College was founded under the will of Richard Churcher in 1722, a wealthy local businessman and philanthropist who made his fortune through interests in the British East India Company. Churcher decreed in his will, dated 1722, that the College was 'to educate ten or twelve local boys from Petersfield, of any age from nine to fourteen, in the arts of writing, arithmetic, and navigation, so they could be apprenticed to masters of ships sailing in the East Indies'. Churcher's College was established as a non-denominational foundation under the terms of Richard Churcher's Will and has remained so ever since.

Subjects taught during Tommy Rose's time there, taken from the Governor's records were: Latin, History, Scripture, French, English, Geography, Mathematics, Art, Gymnastics, Physics and Chemistry, and it was recorded that the school had the best science facility in the south of England. Greek, German and shorthand were taught as optional extras, but it is not known from the school records if these extras were added to Tommy Rose's curriculum. Tommy Rose excelled in the sports that were offered to the pupils, football, cricket, tennis, and swimming in the River Rother.

The fees were £4 for the term and the school motto, *Credita Coelo* literally translated as 'entrusted to heaven'.

Tommy Rose passed the Cambridge local exams Preliminary in 1908, Junior in 1909 and 1910, and left Churcher's at half term during the Summer of 1911 to go to King's School, Wimbledon, then in Surrey, on 19 June 1911. Unfortunately, Kings School have very few catalogued records, so it has not been possible to find any more details about his time there, other than the register showing that he was in the sixth form (VIB) for three terms until the Summer of 1912, and he played Rugby and Cricket for the school teams.

However, tragedy struck the family in 1911 when Tommy's mother Annie died whilst visiting her sister Drucilla in Small Heath, Birmingham, leaving John a widower, with a farm to run as well as the young family to look after, the youngest being my great-aunt Mary who was only four at the time.

The death of Tommy Rose's mother must have had a devastating effect on him; being the eldest of five children, he was very close to her. This possibly created in him the desire to be independent, competitive, and always wanting to excel in any task undertaken.

Losing his wife Annie clearly caused problems for John Rose, then aged forty-six, not only by losing his life's companion so prematurely at the very young age of forty-one, but also as the mother of the children left at home, and the fact that Annie Rose had not only carried out all the domestic duties, but had also helped with the running of a very busy mixed farm. However, John remarried four years later, this time to Charlotte Pricilla aged forty-one who was the assistant schoolteacher at Privett School.

John died in 1929 at the age of sixty, from a brain tumour, in a nursing home in Southsea; he was brought back to Basing Park, where a very large funeral and interment took place at Holy Trinity Church, Privitt. This was reported in the *Hampshire Telegraph* for Friday, 21 May 1929. The funeral was officiated by three clergy, the Rev. W.H. Perritt, Vicar of Privett, the Rev. W.H. Thomas, Vicar of West Meon and A.E. Edge, Vicar of Froxfield. Those present were several generations of the Nicholson family, by whom John had been employed for twenty-five years and by estate workers, villagers, and interestingly, a member of the Toogood family from Southampton, William Toogood, one of my relatives!

Tommy Rose's youngest brother, William, continued farming at Basing Farm after John's death, but in 1937 he gave up farming altogether to take over the freehold of the Colgrave Arms, 145, Cannhall Road, Leytonstone, where he remained until his death in 1958, but his wife continued to run the public house until 1960.

John Rose junior emigrated to Canada in 1938 after William left to become a publican, winding up the Basing Park farm and handing over to new tenants, to start farming there.

Employment

It was usual in rural communities in those days for the eldest son to follow their fathers into the farming community but Colonel Cody decided otherwise! Tommy Rose at the age of sixteen in 1911, cycled from Kings College in Wimbledon with friends to Farnborough, regularly to see the 'bird man' Colonel Cody, testing his Box Kite aeroplane. It was on one of these visits that Tommy Rose was taken for a brief ride with Cody in his Box Kite. Afterwards he stated 'I shall never forget it as long as I live, thrilling is not the word for it. I went back to school feeling like a hero if ever I felt like one and bought a hat one size bigger. Gosh, what a row there would have been at

THE EARLY YEARS

Clockwise from the far left: Tommy Rose, John junior (behind), John senior (centre), William (right, behind), Frederick (in front, standing), Mary sitting on father's lap, taken about 1912.

home, if they knew I had been up in the air.' But they never got to know about it at home. He went many times to Farnborough and 'managed to scrounge a few more flights out of the Colonel', as he stated at the time. This event had a profound effect on Tommy Rose, it was at this point he knew the farming life was not for him, however, his father decided if Tommy was not going to be a farmer, maybe he could join the Indian Civil Service.

Tommy Rose would need to have a suitable training in finance to achieve this goal. There were many articles carried in the national press at this time extolling the virtues of a career in banking, viz, 'The Occupation of the Bank Clerk, how to secure appointments', which undoubtedly John would have read. The article mentioned that the applicant would be settled for life, rewarded with a dignified occupation, with excellent pensions for long service. All that was required by the applicant was to be well educated, presentable in appearance, of good address, and of fair social position, and Tommy Rose met all the requirements.

Good handwriting and mathematical skills were considered essential, the optimum age was 16-17, although the Bank of England and Coutts Bank did not accept applicants under the age of eighteen which was the reason behind sending Tommy Rose to the Inland Revenue prior to applying to Coutts Bank.

Tommy Rose was there for just a year, before becoming a Bank Clerk with Coutts Bank on 8 December 1913.

The interview notes from Coutts Bank, recorded that Tommy Rose was living at 16, St Mark's Hill, Surbiton, had been educated at Churcher's College, Petersfield and Kings College School, Wimbledon, and that he had completed a year at the Inland Revenue. References were given by his father.

The remarks of the interviewer stated he was a pleasant spoken youth, of fair appearance, and had completed a spelling test with only four mistakes, sums five out of eight, writes quietly, and took two hours ten minutes to complete the test, how many hours were allowed for the test is not known. The verdict was Tommy Rose was suitable for employment, at 440, The Strand, London, where he started work in 1913 on an annual salary of £100 (in today's money the equivalent of about £11,000). In August 1914 Tommy Rose was undergoing the ordinary training of a junior clerk, but what if he had continued as a clerk? Would he have reached the exalted rank of Bank Manager, again we will never know.

Tommy Rose's father had hoped that he would follow in his footsteps as a Farm Bailiff, as it was often the case with parents in those days who chose the career their young sons should follow. However, on 28 June 1914, Franz Ferdinand was assassinated and this led to Austria declaring war on Serbia. On 1 August, Germany declared war on Russia, and on 3 August Germany declared war on France. On 4 August the British declared war on Germany, while Tommy Rose was still living and working in London, and no doubt keeping a close eye as these disturbing developments unfolded.

Tommy Rose volunteered to join up, sometime in early August 1914, like many men of his age at that time, to do his bit for his country, by enlisting in the Royal Navy. Why he chose the Royal Navy instead of the Army might have been influenced by stories of William Rose, a great-uncle who, at the time of the 1881 census, was working aboard HMS *Boadicea*. From September 1886 until at least 1891 he was later on the Royal Yacht HMY *Victoria and Albert II* as a rigger, one of a crew of 240, including, strangely, a great-uncle from my mother's side of the family, Chief Petty Officer Oliver, who was the Purser aboard the same ship.

At the age of nineteen years and nine months, Tommy Rose resigned his position on the staff at Coutts Bank; he recalled later, *'At school I had no difficulty in getting into the Rugger or Cricket teams, but it was a very different matter when it came to getting into the Civil Service! After several abject failures, nine months later my release was arranged by Kaiser Wilhelm II, and as far as I know, my frock coat is still hanging up in its locker at number 440, The Strand, London.'*

Tommy Rose was retained on half pay by Coutts Bank, until he officially resigned on 12 September 1919, having decided to continue with his career in the RAF. For the record, his final pay in 1919 from Coutts was £148 - today some £8,264, a reduced value, to his first salary in 1913 due to post war deflation. The Coutts records show that Tommy Rose joined the Royal Navy Voluntary Reserves, as a Despatch Rider, he then served in the RN Armoured Car Service in Belgium, under Commander Samson, later in South-West Africa, under General Botha and lastly in East Africa, under General Smuts.

Tommy Rose formally enlisted on 22 October 1914, and his service record (F804) shows that it was for the duration of hostilities. He was given the rank of Air Mechanic 1 grade, later deleted and replaced by Petty Officer Mechanic. He was to report to Chrystal Palace for induction and basic training and allocated the administration station Pembroke 111, Chatham Docks, Chatham, Kent.

Chapter 2

Tommy Rose joins the Royal Navy
22 October 1914 to 6 May 1917

'First gain the victory and then make the best use of it you can.'
– Horatio Nelson

It has been very difficult to find details of Tommy Rose's Naval years, due to the fact that on 11 March 1941, Admiralty House, Portsmouth, where the First World War records were kept, was twice hit by bombs during the Second World War. Admiral James moved the HQ to HMS *Victory* when a bomb exploded again on Admiralty House on 17 April 1941.

The First World War commenced 28 July 1914, whilst Tommy Rose was a Junior Bank Clerk at Coutts Bank, perhaps during his lunch hour, or on his way to work Tommy Rose passed the Navy recruitment office at 112, The Strand, and knowing that sooner or later he would be called up, decided to join the Royal Navy Volunteer Reserve as a motorcycle despatch rider, for the 'period of hostilities' and given the service number F804.

At the age of eighteen his height and personal details were shown as: height 5ft 8 1/2 inches, chest 37 inches, hair brown with dark eyes and fair complexion.

Coutts Bank staff records stated that they would release him, on 'half pay', for the duration of the war. What Coutts or Tommy Rose did not know, until his formal application had been processed, was that there had been a very successful recruitment drive to enlist motorcycle despatch riders, the London office had 2,000 more applicants than places at the start of August 1914, a similar response was reported in the regional centres around the country.

The first entry on Tommy Rose's brief service record stated the ship, or in this instance a shore establishment or, in Navy parlance, a 'stone ship', to which he would be posted, was HMS *Pembroke III*, starting on 22 October 1914 until 31 March 1915. From there he was posted to HMS *President II* on 10 April 1915. HMS *President II* was another shore establishment, which also acted as the accounting base and pay office for all Admiralty based personnel.

Tommy Rose's first posting was to the Royal Navy Air Service (RNAS) recruitment centre Crystal Palace for basic training, which had been requisitioned and named HMS *Victory VI*. However, Tommy Rose never mentioned his time in the navy to any of his friends and associates, who all assumed (incorrectly) that he joined the RFC from school.

The Royal Naval recruiting officers were tasked to recruit mechanics into this new branch of the Royal Navy, as on 1 July 1914, the Admiralty finally faced up to the insurmountable differences between their aerial needs and those of the British Army and formed the RNAS from the Naval Wing of the RFC, but it was not until late August 1914 that the RNAS joined the war in Europe.

Crystal Palace served as the reception and initial training centre for RNAS and Royal Navy officers in order to further its reconnaissance role and also to rescue downed pilots. The RNAS used armoured cars as early as September 1914. For this task, and although this was not the first use of such vehicles, they were quickly absorbed into the RNAS, whose Commander C.R. Samson was the first instigator of this initiative, which was so successful that on 3 September 1914, the First Lord of the Admiralty Winston Churchill, ordered the formation of an additional wing of the RNAS to be known as the Royal Naval Armoured Car Division (RNACD).

While the RNACD was being put on a formal footing the more able recruits were selected to train for this division. Tommy Rose was then posted to Chatham, where he had a further four weeks specialist training in the maintenance and management required for a motorcycle despatch rider.

Although no detailed records were available from the Royal Navy, fortunately Coutts Bank kept detailed notes on Tommy Rose's personal file. These stated he had joined the Royal Navy Volunteer Reserve (RNVR) as a motorcycle despatch rider and confirmation of this appeared in the *Reading Mercury* for 22 April 1939 see below:

READING AERODROME MOTORCYCLE CLUB ANNUAL DINNER
The second annual dinner and presentation of awards in connection with the Reading Aerodrome Motorcycle Club was held at The Lower Ship Hotel Reading on Saturday, with Flight Lieutenant Tommy Rose as the guest of honour. In a short witty speech, he told of his happy experiences as a motor-cycle despatch rider in the last war, and later proposed a toast to the secretary Mr D. Broughton and the committee for all their hard work over the year.

HMS *Victory VI*, Crystal Palace, was a cast iron and plate glass structure built in Hyde Park, London, to house the Great Exhibition of 1851 but over 125,000 officers and men were trained there during the First World War.

On arrival Tommy Rose found himself in the corner of the enormous transept just behind the great organ. All around him and the other recruits, slender iron pillars rose into a maze of girders and cross stays which merged into a great vaulted glass roof.

HMS *Victory VI* was run as a ship, recruits quickly became familiar with the ways and traditions of the Royal Navy. The vast building was sub-divided into 'decks' such as the Quarter Deck where the recruits mustered and the Mess Decks for meals. Time was measured in 'bells' (the number of bells signifying the subdivision of any given watch). Caps off on the Mess deck was one of the first conventions when wearing their caps. Hammocks had to be 'unlashed and slung', and then 'lashed and stowed', to leave the Palace precincts was 'to go ashore', the issuing of the Naval 'kit' was thrown over the counter for trying on and, if necessary, exchanged. It was a very strange way of living and one the new servicemen had to quickly become used to. No maternity jacket for the RNAS, but a blue jacket with large side pockets, a waistcoat, grey flannel shirt,

TOMMY ROSE JOINS THE ROYAL NAVY

Tommy Rose's Royal Navy record form F804, this is the only record to have survived of Tommy Rose's time in the Royal Navy. The record has very little detail and, without his subsequent interviews with Bert Clarke later in life, it would have been impossible to piece together his time in the Royal Navy.

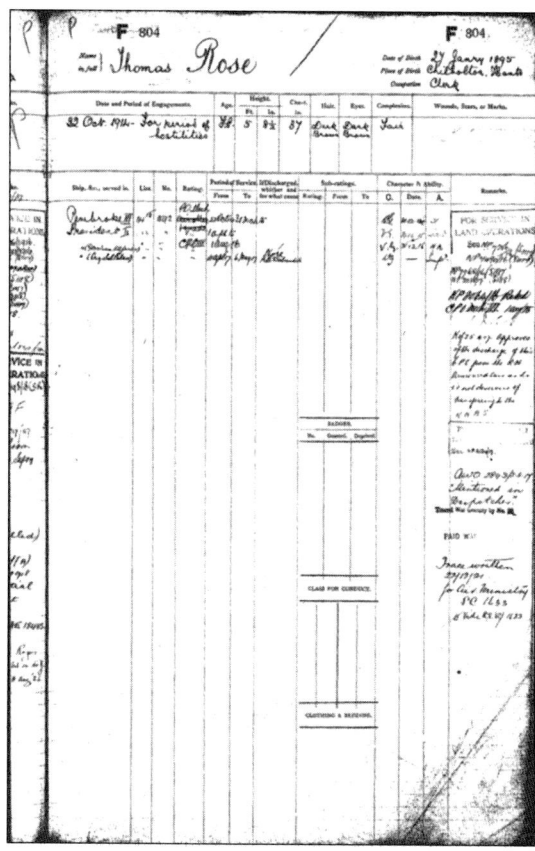

black tie, a peaked cap, breeches, and putties for working, though trousers were worn on Sundays for 'going ashore'. For winter there was a blue jersey worn over a white flannel shirt with its square blue-edged neck. Mechanics (like Tommy Rose) wore the badge of their trade in red embroidery on the right arm. A huge yellow kit bag and a small white-painted 'ditty-box' held kit and personal effects respectively, and the Navy provided a wooden block stencil to mark a man's name, not his number, on his clothing.

The recruits could keep a moustache worn with a beard, but not on its own. Vaccinations and throat swabs were to be endured, PT, drilling and more drilling paced out. Forenoon parades opened and closed with the reading of prayers by the Chaplain. Rifle exercises, physical drill, knot tying and signalling, lectures on seamanship, even a single experience of descending ropes, these were all exercises which formed the foundation for all Service experience no matter how specialist the trade. The new recruits also had lectures on aircraft and engines which would have included stripping down, later in life Tommy Rose took great pride in looking after his aircraft engines, particularly when he was flying solo to South Africa. They were also taught how to use lathes and their abilities were tested, they also had sewing, filing and fitting tests.

Every fortnight a pay allotment was issued from a compartmented tray. So ceremonial was this parade that a rehearsal was held, sometimes a naïve recruit would say 'thank you' upon receiving his pay packet. The response was 'No need to thank anyone, it's yours or you wouldn't get it.'

It was an almost impossible task to get Tommy Rose to talk very much about his early days. In fact it was not until he was over fifty-one years old that he allowed his friends at Woodley to get him to talk, so an article could be included in the *'NEWS' Miles Aircraft Works Magazine* for February 1946, on the occasion of his retiring from his position of company's chief test pilot in January 1946. Without this article we would not have had any idea of his involvement in the First World War, or in what aircraft he made his first solo, it really was a journalistic 'scoop':

> 'At School I had no difficulty in getting into the Rugger or Cricket sides, but it was a very different matter when it came to getting into the Civil Service! After several abject failures, my father bought me a frock coat, and I entered the service of the "Kings Bankers". After nine months my release was arranged by Kaiser Wilhelm II, and as far as I know, my frock coat is still hanging up in its locker at number 440, The Strand.
>
> 'At the beginning of the First World War I was in the Royal Naval Armoured Cars and, with Commander Samson's assistance, I endeavoured to annoy the Huns in Belgium. Later, General Botha helped me clear the enemy out of German South-West Africa, and later still, with the assistance of General Smuts, British East Africa was cleared. From 1916 onwards, it has been flying; little ones and big ones, good ones and bad ones – both men and aeroplanes.
>
> 'My first solo in a Shorthorn was a memorable performance; my astonishment at survival was only excelled by that of my instructor. The RAF tolerated me until the end of 1926, and those ten years and the eleven I have been here, have been the happiest of my young life.
>
> 'There are some who look on fifty-one as being a great age, yet in most ways I feel no different than I did at forty. Of one thing I am certain; it is that friends and friendliness make life worth living. To work for and with people who are one's friends is great good fortune.'

Motorcycle despatch rider training Chatham

At the outbreak of the First World War motorcycles (M/Cs) were little more than crude approximations of the modern bicycle. From the early 'safety bicycles' to the 'motorcycles', most were little more than internal combustion engines mounted onto wooden frames. But most major manufacturers took notice of the early four-stroke engines, like the De Dion Bouton, copying its construction.

The motorcycle had evolved by the time the First World War broke out in 1914, and manufacturers like Clyno, Blackburne, Douglas (who had a contract to supply 300 per month), Triumph, Royal Enfield, Sun, BSA, Phelan and Moore and Norton, were contracted to supply motorcycles to the war effort.

Though production figures are difficult to establish, it is estimated that Douglas alone produced 70,000 motorcycles for the allied forces, 25,000 of which were 348cc twin-cylinder machines, made specially for the Army's new despatch riders. Triumph boasted a British order for 30,000, though it also supplied Greek despatch riders with single-engine motorcycles. Royal Enfield manufactured for both the UK war department and also won a contract to supply the Russians.

However, 1914 motorcycles were mostly belt-driven with side-valve, two stroke engines and very little suspension. Although the seat was fairly well sprung, with two springs underneath, it would move about.

If it rained hard, or if you were riding in the snow, the belt would inevitably slip because it would slide around the pulleys. Riders got used to having a pocket or tin full of sand, which they sprinkled over the belt and the pulleys to help them to grip, if you were in the countryside then you could sprinkle some dry soil over the belt.

The Admiralty at Chatham bought fifty Triumphs in 1914 for despatch rider duties, and many unsuccessful applicants, with or without their motorcycles, were accepted by Scotland Yard on different terms to patrol country districts, these motorcycles carried a plate on the front with the lettering 'OHMS'.

As the war progressed the wide variety of volunteered machinery presented maintenance and spares problems and was progressively replaced by a limited range of military models.

The Triumph Model H was a single-cylinder machine with a 4 hp air-cooled engine of 499cc and proved to be very reliable on the battlefield, earning it the nickname 'The Trusty'. Many of them were fitted with sidecars and machine guns, and 30,000 Model Hs were estimated to be in use on the front lines by the end of the First World War.

At Chatham, Tommy Rose learned what was expected of him as a despatch rider and how to maintain his Triumph Model H, whilst still having to participate in the daily drill, physical activities, the stripping and assembling of his firearms, target practice and of course getting used to riding 'The Trusty'.

The basic kit of spares required for the motorcycle despatch rider in the field was as follows:

- One valve, complete with spring, washer and cotter
- One spark plug
- One piston ring
- A tyre repair kit including spares for valve
- A spare tyre
- A spare tube
- A spare belt and fastener (if belt-driven)
- A spare link and spare chain (if chain-driven)
- Complete set of spares for the magneto
- Selection of nuts and washers
- Two valve cap washers (if used on machine)
- Complete set of tools
- Two gaiters for tyre repairs
- A spare 'cover' to be carried by signal units for each machine (a tyre)

Despatch riders were used by the armed forces to deliver urgent orders and messages between headquarters and military units. They had a vital role when telecommunications were limited and insecure. They also used to deliver carrier pigeons, these were strapped onto the parcel shelf at the rear of the motorcycle in special carriers. They also acted as scouts, carrying out patrol, security, despatch, and courier duties. They also acted as mounted infantry and ammunition carriers, medical supply, casualty evacuation (with side cars), very light transport (again with side cars) and signals. They were also a reasonably quick and secure means of delivering written orders, reports, maps, aerial photographs, signed authorisations and many other items.

Behind the lines despatch riders effectively provided what could be regarded as a military postal service.

After training, Tommy Rose, with his motorcycle, was assigned to Commander Samson who had established a base near Dunkirk sometime mid-December 1914, to support the Royal Marine Brigade, which in turn had been attached to the Belgium Army.

Royal Navy Air Service (RNAS) Armoured Car Section

The Royal Naval Air Service in August 1914 had ninety-three aircraft, six airships, two balloons and 727 personnel and, by August 1915, came under the control of the Royal Navy.

The RNAS Armoured Car Section was set up with nine aircraft and 125 men commanded by Charles Samson, and his brother Felix, recently commissioned as a Lieutenant in the RNVR, was in charge of the motor transport for the squadron, with six cars, ten bus chassis and several other acquired vehicles. One of the cars, his own Mercedes touring car, was equipped with a Maxim machine gun and, after a few frustrating days, they ended up in Dunkirk where they got news of a new kind of warfare.

The first patrol comprised two cars, nine men, and one machine gun. Inspired by the success of the Belgians' experience of armoured cars, Samson's cars were a Mercedes and an armoured Rolls-Royce. These vehicles initially had only partial protection, with a single machine gun firing backwards, and were the first British armoured vehicles to see action. Within a month most of Samson's cars had been armed and some armoured. These were joined by further cars which had been armoured in Britain with hardened steel plates at Royal Navy workshops. The force was also equipped with some trucks, which had been armoured and equipped with loopholes so that the Royal Marines carried in them could fire their rifles in safety.

Both the Mercedes and the Rolls-Royce were equipped with a 0.303 calibre (7.62mm) Maxim machine gun to supplement the lack of aircraft. After a few sorties, they were armoured with boiler plates, and later used in co-ordination with observer aircraft that were available to spot the enemy.

So successful were the armoured car sorties, that a decision was made by the War Office in October (the month Tommy Rose enlisted), to convert all other Rolls-Royce Silver Ghost chassis to armoured cars.

A committee, headed by the Admiralty Air Department, rationalised the conversion and set up new tactical units, creating the Armoured Car 1914 Pattern.

The Rolls-Royce Silver Ghost of 1914 were more expensive than other sedans and coupes and they were built to a very high standard of quality and reliability. Their petrol engines were carefully crafted 6-cylinder, water cooled and gave 80hp and the early series name came from its all over silver finish. The engine ran without vibration and noise, and it was said at the time it was customary for the car salesman to put a customer's coin on edge, right on the central hinge of the bonnet of the engine and start the engine, to illustrate this.

The chassis was a 2 x 4 with a single front and double rear axles, with wire wheels, with two to four spares. The armour was made of 0.47 in (12mm) rolled steel plates, riveted around the chassis to a light frame. Flight Commander T.G. Hetherington defined the armoured bodyworks most important feature: a revolving turret (Admiralty turreted pattern) fitted with folding panels on each side and a small hatch for the commander in the middle. It housed a regular water cooled standard naval 0.303 calibre (7.62 mm) Vickers machine gun. The engine bonnet and radiator were completely armoured. The rear of the chassis, between and above the axle, was for storage boxes, spare parts, and everything else required. There were also the side-walks available for storage.

It is estimated that 120 vehicles were converted for the RNAS by 1915. Rolls-Royce was later requested to build aero engines, which took priority over the armoured cars.

Belgium 18 December 1914 to 2 March 1915

With Commander Samson annoying the Huns in Belgium.
In the late Summer of 1914 Samson took No. 3 RNAS Squadron from Eastchurch to France, where it supported Allied ground forces along the French and Belgium frontiers, and with too few aircraft at his disposal, Samson instead had his men patrol the French and Belgium countryside in the privately owned cars some of them had taken over with them. Despite its early endeavours, armoured car development in the UK was almost zero.

By the end of September 1914, Commander Samson's force had grown dramatically in size and power. The Germans had placed a price on his head, but the British Army in France dismissed this, they felt his unit was just a bunch of clowns, who should go home and leave the fighting to the professionals, hence the unit was given the nickname of the 'Dunkirk Circus'. Closer acquaintance with Samson's men led to the less-friendly epithet 'Motor Bandits', as the RNAS helped themselves to whatever Army transport, stores and equipment they required to fill the shortages in material provided by the Navy. Some people would say they were only using their initiative, others, including the 'Tommies', would christen them the 'Motorised Bastards', as they fell prey to the ruthless relocation of their military supplies, but none of that bothered Samson!

Samson had under his direct command twenty-one aircraft, over twenty armoured cars, 250 Marines and 150 naval personnel. The aircraft were divided into HQ Squadron, based at Morbecque and Dunkirk, No. 1 Squadron (to which Tommy Rose was assigned) and No. 2 Squadron, both based at Antwerp, and No. 3 Squadron at Morbecque, which had just returned from Lille. The armoured cars were divided into three sections by type: No. 1 Rolls-Royce, No. 2 Wolseley and No. 3 Talbot, and then there was a mixed section of armoured lorries and other armoured cars. By trial and error Samson had developed a number of tactics on the best way of using these armoured cars in war and these were beginning to decimate the Germans. He wrote down and reproduced them in a pamphlet that all new men (including Tommy Rose) had to read.

Samson drew up a list of 'Ten lessons learnt from Operations':

1. Five or six cars are enough to work together as any more in the patrol complicated mobility.
2. Lewis guns were by far the best machine gun for motor car work. The problem was that the belts for the Maxim gun jammed when wet.
3. Rifle grenades should always be carried in all cars.
4. No cars should be taken out on patrol unless they could do over 40 mph.
5. Electric lights are a necessity.
6. Rope should always be carried in or on the cars.
7. Not more than five men should be carried in each car, except for the armoured trucks.
8. The Talbot fast lorry was the best available to him.
9. The driver should be able to leave his seat quickly or be pulled from his seat quickly and easily.
10. Boiler plate is not bulletproof at close quarters.

In less than four weeks Samson had created a new and innovative way of fighting, developed the tactics and the means of using these new weapons, and more importantly used it with outstanding success against the Germans. Everyday Samson's aircraft were attacking the enemy using both high explosive and incendiary bombs, these actions helped Samson develop and school his men in these new and extremely effective tactics which they could use to take the fight to the Germans. On 30 September things worsened in Antwerp, the Germans shelled and destroyed the waterworks for the city, and after a month of non-stop fighting, Samson and his force had to take on the new duties around Antwerp.

This aggressive patrolling by Samson's improvised force in the area between Dunkirk, and Antwerp did much to prevent German cavalry divisions from carrying out effective reconnaissance, and with the help of Belgian Post Office employees, who used the intact telephone system to report German movements, he was able to probe deeply into German occupied territory.

Tommy Rose and a few other newly trained RNAS recruits, were sent out to join Samson in mid-December 1914, who was now in command of No. 2 Aeroplane Squadron, later renamed No. 3 Wing. The weather had been terrible, so no useful reconnaissance work could be undertaken either on the ground or in the air. There were also problems between Lord Kitchener, who was against the Royal Navy being involved, and Sir John French, Commander in Chief BEF since war was declared, the ill-feeling between these men kept growing. Asquith had asked Churchill to interfere between these two men for the sake of the Army. Churchill was 'piggy in the middle' between two very powerful men and it was not a good place to be. In the end it would rebound on Churchill and he would lose his position as First Lord of the Admiralty.

Lord Kitchener sent Churchill a letter on 23 December 1914:

> *I am sorry to see in your letter that you have gone back upon what was agreed to between us with regard to the future of the various formations that you have raised at different times for service with the Army.*
>
> *The Navy and the Army have each their definite role to perform, and I think it is a good rule that the Admiralty and the War Office should confine themselves to the supply of the services required by their respective Departments. Armoured trains, bus transport, armoured cars are, or can be, provided by the War Office when required; they are subsidiary services pertaining to the Army on land, and not Naval services.*
>
> *If these irregular formations are only a means to enable certain officers, and gentlemen without military experience and training, to get to the front and take part in the war, then I think it is more important, if they are kept on, that they should form part of the Army, and not claim to be separate entities under the control of the Admiralty; I know how anxious you are to do all in your power to promote the success of our army in France, and when I tell you that the morale of the army in the field is affected by these irregular Naval additions and therefore its fighting power impaired, as well as that they cause discontent and give trouble to the staff entirely out of proportion to their utility, I think you will agree with me that it is essential that something should be done to regularise the situation.*

As far as Kitchener was concerned this was going to be the end of naval units operating in France and naval personnel were to be given the choice of joining the Army and staying in France or staying with the Navy and going back to England.

Faced with this, on 24 December, Churchill shot back a ten-page letter about Naval units in France, just how successful they had been and just how much help the Army had required to save it at Ypres. It was unfortunate, as in many respects the letter rubbed Kitchener's nose in the facts:

> *I cannot for the life of me understand why the various naval units now serving with the Army in France cannot be treated in the same way as naval detachments have always been treated by the Army in Egypt, South Africa and in many other campaigns.*
>
> *On returning to the Admiralty today, I have been shown the numbers of precedents where small and large detachments of sailors under the Naval Discipline Act, serving in their own units and under their own officers in charge of guns, in charge of armoured trains, or as infantry, have all served all over the world side by side with their military comrades, receiving their orders from the military commander. I cannot understand why the precedent of the past should be thrown over entirely now and the choice put to every sailor of either becoming a soldier or being sent home. (PRO30/57/72).*

FLIGHT LIEUTENANT THOMAS 'TOMMY' ROSE DFC

Churchill then went on for most of the letter to list all the successes of all the various naval units in France: the three armoured trains, sixty buses, seventy lorries, aeroplane squadrons at Dunkirk and Antwerp and finally the armoured car section which acted as a fire brigade on the front line helping plug gaps in British, French and Belgium lines and so on. Unfortunately, being right was not enough to rebuild the relationship, especially as he had laid out so comprehensively the extent to which the forces Kitchener and French disliked so much, had done so much to aid the Allies in the field.

On 31 December, Churchill wrote to Kitchener again and basically agreed to pull some of his naval units out of France and to hand others over to the army. His motive in recalling Samson and his men, was that he wanted to retain control of this very successful unit and to keep the men together as they had worked very well. He also had plans for them. The bus section was transferred to the Army Service Corps but remained a single unit serving the Ypres area for most of the war. The armoured trains were handed over to the Army and the Armoured car sections would be held at Wormwood Scrubs until the Army asked for them. The lorries were distributed amongst the Army Service Corps units and possibly, unbeknown to them, some of the vehicles were returned to their original owners. (Churchill Archives: CHAR 13/27B)

This was the beginning of the end for the 'Motor Bandits' in France. Soon they would be going to a place that was much warmer. The demise of this unit was not the fault of the men or the equipment that they had designed and developed, they were the casualties of a political and private war between three very powerful men. Time and again the RNAS in Dunkirk had punched well above its weight to help defeat the Hun. It had helped the Belgium and French Armies, and it had helped the BEF and the RFC. This small force had more decorations than any other British unit and received great honours from the Allied countries they had fought alongside. This small band of men made history every day of the first six months of the First World War. They escorted the largest ever military vehicle convoy for the first time in Antwerp: some 145 vehicles. Samson's pilots could be flying in the morning and in the afternoon commanding an armoured car attacking the Uhlans (German cavalry) on the ground.

But, between the RFC and the RN, the men of the RNAS and particularly this unit, have been forgotten, perhaps some would say even written out of history. Samson pushed the boundaries of innovation and warfare every day when they went out to find and fight the Germans. They fought alongside men from Belgium, France, Britain, North Africa, and India. Today when you ask the Royal Navy, the British Army or the Royal Air Force for information or documents on this unit they come back with the reply 'we have nothing'. Yet this small highly decorated force, at first under 200 men, should not be forgotten, they deserve their place in the memory of both aviation and ground warfare. There is no plaque, memorial or any other kind of remembrance for them, which is incredibly sad for all those men who heroically served in the RNAS, and this included Tommy Rose.

The 27 February was a day of farewells, a sad day for Samson and his officers and men. They had all made a lot of good friends in the Dunkirk area and the thought of leaving the cold, damp and very makeshift billets behind was very upsetting. None of them wanted to end up as instructors or teachers at a training station as they all thought would happen.

TOMMY ROSE JOINS THE ROYAL NAVY

Samson went off to General Bidon's HQ and said his farewells to the general and his staff. After that he went to have his last lunch with the Commandant of the French Squadron that shared the airfield with them, and what a lunch it was. That evening all the pilots met up and a sweep was organised amongst the pilots for the first one back at Dover.

The weather was not at all good on Sunday, 28 February. Samson and his pilots decided one last lunch was required and retired to Café des Arcades, but after lunch the fog was still there and just as bad. However, Samson felt it had cleared a little, possibly due to the wine at lunch, and a number of pilots took off.

Upon landing Samson waited for the rest of the squadron, who started turning up later that afternoon, with the last one landing the next morning.

Tommy Rose arrived back at Dover on 2 March 1915 ready to return to the RNAS base at Eastchurch. Samson was being posted to the Dardanelles and Tommy Rose was being sent with the No. 1 Armoured Car Squadron to South-West Africa.

The RNAS, whilst in Belgium, dropped a total of sixty-one bombs on various targets with a combined weight of 1,620 lb.

They attacked the following:
- Two workshops containing U-boats were damaged and about twenty workers killed and wounded.
- One U-boat damaged in Zeebrugge.
- Several gun batteries to the south of Zeebrugge were badly damaged with a number of guns destroyed. The water tower was also badly damaged.
- The Rombach Central Electric works and the coke works in Zeebrugge were put out of action. This then stopped all the swing bridges from working as they had no power.
- The German seaplane shed on the mole at Zeebrugge was destroyed.
- A breach was made in the mole at Zeebrugge.
- Two trawlers from Zeebrugge used for minesweeping were sunk.
- A large section if the railway track was damaged.
- The Cockerill steel works were badly damaged.
- A train containing stores and U-boat supplies was destroyed at Ostend.
- A railway station and goods yard was destroyed by fire.
- Sheds near the station were also damaged, and the hotel near the station damaged.
- The De Smet de Baeyer bridge was badly damaged.
- One officer and thirty-seven men were killed and a large number of men wounded from the various gun batteries in and around Ostend.
- The station at Blankenberghe was totally destroyed, along with a large section of track.
- A large number of guns around Blankenberghe were either damaged or destroyed and their crews suffered, one officer and twenty men being killed, and over fifty-five men wounded.

The damage recorded above was reported on in various American newspapers and also by various intelligence networks including Samson's own network run by O'Caffrey.

Commander (later Air Commodore) Charles Rumney Sampson CMG, DSO & Bar, AFC

Commander Samson created a lasting impression on Tommy Rose and it is safe to say inspired Tommy Rose more than any other commanding officer did, but who was he?

Commander Charles Rumney Sampson commanded the *first* British armoured vehicles used in combat, he was the *first* British pilot to take off from a ship, on 10 January 1912, flying a Short S.27 from a ramp mounted on the foredeck of the battleship HMS *Africa*, which was at anchor in the River Medway. On 9 May 1912, he became the *first* pilot to take off from a *moving* ship, using the same ramp and aircraft, now fitted to the battleship HMS *Hibernia*, he repeated the feat again, on 4 July 1912, this time from the battleship HMS *London*, while it was under way.

He developed the *first* navigation lights and bomb sights. When the Royal Flying Corps was formed in May 1912 Samson took command of its Naval Wing, and led the development of aerial wireless communications, bomb and torpedo dropping.

Tommy Rose and several others in his crew were then assigned to No. I RNAS Armoured Car Squadron (ACS), who were being made ready to sail to the Campaign in South-West Africa under the command of Lieutenant Commander Whittall, with overall command of the campaign being held by General Botha.

German South-West Africa Campaign 1915

Helping General Botha clear the enemy out of German S W Africa
The No. 1 RNAS Armoured Car Division sent to South-West Africa in April 1915, consisted of:

> Lieutenant Commander Whittall the Commanding Officer
> Two Lieutenants
> Three Sub Lieutenants
> Five Chief Petty Officers
> Sixty-five Petty Officers (including Tommy Rose)
> Total of seventy-six

The voyage out to South-West Africa was on a 13,000 ton Australian troop ship, which had brought over as part of the Australian contingent, to drop the squadron at Walfish Bay on the way back to Australia, where she was bound on another trooping trip. The squadron had the ship to themselves, and with ten officers and about 120 other ratings the ship was rather empty. They saw nothing of other shipping, except a French steamer bound for St Helena, during the whole voyage, with fine weather the whole way down to South-West Africa. Drill instruction and sports made the voyage pass both quickly and pleasantly and by the sixteenth day they were at anchor at Walvis Bay.

TOMMY ROSE JOINS THE ROYAL NAVY

Tommy Rose in Royal Navy tropical uniform on the way to South-West Africa, 1915. (*Harry Toogood*)

Walvis Bay had been made a base for the Northern Force destined to co-operate in the conquest of South-West Africa. Although a British possession, with the only real harbour on the whole west coast of Africa, nothing had ever been done to develop it. It had been for many years a whaling station of some importance.

The most important features of the landscape were two groups of lanky iron chimneys belonging to the whaling station and the condenser plant.

The landing arrangements at Walvis were in the control of Commander Price RNVR, who was a senior naval transport officer.

Price managed to spare four pontoons and was able to have them towed alongside a half finished jetty a mile above the town, and so began the most strenuous two days the squadron had ever experienced. Twelve light armoured cars, with support vehicles. 'Light' was an understatement, since the armour-plated Rolls-Royce touring cars, with Vickers machine guns in revolving turrets, tipped the scales at about four tons. There was also a couple of hundred tons of stores, to be slung over the side of the ship and lashed onto the pontoons, and then landed onto a rickety jetty. To add to this, there was a heavy tidal range alongside the jetty, so the pontoons constantly surged six or more feet in both directions. This made it a very risky business in getting the armoured cars ashore, as the only way to do that was to drive them under their own power across a couple of narrow planks. However, thanks to the skill of the drivers and a lot of luck, everything was landed safely ashore.

During the first few days at Walvis, the squadron had their first experience of the fly plague. Inside the tents you could not put a finger on the canvas without touching a fly, there was nothing that could be done to combat this plague, other that endure it with grim resignation.

Commander Whittall's order came through to proceed to Swakopmund, where General Botha had his headquarters, to discuss the disposition of the squadron in the coming advance, Nalder the second in command was left in charge while Whittall went to Swakopmund via motor trolley over the new railway, he covered the twenty mile journey within an hour.

After declaring war on Germany on 4 August 1914, Britain asked the Union of South Africa, then a British dominion, to invade German South-West Africa. The British hoped their ally would be able to neutralise powerful German radio facilities located in

Lüderitz, Swakopmund and Windhoek, and seize key port facilities; the Union of South Africa agreed to assist.

The Union of South Africa (SAU) troops, commanded by Colonel P.S. Beves landed at Lüderitz on 18 September, and forces commanded by Colonel P.C.B. Skinner went ashore at Walvis Bay on Christmas Day 1914. A Southern Force approached German South-West Africa from South African territory.

Colonel Skinner captured Swakopmund in January 1915, and on 11 February, General Botha landed at Walvis Bay, to assume direct command of the Northern Force, and overall command of all SAU forces, which, a month later, would include the sole British unit to participate in the campaign.

General Botha's Chief of Staff, Colonel Collyer, expressed doubt that the heavy armoured vehicles would be able to traverse the sands of the dry Swakop River bed, which served as the roadway for the first fifty miles toward Windhoek. Collyer instead ordered Whittall to proceed via rail to support Colonel Skinner's Brigade, about forty miles east of Swakopmund.

On 24 April 1915, Whittall and his unit joined South African units at Trekkopje, where patrols had contacted a German unit of unknown strength. Preparing to repulse an attack, five of the Royal Navy armoured cars were situated up to half a mile in front of the South African lines. Two others were placed to directly support infantry units, and two were held in reserve.

The German attack was met with heavy fire from the armoured vehicles, which had not been anticipated, since aerial reconnaissance had mistakenly identified them as water trucks or field kitchens. The German intent was to cross the railroad tracks, take a ridge, and flank the South African trenches. Instead, the steady fire from the armoured cars and the infantry forced them to move parallel to the railroad tracks. When the German troops committed to a frontal attack on the trenches, they were repulsed, and elected to withdraw. A counterattack by Skinner was thwarted by heavy German artillery fire, and the armoured vehicles were unable to overcome the steep railroad embankment to pursue the fight further.

Following the action at Trekkopje, Skinner continued to move east, replacing the rail lines destroyed by the Germans, and becoming the left flank of the northern force's advance toward Windhoek. The armoured cars patrolled the railway lines, providing support to the infantry units protecting the railhead.

In his book, *With Botha and Smuts in Africa*, Lieutenant Commander Whittall describes the back-breaking efforts of his sailors, including Tommy Rose, as they moved four-ton vehicles through near impossible terrain. 'During the whole campaign we did not encounter five miles of road that by any stretch of the imagination could be called even passably fit for cars,' he remarked. Water was always a concern; so heavy was the going the cars were consuming four gallons of petrol and one of water per car per mile covered. Alleged 'permanent' water sources were frequently dry, or the water was so bitter that even animals refused to drink it. Whittall was able to secure a number of steel beer kegs, left behind by the Germans in Swakopmund, which served his unit well as containers for hauling water.

Experience in the off-road driving of mechanised vehicles was virtually unknown in 1915. Encountering deep sand 'as fluid as water', Whittall admits that his unit experienced 'appalling difficulty' in negotiating drifts and riverbeds early in the campaign; manhandling the vehicles over difficult terrain was the cause of the only casualties his squadron sustained during their service. The detachable running boards, with which the cars were equipped, tended to turn over, and were useless in sand. Matting was drawn under by the drive wheels and thrown out the back. Wooden poles broke, and iron piping bent.

The solution turned out to be two-inch angle iron, cut into eight-foot lengths, with a wire rope and toggle attached. The irons were dropped between each of the twin drive wheels in heavy sand, with the crew moving the pieces forward as the vehicle progressed; it was described as 'murderously difficult work', but it proved to be effective. Each vehicle carried four of the angle irons, but occasionally at a wide riverbed, all the iron would be laid in advance, forming a 'continuous railway' for the cars.

Driving tactics improved with experience. Scouts once reported that a 200-yard-wide riverbed with deep sand was impassable, but the cars, being 'well-driven', all made it through. At another 'iffy' crossing, Whittall signalled his number two to come forward to assess the situation, but the officer, misreading the gesture, came at high speed, and 'throwing sand up like the bow wave of a destroyer' made it to the other side, with the other cars then following his example.

While skirmishes with the enemy did occur in other areas, Skinner's Brigade's push through Usakos, Omaruru, Kalkfeld, and finally Otjiwarongo, was more a battle with the terrain, since German forces generally avoided contact and steadily withdrew before them. Past Kalkfeld, the terrain worsened, and the naval squadron's support vehicles had to be left behind, along with tents and personal kit. The sailors suffered from the hard labour of levering boulders out of their path, the night-time cold, and the lack of adequate water.

Because of the increasingly arduous terrain, the squadron was ordered back to Usakos before the German surrender came on 9 July 1915. When they returned to Walfish Bay, one of the squadron's units was detached for service in East Africa; the rest returned to Britain.

No. 1 Squadron, the first armoured unit in history to be deployed in Southern Africa, encountered daunting obstacles during their service. A fitting tribute came in Usakos, before the final push, when General Botha conducted an inspection, which included a pass 'in review'. Many thought the noise and clanking of the awkward armoured cars would add a humorous note, contrasting with the military precision of the infantry and horse cavalry units. Instead, in the words of Lieutenant Commander Whittall, the squadron, 'stole silently past, four abreast, in perfect alignment, their grim outlines relieved by the flaunting White Ensigns we flew on Gala occasions'.

Yorkshire Evening Post for Monday, 5 July 1915, reported:

SAVED BY THE ARMOURED CARS MISTAKEN BY ENEMY AIRMAN FOR WATER CARTS
A Naval Air Service man, serving with the armoured car division in South-West Africa, writes in the London 'Evening News':

'After spending close on a week in Walfish Bay we travelled by rail up country. We had been a few days in camp at Trekkopje when the Germans

FLIGHT LIEUTENANT THOMAS 'TOMMY' ROSE DFC

attacked us at about eight o'clock in the morning. Our field guns (4 inch) had been sent back to the base for replacement, and one of the enemy's aeroplanes had reported that the camp would fall as easy prey to a surprise attack. The observer had taken the "armoureds" for water carts!

'*Well, their artillery (eight guns) rained common shell and shrapnel on us from neighbouring Kopjes. Matters got very uncomfortable. Their infantry and cavalry advanced and let fly with rifles and machine guns. Then the "water carts" got their chance. Our Maxims poured a withering fire into them and mowed them down like chaff. It was horrible. The cars absolutely saved the force, who were very much outnumbered.*'

This was Tommy Rose's unit and thankfully, they all survived.

Leicester Daily Post for Saturday, 10 July 1915, reported:

BOTHA'S DECISIVE VICTORY
CAMPAIGN IN S W AFRICA ENDED
German Forces Surrender
It was officially announced that General Botha has accepted the surrender of the entire forces in South-West Africa. Hostilities have now ceased. The whole of the Citizen Army will be brought back to the Union as quickly as possible. – Reuter
Cape Town Friday.

The German forces surrendered absolutely unconditionally. General Botha presented an ultimatum to the commander, which expired at teatime yesterday. – Reuter

The Central News *says in reference to General Botha's great victory that the latest official despatches which have reached London state that negotiations respecting the terms and conditions of the surrender are still proceeding between General Botha and the German commander-in-chief. A full statement will be issued as soon as these are definitely known.*

Lord Buxton's Dispatch
The Press Bureau last night learned a dispatch from Lord Buxton to the Colonial Office, announcing that General Botha yesterday morning accepted Governor Seita's surrender of all the German forces in South-West Africa. Hostilities have ceased, and the campaign has thus been brought to a successful conclusion.

No. 1 Squadron returned home in the Union Castle liner, RMS *Briton*, leaving Cape Town and arriving in Plymouth on 17 August 1915, Tommy Rose and others were going home to some well-earned rest, recuperation and training, ready to be sent out to Mombasa. In October, No. 2 Squadron, comprising four armoured cars, together with the Lieutenant Commander, were shipped from the Cape to Mombasa, East Africa.

TOMMY ROSE JOINS THE ROYAL NAVY

It was reported in the *Burnley News* for 4 September 1915, an extract from a letter sent from one of J. Blake and Co. drivers, who worked alongside Tommy Rose, '*I never thought that motor cars could do the work they have been put to in this campaign, and I can honestly say I do not think anyone who had not seen it done would have believed it possible. I have been through more hardships in one week here than I have ever been through in my life.*'

East Africa October 1915

Assisting General Smuts, in British East Africa, until it was cleared.
Lieutenant Commander Nalder was in command of No. 2 Squadron, which had been re-designated as No. 10 Royal Navy Armoured Motor Battery, and which now consisted of four armoured cars.

Before the arrival of Nalder and his detachment of armoured cars, the construction gangs had to suspend work on account of the threat of attack by the enemy. Scarcely a day passed without the construction gangs having to suspend work due to the frequency of the attacks. The British patrols were constantly attacked and the Germans from Mbuyuni, or from the post at Kasigau were blowing up the line.

The first ten miles of the line leaves the hilly country and enters the bush, which comprised of an almost impenetrable mass of thorn, ten feet high and many hundreds of square miles in extent. When in the bush the strong tropical sunlight dims to soft twilight, making it almost impossible to find your bearings without a trained navigator, added to this was the unpredictable wildlife that the squadron would have encountered, including deadly snakes, noxious insects, etc, a complexly hostile environment.

A good road fully capable of bearing the heaviest motor traffic had to be built beside the railway, and it was obvious that the armoured cars would prove to be the greatest value when patrolling the line and assisting in the protection of the construction gangs. They were immediately given this duty, and on no occasion after the Germans first encountered the armoured cars were the railway patrols attacked or the line itself seriously damaged.

For nearly two months the detachment patrolled between Voi and Maktau, the boredom varied by the occasional plunge into the bush in the company of the mounted infantry, in the effort to round up the enemy's raiding parties. Long before this period came to an end the German's had learnt to regard the cars and their crews with much respect. The native German troops were not afraid of anything, but they could hardly face the cars, which they called 'the charging rhinoceros which spits lead'.

The Germans tried everything to destroy and capture the cars, they mined the roads. They tried to ambush them by trying to board them, they were driven off with the loss of several of the party killed and wounded, and five Askaries taken to Maktau as prisoners.

Later, when the most advanced post held by the British became the entrenched camp at Maktau, the cars were mostly employed in reconnaissance work and patrols towards Mbuyuniy. There was not a day on which one or more cars was not employed in this way, and very few on which there was not some sort of fight with enemy patrols.

It was in this kind of work that the armoured cars excelled, the combination between them and the mounted infantry being just what was required for keeping the bush clear of enemy parties. When Maktau was first occupied by the British a *boma* (thorn *Zareba*) was built right round the perimeter of the camp, backed by trenches and machine gun emplacements. Outside the *boma* the bush was dense, and there was nothing preventing the enemy from coming right up to the fence unseen.

By the end of 1915 the time of severe crisis was over and fresh British and South African troops began to arrive. General Sir H.L. Smith-Dorrien had been appointed to take over the chief command, and was on his way from England, however, he did not proceed further from the Cape, whether it was illness or something more of a diplomatic nature no one knew, however General Smuts was on his way to replace Smith-Dorien.

The campaign was reactivated in March 1916 with the arrival of South African reinforcements under Lieutenant General J.C. Smuts but, like the Indians, the South Africans were not easily deployable to the western front. However, Smuts's aims were much more extensive than those of London's. He wished to conquer the entire German colony and then to trade territory with Portugal, so as to extend South Africa's frontier into Mozambique at least as far as the Zambezi. He therefore invaded German East Africa from the north, cutting across the axes of the two principal railway lines and neglecting the harbours on the coast. He had earned his military reputation as the leader of a Boer commando and conducted his campaign as though his mounted rifles could move as fast through regions infested with tsetse fly as across the veld. He accorded little recognition to the difference between rainy seasons and dry. His advance, although rapid, failed ever to grip and defeat the German forces. His troops entered Dar es Salaam on 3 September 1916, and were astride the Central railway, running from there to Tabora and Lake Tanganyika. Smuts should have paused but he did not, plunging on to the Rufiji River, and claiming that the campaign was all but over, when in reality it had stalled.

Worrying for Smuts were Belgian territorial ambitions in the west. Debouching from the Congo into Ruanda and Urundi, the Belgians had reached Tabora in August 1916. Smuts's sub-imperialism was challenged even more fundamentally by the contribution of natives to the campaign. The Schutztruppen, although officered by Europeans, were predominantly native Africans, and yet they had proved formidable opponents for the Europeans. On the British side the South Africans were particularly susceptible to malaria, and, by early 1917, they were being replaced in the British order of battle by the natives of the West African Frontier Force and the King's African Rifles. Moreover, the collapse of animal transport meant that supply was largely dependent on human resources; the British ended up recruiting over a million labourers for the campaign. The long-term impact for Africa in the development of the cash economy, in the penetration of colonial rule into areas hitherto unmapped and, in the erosion of chiefly or tribal authority, was immense.

Smuts was recalled to London in January 1917 and handed over his command to A.R. Hoskins. Hoskins set about remedying the worst of the health, transport, and supply problems, but in doing so aroused impatience in the War Cabinet in London, which could not understand why a campaign which Smuts had said was over was still continuing to drain Allied shipping. In April, Hoskins was replaced by Brigadier General J.L. van Deventer, another Afrikaner, who implemented Hoskins's plan but still failed to prevent the rump of the Germans from escaping into Portuguese East Africa in November. For the next year, Lettow-Vorbeck's columns marched through Portuguese territory, fighting largely to secure supplies and munitions. The Allies still had a ration strength of 111, 371 in the theatre at the war's end.

TOMMY ROSE JOINS THE ROYAL NAVY

Virtually nothing remained for Willoughby's cars to do in East Africa. In response to the need for armoured cars elsewhere, they were despatched to Egypt, Mesopotamia, Arabia and Salonika where fresh adventures awaited them.

The campaign for German East Africa was effectively confined to a period of eighteen months, from March 1916 to November 1917. Its commencement had been delayed by the under-appreciated efforts of Lettow-Vorbeck's colleagues in South-West Africa (who had engaged the South Africans until 1915), and in the Cameroons (who had tied down British West African forces until 1916). The inadequacies of Portuguese military administration, rather than the failings of the British, go far to explain Lettow-Vorbeck's continued survival after all political purpose in continued fighting had been removed.

In the Company's history of the Rolls-Royce cars during the First World War, it was stated that:

> *'The Germans were desperately anxious to find a counter to the cars, which were spoiling their guerrilla tactics. All sorts of booby traps were laid for the cars. Mines were laid on the tracks they used; game pits dug in the hope that the cars would fall into them; and on the road (if you could call it that) to Taventa trenches were echeloned half across the track at intervals of a few yards so that there was no room for the cars to get enough lock on the steering to go round without considerable manoeuvre. Several times, when the presence of these traps delayed the cars, the latter were rushed by the enemy, but never with any success, and they generally incurred more or less severe loss for their pains.'*

History also makes the point that, despite the cars being in action so frequently, the crews were unable to carry out the recommended maintenance programme, such was the quality of the engineering that went into their construction, they were not off the road for a single day.

In the Despatches sent by Lieutenant General J.C.Smuts from East Africa 30 April 1916, Tommy Rose was recommended for *'gallant and distinguished service in the field.'* From his despatch regarding the two Royal Naval Armoured Cars, he reported: *'The air services performed valuable reconnaissance work throughout the operations, and on several occasions considerably demoralised the enemy by the use of bombs.'*

Together with Tommy Rose, also mentioned were Lieutenant Commander H.G. Nalder, RNVR, commanding No. 10 Armoured Car Battery, R. Marshall Sub-Lieutenant, RNVR, A. Beacham, Chief Petty Officer Mechanic 3rd grade, and J. Daniel, Petty Officer Mechanic, RNAS.

Daily Mirror for Saturday, 18 March 1916, reported:

CHRISTENED ARMOURED CAR 'RHINOCEROS'
Johannesburg, Friday – A vivid account of the fighting in East Africa shows that the enemy has the advantage of irregular lanes, skilfully cut and designed in the thick, thorny bush, where machine guns were able to engage in crossfire.

FLIGHT LIEUTENANT THOMAS 'TOMMY' ROSE DFC

The War of 1914-1918.

Royal Naval Armoured Cars—
No. F.804 P.O. Mechanic T. Rose, R.N.A.S.

was mentioned in a Despatch from
Lieutenant General The Honourable J.C. Smuts
dated 8th May 1916
for gallant and distinguished services in the Field.
I have it in command from the King to record His Majesty's
high appreciation of the services rendered.

Winston S. Churchill

War Office
Whitehall, S.W.
1st March 1919.

Secretary of State for War.

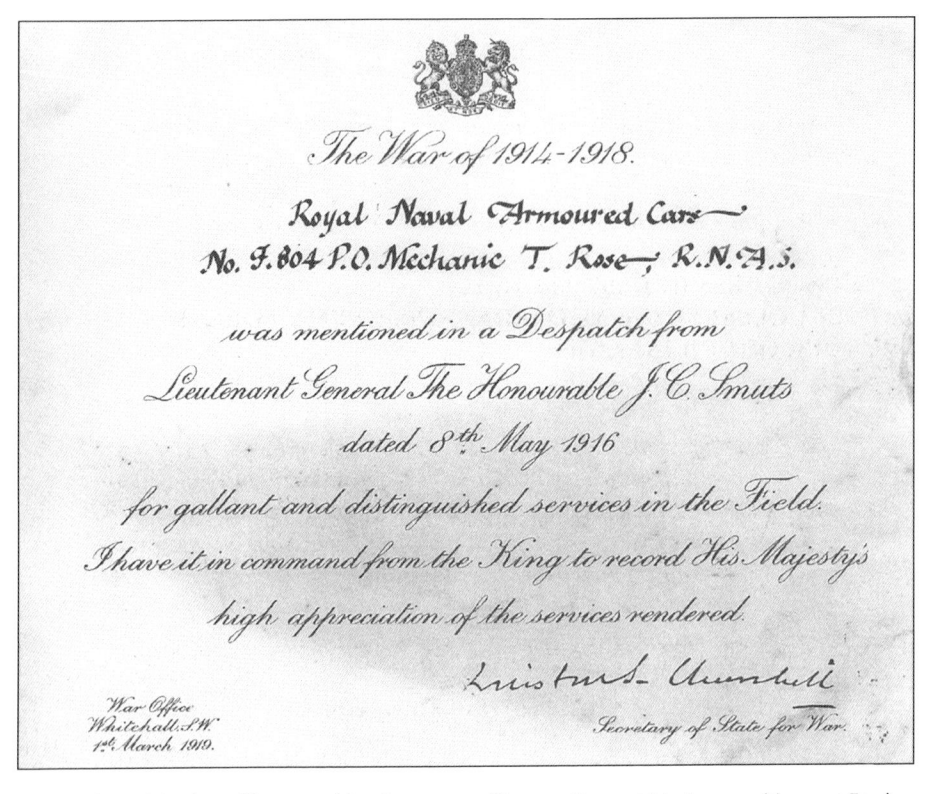

This is the original certificate notification sent to Tommy Rose at his home address at Basing Park, Hampshire. The date on the envelope is 9 September 1920. The notification first appeared in the *London Gazette* on 30 June 1916 (No.29648/6563). (*William Hale collection*)

> Snipers were artfully disposed in trees and in contracted open spaces. The work locating them was slow and risky. The enemy's native troops were formidable but in the open the armoured cars commanded by naval officers created terror in the minds of the natives, who named the cars 'Rhinoceros'.

Portsmouth Evening News for Saturday, 1 July 1916, reported:

BRAVE NAVAL MEN RECOMMENDED FOR AWARDS
In a despatch received by Secretary for War from Lieutenant General the Hon J.C. Smuts, Commander-In-Chief, East Africa Force, the following are among the names of those recommended for gallant and distinguished service in the field:

Royal Navy – Commander Lang G.H., RN, Commander Thornley G.S., RN.

Royal Naval Reserve – Lieutenant Blencowe C.B., RNR.

TOMMY ROSE JOINS THE ROYAL NAVY

Royal Naval Armoured Cars – Commander Nalder H.G., RN, Commanding No. 10 RN Armoured Car Battery, Lieutenant, RNVR, Sub-Lieutenant Marshall R., RNVR,

Beacham, No. F512 CPO Mechanic 3rd Grade A, RNAS, Rose, No. F804 PO Mechanic T, RNAS, Daniel, No. F1084 PO Mechanic J, RNAS

Lincolnshire Echo for Monday, 7 August 1916, reported:

PROGRESS IN EAST AFRICA
SUCCESSFUL NAVAL OPERATIONS ENEMY FORCES DISLODGED INLAND
The London Press Bureau issued the following this afternoon:

The War Office announces with regard to the operations in East Africa that a report received from Lieutenant General Smuts states that the minor port of Sadani was occupied by naval forces on 1 August, slight opposition only being experienced. Other naval operations are in progress at various points on the west line.

Page one of the Army Form B.103, which gave his new service No.82642, covering Tommy Rose's discharge from the Royal Navy and entering the RFC on a temporary commission.

FLIGHT LIEUTENANT THOMAS 'TOMMY' ROSE DFC

Having reached the German central railway at Kilimatinde, Dodoma, and Kikombo, Major General van Deventer is pursuing the enemy forces dislodged from this area in the direction of Mpapuea.

A detachment operating in the direction of Ssingida (west of Kondon Jrangi) was engaged with an enemy party, which surrendered after making a stubborn resistance in a blockhouse amounted to the substantial total of 150, exclusive of prisoners. After this engagement Brigadier-General North's column advanced to Madibira, thirty miles further north on the road to Jringa.

Tommy Rose and some of his unit were sent home in late May 1917, the Armoured Car division was to be disbanded. On 20 May, Tommy Rose was given a new service number 82642, which replaced his Naval number F804, which stated he was '*not desirous of transferring to the RNAS*' and was approved for discharge to the Royal Flying Corps, as an officer cadet on appointment to a commission.

On 29 May, Tommy Rose was posted to South Farnborough, a recruit's depot for training in ground school activities awaiting transfer to flight training school. He was finally going to learn to fly.

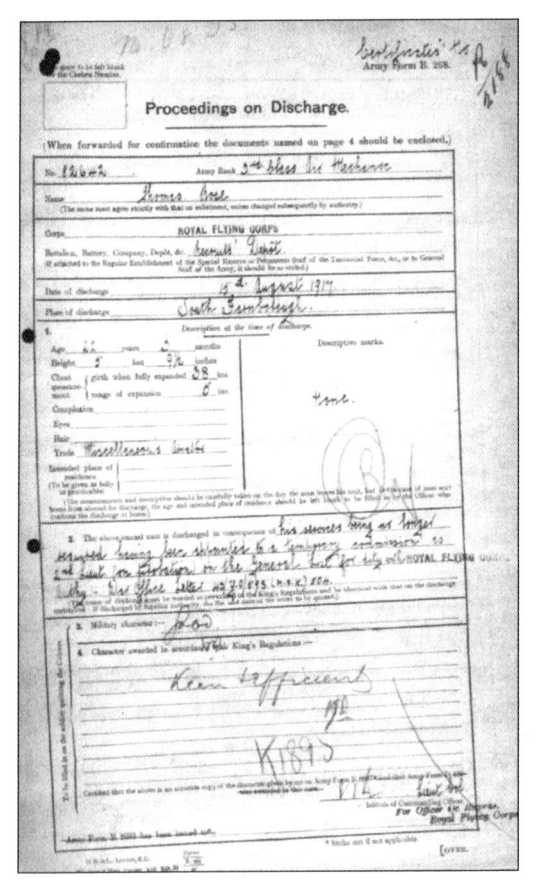

The first page of Tommy Rose Rose's discharge from the RN document, dated 15 August 1917.

Chapter 3

The Royal Flying Corps 1917–1918
Learning to fly, active service and a DFC

'We thought we were introducing into the world an invention that would make further wars practically impossible.'
– Wilbur Wright

On 25 April 1917, Tommy Rose was approved for discharge from the Royal Navy on 6 May 1917; he was discharged as a Petty Officer Mechanic 3rd Grade, on the disbandment of the Armoured Car Section.

South Farnborough – Recruits Depot 30 May 1917 – 18 June 1917

This was formed at South Farnborough in May 1916 for training RFC officers in ground subjects while awaiting flying training. On 20 May 1917, Tommy Rose was given a new service number 82642 and trade, as Air Mechanic 3rd class, he was listed as a Cadet in the RFC at the age of twenty-two years. He was recorded as playing the following sports: Tennis, Squash, Hockey, Cricket and Rugby, he was also in the Junior XV for Harlequins. Several of these sports would continue to influence and impact on his life in the future. On 30 May 1917 Tommy Rose was sent to South Farnborough where he remained for nineteen days. On arrival at the camp, which lies on a sandy, barren hill overlooking the aerodrome, he was directed first to one tent, where he was given a knife, fork, and towel, then to another where he was presented with three dusty blankets. He was then allocated a tent, eventually there were eight billeted in most tents.

Farnborough at that time was an awful place, there were 1100 air mechanics and 600 cadets, the washing facilities consisted of twelve cold water taps outdoors, and a shower-bath tent for cadets only. The showers had very little pressure behind them, the so-called showers were little tins with a rose and tap screwed into them. Before use one had to fill them from a tap, then climb up a ladder and put them on the top of a stand. By the time you got it there it was nearly empty again!

The meals at Farnborough were considered basic, the first tea could also be rather a shock and one memorable meal consisted of lettuce and onions mashed up in a very battered tin dish and covered with vinegar, a slice of bread with some very questionable margarine, and a tin mug of tea.

The usual time spent at Farnborough was about a fortnight, but whilst there, the average recruit/cadet was sworn in, had to fill in numerous forms, and was issued with his basic uniform, plus sundry items of equipment. The cadets were given a cursory medical, interviewed, given the required inoculations and vaccinations, these were really nothing much to worry about, scare stories were rampant, but it was usually just banter. They were taught how to drill, parades were taken most mornings and afternoons, these parades were taken by Regimental Sergeant Majors, who had already served in the Boer War with the Army and who gave raucous roasting to these recruits, it was easy but monotonous.

The men were allowed out after five o'clock in the afternoons, the time was usually spent in either going and getting a good meal at a restaurant or having a good bath. For the first few days a new arrival does not do much, after about a fortnight, one draft leaves and more new recruits arrive.

The cadets were then posted to the Cecil Hotel, London, where part of the hotel had been taken over by the medical personnel, for their medical examinations and to certify them physically fit for pilot training.

The medical examination undertaken by each recruit was considered extremely thorough, each doctor visited had their own speciality and each recruit had to pass every stage to be declared physically fit, and of course Tommy Rose passed this stage.

During the training at Farnborough, the men learned about Service procedures, they had sewing tests, lathe tests, filing and fitting tests, very similar to the RN tests.

The strictness of the training did not slacken as the months went by, the living areas were inspected at 7 am and everything had to be spotless, tables, beds, lockers, floors, showers and wash basins. Every day the men had to clean the classrooms at the end of instruction, likewise the Mess tables, which had to be scrubbed after meals, the floors washed, and polished and clean cutlery set out.

No. I Cadet Wing, RFC Denham 18 June 1917 – 13 July 1917

'The first necessity of an airman is that he must have discipline.'

Schools of Instruction
Schools of Instruction were formed to provide training in ground subjects for RFC officers awaiting flying training and were usually equipped with a small number of ground instructional airframes. They became Schools of Military Aeronautics on 27 October 1916, then Schools of Aeronautics on 1 April 1918.

On 18 June 1917, Tommy Rose was posted from Farnborough to the Cadet Wing, RFC Denham, where he remained until 13 July 1917. The training syllabus consisted of foot drill, military law, military organisation, Morse code, guard duty etc. When part way through the course the cadets qualified for officer-pattern uniforms, bought from Gieves and Co of No.1 Saville Row, London, by way of a uniform allowance of £50. Gieves representative visited the cadet wing to measure and take orders.

The school was a hutted camp, with hangars and a real airplane, a BE2e of 1913 vintage. More instructional ground training continued, usually undertaken during a two-month course, including once-a-week drilling, physical training, King's regulations, Military Law, aerial navigation, compass theory, theory of flight, map-reading, and rigging of aeroplanes.

The construction and functions of various types of aeroengines were taught, although Tommy Rose would have been familiar with the workings of engines, having spent three years in the Royal Navy Armoured Car Service. All the engines were fitted with propellers and set up on beds of concrete so that the cadets could start and run them. The Lewis and Vickers machine guns were also studied and fired, each cadet was expected to be able to take them apart and re-assemble them at speed and become so familiar with them that when they were blindfolded, others had to guess how long each would take to reassemble the guns. This taught the cadet familiarity and speed which would be vital in the combat zones.

This was the first school in which the cadets had their meals at tables, with tablecloths, where all meals were served by members of the Women's Army Auxiliary Corps. At the end of the course, another physical examination involving balance and co-ordination tests were undertaken and passed.

The final examinations were prepared and set at the behest of the Air Board, the examination papers were brought from London, with the only identification being by numbers, not names, and three days after the examinations were taken, the cadets were paraded to hear the numbers read out of those who had failed. Tommy Rose's number was not read out, and the parade descended into chaos as the cadets who had passed flung their caps in the air. The trainees were now able to put a white band around their caps which now signified they were flight cadets.

From the cadet wing, trainees were posted to the School of Instruction, Hendon (formed by 1916), where the equipment included Graham-White, Caudron C.3 and Beatty Pusher aircraft.

By 1917, cadets were doing a four-week course in artillery spotting, use of wireless, photography and machine gun instruction, practical training being by lodging old aircraft fuselages in trestles, lining the Upper Redlands Road, near Wantage Hall. This startling sight was only matched by the activities on the playing fields alongside Elmhurst Road, where wingless aircraft were used to provide taxiing experience.

No. 2 School of Instruction, Oxford, also known as the School of Military Aeronautics 18 June 1917 – 13 July 1917

On 18 June 1917, Tommy Rose was next posted to No. 2 School of Instruction, Christchurch College, Oxford, where he stayed until 13 July 1917. On arrival at Oxford the recruits were dealt out to different colleges. Tommy Rose was sent to Queen's, which was the best in many ways and, after a week, some of the cadets were moved to Brasenose, which was not nearly as comfortable. The cadet's typical day started with a 6 am wake-up call – reveille – then breakfast, followed by parade to a large open space, where the assembled cadets were inspected. They then broke-up into squadrons of ten to go to the classrooms. There were two lectures and two periods of practical work each day, with two fifteen-minute recesses, and classes ended at 4 pm. From then on until the following morning, their time was their own, unless the CO had instituted Study Parades, in which case cadets were expected to remain in their rooms studying. Lights out was at 11 pm.

All RFC candidates, whether direct entry or transferred in, were considered as cadets and their ranks were strictly probationary; rank badges could not be worn. To demonstrate their cadet status, candidates were required to wear a white band around their peaked caps, this band covered the normal hat band just above the rim. A typical cadet class would see a mix of uniforms, transferees wearing their regimental jackets, and the direct entry cadets wore the tunic jacket. Regulations stated that breeches and puttees were supposed to be worn while on duty, long stockings in place of puttees were not permitted, ordinary trousers could be worn when off duty.

Cadets had come for further technical tuition, on engines, machine guns, bombs, instruments, rigging machines, aerial observation and navigation. The latter was very interesting: they would go up in a gallery and on the floor was a model of the Ypres Salient. They then saw guns flash, the shell burst and a puff of smoke rise; the message was then sent down to the Battery.

The School of Military Aeronautics presented a concentrated university course and was compressed into a month. Courses were initially four weeks, but they were increased in mid-1917 (August – September) to six weeks. Cadets were under parade discipline at all times while being instructed and were required to salute an instructor at all times when speaking to him, even if their probationary rank was higher than the instructor's.

Cadets almost universally seemed to have regarded ground instruction as complicated and pointless, while practical courses in aerial observation and wireless telegraphy were vital. It is doubtful anyone learned anything useful about aneroid barometers, the manufacture of engine parts or the proper method of stitching linen to cover aircraft, a course called 'sail making'.

The second page of the discharge from the RN document, dated 15 August 1917 processed after Tommy Rose had already commenced his Royal Flying Corps training.

Cadets were required to know all the parts of a Lewis gun, and be able to replace a broken bolt, even though it was common knowledge that it was impossible to do this whilst flying, the replacement parts were not even carried in the aircraft. The information was taught not because it had proven useful, but because it was always taught as part of the ground-school curriculum. Cadets also took courses in mess room etiquette, something they probably would have forgotten once they reached the front lines.

There were no classes in the theory of mechanics of flight, until Smith-Barry introduced his Gosport system in the Autumn of 1917.

Tommy Rose's previous training in the RNAS clearly enabled him to be hurried through this training, which usually took at least six weeks, with final examinations being taken in the sixth week. Tommy Rose spent just over three weeks at Oxford.

The Flying Kit

By the start of 1914, aircraft were becoming more refined, the pilots were being contained more within the fuselage of the aircraft, rather than just perched on a wicker seat and fully exposed to all the elements. At this stage in the evolution of the Royal Flying Corps, there was no formal issue for clothing specifically for flying, but the Army motor transport division had a wide range of readily available motoring garments, which they supplied to the RFC and RNAS pilots. At the start of the war pilots were provided with weatherproof coats, goggles, gauntlets, and leather boots, all of which were worn over the uniform.

The soldier-pattern uniforms were exchanged for flying kit; a full-length leather coat, sheepskin flying boots which reached the waist, rather like a fisherman's waders, leather flying helmet, pair of goggles, silk inner gloves and leather gauntlets. Then the students were assigned to the type of aeroplane they were to fly; scout, bomber or artillery observation, Tommy Rose was assigned to be a scout as his visual accuracy was amongst the best in his class.

Although pilots were able to use the military issue, which had probably been worn before and then recycled to the new pilots, it was reported by many pilots that these items were so essential for their survival in the air, that they were reclaimed very speedily from those who had lost their lives. Those who were able to, were also free to purchase their own clothing, and these commercial companies continued to develop the motoring clothing into the more specialised clothing better suited to the airman.

The Sidcot suit

In the winter of 1916, the first significant step forward was made in providing effective protection for the pilot, and this was the brainchild of Sidney Cotton, an RNAS pilot with No. 8 Squadron. Cotton had been working on his own aircraft when a 'scramble' was called and he flew in his dirty overalls for an hour or so, and upon landing, found that, unlike his fellow pilots who were shivering with the cold, he was quite unaffected. Having reflected on this unusual effect, he realised that it was the oil and grease soaked into the overalls that had retained his body heat.

Picking up on this idea, he took leave and travelled to London, to Robinson and Cleaver, where he had a flying suit made for him with his design. The suit had three layers, a thin lining of fur, a layer of airproof silk, and an outside layer of light Burberry material, all made into a one-piece suit, just like his overalls. Robinson and Cleaver were asked to register the design made on behalf of Cotton and the flying suit took its name from the inventor and was called the Sidcot Flying Suit - SIDney COTton.

By the time Tommy Rose was learning to fly, in late 1917, tests had shown the Sidcot flying suit No. 5 was regarded by pilots as the most suitable for operational use. Robinson and Cleaver were then asked to make 250 suits per week, just fourteen days after the original order, and deliveries were later expected to reach 1,000 per week just four weeks after the initial order. By December 1917 the orders for some 3,000 leather flying coats were cancelled in favour of the Sidcot suit. This revolutionary new suit met virtually every requirement for protection against the cold and was in service in various forms, right through the Second World War, and only ceased being used as cockpits were enclosed.

'Fur boots' were largely discarded with the introduction of the Sidcot suit, but they continued to be used in the 1920s in combination with the Sidcot in the Middle East and Far East and when flying at high-altitude.

Prior to the introduction of the Sidcot Flying Suit, the necessary levels of protection from the cold earlier in the War were as follows: Clothing had to be put on just before flying, otherwise the body would give out moisture which would freeze again at altitude. Dressing would then be in strict sequence. Silk underwear, close-woven woollen underwear duplicating the silk and worn loose, cellular two-inch squared vest, silk inner shirt, Army khaki shirt, two pullovers, tight woven gabardine Sidcot Suit lined with lamb's wool and muskrat-lined gauntlets with silk liners.

Dressed thus the pilot could tolerate temperatures of minus fifty degrees Centigrade through high wind, poor fit, sweat before dressing or poor circulation of an unfit man, all of which could chill him to the point of tears at ten degrees Fahrenheit. One final military touch before leaving the dressing hut, the presentation for signature of an Army form FS20. 'Date, time, pilot's name, thigh boots, fur line boots, gauntlet, fur-lined goggles with Triplex glasses, Sidcot suit and over-sleeves.' These were the property of the RFC and losses due to exigencies of service campaign had to be certified by the Officer Commanding.

The final adjustment would be to the head area. A silk scarf would be wound carefully around the throat, to prevent air entering the vulnerable neck area and getting inside the flying suit as well as preventing skin chaffing from that constant turning around in flight to check for enemy behind the tail. The face would then be smeared with whale-oil, and then covered with a mask which was made of either Chinese dog-skin or of Canadian wolverine fur, since breath could not freeze on it. The triplex goggle, which covered the single gap in the mask (32s 6d over a

London shop counter), were fur lined moulded sponge-rubber with sage green tinted glasses to absorb the ultra-violet rays. Various preparations would finally be rubbed on to the glass to counter the fogging below ten degrees Fahrenheit and frosting at minus ten, with perhaps a touch of ointment on the lips, though pilots philosophically accepted the facts that all chapped lips cracked at altitude whatever specifics were used. Fully dressed, the pilots would walk together to the CO's hut, stamping noisily.

One can only image the immobility of the pilot with all these layers of clothing, but he then had to climb into the cockpit and sit down, get comfortable and prepare to take-off, once airborne over the front to manoeuvre the aeroplane into a position to attack the enemy and also use the machine gun.

Tommy Rose, even throughout his later life, always wore a silk scarf or a cravat, around his neck to prevent it from chaffing.

Parachutes

Parachutes for pilots were discussed at the Royal Aircraft Factory, and tests were successfully carried out on the Calthrop parachute in 1917 (N.A. AIR 5/1348). Parachutes were also used to drop agents behind enemy lines (N.A. AIR 2/181), but there was no British order for free-fall parachutes until September 1918. Parachutes were simply not adopted by the British Army for aeroplane pilots and their observers, although every effort was made to improve the design of the aeroplanes themselves under the exigency of war.

First World War aeroplanes were made of wood and doped fabric, and were, therefore, highly flammable. From reading pilot's diaries, letters and books, it was clear that the absence of a parachute caused considerable consternation. Such writings reveal the true personal feelings, which were very emotional, and they dreaded the reality of having no parachute, one pilot stated; *'what a way to die, to be sizzled alive or to jump and fall thousands of feet. I wonder if you are conscious all the way down. I would much prefer a bullet through the head and have done with it'.*

Pilots saw the reality of seeing fellow pilots dying in a flaming aeroplane, witnessing them going down in flames, one commented, *'it was a horrible sight and made me feel sick'.*

One diary entry stated, *'They could see him struggling to get clear of his harness, then half standing up. They said it was horrible to watch him trying to decide whether to jump. He didn't and the machine and he were smashed to nothingness, imagine his last moments, seeing the ground rush up at him, knowing he was a dead man, unable to move, unable to do anything but wait for it. A parachute could have saved him, there is no doubt about that. What the hell is wrong with those callous dolts at home, that they won't give them to us'?*

Pilots in the RFC were not issued with parachutes, initially due to the design of the aeroplane cockpits, which meant there was barely room for the pilot as it was, wearing all his bulky flying equipment, with no room for an equally bulky parachute.

Officially, however, parachutes were seen as being an easy escape route for pilots if their aeroplane ran into difficulty. In a report into the possible use of parachutes the Air Board declared:

> *'It is the opinion of the board that the presence of such an apparatus might impair the fighting spirit of the pilots and cause them to abandon machines that might otherwise be capable of returning to base for repair.'*

With the option of escaping a burning aircraft removed, it was thought pilots would fight harder to ensure they landed safely. In reality, many pilots had to face the option of what to do in an event of their plane being heavily damaged. Some ensured their revolver was to hand to provide a less painful option than burning to death.

War Office files appear to lack specific statements made by any officer which collectively smothered the developments of the parachute. In fact, Commander Boothby RNAS, wrote: *'We don't want to carry additional weight merely to save our lives'*. Other commentators suggested that one parachute was sufficient to rescue both the observer and the pilot. One of the notable exceptions was General Longcraft, Commander of the Third Brigade RFC in France. A pilot himself, he wrote: *'I and my pilots keenly desire parachutes and recommend the Calthrop method of fitting the pack to the top of the fuselage'*. All was to no avail, the official reply being: *'This will impose a dangerous strain on the pilot'*. One might ask – more dangerous than being killed? Another rebuff to Calthrop was made by Air Board member, General Leo Charlton, who wrote on the minutes of his request for parachutes to be used at least in flying schools and received the reply; *'No'*. When Calthrop persisted, the reply was; *'Not many'*. Judging from the statistics provided below (thirty per cent of aircraft flamed in mid-air) this seems to have been a poorly informed reply.

Finally, on 16 September 1918, a declaration from the headquarters of the RAF in the field gave authorisation that *'all single-seaters are to be fitted with parachutes forthwith'*. One has to ask why it took so long to arrive at this decision?

Hendon 19 August 1917

Air Flying Squadron
By 1916, Hendon had become a School of Instruction, the War Office having commandeered all the flying schools there. On 22 September 1916, it came under the OC 18th Wing, and some 490 pilots were trained there. Its purpose was to provide pupils with their initial flying training.

Tommy Rose at Hendon
The main type of aeroplane used at Hendon appears to have been the Graham White XV, this was a two-seat trainer, powered by an 80hp Gnome rotary engine (which was very similar to the Maurice Farman Shorthorn in appearance), Caudron C.3 and Beatty Pusher.

THE ROYAL FLYING CORPS 1917–1918

Tommy Rose was posted to the Air Flying School at Hendon on 19 August 1917 and the next few weeks were taken up with more ground school and firing the machine guns from aircraft fuselages on the ground. Their flying time was very low, and someone senior had noticed their lack of progress. They were then assigned to the Wing Examining Officer, a Captain Oliver.

Four pupils were assigned to a new instructor, Lieutenant Keevil, who was very keen, and the pupils all began to make progress. There was much activity on the aerodrome and Tommy Rose, much later in life, stated he in fact learnt to fly and made his first solo in the Maurice Farman MF.11 Shorthorn. He described his first solo exercise as being a take-off, two level turns and a landing, which nowadays would be a considered a circuit of the airfield.

It would appear from later newspaper articles that Tommy Rose was a natural aviator.

In an interview with Bert Clarke given by Tommy Rose upon his retirement from Miles Aircraft in January 1946, he candidly remarked: '*My first solo in a Shorthorn was a memorable performance; my astonishment was only excelled by that of my instructor. The RAF tolerated me until 1926 and those nine years and the eight and a half I have spent here, have been the happiest of my young life.*'

Learning to fly
Just what was on the syllabus for the student learning to fly?
The following is taken from the 'first flying instructor's course' dated September 1917:

Lesson 1
Demonstrate use of controls and their effects on the machine.
Straight flying, level and climbing.
Turns (with engine on):
    Use and effect of controls in turning.
    Getting into the turn and keeping the machine turning.
    Getting out of the turn.
    Misuse of the controls and detection of faults.
Turns (with engine off):
    Difference in effect of controls of machine.
    Faults in turning.
Glide.

Lesson 2
Taking off into wind.
Repeat lesson landing into wind.
Normal and short circuit landings.

Lesson 3
Brief repetition of lessons 1 and 2.
Steeper turns, with and without engine.
Taking off across wind and climbing turns.

Landing crosswind.
Side slipping, various degrees and uses of.
The approach for landing on a fixed mark.
Flatter Glide.

Lesson 4
Lesson 3 repeated, but not that part taught in lessons 1 and 2.
Forced Landings: Practice in choosing the right field.
Detection of wind.
Approach.

Lesson 5
General repetition of advanced training.
Harder Manoeuvring:
    Looping
    Rolling
    Spinning
    Stalling turns
    Manoeuvring against another machine.

The instructor should, when possible, remain in the air half an hour with a pupil, the lessons had been set out to occupy about that time.

It was the unspoken consensus of RFC instructors, before the autumn of 1917, that students had a better chance of becoming good pilots if they taught themselves. This amounted to an admission that there was little that an instructor could teach beyond the rudiments of taking off, turning, simple manoeuvres and landing.

Accordingly, students spent ten times as much flying time solo than they did under instruction. The cadets were encouraged to fly higher and further as they became more comfortable with the process, and the duration of solo flights increased to forty-five minutes, an hour, or more. Cadets flew as high as 3,000 feet, one student reached 9,000 feet, which his CO told him was a record for his training squadron.

Most pupils were reluctant to push themselves too far, they feared the cloud base, and did not have enough nerve to try and get above them. Elementary training was considered to have been completed once they had spent between ten and twenty hours in the air.

The following extracts were taken from *'Learning to Fly'* a practical manual for beginners, written by Claude Grahame-White, which was first published in 1916.

Flying instruction was usually conducted in the early morning and again in the evening, when the wind blows with the least violence, it was vital for every pupil handling craft for the first time, they should have weather conditions that were favourable.

The pupil found that during the first stage of his flying tuition he was given the task of familiarising himself with the controls of the school biplane. Firstly, whilst the aircraft was on the ground the pupil in the driving seat was able to get used to the levers and resting his feet on the rudder-bar, making various movements of control, until he was accustomed with them.

The next stage was a more interesting one, where the pupil occupied the seat directly behind the instructor and was taken for a series of rides as a passenger. This allowed the pupil to get accustomed to the sensation of flying, and the sensation of being in the air, also being able to judge heights and distances. Whilst the pupil was with the instructor, the pupil would be analyzing and observing the lever movements required to fly the aircraft.

This was followed by the pupil to handle the moving aircraft on the ground with the motor giving sufficient power to render the control surfaces effective, but it did not permit the aircraft to rise in the air. A pupil continued this practice until he could drive the aircraft to and fro across the aerodrome on a straight course, with its tail raised off the ground. Once this was mastered, the pupil was then ready for his first short flight across the aerodrome, rising only a few feet, flying a straight course, alighting each time before he turns and running the machine round on the ground. This was repeated until the instructor was confident in the pupil's progress.

Then came a succession of straight flights, taking the machine into the air with precision and landing without awkwardness and the problem of turning the aircraft in the air. Turns to the left are attempted first, and the reason for that was that the propeller of the aeroplane was revolving to the left – and the motor too if it was a rotary engine – the machine had a tendency to turn in that direction. Half turns tried first working the rudder-bar and if necessary, the ailerons slightly so as to prevent the biplane from tilting sideways. This manoeuvre was to teach the pupil the safe 'banking' technique.

After the pupil could make a full left-hand turn, he then goes on to perfect himself in this movement. Flying alone now, and repeating the turn he feels he can make it with confidence, and at a fair height. This exercise is then repeated, but with a right-hand turn, then onto a descent when his engine has stopped, remaining in full control, maintaining the appropriate rate of descent so it is stable and he is in full control of his machine, the control services, and turning the aircraft to reduce the rate of descent, bringing the aircraft safely down to land.

Next are the test flights in order to grant certificates, and to demonstrate that the pupil is in full control over his actions in normal conditions. He would be asked to ascend to a fair flying altitude and make such evolutions that would demonstrate his command over the control surfaces of the machine. Finally, and with the motor switched off, to carry out a vol-plane (gliding flight) and bring his machine to a halt within a specified distance of a mark.

Tests A and B: two distance flights, consisting of at least five kilometres each in a closed circuit, without touching the ground.

Test C: altitude flight, during which a height of at least 100 metres above the point of departure must be attained, the descent made from that height with the motor cut-off. The landing must be made in view of observers, without re-starting the motor.

The rules to govern these flights:

The candidate must be alone in the aircraft during the tests.

The course on which the aviator accomplishes test A and B must be marked out by two posts situated not more than 500 yards apart.

The turns around the posts must be made alternatively to the right and to the left so that the flights will consist of an uninterrupted series of figures of eight.

The alighting after the two distance flights in tests A and B shall be made:

By stopping the motor at or before the moment of touching the ground.

By bringing the aircraft to rest not more than fifty metres from a point indicated previously by the candidate.

All alighting must be made in a normal manner, and the observers must report any irregularity.

The test flights for the certificate were to be undertaken only in such weather conditions as the pupil's instructor may think suitable and watched by official observers appointed by the Royal Aero Club. It is the business of these observers, when the prescribed flights have been made, to send in a written report concerning them to the Club and, acting on this report after it has been considered, and shown to be in order, the Club issues to the pupil his numbered certificate. With the successful passing of his tests the pupil's tuition is at an end. He is regarded no longer as a novice, but a qualified pilot.

It is well documented in several ex-RFC pilot's biographies where they comment on the 'glamour' of being an RFC pilot, 'the aura surrounding the life, the pretty girls who flocked around the khaki-clad wing-sprouting hero. They all loved the attention, and some strutted around like young peacocks relishing in the attention.'

Tommy Rose was granted a temporary commission, with effect from 16 August 1917, and placed on the general list for duty with the Royal Flying Corps as a Second Lieutenant (probationary). While at training school his daily pay had been seven shillings and sixpence, but as soon as he graduated and had been posted to a training squadron his daily pay increased to eleven shillings and sixpence. The extra four shillings was flying pay, plus four shillings and two pence daily allowance, this of course was on top of the half pay Tommy Rose was receiving from Coutts Bank. The *London Gazette* for 11 September 1917, stated that he was no longer on probation, as he had achieved his 'solo' and completed the first phase of his training.

Bramham Moor (Tadcaster) 28 August 1917

No. 68 Training Squadron, Bramham Moor
Tommy Rose at Bramham Moor
The aerodrome at Bramham Moor adjoined a main road and the aeroplanes were housed in tents.

Tommy Rose then moved on to more specialized flying training instruction, one of the main elements of the Gosport System was that the training regime became increasingly specialized as it progressed, until by the time a pilot or observer was ready to be posted to a frontline squadron, he had spent thirty hours or more flying the type of machine he would use at the front. This flying was normally done at schools specialising in one particular aspect of military aviation, where the pupil practiced the kinds of work he would be doing on duty. Of necessity this meant that aircrew were streamed before going to these specialist schools. This was possible because the Gosport System was designed to evaluate pupils at every stage.

No. 68 Training Squadron was formed on 7 April 1917 out of No. 14 Reserve Squadron at Catterick. On 14 April 1917 it moved to Bramham Moor, by which it was known. The aerodrome was opened as a Home Defence (HD) and First-Class Night Landing Ground (NLG1) for No. 33 Squadron, which arrived from Filton on 18 March 1916. Responsible for the defence of Leeds and Sheffield, No. 33 (HD) Squadron was equipped for this task with BE2C and BE2D and later BE12.

Tommy Rose gained his wings on the Farman Shorthorn, between 26 September 1917 and 22 October 1917, he was then a fully-fledged pilot, ready for more advanced training.

It was at this point Tommy Rose was given the following information to keep with his flying records and pilot's logbooks:

Notes to Service Pilots

A. To graduate, a pilot must have:

1. Received certificate A.
2. Had twenty hours solo in the air.
3. Flown a service aeroplane satisfactorily.
4. Carried out a cross-country flight of at least sixty miles successfully – during which he must have landed at two outside landing places under supervision of an RFC officer.
5. Climbed to 8,000ft and remained there for at least fifteen mins, after which he will land with his engine stopped, the aeroplane first touching the ground within a circular mark of 50ft in diameter.
6. Made two landings in the dark, assisted by flares (only applicable to BE2 and FE2 pilots; pilots of other machines may do this at the discretion of Wing Commanders and Commandant CFC).

B. Pilots will not wear wings until they are qualified for service overseas as under:

1. Passed test applicable.
2. Have had air experience thirty hours solo, of which not less than five hours must be done on a service type.
3. Carried out fifteen 'tails down' landings on service type.

He will then be known as a service pilot and will wear wings.
If a service pilot is required for overseas on a type other than on which he qualified as such, he must do a further five hours solo and fifteen 'tail down' landings on new type.

To Pilot …………………………..

AT HOME

1. Do not lose this card or your graduation will be delayed.
2. On being transferred from one Unit to another, show this card to the Officer Commanding the Unit you are leaving, who will fill in what sections you have passed and will leave others blank.
3. On arrival at your new unit show it again to the Officer Commanding your new unit and ask him to fill it in before you leave. If you fail to do this you are liable to be sent back to pass again.

ABROAD

On being posted to a unit with the EF show this to the Officer Commanding there. He will dispose of it as he thinks fit.

Beverley, Yorkshire, 26 September 1917

No. 36 Training Squadron, Beverley
Beverley airfield was classified as a Training Squadron Station from April 1916 and was recognised as a second-class Landing Ground on 31 March 1917.

Tommy Rose at Beverley
Tommy Rose's time at Beverley was spent gaining experience on each of the aircraft, and on scouting exercises, Beverley aerodrome was like a grassy pimple; if one flew in too low one ran the danger of hitting the rising ground; and if too high, the ground receded on the far side of the pimple and, instead of touching down, pilot's wheels went higher and higher and another circuit became imperative.

    The Avro 504 was the primary trainer used there and it was powered by an 80 horse-power rotary Gnome engine, manufactured in France. The 7-cylinder engine, which revolved round a stationary crankshaft, had automatic inlet valves (which sometimes refused to open) and mechanically operated exhaust valves. There was no means of controlling the speed of the engine before taking off (or landing), so it was necessary to 'blip' the throttle to adjust the speed by means of the button on the top of the joystick to switch the engine on and off. To protect the propeller on landing a skid jutted out from, and was fixed to, the axle of the landing wheels. The engine was lubricated with castor oil and the centrifugal force of the rotating cylinders spewed out a thin film of oil, some of which found its way aft to the discomfort and odour of the pupil and instructor. The Avro 504s were not difficult to fly, provided the engine behaved itself, and were much lighter on the controls than the relatively heavy-handed Maurice-Farman Shorthorns that Tommy Rose made his first solo on.

Many of the exercises involved cross-country flying and landing away at other stations, passing set exercises and practicing 'scouting' while gaining sufficient proficiency to move on to the next squadron, which was to be No. 45 Training Squadron based at South Carlton, Lincolnshire.

South Carlton, Lincs, 22 October 1917

No. 45 Training Squadron, South Carlton

No. 45 Training Squadron was tasked with carrying out single-seat fighter training and it operated more than seventy aircraft, comprising Avro 504J/K, Sopwith Camel, Sopwith Dolphin and Sopwith Pup.

Tommy Rose was posted to South Carlton to train as a fighter pilot, to include reconnaissance, with No. 45 Training Squadron and, on 27 October 1917, he was promoted to Flying Officer RFC, and confirmed in rank with the appointment being confirmed in the *London Gazette,* for 20 November 1917.

Ayr, Scotland, 15 November 1917

No. 1 School of Aerial Fighting, Ayr, 24 November 1917

No. 1 School of Aerial Fighting was formed on 17 September 1917, under the Training Division, and was equipped with: Sopwith Camel, DH2, Spad S7, Avro 504J, SE5A, Bristol M1C and F2B Sopwith Camel.

It was at Ayr that Tommy Rose developed his aerial skills in 'dog fighting' that would be so essential when he and his squadron took part later in the battle of Cambrai.

From there he was posted, on 24 November 1917, to No. 2 Aeroplane Supply Depot, which had formed on 1 November 1917 within No. 1 AD at Fienvillers, a commune in the Somme department of Hautes-de-France region of France, and it was here that the pilots learnt about battle plans and made their wills in case the worst happened.

On 4 December 1917, Flying Officer Tommy Rose joined No. 64 Squadron which was based at Saultain, a commune in the Nord department in northern France.

Initially equipped with a variety of types for training purposes, in June 1917, the squadron re-equipped with the DH5 fighter, and began to work up ready for operations.

FLIGHT LIEUTENANT THOMAS 'TOMMY' ROSE DFC

No. 64 Squadron's DH5s lined up prior to take-off for France, 14 October 1917. (*via Peter Amos*)

The DH5 had poor altitude performance and so the squadron extensively practiced low-level flying prior to, and following its move to France, on 14 October 1917.

On 20 November, the British launched the Battle of Cambrai, an offensive supported by the use of a large number of tanks and No. 64 Squadron supported the British troops flying many low-level ground attack missions, both during the British attack, and during the German counterattack that followed.

The DH 5s were replaced by SE 5As in March 1918 and with these superior machines, they conducted both fighter and ground-attack operations for the remainder of the war. Tommy Rose ultimately became deputy flight commander.

After three and a half months of bitter fighting up to November 1917, causing 250,000 casualties on each side, Haig's Flanders offensive had finally floundered in a morass of liquid mud at Passchendaele, leaving his armies with inadequate resources for further adventures that winter. By mid-November, the pilots of III Brigade RFC under J.F.A. 'Josh' Higgins, one of the original flight commanders from August 1914, had reason to suspect something unpleasant was brewing.

First of all, the brigade was hastily reinforced with two Camel squadrons, Nos. 3 and 46, two new DH5 squadrons, Nos. 64 and 68 (Australian), two flights of a newly arrived day-bombing squadron (DH4s), and Sholto Douglas's No. 84 Squadron (SE5A). The 3rd Brigade now comprised the bulk of fifteen squadrons of nearly 300 aeroplanes, giving it an advantage on the Third Army's front, opposite Cambrai, of three and a half to one.

For the pilots going into action for the first time, including Tommy Rose, who up to this point had only seen action with the Royal Navy armoured cars, this was going to be his first taste of aerial battles. Many casualties occurred through pilots flying into the ground, the majority being shot out of the skies by ground fire.

The Commander of No. 64 Squadron (DH5s), Major Bernard Smythies, formerly of No. 9 Squadron, realised from an early stage that he was ignorant of what was happening on the ground and was likely to remain so. This was typical of the Army squadrons; they had their specific objectives and were fully occupied with those. Only the corps squadrons could normally hope to follow the course of the battle. The pilots of the DH5s, in their first taste of action, scattered troops with bombs and machine-gun fire, routed horse-drawn gun teams, silenced batteries, pounded dug-outs, blasted fortified shell-holes, and fired into trenches and gun emplacements. Those who escaped more or less unscathed re-armed and went again. But their single Vickers machine guns, although synchronised to fire through the propeller and supplemented by a bomb rack carrying four 20lb bombs, combined with other inadequacies made the DH5 a somewhat disappointing successor to the DH2.

The change to a tractor configuration gave a good forward view, but the rear view, where hostile attacks mostly originated, was obstructed by the wings. A poor performance above 10,000ft did not matter for low-level strafing, but bombs could only be aimed in a dive. This put a particularly severe strain on the newer pilots, and casualties were heavy.

On that first day alone, the squadron had one man killed, one wounded, and two missing. No. 64 Squadron was notable for having three of the first pilots to be trained in Canada under a scheme first examined by RFC veteran C.J. Burke *(nicknamed 'Pregnant Percy')*, was established in January 1917 together with veterans C.H. Hoare and Dermott Allen.

Others who helped to restore the squadron's confidence included Captain Jimmy Slate (thirty-four victories) and E.R. Tempest (seventeen victories). These victories were mostly gained after the DH5 was replaced by the SE5A. The DH5s of Nos. 64 and 68 squadrons, for all their deficiencies as fighting machines, were well led and well handled.

The rush to reinforce the Cambrai front had contrasting effects on the men drafted from England. However, despite the efforts of Smith-Barry and other pilots, some squadrons were still being sent to the front in answer to emergency calls before they were operationally ready.

No. 64 Squadron suffered high casualties whilst performing these low-level bombing/strafing missions during the Battle of Cambrai in November 1917. News arrived that the SE5As were arriving at Le Hameau, this was greeted with great enthusiasm. However, it took some time to convert the existing pilots to the new aircraft, but also to the new fighter role, so 64 Squadron did not begin operations with the SE5A until early March 1918. The unit had claimed just two aerial victories in several months of frontline flying with the DH5, and both of these had been claimed by Captains J.E. Slater and E.R. Tempest.

No. 64 Squadron was much happier after their DH5s were exchanged for the SE5As in which Flight Commander Jimmy Slater claimed two Albatross D.Vs, and half a share of a Fokker Triplane. Walter Daniel, a Canadian described the action at the time, 'We were really in the thick of it, flying and sleeping and flying again, the turbulence from passing shells and bursts on the ground and in the air made me more airsick than I have ever been before', and to the 19-year-old Walter Daniel, who was one of the pupils, the early casualties imposed an additional strain. He was passing over an ammunition dump when it blew up; 'I went up over a thousand feet with the blast and debris before I righted the plane and found it to be all in one piece.'

FLIGHT LIEUTENANT THOMAS 'TOMMY' ROSE DFC

Many squadrons received attention from the German bombers in this period and 64 Squadron was no exception. Daniel was blasted from his hut one night to find a huge crater outside, with a visiting chaplain lying face down peering into it, evidently looking for victims to rescue, this obviously profoundly affected Daniel, who later served with the RCAF as a chaplain in the Second World War.

Tommy Rose flew on many occasions with Captain Edmund Roger Tempest in 1918 and when he corresponded with Norman Franks, the author of *'SE5/5A Aces of World War I'*, later in life, he told him:

> 'Edmund Tempest was the brother of Wulston, who got the Potters Bar Zeppelin. Edmund was the greatest patrol leader I have ever known. I was in his flight initially, and I am certain that if the opportunities had come his way he would have been known as one of the greatest. Jimmy was the opposite type. If an "archie" burst was close enough, he would loop round it. If one of his flight habitually left the patrol with "engine trouble", he would follow him down firing both guns.
>
> 'It is all so very difficult, one gets so many thrills in life, most of them outside flying and a great many unsuitable for publication, even in a journal read exclusively by those interested in Aviation.
>
> 'I suppose the most completely thrilling experience I have ever had happened in France in early 1918. There were the usual hair-raising odd moments when death was expected every next breath, followed by such a totally unexpected and glorious act of self-sacrifice that one was completely overcome.
>
> 'No. 64 Squadron, to which I belonged, was equipped with SE5As and operated mostly on the Arras-Bapaume front on routine flight ops. To my flight was posted quite an ordinary young man, who we will call Smith. He was not a product of Eton or Harrow, but he was an average pilot, quite clean about the house and able to do his share in cutting up any Tipsy cake that was available.
>
> 'He had several practice flights, was shown the lines a couple of times and eventually took his place at the tail end of the Flight formation. The first time we crossed the lines with him, "archie" (anti-aircraft fire – SC) was particularly naughty and very accurate. I suppose that "archie" frightened ninety-nine out of every hundred pilots that suffered from his attentions, but most of them managed to pretend successfully that they didn't care. Personally, I know that I always got an acute sinking feeling in the pit of my stomach every time those "woofs" used to start up.
>
> 'On this particular occasion we got it good and hard for five minutes, and on looking round I found Smith about 600 yards behind the formation turning right and left like a lunatic. I did a gradual sweep to pick him up, but he started to lose height and fly back towards home.
>
> 'After an uneventful patrol we got back and he was on the aerodrome. I found there was nothing wrong with his machine, and in the privacy of my room, he confessed that it was sheer wind up. The riot act was

read and he was reminded that his one and only duty was to keep close formation, not only for his own sake, for he had been told many times what happened to stragglers, but for the sake of the rest of the flight. A combat with one machine missing might have disastrous results. If it went on, of course he would be sent home in disgrace, but I assured him that if he left the Flight again without good reason I should turn and warm my guns in his direction, and it was a well-known fact that my shooting was not of the expert type, but the bullets covered a very large area.

'Late in the afternoon we did another patrol and everything was comparatively peaceful. Smith kept a tight formation and showed no sign of noticing the odd shots that "archie" sent up, and I thought he was settling down to it.

'Next day we were off at midday and on crossing the lines received a right royal plastering! The shooting was very accurate, and suddenly, out of the corner of my eye I saw Smith turn away from the formation and dive towards the lines. It was impossible to carry out my threat and we carried on. After half an hour we ran into seven Huns and after a hectic quarter of an hour drew off and reformed, having no victory to record, and one of our own machines having spun down to destruction.

'It was a pitifully disappointed four pilots that landed back at the aerodrome and the most unpopular man in the world at that moment was Smith. I have reviled people in my time, and heard others speaking their minds in anger, but this unfortunate fellow had a continuous attack from the whole squadron. After much deliberation, the CO decided to give him one more chance on the morrow and we turned in, in a most disagreeable frame of mind.

'My Flight left the ground in the morning at about 10.30 am, with the five old pilots and a new arrival to replace the casualty of the day before. I had five minutes with Smith beforehand and told him that he simply had to do his stuff this time, as we were carrying a novice with us. He was very strained and pale but promised he would do his best. I had moved him up to the inside right position of the V to give him confidence, and although we were greeted quite normally by "archie" when crossing the lines, he stayed with us. After half an hour at 16,000 feet, I suddenly saw Pfalz Scouts quite close to the lines and about 8,000 feet below us. This seemed almost too good to be true, as this particular machine was always looked upon as easy money by SE pilots, and they were very seldom near the lines.

'Having had a good look round for enemy machines up above and finding none, I gave the usual signal and down on the Pfalz we went. There followed a very pretty five minutes of dog fighting; we had the legs and climb of them and I had seen two go down, one in flames, when, on my tail from above came three Fokkers. We had been caught in the old, old trap and now we were suddenly for the high jump. Before I realised, they were there I had got a burst of machine-gun fire through the fuselage, which put the Vickers out of action and ripped a large hole in the bottom plane in the process. I half rolled and did everything I knew, but every time I tried to fly straight one of them was in position on my tail making shooting practice. There was nothing for it but to spin right down and try to get back by hedge hopping.

'Down I went in a spin, sick as blazes and expecting the worst at any moment. Flattening out at fifty feet, just over the shell area, I opened the throttle wide and started west towards the lines. After just one minute, there was another burst of firing on my tail and one of the Fokkers was with me again. There was now apparently nothing to save me; I had one gun out of action, the Lewis drum was empty and there was no chance of changing it, and petrol was getting low. As I swung round a ruined tower a burst went through the fairing behind my head, just missing my left shoulder. In desperation, I flew the machine round in a steep right-hand turn and as the Fokker turned to follow, out of the blue hurtled an SE 5. Its guns were not working but it came straight on in a colossal dive and crashed into the Fokker in about the middle of the fuselage. From this height they hit the ground with a tremendous crash almost immediately, but the SE was on top, and on the side of the fuselage was the figure 5.

'Five was the number of Smith's machine.'

That lesson of self-sacrifice stayed with Tommy Rose for the rest of his life.

The Reading Chronicle for 13 March 1981, carried an article about Tommy Rose's career in the RFC, about *The Man who wore a blackbird feather*:

To all who met him, Tommy Rose was in every sense a gentleman. Immaculate in his dress, courteous, modest, generous to a fault, gentle and attentive, he possessed a rare skill of bringing together complete strangers and leaving them moments later as if they had known each other for years.

But what none of them knew was that his fastidious attention to dress each day was never completed without the final tucking into his top handkerchief pocket of a blackbird's feather. It was a daily ritual he had practiced since the First World War and from the day the bird had saved his life.

For some weeks, from his open cockpit, Rose had cursed the bird's habit of flying across his path either as he took off or was about to land from a patrol of the German lines, He came to know the bird well.

One day, as he was making his return approach to the airfield in worsening visibility, he saw his feathered friend flying straight towards him. Fearing they would collide, Rose side slipped violently but failed to miss the bird, which struck his aircraft and was killed. At the moment of impact Rose heard the chatter of a machine gun and looking up saw a

THE ROYAL FLYING CORPS 1917–1918

German fighter aircraft pass close above him and climb off into the low cloud.

Ever afterwards Rose swore that had it not been for the sudden evasive action he had to take in trying to avoid the blackbird, he would never have lived to tell the tale. From the remains of the bird on his aircraft he took the feather which he was to carry with him for the rest of his life.

The war was coming to an end and Tommy Rose returned home on 8 October 1918, while No. 64 Squadron returned to Narborough on 14 February 1919, where it was disbanded on 31 December 1919.

At the 11th hour of the 11th day of the 11th month of 1918, the First World War ended. At 5 am that morning, after three days of negotiation, a German delegation signed the Armistice in Allied Supreme Commander Ferdinand Foch's railway carriage in Compiegne. The agreement they signed would, six hours later, end one of history's bloodiest conflicts.

After four years of slaughter, the British and French were in no mood to let Germany off lightly. So, among the terms of the Armistice were the demands that the Germans give up all territories they had occupied during the conflict, hand over thousands of pieces of military hardware (including virtually their entire navy) and promise to pay the victors substantial reparations.

The First World War left nine million soldiers dead, twenty-one million wounded, with Germany, Russia, Austria-Hungary, France and Great Britain, each losing nearly a million or more lives. In addition, at least five million civilians died from disease, starvation, or exposure.

During the war No. 64 Squadron had claimed in excess of 130 victories and produced eleven 'aces', who were:

Captain J.A. Slater 22 (24)	Captain C.W. Cudemore 10 (15)
Lieutenant B.A. Walkerdine 6	Captain E.R. Tempest 17
Captain W.H. Farrow 9 (10)	Captain E.D. Atkinson 5 (10)
Captain P.S. Burge 11	Captain D. Lloyd-Evans 8
Captain R.S. McClintock 5	Lieutenant T. Rose 11
Lieutenant C.A. Bissonette 6	

The final amended total is shown in brackets.

Tommy Rose soon became deputy flight commander and when his DFC was gazetted, in November 1918, he had claimed eleven victories.

The *London Gazette*, 1 November 1918, 12972 supplement reported:

Lt Thomas Rose
This officer has accounted for nine enemy machines during recent operations. Possessing a marked degree of real offensive spirit, he sets a notable example to the other pilots of his squadron by his utter disregard of personal danger.

FLIGHT LIEUTENANT THOMAS 'TOMMY' ROSE DFC

Victory No	Date 1918	Aircraft (German)	Aircraft (British)	Squadron	Where	Time	Claim	Combat Report
1	8 March	Alb DV	C9602	64	Graincourt	12.30	OOC	CR/RAF 8.3
2	13 March	Hispno Suiza	C9602	64		17.50	DES (F)	CR/ORB not unknown
3	23 April	C	C5393	64	Ervillers	17.50	DES (F)	CR/RAF 23.4
4	29 April	Pfalz DIII	C5392	64	Wancourt	17.35	OOC	CR/RAF 29.4
5	3 May	Rumpler C	C1860	64		10.40	DES	CR/ORB not known
6	9 May	Rumpler	C1860	64	Boiry	10.40	DES	CR/RAF9.5
7	9 May	Halb C	C1860	64	Boiry	10.42	OOC	CR/RAF 9.5
8	22 May	C	C1860	64	Bauvin/Carvin	11.20	DES	CR/RAF 22.5
9	25 July	Fokker DVII		64	W Aubers	08.10	OOC	CR/ORB not known
10*	10 August	Fokker DVII	C1860	64	Roye	08.40	OOC	CR /ORB not known
11	11 August	Fokker DVII	C1860	64	Roye	08.15	OOC	CR/ORB not known
12	12 August	Fokker DVII	D6978	64	Chaulnes	07.15	DES	CR/RAF/12.8
13 **	14 August	Alb C		64	N Roye	09.10	OOC	CR/ORB not known

Although Tommy Rose was credited with thirteen victories he, in fact, shared two with other officers. In combat it is very difficult to confirm just which aircraft from the squadron actually shot down the enemy aircraft claimed, and, in these cases, all pilots involved were often credited with the same victory.

    *   Shared with Captain E.R. Tempest (B74); Lieutenant G.L. Wood (E1391); Captain T. St P. Bunbury (E5977), Captain A.F. Buck, Captain C.W. Cudemore (D6952).
    ** Shared with Captain E.R. Tempest and Lieutenant G.A. Wood.

OOC   Out of control
DES   Destroyed in flames.
CR   Combat report
ORB   Operational record book

THE ROYAL FLYING CORPS 1917–1918

The above information was taken from *Above the Trenches* by Christopher Shores, Norman Franks and Russell Guest.

On 8 October 1918, Tommy Rose was posted to No. 30 Training Depot Station, Northolt and on 3 November 1918 he was posted to the South-Eastern Area Flying Instructors School, Upavon, which, according to official records, was not formed until 23 December 1919. On 16 November 1918 he returned to No. 30 Training Depot Station, Northolt. His next posting was to CDP, which probably meant the Central Despatch Pool of Pilots, which had been formed at Orchard Hotel, 5, Portman Street, London, W1, on 1 April 1918.

Chapter 4

The Royal Air Force 1918–1926
The Distinguished Flying Cross, Flying Instructor training, the Waziristan Campaign and medal and the return to civilian life

Per Ardua ad Astra (Through Struggle to the Stars)

By the end of the First World War, the RFC had more than 30,000 officers and over 17,000 aircraft and had trained more than 22,000 pilots. More than 15,000 British pilots had become casualties of war – more than Germany, and more than double France's losses (Morrow, *The Great War in the Air*, p367). Despite these losses and the RFC's struggles throughout the war, historians have argued that the air was one front on which the Allies could claim they had been victorious. They had achieved part of what Churchill had prophesised would be necessary: 'command and perfection in aerial warfare'. (Churchill, *His Speeches*, 2184).

After the war, the RAF were reduced from some 304,000 personnel to 29,730 by January 1920, by the end of 1918 there were 22,647 aircraft. The forty-four flying schools in Britain were mostly closed, only the Central Flying School, along with a number of other satellites, was kept open.

Foundation of the Royal Air Force

The RAF was founded on 1 April 1918, by the amalgamation of the Royal Flying Corps and the Royal Naval Air Service, and was controlled by the British Government Air Ministry, which had been established three months earlier.

The Royal Flying Corps had been born out of the Air Battalion of the Royal Engineers and was under the control of the British Army. The Royal Naval Air Service was its naval equivalent and was controlled by the Admiralty. The decision to merge the two services and create an independent air force was a response to the events of the First World War, the first war in which air power made a significant impact. The creation of the new force was based on the Smuts report, prepared by Field Marshal Jan Smuts for the Imperial War Cabinet in which he served.

The squadrons of the new RAF kept their numerals, while those of the RNAS were numbered from 201 onwards. At the time of the merger, the naval air service had 55,066 officers and men, 2,949 aircraft, 103 airships and 126 coastal stations, the remaining personnel and aircraft came from the RFC.

With the accompanying British defence cuts, the newly independent RAF waited eight months to see if it would be retained by the Cabinet. While 6,500 officers, all holding temporary commissions or seconded from the Army and Navy, applied for permanent commissions. The Cabinet sanctioned a maximum of 1,500 and the Air Ministry offered 1,065 to the applicants, publishing the first list on 1 August 1919, seventy-five per cent of them short-term (two to five years).

Tommy Rose started his flying instructors' course at No. 30 Training Depot, Station Depot, Northolt, on 8 October 1918, and on 1 November 1918, the *London Gazette* 912972) stated that Tommy Rose had been awarded the Distinguished Flying Cross (DFC). The citation read:

Lieutenant Thomas Rose

This officer has accounted for nine enemy machines during recent operations. Possessing in a marked degree the real offensive spirit, he sets a notable example to the other pilots of his squadron by his utter disregard of personal danger

The DFC was the first of the flying decorations and replaced the Military Cross which had been awarded to some early military aviators. The DFC was instituted by King George V on 3 June 1918. It was awarded for displaying valour, gallantry and devotion to duty on one or more occasions, while flying on active operations against the enemy.

Tommy Rose's other medals:

1914-1915 Star, British War Medal, Victory Medal

This, and the following two medals known fondly as Pip, Squeak and Wilfred, the nicknames coming from a popular comic strip of the time from the *Daily Mirror* newspaper. Pip was a dog, Squeak a penguin and Wilfred was a baby rabbit.

1914-15 Star (ribbon only, the medal has been missing since 1925)
This bronze medal with a red, white and blue watered silk ribbon was awarded to those who served in any theatre of war between 5 August 1914 and 31 December 1915. Total number of medals awarded 2,350,000.

British War Medal
This silver medal with an orange centred ribbon with black, white and royal blue edges was introduced to record the successful conclusion of the war and awarded to anyone who saw service at any time between 1914 and 1918. Total number of medals awarded 6,500,000 in silver.

FLIGHT LIEUTENANT THOMAS 'TOMMY' ROSE DFC

Tommy Rose's medals on display at the Alderney Museum. From left to right: the Distinguished Flying Cross, the 1914-1915 Star (missing since 1925), the British War medal, Victory medal and the Indian General Service Medal with two bars: one for Waziristan 1919-1921, and the other for Mahsud 1919-1920. (*Sarah Chambers*)

Victory Medal
This yellow bronze medal with a double rainbow ribbon was awarded to all who had received the Star medal and most of those who had received the British War Medal. Total number of medals awarded approx. 6,000,000.

Medals awarded for overseas service post First World War

The Indian General Service Medal
The medal is 1.4 in (36 mm) in diameter. It was struck at both the Calcutta and London mints and was for Indian and British forces respectively. For early campaigns it was awarded in silver to combatants from 1919 onwards. The name and details of the recipient were engraved or impressed on the edge of the medal.

The Mahsud 1919-1920 clasp
The Third Afghan War set the Frontier alight, with no tribe being more dangerous than the Mahsuds. This clasp was awarded for service in the Mahsud punitive Derajat Column under Major General Skeen between 19 December 1919 and 8 April 1920. This clasp is usually found with the Waziristan 1919-1921 clasp, as in Tommy Rose's medal.

Waziristan 1919-1921 clasp
Awarded for service against the Tochi Waziris, Wana Waziris and Mahsuds on the North-West Frontier, between May 1919 and January 1921.

THE ROYAL AIR FORCE 1918–1926

An AW Atlas at Netheravon, being worked on in 1926. (*via Peter Amos*)

On 3 November 1918 Tommy Rose was posted to Shoreham, the home of the South-Eastern Area Flying Instructors School, which was formed on 1 July 1918 with a miscellany of aircraft, including Avro 504A/J/K, SE5A, Bristol F.2B Fighter, Bristol M1c Monoplane Scout, Sopwith Pup, Sopwith Triplane, Sopwith Camel Two-seater, and Sopwith Snipe. On 10 November 1918 Tommy returned to No. 30 Training Station Depot, at RAF Northolt.

Tommy Rose was then posted to the Central Despatch Pool of Pilots on 14 February 1919. This unit was formed on 1 April 1918 at the Orchard Hotel, 5, Portman Street, London and, as a ferry pilots pool it was responsible for giving details of postings to pilots, it was disbanded on 1 July 1919.

On 1 March 1919, Tommy Rose was posted to No. 2 Depot, RAF Uxbridge, then on 10 September 1919, he was posted to the RAF Depot, Halton.

The *London Gazette* (11468) reported that, with effect from 12 September 1919, Tommy Rose had been granted a three years short service commission with the rank of Flying Officer.

The Waziristan campaign 1919-1920

This military campaign was conducted in Waziristan by British and Indian Forces against the fiercely independent tribesmen that inhabited this region. These operations were conducted in 1919-1920 following the unrest that arose in the aftermath of the Third Anglo-Afghan war and *Flight* for 7 November 1919, reported:

> **INDIAN FRONTIER AIR WORK**
> *From messages to hand from Waziristan, it appears the air raids against the Waziris and the Mahsuds have proved effective. The air operation commenced on 13 November when Kaniguram, Makin and Marobi were bombed by twenty-five aeroplanes which dropped five tons of bombs. Operations continued daily, and although machines had been heavily fired at, all returned safely. The offending section of the Wazirs have accepted unreservedly the British terms, and against the Mahuds air operations continue.*

On 3 January 1920, Tommy Rose joined No. 99 Squadron, based at Mianwali, India, equipped with DH9As, and their brief job was to patrol the North West Frontier.

Birmingham Daily Gazette for 25 March 1920, reported:

> **FLYING FOR TAXES**
> *It was mentioned in the House of Commons a few days ago that RAF aeroplanes had been recently used for the collecting of taxes in Mesopotamia. This method, although novel, is by no means new, during the troubles on the North-West Frontier of India in the early part of 1919, the scheme was carried out.*
>
> *The Mahsuds and the Waziris in the wild mountainous and roadless 'buffer state' of Waziristan had been 'naughty', and as a punishment heavier taxes were levied upon them, but the first attempt to collect them, by armoured motor car, although not ending disastrously, was a complete and ignominious failure for the collectors. Other attempts on similar lines met with no better success, and the idea of collecting the money was for a time abandoned.*

The Politics

The North-West Frontier represented a natural geographic boundary to the British Raj. A barren, mountainous chain rising up from the fertile Indus plain it also marked a cultural and economic boundary. This discontinuity generated long-lasting unrest that erupted in waves of extreme violence.

Frontier strategy balanced three interconnected issues: the 'Great Game' with Russia, Afghan intrigue, and tribal unrest. Britain went to extreme lengths to ensure that Afghanistan remained within its sphere of influence (and outside Russia's), including the 1838 First Afghan War and the 1878 Second Afghan War which, in turn resulted in the Third Afghan War, in which Tommy Rose and No. 27 Squadron were to become involved.

The prelude to the 1919-1920 campaign was an incursion by the Mahsud Tribe in the summer of 1917 while British forces were engaged in fighting in the First World War. The British forces eventually restored calm, but in 1919 the Waziris took advantage of unrest in Afghanistan following the Third Anglo-Afghan War to launch more raids against British garrisons. It has been asserted that one of the reasons for these raids was that a rumour had been spread amongst the Wazirs and the Mahsuds that Britain was going to give control of Waziristan to Afghanistan as part of the peace settlement following the Third Anglo-Afghan War. Buoyed by this prospect and sensing British weakness, the tribes were encouraged to launch a series of large-scale raids in the administered areas and by November 1919, they had killed over 200 people and wounded a further 200.

Geographical

Waziristan lies in the western border in the Indian Empire and forms the connecting link on the Afghan frontier between the districts of Kurram and Zhob. For political and administrative purposes, it was divided into Northern and Southern Waziristan, its shape resembling a rough parallelogram, 5,000 square miles in extent, practically the whole of which is a tangled mass of mountains and hills of every size, shape and bearing.

The two chief highways of Waziristan are the Tochi and the Gomal Valleys, the former giving access from the Bannu district to the Afghan district of Birmal, and the latter connecting the two British districts of Derajat and Zhob and forming the principal route used by Powindah caravans in their annual migration from Afghanistan to India.

The Waziristan troubles 1919-1920

The first attempt to subdue these warring tribes was made in November 1919, when Major General Sir Andrew Skeen launched a series of operations against the Tochi Wazirs. These operations were largely successful, and terms were agreed. In December 1919, Skeen turned his attention to the Mahsuds. As the 4th and 67th Brigades were grouped together as the Derajet Column, and committed to the fighting, they met with heavy resistance as the largely inexperienced Indian units came up against determined and well-armed tribesmen. Due to the denuding of the Indian Army caused by commitments overseas during the First World War, many of the battalions employed in the campaign were second-line units with disproportionately large numbers of very young soldiers and inexperienced officers.

The fighting continued for about twelve months in this vein, and the British had to resort to using aircraft on a number of occasions to supress the tribesmen. There were a number of successes though, notably the 2nd/5th Gurkhas stand during the eight-day battle in January 1920 at Ahnai Tangi, and efforts of the 2nd/76th Punjabis, who fought their way through to support them. Equally notable was the counter-attack launched against the Mahsuds by just ten men of the 4th/39th Garhwal Rifles, led by Lieutenant William David Kenny, who received a posthumous Victoria Cross for his actions.

The Mahsuds took heavy casualties during the fighting at Ahnai Tangi, and it was these casualties, as well as the destruction of their villages a month later by the RAF bombers, that temporarily subdued the Mahsuds. When the Wana Wazirs rose up in November 1920, they appealed for help from the Wahsuds, but still recovering from their earlier defeat, no support was forthcoming and the Wazir opposition faded away. On 22 December 1920, Wana was reoccupied.

Air operations

During December 1919, a month before Tommy Rose was posted to No. 99 Squadron, the RAF had been carrying out a programme of intensive activity including night raids, against the Mahsud villages, until it was confirmed that these had been vacated. Damage was done to material and personnel; throughout the country the greater proportion of the inhabitants had left their homes and took to the caves or the hills.

To enable the harassing of the tribesmen to be carried out, the Mahsud country was divided into three sub areas, each of which was allocated to one squadron, at least one machine being over each area all day. This proved effective, and much damage was done to flocks and personnel.

Three more Bristol F.2B Fighters were lent to the Force and a specially intensive programme of aerial bombardment was made, with a daily average of over 10,000lbs of bombs being dropped, despite all these efforts, at no time did it appear that the Mahuds would submit from the effect of the air operations alone.

The ability to fly at low altitudes depended on the employment of suitable machines, the dispersion of targets and consequently of fire. The sight of a flight of low flying machines at close quarters, and the feeling of danger induced by the noise they made, militated against the accurate fire from the tribesmen.

The conclusion of the 1919-1920 Waziristan campaign resulted in a comparatively peaceful state and Sir Sefton Brancker wrote in 1921:

'It seems obvious that the garrison in India can be reduced to the strength necessary for purely defensive work, and that all offensive operations, both on the frontier and internally, can be entrusted to the Royal Air Force, with a great saving in money and far greater saving in men'.

No. 27 Squadron moved to Risalpur, India on 15 April 1920 (now in Pakistan).

Tommy Rose returned home, departing from Bombay, on 7 January 1922, and arriving at Southampton on 28 January 1922. On 13 March 1922, he was posted from the RAF Depot, Uxbridge, to the Central Flying School at RAF Upavon, to train as a flying instructor.

RAF Upavon 13 March 1922 – 1 July 1922

Referred to as 'the birthplace of the Royal Air Force', Upavon was where the Central Flying School (CFS) was formed on 13 May 1912. The CFS was under the command of Captain G.M. Paine RN, with Major H. Trenchard (the future father of the RAF) as his assistant. The site was originally an Army training gallops and considering the number of potential locations across Salisbury Plain, Upavon was far from the best, the site was split by Andover Road, with its flying area to the south and domestic area to the north.

RAF Netheravon 1 July 1922 – 28 July 1924

RAF Netheravon at that time were using Avro 504K, Avro 504N, Sopwith Snipe, DH9A and Bristol F.2B Fighter aircraft. Tommy Rose was to spend two years there, mainly training officers of the Fleet Air Arm.

On 1 July 1923 Tommy was posted to RAF Netheravon as a Flying Instructor and *Flight* for 5 July 1923 reported:

*The fourth Aerial Pageant took place with the usual punctuality and freedom from accident of any kind at Hendon last Saturday (*4 July*), and this presented an entirely new and different atmosphere.*

THE ROYAL AIR FORCE 1918–1926

During the morning, with its blue sky and bright sunshine giving promise of real summer conditions, Hendon aerodrome presented a busy appearance, what with machines arriving, making trial flights and sundry eliminating trials for certain of the afternoon's events being held.

The relay race, for the challenge cup, presented by HRH the Duke of York, consisted of Avros, a Bristol Fighter, and Sopwith Snipes from each of the six RAF stations, competed (eliminating heats having been flown in the morning). The Avro started first over one lap of the course previously flown, and on landing each had to hand over the tally disc to its respective Bristol Fighter, which then took off and flew over the same course, handing the disc to its waiting Snipe as before. The Snipes then started off (Flight Lieutenant T. Rose DFC, V.P. Feather and Flight Lieutenant J.W. Woodhouse DSO).

The final lap, finishing past the Royal Box, in the following order: Farnborough, Netheravon, Halton, Spittlegate, Northolt and Upavon.

Flight for 26 March 1964 included a letter, dated 1 December 1923, to the editor, by an old student from RAF Netheravon, Captain J.S. Sheppard of Leixlip, County Kildare, when he was learning to fly at RAF Netheravon in 1923 and this is reproduced below:

Sir,
Your picture of the DH 9a in 'Straight and Level' (March 12) vividly recalls to me certain excitements at Netheravon on 1 December 1923. On that day, under the supervision of my flight commander, Flight Lieutenant Jack Woodhouse, I took off in DH 9a E209 to be tested on my fitness to go solo. I made two successful landings and was gliding in for my third when I was roused from a deep sleep by Flight Lieutenant Tommy Rose shaking my shoulder (both pilots were found unconscious by Tommy Rose – SC).

There was a curious sort of silence, and a strong smell of petrol and new-mown hay, but it took me some time to realise that I had flown into the side of a hayrick. Flight Lieutenant Woodhouse had also been knocked unconscious – and small wonder, as we had decelerated from 80 mph to full stop in three yards at an estimated 12g.

My safety belt came adrift on impact so that I shot forward and through the instrument panel. We were indestructible in those days, both occupants being back on flying duties in less than a week.

I should like to pay tribute to that legendary hero Tommy Rose, who, seeing the crash from his Avro 504K, landed close to the hayrick and rushed over in time to switch off the ignition before a fire started. The rick being saturated with petrol, and the ignition of the Delco-Remy battery type, it was only a miracle that prevented our incineration.

I enjoyed another 14,000 hrs of flying before retiring from BOAC in 1946. I have not heard recently of the other two pilots in the story, but I hope both are well and flourishing. At the time Flight Lieutenant Woodhouse was one of the great DH 9A pilots in the RAF, and it was ironic that he should have allowed a fool to fly him into a hayrick.

CFS RAF Upavon 28 July 1924 – 1 September 1924

On 28 July 1924, Tommy Rose was posted back to RAF Upavon to attend a course at the Central Flying School. It was whilst Tommy Rose was stationed at Upavon, that it is thought he met, and courted, Margaret Elizabeth Ashford, a farmer's daughter from Laverstock, near Salisbury. He was playing competitive Rugby for the RAF, and later for Bath, Somerset and Richmond, but the season ended in March, he also played cricket, Tommy and several other friends, decided to join the Salisbury Tennis Club, introduced by a couple of the pilots who were already members.

The club was well known in the area for putting on dances and whist drives over the winter period, and it was an ideal opportunity to have a break from the all-male environment on the base. Tommy Rose was then settled into his career and it would be an ideal opportunity to keep his fitness levels up in the summer months.

Rugby Years 1921–1926

One little known fact about Tommy Rose was he played Rugby not only for the RAF from 1921, but also for Bath, Somerset and, in 1926/1927, Richmond. He had all the attributes, a team player, stamina, determination and above all he was a good sport. Tommy was also awarded four caps for his participation in the Inter-Services Rugby Football games against the Army. He continued playing Rugby after leaving the RAF in October 1926, joining Richmond and playing his first match with them on 4 October, until the end of the season on 26 March 1927, during this season with Richmond, the team had fifteen wins, and seven losses.

Competitive air racing took over from competitive rugby, Tommy once stated 'flying is the only sport you can compete in sitting down'!

Tommy joined the Bath team and played his debut game with them, against Gloucester, on 15 November 1923, an away match played at the Gloucester ground. He played a total of thirty matches for Bath and his final match was on 3 January 1925, against Richmond, which Bath won 6-1.

A note from the Bath Rugby Heritage website, stated:

Tommy Rose was an RAF flier, stationed on Salisbury Plain. He played anywhere in the forwards, thirty times in all. Rose was a good footballer, and a good sport, and one of the best fellows who ever wore a Bath jersey.

THE ROYAL AIR FORCE 1918–1926

The fixture list for the 1920-21 season showed matches against Blackheath, Cambridge University, Harlequins, Leicester, Llanelly, Northampton and Devonport Services, played at Devonport and this was the first recorded match Tommy Rose appeared in for the RAF on 2 February 1921. All of these matches were played between 27 December 1920 and 5 March 1921.

The 13 October 1922 saw Tommy Rose playing for the RAF against Seaton, which they won 18-15, and on 17 April 1923 Netheravon against Duxford played at the Richmond ground.

The *Western Morning News* for Friday, 18 October 1922, reported:

AIRMEN GIVE SEATON A FAST GAME
At Seaton yesterday about 1,000 spectators saw a fine game between Seaton and the Royal Air Force (Netheravon). The Airmen played with the sun and wind behind them in the first, and tries were scored by Rose, Usher, Coventry, and White. Half-time: RAF 18 points Seaton Nil.

On resuming, Seaton played much better, and tries were scored by Richards (Honiton), W. Summers (Honiton 2), Campbell (Plymouth), converted game ended with the score: RAF 18 points; Seaton, 15.

On 15 September 1923, Tommy joined Bath Rugby Club, and made his debut in the Bath v Gloucester match.

The RAF won nearly all their Inter-Services matches; they beat the Army in 1924 as well as the Royal Navy, and drew with the Army in 1925. Tommy Rose competed in seven Inter-Services matches, between 1923 and 1926.

On 12 January 1925, Tommy was posted to No. 29 Squadron at Duxford.

The RAF football side who beat the Army 8-3 in 1924. The light blue, dark blue and maroon striped shirts were still being worn, and the newly established convention of RAF crests, for Inter-Service matches only, was being observed. Tommy Rose is seated to the right of front row.

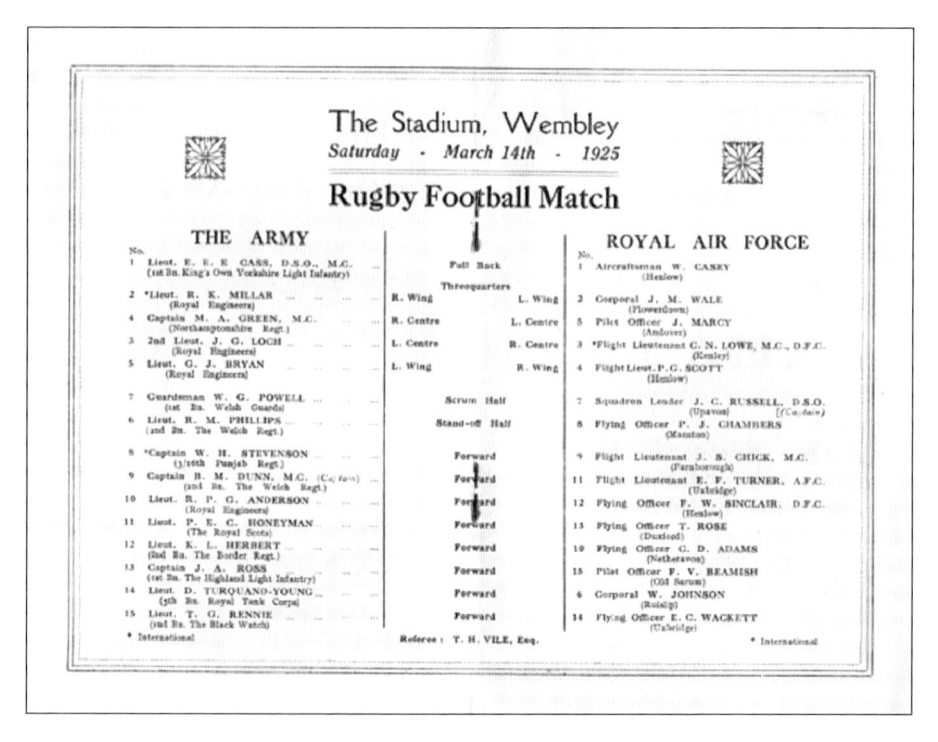

> **The Stadium, Wembley**
> Saturday · March 14th · 1925
> **Rugby Football Match**
>
> [Programme listing THE ARMY vs ROYAL AIR FORCE teams]

The middle pages from the official programme. Dated 14 March 1925, Tommy is listed as number 13 under the RAF section.

No. 29 Squadron at Duxford

The squadron was equipped with Gloster Grebe II.
Meanwhile, on 27 June 1925, the *Bath Chronicle and Weekly Gazette* reported:

> *The Bath footballer, Flying Officer T. Rose DFC RAF, is getting married on 16 July at Laverstock. His bride is Margaret Ashford.*

The time spent at the Salisbury Lawn Tennis Club, and at other social venues, helped Tommy Rose get to know Margaret Ashford and her family well, but it is not known when they became engaged, but they were married on 16 July 1925 at St Andrews Church, Laverstock, near Salisbury, Wiltshire.

Bath Chronicle and Herald for 17 July 1925 reported:

> **FLYING OFFICER T. ROSE AND MISS M. ASHFORD**
> *The marriage took place yesterday at St Andrew's Church, Laverstock, of Flying Officer, Thomas Rose, DFC, RAF, son of Mr John Rose, Basing Park, Alton, Hampshire, and Miss Margaret Ashford, daughter*

of Mr and Mrs W.T. Ashford, Mill House, Mill Lane Salisbury, the Vicar was Reverend A. Aldworth.

The church had been nicely decorated with beautiful arrangements. The hymns sung during the service were 'Heavenly Father' and 'O Perfect Love', at the end of the service the organist played Mendelssohn's wedding march. The bride who was given away by her father, wore a dress of white georgette embroidered with pearl with silver tissue train covered and embroidered with tulle, the veil was trimmed with old lace and orange blossoms. She carried a bouquet of harrisii lilies and white heather. The bridesmaids were Miss R. Lush (cousin of the bride), D. Sargent and P. Reid, their headdresses were mauve georgette with pearl trimming, finished with bunches of mauve and pink flowers, they carried bouquets of mauve sweet peas. Their gifts from the groom, were gold vanity boxes. Mr R.S. Blucke, RAF, acted as best man. A reception was held afterwards at the County Hotel, and later the bride and groom left for their honeymoon, which is being spent in the West of England. The bride wore a dress of grey georgette. The bride gave the groom a gold wristwatch. The groom gave the bride a fur coat.

Tommy's fellow officers at Netheravon all attended the wedding and they had all clubbed together to buy a silver cigarette box as a wedding gift, with the inscription 'from old friends at Netheravon 16 July 1925'.

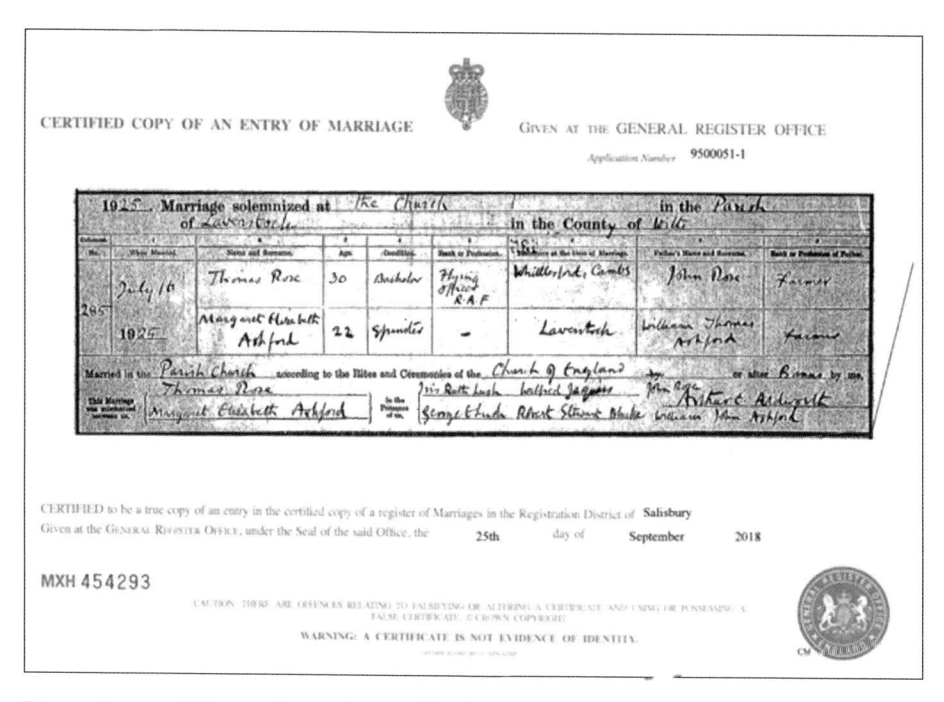

Tommy Rose and Margaret's marriage certificate.

FLIGHT LIEUTENANT THOMAS 'TOMMY' ROSE DFC

Taken at the County Hotel, Salisbury. Best man Robert Blucke, Margaret and Tommy Rose, and bridesmaids Miss R. Lush (Margaret's cousin), Miss D. Sargent and Miss P. Reid (Margaret's friends). (*William Hale Collection*)

No. 43 Squadron, Henlow 7 August 1925 – 12 September 1926

Tommy Rose was posted to No. 43 Squadron, based at Henlow. which was equipped with Sopwith Snipe and Gamecock aircraft, and the *London Gazette* reported that, with effect from 1 January 1926, Tommy Rose had been promoted from Flying Officer to Flight Lieutenant.

On 26 March 1926, Squadron Leader Brooke flew No. 43 Squadron's first Gloster Gamecock I in to Henlow – and so they became known as 'The Fighting Cocks'.

The Gloster Gamecock was a development of the earlier Gloster Grebe. Powered with an un-supercharged Bristol Jupiter VI, nine-cylinder radial of 450hp, it had a top speed of 155 mph, climbed to 10,000ft in seven and a half minutes and was armed with twin Vickers Mk I machine guns synchronised to fire through the propeller.

Although there was provision for oxygen equipment and a wireless receiver/transmitter unit, both of which existed at the time, these were rarely fitted. To quote Tommy Rose, '*recovery from a spin was not an even money bet*'. The poor spin recovery characteristic was probably due to the already small rudder being made even less effective by the blanketing effect of the deep fuselage.

The Army breaking away from the scrum. Match against the Royal Air Force at Twickenham. Though this is unfortunately a poor quality image, Tommy can be seen on the right, behind the player who is in possession of the ball. The match was played on Saturday, 27 March 1926.

Tommy Rose also said that, *'for its purpose the Gamecock was the best aeroplane of its generation, a real gentleman's aeroplane'*. The performance of the Gamecock at the Hendon Air Pageants was never quite equalled by its later and heavier successors.

Re-formed four days after the 1925 pageant, No. 43 Squadron began preparing for the 1926 show, using a reservoir near Biggleswade as the target. They spent all their time practicing formation dive bombing, as the particular part allocated to 43 was to attack the set piece 'hostile aerodrome' with bombs, and then make another attack with machine guns, before retiring and allowing the 'heavies' Vickers Vimys to finish off the job. This was the part that No. 43 Squadron did to perfection at the actual display but more, they concluded their performance by doing what nobody had done before at Hendon, and that was landing in formation.

'Actually', said Tommy Rose, *'it was a close-run thing for we never succeeded during the rehearsals but, on the great day itself, everything was spot-on'*. The subsequent signal, *'My hearty congratulations on the magnificent display given by your squadron in the set piece. Give my personal congratulations to all your pilots and mechanics,'* was received from Air Chief Marshal Sir Hugh Trenchard.

In July 1926 the RAF Pageant was held at Hendon, although Tommy Rose was not mentioned by name in any of the press articles, it is known he took part in it from the history of No. 43 Squadron, and the *Sphere* for 10 July 1926 reported:

> *The RAF Pageant at Hendon on Saturday last was easily the most important of the many outdoor functions held over the weekend. It is estimated 100,000 spectators witnessed the thrilling display, and that more machines were seen in the air at one time than ever before in England.*

Tommy Rose was transferred into the RAF Reserve on 17 September 1926, and he left the RAF at the end of October 1926. The following few months were spent looking for a career outside the constraints of military life.

He eventually started work for the Anglo-American Company at Brooklands, overseeing the installation of the first aero pumping station for aircraft, also obtaining his Commercial Pilots 'B' Licence, whilst working at Brooklands.

Taken at the time Tommy Rose left the RAF in 1926. (*William Hale Collection*)

Chapter 5

Anglo American Oil Company January 1927 – February 1928
The first aviation fuel pump in the UK, Rugby Matches

'Adventure is the essence of life.'
– Dick Rutan, piloted Voyager aircraft
around the world non-stop

Tommy Rose left the RAF in October 1926 and for the next couple of months he was having a well-earned holiday as well as looking for his first civilian job. He knew he could never take up a permanent 'desk bound' job and whatever career move he made would have to somehow include flying.

Despite his considerable piloting skills, he had to somehow raise his profile within the influential flying circles, to catch the eye of potential wealthy sponsors and patrons, to do this he needed to be based at an airfield, either teaching students to fly or have access to suitable aircraft with which to display his acrobatic skills, and also be able to compete in races and pageants.

This was not going to be an easy task, aerodromes, flying and flying schools were only just beginning to become established in the 1920s. In 1923, Sir Sefton Brancker, the first Director-General of Civil Aviation at the British Air Ministry, announced Britain's 'future lies in the air, just as our past has come from the sea'. Sir Sefton Brancker continued to be an avid pioneer supporter of the civil and military aviation and in particular, fledgling flying clubs, right up to his untimely and tragic death in the airship R101, which crashed on 5 October 1930.

The flying community in those days was a very close knit one, and if a job was to be found, particularly one that would involve flying, the best place to start would be a fledgling aero club, or perhaps at one of the first established airfields in the country such as Brooklands in Weybridge, Surrey.

Tommy Rose needed to obtain his commercial 'B' licence if he was to be able to offer his services as a professional pilot, and to be able to carry fare paying passengers. This requirement was fulfilled in 1926, Anglo-American Oil Company were looking for someone to oversee the installation and management of the first aero fuel pump in the country at Brooklands.

Shortly after Brooklands motor-racing track was opened it soon also became an aerodrome, although it was some time before it was generally referred to as such. It was first known as the 'Brooklands Aviation Ground'. As far back as September

ANGLO AMERICAN OIL COMPANY

1907, A.V. Roe (Sir Alliott Verdon-Rose), was experimenting with his first aeroplane. There were other early pioneers experimenting with aeroplanes elsewhere in Britain, but the fact that manufacturing companies, attracted by the efforts of A.V. Roe, were establishing themselves at Brooklands is justification for regarding the place as the original home of the British Aircraft Industry.

After the war the airfield grew from strength to strength, and even motor racing returned, making Brooklands a very exciting place to be. The first flying school to operate at Brooklands was the Henderson Flying School, which was registered early in 1927, as a successor to the business which Lieutenant Colonel G.L.P. Henderson had been operating in Croydon.

In 1926, Brooklands held its first international motor race – the first British Grand Prix, which raced in an anti-clockwise direction and made use of the Finishing Straight, to reflect the characteristics of the road circuit. In the following year the aerodrome followed. The school began operations with three 'Avro' biplanes – two 548s and a 'Mono-Gnome 504K'. Grahame Henderson was the chief flying instructor.

In 1927, the school started an air-taxi service at the rate of £4 per hour, flying the 'Avros' at 75 mph to 80 mph. These machines were also used for banner-towing, a single horizontal banner trailing behind the top of the plane and over the rudder.

What was the importance of 'Pratts' aviation fuel? The following article from *Flight* gives the background to Anglo-American Oil's rise in the field of aviation fuel.

Flight, 9 December 1926, ran an article on Anglo-American Oil Limited:

> *Successful aircraft performance relies upon the qualities and characteristics of fuel used as much as any other item forming a part of the design of the machine concerned. The production of a fuel that will give the best results under a variety of conditions is a vast problem in itself, and that this problem has been tackled with success by the Anglo-American Oil Co Ltd, of 36, Queen Anne's Gate, SW 1 – who started marketing motor spirit suitable for aviation as early as 1896 – is demonstrated by the large number of big aviation events, from the early days up to the present time, that have been accomplished on 'Pratts'.*
>
> *'Pratts' was also successful in several of the big post-war racing events, for instance, the 1926 King's Cup Race was won on this fuel by Captain H.S. Broad, who achieved a remarkable win in this annual event on a DH Moth light plane fitted with a 27-60hp, 'Cirrus' engine, after a splendid fight against bigger and more powerful rivals. He completed the two days 1,464 miles in 16 hours 22 minutes 20 seconds, or at an average speed of 90.4 mph.*
>
> *Another 'Pratts' success in the sporting side was at Lympne during this year's light plane competitions when Mr L.P. Openshaw made the fastest time (105.5 mph) in the Grosvenor Cup Race on the Westland 'Widgeon' monoplane, fitted with an Armstrong Siddeley 'Genet' engine. 'Pratts' has also found success amongst the recently formed Light Aeroplane Clubs in their sporting events.*

FLIGHT LIEUTENANT THOMAS 'TOMMY' ROSE DFC

> *Last, but by no means least, the Anglo-American Oil Co. has important business in connection with the commercial side of aviation and it is hardly necessary to point out that as regards an air service, carrying passengers, mails and goods, reliability is of the utmost importance. One of the factors necessary in obtaining the reliability is, of course, the use of a suitable fuel – and, incidentally, its supply. In this connection, the Anglo-American Oil Co, has built up a sound reputation, and it may be of interest to note that this firm handles the total business in this country of the French Air Union Co, who operate the commercial air service between Paris and London.*
>
> *They have an efficient organisation, both at Croydon and Lympne, for replenishing with 'Pratts' spirit the fuel tanks of the Air Union machines during their comings and goings. At Paris and other French airports, the Air Union's requirements are looked after by their associated company, Messrs L'Economique of 82, Champs Elysees, Paris.*

Five leading oil companies supplied the drivers at Brooklands with their fuel in the 1920s and 1930s, these were BP, Cleveland Discol, Pratts (Esso), Redline and Shell. All built their pumps in 1922, each had their own petrol filling station built in the 'pagoda' style. Anglo-American Oil Company Limited (Pratts) who had been developing motor spirit suitable for aviation engines as early as 1896, spotting a niche in the market, wanted to install the *first* aviation fuel station in the UK, and more importantly, one that sold 'Pratts' in the UK and Brooklands, with its significant reputation, would be a perfect place to install one. The fuel station had underground tanks and electric delivery pumps, therefore getting the edge on their competitors already established at Brooklands who delivered their fuels to motorcars.

Anglo-American Oil Company was the first company to install petrol pumps and give its support to bulk storage installations, by 1927 they had over 20,000 Pratts pumps in operation throughout the British Isles and were considered the leaders in the field of fuel distribution at this time.

Brooklands was considered to be the birthplace of British aviation so where better than to install Great Britain's first dedicated aero fuel pumping station. Anglo-American had been the leaders in motor spirit but now turned their attention to aviation spirit, Brooklands was an important growing aerodrome and they wanted to be able to claim they had installed the first aviation filling station.

In January 1927, Tommy Rose was at Brooklands obtaining his 'B' Licence, Number 1257, and this led to him being offered a job at Brooklands when the area Manager for Anglo-American was looking for a suitable candidate to not only oversee the installation of the very first UK 'Pratts' fuel station, but also to manage and dispense the aero fuel. There he would be well placed to meet fellow aviators whilst refuelling the flying school's aircraft, and with his magnetic personality and warm cheery nature, he would be bound to secure something more suitable later.

From the book '*Brief history of Brooklands Airfield*' p192:

> *The first flying school to operate at Brooklands after the First World War was the Henderson Flying School, which was registered early in 1927, in*

ANGLO AMERICAN OIL COMPANY

The first UK Aero Filling Station, installed March 1927, at Brooklands. The Henderson's Flying School Avro shown in the illustration. (*Flight* for 26 May 1927)

the Summer of 1927, the school started an air-taxi service, which would need regular refuelling.

The first filling station primarily for aircraft refuelling was officially opened at Brooklands by the Anglo-American Oil Company Limited, whose painted sign 'Pratts Air Service' became a familiar sight, came into use in March 1927.

From the book '*Fifty Years of Brooklands*' p 96:

The first filling station intended primarily for aircraft, was installed at Brooklands by the Anglo-American Oil Company Limited, whose painted sign, 'Pratts Air Service', became a familiar sight. In charge of the station was Flight Lieutenant Tom Rose. This station first came into use in April 1927 and was of great service during the King's Cup Air Race flown on 20 and 21 the following year.

Tommy Rose at this time was also continuing with competitive rugby matches. The season opened late, on 4 October 1926, the month Tommy Rose left the RAF, but this time he was playing for Richmond Rugby Club for the 1926/1927 season, the last season he played rugby, as his future interests would lean towards competitive air racing.

The first mention of Tommy playing Rugby was in an article in the *Western Daily Press*, for 13 December 1926:

PALMER GETS 12 POINTS AGAINST BATH
Two old Somerset and Bath forwards – Tommy Rose, the RAF forward, and H.W.H. Considine, brother of the International. Palmer in the first half was allowed to get three tries, and Barr added a goal kick, while Bath, except for brilliance in occasional efforts, looked on. Even the forward's work was not up to standard.

The next match reported upon in the *Western Daily Press* for 3 January 1927:

FOUR POINTS DOWN
Bath played much better football than they did in the two preceding matches, when they met Richmond on the recreation ground, and eventually lost to a strong side by 1 penalty goal and 4 tries (15 points) to

FLIGHT LIEUTENANT THOMAS 'TOMMY' ROSE DFC

Aerial photo taken in 1929 of the first aviation fuel station at Brooklands. (*Brooklands Museum J Temple*)

a goal, a penalty goal, and a try (11 points). Richmond were without A.R. Aslett and two of the selected forwards and Bath turned out without D. Janes, their full back, for whom W. Bishop, a junior player from Walcot OB deputised, and did very well, together with R. Banks. They included in their side Hector Mackay, a Lancashire centre, who is staying at Shockerwick, and who made a good impression. I.J. Pitman operated as standoff half, but this does not seem to be his position. Eric Chard came in as an extra three quarter. Included in the visitors' side were H.W.H. Considine brother of S.G.U. Considine, an old Bath player himself, and Tommy Rose of Somerset, the RAF, and Bath, who was glad to renew acquaintance with Len Bisgrove, the Weston-super-Mare forward who was assisting his old club.

By the second half Bath woke up and pressed Richmond hard, but Pitman was slow in getting his three's off the mark, while many passes went astray. While Richmond rested through good tough kicking, Bath's kicking was never the same. Bishop showed style and speed and is a young recruit that should be useful. Turguand Young dribbled the ball away from his own line, and the Richmond three's got in a delightful bout of passing – not the first of the afternoon by any means. Tommy Rose dived over for another try, Considine hitting the post with the shot. Goold got through, dribbled on and scored a great try for Bath on time. Richmond defended hard in the last minutes. It was a keen open game.

An interesting article appeared in the *Chester Chronicle,* for Saturday, 5 May 1945, regarding Tommy Rose in the back of a Mercedes, the event was thought to have taken place in 1927, see below:

ANGLO AMERICAN OIL COMPANY

TURF PRODUCTION

In 1914 Mr Claude Pierrepont Hunter's specialist knowledge of turf production was early requested by the Government. Between 1914 and 1918 over thirty aerodromes and acceptance parks were seeded. Later he evolved a technique of aerodrome construction, so specialised and so successful as to receive unsought at the hands of C.G. Grey the Editor of 'The Aeroplane', the designation 'Hunterising'. From this starting point 'hunterised' became the recognised standard of smooth and firm excellence, as Macadam, called after its inventor, was indicative of high road perfection.

It may be of interest to add that Mr Hunter held the still unbroken speed record for driving a car on one of his own Sussex aerodromes at 72 mph. The car was his own 36/220hp supercharged Mercedes, one of the passengers being the great flier Tommy Rose.

After just over a year, during which time Tommy Rose had also obtained a 'B' licence, he was ready to start work with a flying club as a flying instructor.

Chapter 6

Midland Aero Club, Castle Bromwich February 1928 – June 1929
Air Pageants, Races and the birth of a Daughter

'There is an art to flying. The knack lies in learning how to throw yourself at the ground and miss.'
– Douglas Adams, The Hitchhikers Guide to the Galaxy

Tommy Rose once told a friend, *'there was nothing more rewarding, than to see months of nurturing a student through the processes of learning to fly, than to see them perform their first solo flight and obtain their wings'.* An opportunity came to do just this when the Midland Aero Club were looking for an experienced instructor, so at the age of thirty-three he moved with his wife Margaret to 25, Eachelhurst Road, Erdington, Birmingham, ready for his next career move.

Castle Bromwich Aerodrome was an early airfield, situated to the north of Castle Bromwich in the West Midlands. A large piece of Warwickshire grassland (Castle Bromwich playing fields) then became the privately-owned Castle Bromwich aerodrome, and Midland Aero Club established itself there.

Midland Aeroclub taken around the time Tommy Rose was at the club. (*Martyn Chorlton*)

MIDLAND AERO CLUB, CASTLE BROMWICH

Flight for 22 January 1925, reported:

> The Midland Aero Club, which was formed in 1909, has now been officially appointed by the Air Ministry as the authority for control of the Air Ministry Light Aircraft Scheme in the Midland area. The Club is being reorganised, and the Lord Mayor of Birmingham (Alderman P. Bower) has consented to become President.
>
> Since the war the Club has organised for the Royal Aero Club at Castle Bromwich 'controls', in connection with the various long-distance races, such as the King's Cup and the Grosvenor Cup. These meetings were very popular and exceedingly well attended and gave ample proof of the interest existing. Since the advent of the Air Ministry Light Aeroplane Scheme, the Club has received a large influx of new members, a large proportion of who possess expert knowledge and experience gained in the Air Force, and it is anticipated that the Club will obtain a very live and enthusiastic membership.
>
> The annual subscription is fixed at £1 1s for the first 500 members, after which there will be an entrance fee of £1 1s. Ladies and boys under 18 are admitted at a subscription of 10s 6d.

Flight for 15 October 1925, reported:

> The Lord Mayor of Birmingham, Alderman Percival Bower, president of the Midland Aero Club, reopened the aerodrome at Castle Bromwich on 6 October, for flying in connection with this club – one of those formed under the Air Ministry's Light Aeroplane scheme. He also accepted three Sopwith 'Pups', with 80hp engines, the gift of Mr James Palethorpe, a Midland flying enthusiast. The Club has two De Havilland Moth light aeroplanes, and the Siddeley Company have sent over two of their latest machines for the use of members.

1928

Flight for 1 March 1928, reported:

> The club under the presidency of Mr Herbert A. Pepper, chairman of the council, on Friday evening entertained to dinner Mr McDonough, who had been flying instructor for the past two and a half years and has received an appointment in Canada. Many tributes were made to the exceptional abilities of Mr McDonough as an instructor, and also to Mr E.J. Halland the ground engineer, for having maintained such a high standard of aircraft maintenance.
>
> Flight Lieutenant T. Rose DFC, the newly appointed instructor, replied to the toast of 'The Visitors', proposed by Major Gilbert Dennison.

Hadleigh Rally, Suffolk

In 1928, the first rally of the season, in which Tommy Rose competed, was the Hadleigh Rally, held at the Suffolk Aero Club at Easter.

Flight for 12 April 1928, reported:

> **THE HADLEIGH RALLY**
> **SUFFOLK AEROPLANE CLUB'S FINE DISPLAY**
> *The blanket of grey cloud which usually spreads over our Island, was mercifully lifted at Hadleigh aerodrome, Suffolk, during the Easter, and we had two of the brightest days this year. Such extraordinary meteorological behaviour put everyone in a state of constant mild surprise, so that the chief topic at the meeting was the weather. The surprise was more acute because the weather expert's theory had led one to expect at least a gale.*
>
> *The chief flying event of the meeting was joyriding. The demand for 5 shilling flights was so persistent that it could not be entirely met despite generous voluntary services given by most of the visiting pilots.*
>
> *The visiting pilots included many private owners. There were Mr Nigel Norman in his slotted-wing DH Moth G-EBWY with Dr Whitehead Reid as a passenger; Mr Norman Jones in his DH Moth G-EBWC, named 'Camberwell Beauty'; Mr R.G. Cazalet, in his Westland 'Widgeon III' G-EBRM, with Flight Lieutenant Rose, the Midland Club instructor as passenger; Dr G. Merton in his DH Moth G-EBQZ; Flight Lieutenant F.O. Soden in his 'Genet-Moth' G-EBOU; Miss W.E. Spooner in her DH 'Moth Mk I' G-EBOT: Miss S. O'Brien in her DH 'Moth Mk I' G-EBOS; Flight Lieutenant N. Comper, in CLA.4 GEBPB; Mr F.P. Raynham, in Avro 'Avian' G-EBWW, with passenger; Mr G. Linnell, in DH 'Moth' G-EBSA; Mr L.G. Richardson, in DH 'Moth' G-EBPQ; and Captain S. Burt in DH 'Moth' G-EBTI.*
>
> *The industry was represented by Captain N. Stack in the ADC Aircraft, DH 'Moth' G-EBUF; Captain M. Blake, the Blackburn Aeroplane Company's test pilot, in the Blackburn 'Bluebird' G-EBTB' Mr J. Stockbridge, instructor at the RAF Reserve School at Brough aeroplane, in Blackburn 'Bluebird' G-EBTA; Captain A.S. White, with Mr Ballantyne, in DH 'Moth' G-EBRY; and Mr Malcolm with Mr Elliott, in DH 'Moth' G-EBNO, represented the De Havilland Company; Squadron Leader T. England, the Handley Page Company's test pilot, was in the slotted-wing DH 'Moth' G-EBWS; Mr Penrose, of the Westland Aircraft Company, brought over a Westland 'Widgeon III' G-EBRO; and the British Airships Limited pilot, Captain Lines, flew the company's Avro 'Avian' G-EBWU.*
>
> *The first event on the opening day was the exhibition flying. The display really began to liven up with the arrival of the visiting aircraft,*

later engaged in the 'On to Hadleigh Rally'. The miles each machine had flown to the aerodrome in a straight line were divided by the number of minutes before or after 11.30 am at which they crossed the finishing line.

This calculation gave a number of points gained by each competitor. The first prize was £10; second £7 10s and third £5.

The winner proved to be a private owner, Mr R.G. Cazalet, who flew his Westland 'Widgeon', in which he was accompanied by Flight Lieutenant Rose. They had flown from Lympne and crossed the line 15 seconds before zero hour.

Tommy Rose also attended the Hampshire Air Pageant, organised by the Hampshire Aeroplane Club, Hamble, at Whitsun 1928.

This time Tommy Rose entered the Morris Open Handicap, where competitors of this event started in the following order: Flight Lieutenant Swoofer in DH 'Moth' (Cirrus) 'OI' (handicap allowance 7 minutes 0.02 seconds). Flight Lieutenant Rose in DH 'Moth' 'LW' (handicap allowance 6 minutes 50 seconds); Mr Lowdell in the Blackburn 'Bluebird' 'SZ' (6 minutes 01 seconds); Captain Brown in Avro 'Avian' 'XX' (4 minutes 54 seconds); and Flight Lieutenant Luxmoore in Avro 'Avian' 'XY' (4 minutes 54 seconds; and Captain N. Stack was scratch on his Martinsyde-Nimbus 'OJ'.

It was an exciting, closely fought race and at the finish, as expected, Stack flew home first at 129.75 mph, 20 minutes 14 seconds, well ahead of Lowdell's 'Bluebird', which was second at 88 mph, 20 minutes 26 seconds, and Tommy Rose, in the 'Moth', was third at 84.5 mph, 20 minutes 26.5 seconds.

Tommy Rose then attended the Midland Air Pageant:

Midland Air Pageant – Castle Bromwich, Saturday, 9 June 1928

Lichfield Mercury for Friday, 15 June 1928, reported the event:

The Midland Air Pageant at Castle Bromwich on Saturday was carried through without a hitch, and programming times were maintained throughout, despite a high and boisterous wind, which only a year or so ago, would have been sufficient to have kept all the light aircraft in the hanger. The carrying through of the programme under prevailing conditions is a striking tribute to the advancement in the reality and efficiency of the type of the small 'owner driven' machine which has so greatly added to the popularity of civil aviation. All officials of the Midland Aero Club, who were solely responsible for the organisation of the meeting, are to be congratulated on their complete efficiency of the arrangements.

There were three races during the day. Owing to the large number of entries, the preliminary heats were decided on Friday.

FLIGHT LIEUTENANT THOMAS 'TOMMY' ROSE DFC

Above left: Tommy Rose, flying instructor of the Midland Aero Club, 1928. (*William Hale Collection*)

Above right: Tommy Rose's personal silver metal model of the souvenir, as presented to the donors, by the Lord Mayor of Birmingham. Tommy Rose originally had this model attached to the bonnet of his car, and later had it incorporated into a silver ashtray above. (*William Hale Collection*)

The results are as follows:

Midland Inter-Club Handicap Final (12 miles two furlongs); First, J.D. Parkinson, Newcastle Aero Club, Moth (handicap 27 seconds), 10 minutes 24 seconds, speed 80 mph; Second Norman Jones, London Aero Club, Moth (scratch), 10 minutes 28 seconds, speed 83 mph; Third Miss Winifred Brown, Lancashire Aero Club, (26 seconds), 10 minutes 37 seconds, speed 78 mph.

Air League Challenge Cup Final (24 miles 4 furlongs): First H. Brooklyn, Halton AC, Widgeon, 20 minutes 10 seconds, speed 90.5 mph; second Norman Jones, Moth, 21.5 minutes, 87.5 mph; third R.I. Jackson, Midland AC, Moth, 20 minutes 40 seconds, 75 mph.

Midland Open Challenge Cup (24 miles 4 furlongs): First Captain T.N. Stack, ADC Aircraft Ltd, Moth, 17 minutes 5 seconds, 88.5 mph; second B. Martin, Nottingham AC, Moth, 17 minutes 12 seconds, 87 mph; third H. Brooklyn, Widgeon, time 17 minutes 36 seconds, 90 mph.

Balloon Bursting Competition: A.C. Ball, Nottingham; G.E. Lowdell, Suffolk and Eastern Counties; and Flight Lieutenant T. Rose, Midland AC, all equal.

The prizes were presented by the Lord Mayor, who said he could visualise the day when every municipality would have its own aerodrome.

Tommy Rose also attended the Blackpool Air Pageant and *Flight* for 12 July 1928, reported on the event:

MIDLAND AERO CLUB, CASTLE BROMWICH

Blackpool Air Pageant Friday, 6 July 1928
The Air Pageant at Squires Gate, Blackpool, started on Friday, 6 July, in temporary chaos owing to a minor gale, which even threatened the machines picketed down in the machine parks. Early in the morning an Avro 'Avian' belonging to the Liverpool Club was blown on its back after landing, causing damage to the propeller, rudder and top centre plane. These adverse conditions led to an order banning amateur pilots from flying, and the balloon bursting competition scheduled to start the meeting, was of course, out of the question. The wind was reckoned to be nearly 50 mph, and when the flying did commence towards noon, the landings of the machines produced excitement among the spectators. It required considerable skill and luck to put the wheels on the deck instead of the wings. When a Westland 'Widgeon' monoplane started in the first race it almost lifted off from the starting position.

Owner Pilot's Handicap Race was another close race, Flight Lieutenant Soden with a speed of 91.25 mph, Miss Brown second, with a speed of 85 mph, and Flight Lieutenant Rose third, with a speed of 92.5 mph.

The first heat of the Open Handicap Race was won by Flight Lieutenant Rose on a DH 'Moth' 'LT' (Cirrus) (handicap allowance, 11 minutes 27 seconds at 83.5 mph in 21 minutes 17 seconds.

In the final of the Open Handicap Race, Miss W.S. Brown in her Avro 'Avian' (Cirrus) at 99.5 mph, came in first; Second place went to Captain Baker in the Avro 'Avian' at 102 mph, and Third was Flight Lieutenant T. Rose in the Midland Club's DH 'Moth' LT' at 89.5 mph.

Other reports mentioning Tommy Rose included:

Flight for 19 July 1928, who reported:

MIDLAND AERO CLUB
Report for the week ending 14 July: Total flying time was 42 hours 49 mins. Dual 21 hours 34 mins. Solo, 12 hours 15 mins, Passenger, 8 hours 4 mins.
  Dual Instruction was given by Flight Lieutenant T. Rose and Mr Sutcliffe.

Flight for 6 September 1928, reported:

MIDLAND AERO CLUB
Report for week ending 1 September: Total flying time, 41 hours 22 minutes. Dual 22 hours 30 minutes; solo, 14 hours, passenger, 3 hours 20 minutes, test 1 hour 12 minutes.

During 1928, Margaret, Tommy Rose's wife, became pregnant and the growing family moved to 125, Kingsbury Road, Erdington, where on 23 January 1929, Elizabeth Ann Rose was born.

FLIGHT LIEUTENANT THOMAS 'TOMMY' ROSE DFC

Flight for 4 April 1929, reported:

CINQUE PORTS FLYING CLUB'S EXCELLENT EASTER PROGRAMME
The first important flying of the year was one of the best attractions at Easter. It had an interesting international aspect, thanks to the enterprise of the organisers, the Cinque Ports Flying Club, and the programme had a note of good variety. The aviation community in all its divisions gave ready support, and they and the club deserved a far greater public interest.

Lympne aerodrome is ideally situated for the entrance of machines from the Continent, but that does not detract from the good flights put up by the foreign visitors. Our own machines turned up in large numbers and included one or two unexpected types of particular interest.

There were at least thirty machines on the field on both days, Good Friday and Saturday, and the number was briefly increased at intervals by aircraft calling in before going to the Continent. Then the air liners circled occasionally and helped fill up the crowded sky.

The only competitive event held on Good Friday was the 'Alight at Lympne'. Although so many machines arrived, comparatively few entered this. The winner was Captain R.G. Cazalet, the private owner in his Westland 'Widgeon', he flew 156 miles from Castle Bromwich and landed at 12 hours 31 minutes 5 seconds. He not only won the silver cup, presented by the Hythe Chamber of Commerce, but a special prize for the best performance of a private owner flying his own machine. Second in this event went to Mr G. Merton, another private owner, in his DH 'Moth', he flew from Stag Lane aerodrome Edgware, a distance of 66 miles, and landed at 12 hours 30 minutes. Third place was won by one of the Rotterdam visitors, Mijnheer L.M. Redele on a Pander machine, he flew 172 miles from Rotterdam and landed at 12 hours 33 minutes 5 seconds.

Frightfulness, or Bombing the Baby, as the programme described it, had Squadron Leader F.O. Soden in his Gipsy Moth and Flight Lieutenant T. Rose, chief instructor of the Midland Aero Club, also in a Gipsy, put up an excellent entertainment in their attempts to bomb an elusive Austin Seven with flour bags. This car, of course can wriggle like an eel, and an alert driver can easily evade a machine once it has started its dive on him, but although no hit was made by the two pilots on this afternoon, they improved considerably towards the end. The rapidity and angle of their dives were like those converging attacks at the RAF display, and more than once they succeeded in getting on the mark almost before the driver was aware of it, but their aim was not quite as accurate. Flight Lieutenant Rose is particularly good at this sport, as he showed at meetings last year. It is a good item at a public display, as it can induce excellent flying and entertainment.

On 24 May 1929, Tommy Rose's father, John Rose, died at the age of sixty, at a Nursing Home in Southsea. Tommy Rose and his wife Margaret, attended the funeral.

MIDLAND AERO CLUB, CASTLE BROMWICH

The *Hampshire Telegraph* for Friday, 31 May 1929, reported:

BAILIFF TO COLONEL W.G. NICHOLSON
We regret to record the death of Mr John Rose of Home Farm, Basing Park, which occurred in a nursing home at Southsea last Friday.

Mr Rose, who was sixty years of age, had been bailiff for Colonel the Right Honourable W.G. Nicholson, and his father before him, for thirty-four years, first one year at Bordean Farm, and afterwards at the Home Farm, and was well known and respected throughout the neighbourhood. He had not enjoyed good health for the last two or three years, and about a month ago was removed to the nursing home.

He leaves a widow, four sons and one daughter, and much sympathy will be felt with them in their bereavement.

The funeral took place at Privett Church on Tuesday afternoon in the presence of a large gathering of farmers, employees and other sympathizing friends. The remains were borne to the church in a farm wagon, drawn by two horses, followed by some sixty estate workers on foot and another wagon laden with beautiful floral tributes.

The chief mourners were the widow, Thomas, William and Frederick Rose (sons), Miss Mary Rose (daughter), W. and T. Rose (brothers), Mrs Gould (sister), Mrs T. Rose and Mrs W. Rose (sisters-in-law)

In June Tommy Rose excelled himself by winning many balloon bursting competitions, using skills he had developed in the RFC.

Flight for 18 June 1929, reported:

The Cambridge Aero Club, which is a branch of the Suffolk and Eastern Counties' Aeroplane Club, held an air display at Connington Aerodrome on June 10 and 11. The display was officially opened by Mr C.R.W. Adeane, Lord Lieutenant of Cambridgeshire, and members of the Cambridge Club gave exhibition flights in Blackburn 'Bluebirds' (Genets).

In the afternoon there was a Grand Parade and fly-past, headed by Lady Bailey, the Club's President, in her Coupe Gipsy Moth.

A balloon bursting competition followed, in which Flight Lieutenant T. Rose was judged the winner on his Gipsy Moth, with Flight Lieutenant Le Poer Trench, on the Halton monoplane second.

However, on 1 July Tommy Rose participated in quite a different flying race.
The Northern Star for Monday, 1 July 1929, reported:

DASH TO WEDDING
Fathers Race by Aeroplane
A 90 miles-an-hour race against time from Birmingham to Manchester in a light aeroplane, was made by Mr S.L. Huins, of the firm of Messrs J. Huins Limited, shoe dealers, to attend the wedding of his son, Dr Proctor Huins, at Bowden Church, near Manchester.

FLIGHT LIEUTENANT THOMAS 'TOMMY' ROSE DFC

Mr Huins left Birmingham with barely an hour to reach Bowden 70 miles away. A motor car took him to Castle Bromwich aerodrome, where he entered a Moth aeroplane, piloted by Mr T. Rose, of the Midland Aero Club.

When the aeroplane landed at Wythenshawe, Manchester's temporary municipal aerodrome, a motor car rushed Mr Huins to Bowden. The journey was completed in 55 minutes.

His efforts failed by a few moments, but he was in ample time to change and be present at the reception held after the wedding. His son, who is a former footballer, was married to Miss Irene Crossland, daughter of Mr and Mrs Frank Crossland of Hale.

Tommy Rose left the Midland Aero Club in early July, to join the Anglo-American Oil Company Limited, in their Aeronautical division based at Croydon aerodrome, this time as one of their flying representatives, enticed back to his previous employers with a salary increase and a hope to meet some future sponsors.

Chapter 7

Anglo American Oil Aeronautical Division, and the first King's Cup Air Race
July 1929 – September 1931

'Pilots are a rare kind of human. They leave the ordinary surface of the world, to purify their soul in the sky, and they come down to earth, only after receiving the communion of the infinite.'
– Jose Maria Velasco Ibarra

Tommy Rose left the Midland Aero Club to join Anglo-American Oil, a subsidiary of the gigantic Standard Oil Company of New Jersey USA, who had developed a more efficient anti-knock petrol called Pratts 'Ethyl Petrol'.

This came about as a result of the early aircraft which had engines that just about kept the aeroplanes to which they were attached, in the air. This soon became a problem as aeroplanes tended to move around in the air, rising, falling, together with many other manoeuvres, completely unlike the average engine mounted in the chassis of motor cars; different lubrication oils and more efficient fuels had to be developed for reliability and aeroplane engines, no longer just in the horizontal plane.

The chemists at Anglo-American Oil, therefore developed Pratts 'Ethyl Petrol' and *Flight,* for 12 January 1928, reported:

> *During the last few weeks many have been puzzled by enigmatic advertisements in the general press warning all that Ethyl is coming. Ethyl is a new fuel which is now being placed on the market by the Anglo-American Oil Company, who claim that it is a fuel which eliminates what is commonly known as 'engine knocking'.*
>
> *Its history really began about fifteen years ago when it was found that increased compression brought a corresponding increase in 'knocking'. Investigation proved that while some petrol's 'knocked' more than others, all discovered that the trouble could be overcome, or at any rate considerably reduced, by the addition of certain ingredients, the first of which was iodine.*

FLIGHT LIEUTENANT THOMAS 'TOMMY' ROSE DFC

> *But the ultimate remedy had to be commercially practicable, and this objective was attained in the discovery by Mr Midgley, a leading American chemist, which won him the Nichols medal in 1924. He produced what is now known as the 'Ethyl Brand of Anti-Knock Compound', which is a constituent part of Pratts Ethyl petrol.*

As part of the publicity exercise behind this new aviation fuel, the Anglo-American Oil Company leased a Westland Widgeon IIIa, G-AAFD on 12 March 1929, and named it 'Miss Ethyl', basing it at Croydon Aerodrome.

Flight for 9 May 1929 reported:

> *A sign of the times is the inauguration last week of a new Pratts fuel supply station by the Anglo-American Oil Company, at Croydon Aerodrome, just adjacent to the old 'ADC' sheds. In addition to the installation of the fuel depot the occasion was also marked by the christening of a Westland 'Widgeon' monoplane fitted with HP slotted wings, which the AA Co, have put into regular use for their representatives to fly wherever it may be necessary, whether in England or the Continent in connection with the distribution of Pratts fuels. The 'christening' was performed by Air Vice-Marshal Sir Vyell Vyvyan, a director of Imperial Airways. 'Miss Ethyl' is the appropriate name which this red-coloured machine bears upon its nose, so that none may mistake its origin.*

Such was the novelty of the aviation fuel pumps, with their underground fuel tanks, that Tommy Rose soon found himself at this proliferation of fuel pumps nationwide. He looked forward to returning to the Anglo-American Company who had created the Aeronautical Division and were looking for adaptable, experienced pilots to fly a few of their newly purchased aircraft, as their flying representative.

Tommy Rose's brief was to fly the Oil Company's VIPs around the UK and Europe to their various meetings and exhibitions, including attending his own sales meetings as well as transporting important 'air mail' documents and packages to their destinations in a fraction of the time any of the existing modes of transport could guarantee delivery. To speed up sales fulfilments as well as important managerial decisions, the general Company attitude was anything that gave them the edge on the competitors was good management practice as previous posted documents sent worldwide had to rely on lengthy sea journeys in the mail ships.

Flight Lieutenant T. Rose, a Pratts representative with his Cirrus III Moth. (*Flight*)

ANGLO AMERICAN OIL AERONAUTICAL DIVISION

The Anglo-American Oil air fleet started with 'Miss Ethyl', G-AAFD, but this was soon followed by a DH 60X Moth G-AAKJ 'Sam' in July 1929; DH 80A Puss Moth G-ABUJ on 4 March 1932, a DH Dragon Rapide G-ADCL in February 1935 and Percival P.10 Vega Gull, G-AELW, on 28 July 1936.

However, they leased G-ABIE, a red single seat Avro 616 Avian Sports IVM, from R.A. Gardner of Brooklands which they called 'High Test', in January 1931, to enable Tommy Rose to fly to Cape Town, South Africa. This was not only to complete an important three-week business trip, but it also gave Tommy Rose the opportunity to make an attempt on the England to Cape Town record. This was something the Board in London thought an excellent idea as this would give the necessary publicity to the 'High Test' Petrol in the press of this country and also within the Continent of Africa if it could be claimed that he achieved the record in an aircraft called 'High Test' while using the fuel 'High Test Petrol', this would certainly raise the profile of the Company and give them the edge above their competitors.

The Americans were also experimenting with high alcohol and methanol content fuels for their record-breaking attempts, whereas the UK got up to 140 research octane number (RON) petrol (Avgas type today) fuels with huge lead content that were giving better results. The high octane and large amount of lead were necessary to stop detonation and preserve the valve seats (sic) in highly supercharged power units etc.

Tommy Rose, therefore, was not only flying the company's personnel around the UK and Ireland for their various sales meetings, but he was also visiting the fledgling aerodromes mushrooming around the country to sell Pratts fuel and associated distribution equipment.

However, as other companies such as Shell-Mex and British Petroleum were 'snapping at the heels' of Anglo American, they then installed a Pratts fuel station at Croydon.

Not only did these fuel companies set up pumps at the main aerodromes, but they also backed up all the flying meetings with a system of service that played a very important part in the success of the various race meetings. It was said at the time that without the co-operation of the petrol companies there would have been no meetings.

The supply of fuel and oil at aerodromes and at airports throughout the country was obviously of prime importance, so Pratts Motor Spirit Company established service stations at Brooklands and Croydon where they erected pumps from which all types of fuel could be obtained and an attendant was always on duty.

By then all the main petrol companies were represented at the smaller aerodromes, as a general rule, and each had a pump of the usual type. This was, in many cases, backed up by a portable pump, such as those of British Petroleum Company and Shell-Mex Ltd. The actual delivery from the pumps varied according to the requirements; in some cases a swing arm was erected for the delivery hose, which was able to be swung back out of the way when not in use and at the same time of sufficient height to clear the top of the aircraft, making refuelling easy; the other type was from an underground tank on the aerodrome, having a long hose through which the fuel was delivered by an electric pump situated in a convenient shed near the storage tank. The old method of filling from cans was, of course, only used where pumps were not available.

For the supply of lubricating oil, the methods were rather varied. Pratts and Shell arranged for their products to be available in a cabinet type of supply pump, in this case the particular grade of oil was pumped into a can and then poured into the engine sump, or tank.

C. Wakefield & Co, who supplied the Castrol branded oils, and Shell-Mex, had a mobile pump which saved the journey between the machine and the pump, which was necessary with a fixed cabinet. In this type a semi-rotary pump was mounted on top of a 50-gallon reservoir and the whole outfit was wheeled out to the machine and the oil delivered by a flexible hose.

Another part of the organisation, which had a direct bearing on the whole problem, was the transport of the firm's representatives to the scene of action. Shell-Mex and Pratts used aeroplanes for this purpose and these machines became quite a feature of the meeting in the late 1920s. BP however, and the oil companies, always had their representatives there in their cars, and many pilots were pleased to take advantage of the lifts offered to the neighbouring towns. Both the aeroplanes and the cars were readily used by their pilots and drivers for the benefit of not only being able to sell their products, but also to give a real service to their end users, anything to give these companies an edge over their competitors.

Between the wars the most important annual air race around Britain was the King's Cup Air Race, originally established by King George V as an incentive for the development of light aeroplanes and engines of British design and manufacture. It was first contested on 8 September 1922 as a handicapped, cross-country air race, organised by the Royal Aero Club, and was open to British light aeroplanes only, whose pilots also had to be British, or from the Commonwealth.

Most pilots complained about the handicapping system, which could, at times seem to be rather boring for the spectator, 'but everyone who was anyone' competed in the race at some stage in their flying careers. The race had a mix of aeroplanes and aviators, with aircraft that could barely get off the ground, let alone do an 800 plus miles around Britain, and only half of the aircraft actually finished the 1922 race.

As Tommy Rose was still serving in the RAF until October 1926, competing in the annual RAF Pageants, and had also been teaching future pilots to fly, he had been unable to compete in the race. However, in 1929 he flew an ex-RAF S.E.5A, G-EBTO, an aircraft that he was familiar with.

1929 King's Cup Air Race

The race took place at Heston on Friday, 5 July and Saturday, 6 July, which also coincided with the official opening of the Heston Air Park, the brainchild of fellow pilots and aircraft co-owners Nigel Norman and Alan Muntz who conceived the idea in 1928, and later formed a new company, Airwork Ltd.

The weather over the weekend was cold, windy and rain threatened on the morning of the race.

On Wednesday, 28 August 1929, Tommy Rose attended the third air pageant at Clacton aerodrome, organised by the Brooklands School of Flying. Tommy Rose, together with Mr Handstock of Pratts, made a flying visit to the event on their way to the Northampton Aero Club for this last flying meeting of the year.

The next race in which Tommy Rose competed in was the Hadleigh Rally on Saturday, 31 August and Sunday, 1 September 1929, and *Flight* from 6 September reported:

> *The Suffolk Aeroplane Club held their International Air Rally at Hadleigh on Saturday and Sunday, 31 August and 1 September.*
>
> *Zero hour was noon, and first prize of £25 was won by Colonel Richardson in his Klemm, second prize of £10 was won by Mr B. Wilson in a Gypsy Moth and third prize of £5 was won by Tommy Rose in a Cirrus Moth.*
>
> *During the afternoon there were exhibitions of aerobatics, slow flying, crazy flying, formation flying, aerial golf, and various amusing events, including a motor-cycle gymkhana.*
>
> *In the aerial golf the competitors were provided with three bags of flour, which they had to aim at a mark on the aerodrome from their machines in flight, within five minutes of being given the word 'go' on the ground. They were not allowed to carry passengers and the pilot who got the shots nearest the mark was the winner. This was won by Flight Lieutenant Rose, second Mr Murray of the London Club, and third, Mons. Maus in his St Hubert, who had flown over with Comte Arnolide Looz Corswarem from Brussels.*
>
> *Flight Lieutenant Rose, in the Anglo-American Widgeon 'Miss Ethyl', and Mr R. Quilter in his Moth, showed how slow an aeroplane can be flown. Mr Quilter made two completely stalled landings and many times stalled down to within a few feet of the ground, and then with a burst of the engine, went away as if it was the most ordinary proceeding in the world.*
>
> *Flight Lieutenant Rose went rather higher, where there was more wind, and then appeared to hitch a couple of skyhooks on to his wings and just hung there. The Widgeon of course has a medium section wing (RAF 34) which is very stable and enables the pilot to retain lateral control to a very large degree at or beyond the stalling point. This machine was also fitted with Handley-Page slots, but with such a wing section in which the centre of pressure has practically no movement it is doubtful whether this is any advantage.*

Flight 4 October 1929 reported:

> *The Northamptonshire Aero Club held their last flying meeting for this year at Sywell last Saturday, 28 September. They have gained a name for cheery meetings, and this was no exception. The spectators were not very numerous, but they were really interested and hung right to the end of the meeting, even though things dragged a bit after teatime.*

FLIGHT LIEUTENANT THOMAS 'TOMMY' ROSE DFC

It is becoming difficult to be original at these meetings, but the committee responsible for arranging this one certainly produced in the Novelty Race a 'turn' which received the approbation of the onlookers.

In this race each pilot selected a lady passenger by drawing lots for her. Having secured his passenger and instructed her in the mysteries of folding wings, the pilot lined up his machine with the engine ticking over. The passengers were then arranged between the machines and the spectators with three empty beer bottles standing in front of each of them and about 10ft away from them.

At the word 'go' they had to knock over the bottles with tennis balls: as soon as the third bottle was down the pilot had to run to an official car nearby and secure a needle and length of cotton which he could exchange for a ticket as soon as the needle was threaded. While the threading was in progress the passengers were scrambling into their respective machines in readiness for the pilots who came dashing across when they had secured their tickets. The machines had next to be taken off and flown once round Sywell reservoir and landed again near a car. The engine turned off, and the wings had then to be folded and the first passenger to reach the car after this was done was the winner.

Two heats were necessary as there were eight entrants, and the first two in each heat completed the final. Flight Lieutenant T. Rose, with Miss Harris, were the winners, a result which was largely helped by the magnificent piloting of Mr Rose, who put the machine down close to the official car in spite of a certain amount of crosswind.

On 10 October 1929 Tommy Rose was at the Air Pageant at Hedon, Hull, and *Flight* for 18 October 1929 reported:

PRINCE GEORGE OPENS THE HULL MUNICIPAL AERODROME

Hull's population enjoyed themselves on Thursday last, 10 October, the city was decked with all manner of decorations and the air of enthusiasm was very marked.

The Air Pageant itself was the terminating event of the opening of the Hull Civic and Empire Week by HRH Prince George and immediately followed by the official opening of the Municipal Aerodrome.

In declaring the aerodrome open Prince George said, 'It is with great pleasure that I accepted the invitation to open this aerodrome and though I had little experience of flying, I at once decided to increase my knowledge of modern methods of transport by undertaking the journey by air. It has been a most enjoyable experience and one which I hope to repeat when visiting other parts of the country'.

ANGLO AMERICAN OIL AERONAUTICAL DIVISION

Tommy Rose entered into the Kingston-upon-Hull Aeroplane race, in which there were eight entries. First was Flight Lieutenant Trench in his Avian (Hermes), second was R. Kemp in a Moth G-EBPT, third was Tommy Rose in the Pratts Moth, and fourth was Captain Percival in an Avian (Cirrus III).

On 16 November 1929, Tommy Rose was at the Hanworth Club, *Flight* for 22 November 1929 reported:

> *Mr Parkhouse has evidently incurred the displeasure of the clerk of the weather who did not bless his meeting last Saturday. The morning turned out with low clouds and general murkiness and Mr Parkhouse thought it wiser to wire those who had promised to come that the conditions were not favourable, however, that indefatigable worker in the cause of private flying, Tommy Rose, managed to get through on 'Sam', the Pratt's Cirrus Moth, and during the afternoon he and Mr Parkhouse took up spectators for free joyrides. A good contingent from the Plymouth Club, to wit, Mr Deane, the chairman of the flying committee, secretary of the club and Mr Sholbrook a member, came over by road, and lent their support and during the evening all enjoyed themselves at the subsequent dance which Mr Parkhouse had arranged; he even engaged two experts, Eve and Ramon, to give exhibition dances and we hope that his enterprise will be better favoured the next time.*

The first meeting of the proposed new Guild of Air Pilots and Air Navigators, was held at the annual dinner of the Veteran Air Navigators, held at Rules Maiden Lane WC2 on Wednesday, 5 December 1928, where over dinner Sir Sefton Brancker discussed with all those present the possibility of setting up a Guild to include air pilots together with air navigators, the objectives of this new company would in the future encompass the following:

- To establish and maintain the highest standards of air safety through the promotion of good airmanship among pilots and navigators.
- To maintain a liaison with all authorities connected with licensing, training and legislation affecting pilot or navigator whether private, professional, civil, or military.
- To constitute a body of experienced airmen available for advice and consultation and to facilitate the exchange of information.
- To strive to enhance the status of air pilots and air navigators.
- To assist air pilots and air navigators in need through the Benevolent Fund.

In the Minutes of the second meeting of the new Guild held at the Royal Aero Club, London, on 12 March 1929, the Committee accepted the Articles of Association, and the conditions within which new members would be considered for membership to the Guild.

FLIGHT LIEUTENANT THOMAS 'TOMMY' ROSE DFC

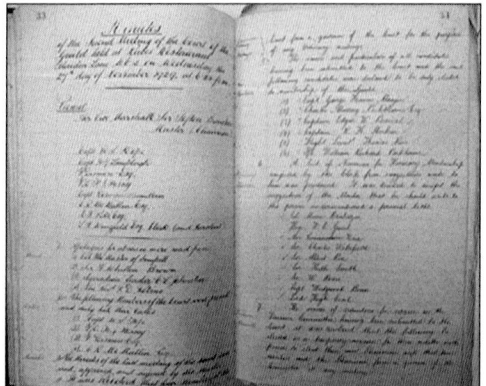

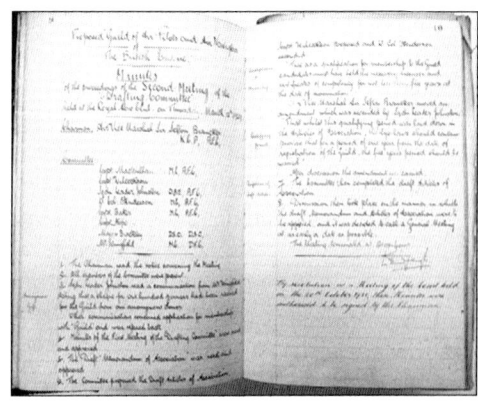

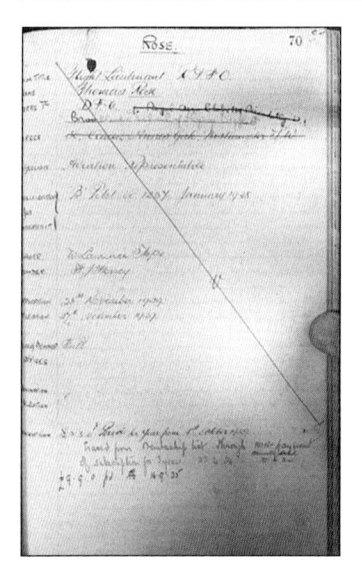

Above left: GAPAN, and the Minute book entry (held in the archives of GAPAN in London) documented a second meeting, which was held at Rules Restaurant, London, with the newly formed committee, the Master (Chairman), who was Air Vice-Marshall Sir Sefton Brancker. Tommy Rose was the fifth new member to be considered and voted upon. (*GAPAN Peter Bugge*)

Above right: The Minute book regarding the second meeting of the proposed Air Pilots and Air Navigators. (*GAPAN Peter Brugge*)

Left: Tommy Rose's page from the members records book. (*GAPAN Peter Brugge*)

The Guild decided and voted upon *'there is a qualification for membership to the Guild, candidates must have held the necessary licences and certificates of competency for not less than five years of the date of nomination.'*

In order to embody the resolution by the International Convention for Air Navigation (the Paris Convention) of 1919, the British Government passed its Air Navigation Act, 1920. The regulations that followed from this required all civil pilots to hold one of three licences. The Class 'A' licence, which Tommy Rose obtained while he was in the RAF, covered private pilots; commercial pilots required a Class 'B' Licence or a Master Pilot's Certificate, the latter being based on the Class 'B' but reflecting extensive practical flying experience and additional formal certification as an Air Navigator, this Certificate was obtained by Tommy Rose in January 1928 (No 1257).

There were two forms of Navigator's Licence. The First and Second Class, the main difference being the number of flying hours logged. In essence, any civil aircraft carrying passengers or goods for hire or reward on an international flight of more than 625 miles over high seas or uninhabited terrain was required to have on board the holder of a First-Class Navigator's Licence. For flights between 100 and 625 miles a Second-Class Licence sufficed.

On 27 November 1929, Tommy Rose became one of the founding members of the Guild of Air Pilots and Navigators (GAPAN) as he had a First-Class Navigators Licence, the Minute book entry (held in the archives of GAPAN in London) documented a second meeting, which was held at Rules Restaurant, London, with the newly formed committee, the Master (Chairman), was Air Vice-Marshal Sir Sefton Brancker, Tommy Rose was the fifth new member to be considered and voted upon. His proposers were W. Lawrence Hope and H.J. Horsey, and his occupation given as Aviation Representative, as he was employed by Anglo American Oil at the time.

It is interesting to note that although Tommy Rose paid his subscription of £3 guineas on 1 October 1929 (about £190 today), by 1934 he was 'erased' from the membership list due to non-payment of subscriptions for three years. Having just won the King's Cup Air Race ten days earlier, one would have thought that he had sufficient funds to pay his back subscription of £9 guineas (about £580 today)! However, this was paid on 16 September 1935, and it should be mentioned that Tommy Rose was notoriously inconsistent with the management of his finances. This was possibly one of the reasons voiced by his ex-wife Margaret during and after their divorce.

The start of the flying season for 1930 commenced in March, when the Brooklands School of Flying opened their season with a flying meeting on Sunday, 2 March. The weather was poor with low clouds, over forty machines turned up, and the local populace showed that they too, had not lost their interest in flying. They attended in large numbers, and though cold, they all enjoyed themselves. The cast from 'Silver Wings' from the Dominion Theatre were there, which also swelled the numbers of spectators.

A short and comprehensive programme was arranged with aerobatics and crazy flying by Tommy Rose, Captain H. Broad, and Mr G. Murray. There was wing walking by Jock Anderson, a parachute descent by Mr John Tranum and 'bombing the car' by Captain H.D. Davis and E.A. Jones.

Then on 1 May 1930, Tommy Rose flew to Malone Airport, Belfast, with David S. Paul, chief of the research department at Anglo American Oil, in connection with the introduction of Pratt's Ethyl Spirit in Ireland.

The extract below is taken from *Fifty Years of Brooklands,* p100:

> *The Brooklands Aero Club came into being in the Spring of 1930, and with A. Percy Bradley, the Track manager as chairman and C.S. Burney as secretary, from the very beginning worked closely with the school.*
>
> *To mark the opening of the club, an air display was held on 17 May, and it was a memorable occasion; no less than ninety-seven private aeroplanes flew in, and the job of parking them was mainly the responsibility of Oliver J. Tapper, then with the Automobile Association and later of de Havilland and later of de Havillands publicity office. Jimmy Jeffs was control officer.*

FLIGHT LIEUTENANT THOMAS 'TOMMY' ROSE DFC

> *The flying programme opened with Tommy Rose giving an aerobatic demonstration, followed by John Rogers in a Salmson-powered Klemm, a German ultra-light design of amazing quietness and high safety factor. A Scorpion powered Swift, designed by Flight Lieutenant Nicholas Comper, was flown by Flying Officer L.S. Snaith, who proved how easily controllable it was.*

The next event was a private owner's day at Brooklands, and *Flight* for 23 May 1930 reported:

> *Ninety-seven private owners attended the Brooklands Aero Club. This club was formed as an offshoot of the Brooklands Aviation Racing Club and flying in the club's Moth will be confined to pilot members; those wishing to have instruction will do so with the Brooklands School of Flying, through the club.*
>
> *The programme opened with Flight Lieutenant T. Rose, who gave one of the aerobatic shows, which we always expect from him. His loops were perfectly done as anyone could wish to see.*

Peterborough's private aerodrome at Horsey Toll, near Whittlesea, owned by Mr K. Whittome, held its first flying meeting on Saturday, 24 May and a crowd of 6,000 watched the flying from an adjoining field, which was slightly higher than the aerodrome.

The programme was opened by Tommy Rose, with one of his perfect exhibitions of crazy flying, followed by some expert formation flying, also by Tommy Rose, who went on to win the balloon bursting competition.

The next meeting was the opening of Bristol Airport on 31 May 1930 and *Flight* for 6 June 1930 reported:

> *Bristol arranged a truly international meeting with which to herald the opening of their Municipal Airport at Whitchurch by Prince George on Saturday last, 31 May. On the Friday morning several foreigners arrived, and a continental rally was held for their benefit. There were two prizes for the competitors starting from the farthest point, the first being the 'Mobil Oil' Cup and £15, the second £5. These were won by R. Neininger on the Darmstadt d-1561 (Genet engine) and J. Mans on a St Hubert (Walter engine).*

Tommy Rose entered into the Bristol Aerial Derby, flying the Cirrus Hermes powered Blackburn Bluebird G-AABV.

The final of the Bristol Aerial Derby took place at 3.55 pm, and was classed as an International Handicap Race, open to all comers, distance approximately thirty miles.

The first prize was the Merlyn Cup and £100, and this went to J. Wentworth in his Westland Widgeon. Second prize of £50 was won by the Bristol and Wessex Aero Club in a DH 60X Moth, and the third prize of £25 went to the Bristol Aeroplane Company, with a Bristol Bulldog. It is not recorded where Tommy Rose competed, but he was not in the first four places.

The 1930 King's Cup Air Race

On 5/6 July 1930, Hanworth hosted the third King's Cup Air Race. The race had started two years previously at Heston (1929) and Hendon (1928). This was a 750-mile race around Britain in a single day, with stops for refuelling. It was also recognised as a testing place for new machines and proving ground for amateur pilots and it usually attracted all the famous aviators of the day. In 1930 most of the aircraft were biplanes which were handicapped on speed with the slowest starting first. Tommy Rose came sixth flying the Blackburn Bluebird G-ABCC, see report below.

The Telegraph for 10 July 1930 reported:

THE KING'S CUP AIR RACE – A WOMAN'S WIN
LOWER SPEEDS BUT MORE RELIABILITY

The King's Cup race over a 750 mile course around England was won on Saturday for the first time by a woman, Miss Winifred Brown, in an Avro Avian aeroplane fitted with a Cirrus III engine, at an average of 102.7 mph. Mr A.S. Butler, flying a Moth with a Gipsy engine, was second, and won the prize for best average speed of 129.7 mph; and Flight Lieutenant H.R.D. Waghorn, a member of last year's Schneider Trophy team was third on a Blackburn Bluebird fitted with a Gipsy I engine in an average speed of 99.47 mph. Out of a field of eighty-eight starters, fifty-nine machines finished, a much higher percentage than in previous years.

The comparatively small number of failures is a tribute to the reliability of the modern light aeroplanes which were most largely represented in the race and to the lower average speeds. Last year's winner was more than 20 mph faster than the machine which made the best time on Saturday.

The race, if it produced a less great achievement in speeds, was remarkable for the number of amateur pilots it attracted and for their success. In the first four, three were private owners flying their own aircraft, and two of these were women. Most of those who finished were amateurs who have taken up flying since the birth of the light aeroplane club movement. Miss Brown, for instance, has been flying only since 1926, and her longest flight in one day hitherto had been from London to Amsterdam.

MISS BROWN'S FLIGHT

Miss Brown started fourteenth from Hanworth, 2 hr 25 min ahead of the scratch machine. At Bristol she had overtaken the four Bluebirds and one of the Moths ahead of her; and through one failure, she took seventh place there. At Manchester two Moths only were still ahead of her; and

> *after that she led the field and saw no more of her competitors while she was in the air. She reached Hanworth at 6.15, just over 12 minutes before Mr Butler.*
>
> *The next eight of nine arrivals quickly followed one another. Flight Lieutenant Waghorn was 2 min behind Mr Butler; Mrs Butler came less than 7 min later; Mr Green was 5 minutes behind her and was followed, 10 sec later by Flight Lieutenant Bruce, who again was followed after 14 sec interval by Mr Tommy Rose. Within 2 min Prince George's machine came in to seventh place, and in the next minute four more machines had arrived. Half an hour after the winner had arrived, the first sixteen machines had crossed the line, and the Prince of Wales's Tomtit came in neck and neck with Mr R. Cazalet's Widgeon to beat it by one second for eighteenth place.*

On Sunday, 13 July 1930, the Leicestershire Aero Club arranged a demonstration of commercial types of aircraft at the aerodrome at Desford.

The occasion was mainly by invitation, but large numbers of the public were there. The idea behind the demonstration was to encourage businessmen in the district who had been slow to embrace the pleasures of flying, to go along and have the opportunity to see the types of machines that were available for their use, and to sign them up as potential new students of the aero club.

Among those who came with their machines were Sir Alliot Roe and John Lord in an amphibian Cutty Sark flown by Mr Scott; Flight Lieutenant T. Rose in an Avro 619 Five, a five seat, three engine, passenger aircraft; Mr Trost with a Junkers Junior; Captain Robinson in a Redwing; Miss Slade, the Secretary of Airwork, who was very knowledgeable about commercial aircraft, was there with her wooden Gipsy Moth, the club had available their metal Moth and Mr Everard's Puss Moth, and also an Avian and Bluebird.

The broadcasting arrangements were unique as Mr Everard brought his own private broadcasting van which he used for political activities.

Next the Yorkshire Air Race 13 July 1930

Flight for 18 July 1930 reported:

> *The Yorkshire Air Race, as it was called, was a handicap race from Sherburn to Hedon and back. This resulted in a win for the scratch man, Mr J.D. Irving, who was flying his Moth, all cleaned up, the same as it was in the King's Cup Race. The handicapping was another triumph for Messrs Dancy and Rowarth, who got the first seven machines home out of a field of twelve in a space of forty-three seconds.*

Tommy Rose flew G-AACC Bluebird (Hermes) with a handicap of 36 seconds, time over the course 60 min 22 seconds speed 110 mph and came in second place.

ANGLO AMERICAN OIL AERONAUTICAL DIVISION

Tommy Rose beside the Bluebird G-AACC 1930 'King Cobra'. (*William Hale Collection*)

Flight for 18 July 1930 reported:

> *According to the rules and regulations competitors in the International Touring Competition for Light Aircraft, organised this year by the Aero Club of Germany, and starting and finishing in Berlin, will be free to start their circuit of Europe at 9 am on Sunday next, July 20. A total of ninety-eight entries had been received by the Aero Club of Germany. Of these, no less than forty-seven are German entries.*
>
> *France comes next with sixteen entries, Poland with fourteen, Spain with nine, England with eight, and Switzerland with four. That all the entries will start, is of course, extremely doubtful. Of the eight English entries one at least, the Robinson Redwing, (*Tommy Rose's entry) *was not expected to start.*

Norfolk and Norwich meeting Saturday 26 July 1930

Flight for 1 August 1930 reported:

> *The Norfolk and Norwich Aero Club got through their third annual meeting at Mousehold Aerodrome very credibly on Saturday, 28 July.*
>
> *It was one of those fairly quiet meetings where visitors were well looked after without being fussed over, and where people are made to feel at home.*
>
> *The Norwich meeting started with a rally for the first pilot to cross the line after 12.30 am according to the programme! At 2.30 pm our indefatigable Director of Aviation, Sir Sefton Brancker, formerly opened the meeting with a few well-chosen words.*
>
> *The comic turn was nobly undertaken by that indefatigable friend of all those who want help of any kind at air meetings to wit, Tommy Rose, on this occasion, he allowed himself to be dressed in a top hat and incarcerated in the 'target' at which a Mexican Chief was to aim his fearful looking shotgun as he flew past. The bottles suspended from*

> one of the sides of the target duly broke after each shot, until the last one, which remained intact until our behatted hero broke his way out of the target and finished it with a hammer. For this dastardly exposure of the hoax, the Mexican landed and proceeded to attack him with a pistol, but Tommy Rose had evidently learnt to fly as well as break the necks off bottles, so he raced our bellicose chief to the Moth and flew off rejoicing.
>
> Before landing, he duly gave the impression that the ambulance would be required when he landed, but after several hair-raising episodes in front of the crowd – no lack of showmanship this time – he went away and landed in a far corner in faultless style. It was well done, but on the whole, it was a shock to see his prowess at 'necking bottles', we had always thought him so abstemious.

Norfolk and Norwich Aero Club 27 July – Tommy Rose won the take-off and landing competition 1930

The day after the excitement of the air pageant and Tommy Rose escaping the wrath of the Mexican Chief, there was a variety of competitions: message bag dropping; balloon bursting; aerobatic competition for the Mobil Oil Cup, and the take-off, landing and folding competition, which was won by Tommy Rose.

The Shanklin Isle of Wight meeting 17 August 1930

On Sunday, 17 August, 8,000 paid for admission to the Isle of Wight Flying Club meeting held at Shanklin, all flocking to the airfield the see the 'superstars' of the skies, and *Flight* for 22 August 1930 reported:

> The programme opened with a fly-past and parade of some of the many machines present. Actually, about thirty visiting aircraft arrived and gave the islanders quite a good idea of the size to which the private-flying movement has now grown. Mr Tommy Rose led the fly-past in a Sports Avian (Hermes), both he and Mr Handstock, who came in his Widgeon (Gipsy) are aviation representatives for Pratts; following him came Mr Piercy in the Puss Moth belonging to Mr Freeman who markets the Arens control; Mr Brett, a French representative of DH's in a Moth; Mr Talbot Lehmann in a Widgeon (Cirrus III); Mr Olley flying a Robinson Redwing (Hornet); Mr Rogers in a Klemm (Cirrus III) and Mrs Victor Bruce in her Bluebird (Gipsy II). After the fly-past Mr Bentley, in the Shell companies Moth (Hermes), gave an exhibition of crazy flying. He skidded about the aerodrome, flying sideways and in fact all ways except the normal way, and showed what liberties a skilled pilot can take when he knows how far he can go.

ANGLO AMERICAN OIL AERONAUTICAL DIVISION

A balloon bursting competition was the last item on the programme. Bunches of balloons were let up, and Messrs Brown, Bentley, Rose and Dick were the contestants who endeavoured to break up the whole of their respective bunches. The first two named were successful in doing so and shared the prize. The air above the aerodrome was somewhat tricky and the balloons went in different directions, making this event very difficult.

Saturday, 6 September 1930 – Ratcliffe-on-Wreak aerodrome.

The opening of Mr Lindsay Everard's private aerodrome at Radcliffe-on-the Wreak, took place on Saturday, 6 September. Many suggested it should have been a total immersion Baptism party. The day started well and the number of machines visiting was unprecedented, but after lunch when the real programme commenced, the rain started and continued at intervals until Sunday morning.

Mr Lindsay Everard was one of the outstanding benefactors to private and club flying, he was also MP for Melton Division of Leicestershire and President of the Leicestershire Aero Club, plus he was connected with the production of Everards beer.

Flight for 12 September 1930 reported:

The meeting, taken as a whole, was a most excellent party, and the hospitality of the club quite beyond comment; as regards the organisation of the races, we certainly heard a good deal of complaining from the pilots, and in the Grosvenor Cup, in particular, it seemed as if the arrangements lacked the attention to detail which characterised all other arrangements made by the club. A turning point was, in at least one case, at a different spot to that marked on the map, which was prepared for each pilot, while the general opinion seemed to be that they were all insufficiently visible from the air, especially as the weather was bumpy, and some of the heats were flown in rainstorms. No explanation was given as to why that particular course was chosen for the Grosvenor Cup Race, and one must assume that there was some very good reason, but a course around the valley on the north side of the aerodrome would have allowed the competitors to be in view for most of the race, and it would be interesting to know why it was not chosen.

The Grosvenor Cup is the Private Owners' Race of the year and ranks second only to the King's Cup Race, and it was difficult to see any justification for relegating it to the day following the main meeting, when there was practically no public to witness it.

Tommy Rose entered the race, with G-AACC the Bluebird IV (Hermes), but in Heat 1 he was unplaced, in Heat 2 he was second, at a speed of 106.5 mph. In the final race Tommy Rose came in sixth place with a speed of 105.5 mph.

Next on the aviation calendar was the Antwerp Meeting and *Flight* for 26 September 1930 reported on it as follows:

> *A Desoutter Mark II made the fastest time of the Concourse de Grande Vitesse at the second International Meeting of the Antwerp Aviation Club, September 13, 14, 15, and also won the third prize for aerobatics at the same meeting.*
>
> *The latter prize was presented to Mr Styran, who gave a rather amusing account of his flight as follows: Mr Styran, the pilot, who had no idea that he was competing in an acrobatic display, but having seen a well-known German give a demonstration, he decided to go up and show them what he could do with an ordinary British cabin aircraft. On landing, and to his great surprise, he was presented with the third prize for an acrobatic display.*
>
> *Other English visitors to this meeting were Mr Jackaman in his Puss Moth (Gipsy III), who won some four prizes, after having a hectic journey from Berlin. In spite of rough weather his passengers found the ventilating arrangements admirable, also Flight Lieutenant T. Rose, on a Sports Avian (Hermes), who came away with six prizes, including second in the acrobatic competition and first in the take-off and landing competition.*
>
> *Miss Winnie Brown, in her Avian (Cirrus III), won the arrival competition and also gained three other prizes. So the English contingent distinguished themselves by gathering a large percentage of the total prizes.*

Most of 1931 was taken up with the flight to Cape Town, detailed in the next chapter. Tommy Rose was carrying out a business trip to Cape Town on behalf of Anglo-American Oil, the culmination of which was the last flight he made for the Company.

It is not known why Tommy Rose's career with the Anglo-American Oil Company came to such an abrupt end, as Anglo-American archives (now housed in the Texas Archive), have no records from the period covering such an event, as they were

Tommy Rose beside the Sports Avian (Hermes), taken at Antwerp Airport. In the background, the Drakenhof, a local castle. (*Antwerp Aviation Club*)

destroyed prior to being lodged at the Archive, only vital milestones of the company records were kept, and no staff records were handed over after 1919.

Tommy Rose possibly lost his job due to his disastrous attempted record, or possibly to the subsequent lack of successful sales anticipated by the trip. The company had hired the aircraft (Avro 616 Avian IVM G-ABIE) on 30 January 1931, had it named 'High Test' and the names of towns Tommy Rose was due to visit to refuel painted on it. This was no spontaneous trip, as it had been meticulously planned and therefore the company hoped to get more out of this venture than just a 'sales trip', and 'urgent commercial despatches'.

By April 1931, the newspapers were reporting that Tommy Rose was going to try and beat the time set up by the Duchess of Bedford, but this ended in failure, something Tommy Rose had never experienced before.

Tommy Rose certainly had the undoubted ability and qualifications than many of the other pilots to fly to the Cape, so the failure was not due to his lack of ability, planning or capability. There was just a catalogue of problems encountered on the way down, and the aircraft was quite simply not capable of enduring this arduous journey, particularly when being confronted with unexpected sandstorms. An RAF friend (not named) arrived to take him home, bringing the letters still stamped 'Cape Town to London by air mail with Tommy Rose in the 'High Test' in six days'.

Tommy Rose left the aircraft at Esna to be repaired, but how he returned to the UK is explained in the article from the *Hull Daily Mail* for Friday, 8 May 1931, which is reproduced below:

PILOTS DILEMMA
HOW TO LAND IN A CROWD
Cairo Friday
An interesting story of how the RAF relief plane sent out to pick up Flight Lieutenant Tommy Rose, when he made a forced landing here on Tuesday (5 May – SC), *itself nearly came to grief, is told by Reuter's Luxor correspondent, who visited Esna, where the airman came down.*

The RAF pilot was preparing to land when he noticed that several score of natives mounted on their usual donkeys had collected beneath him and were gazing up in stupefied amazement.

BEWILDERED DONKEYS
The donkeys, bewildered by the roar of the engine, dodged uneasily about underneath the airman, but would not get out of the way. With the engine boiling, the pilot had no alternative but to land at the risk of killing several of the natives.

He succeeded in missing the crowd, but his machine nearly overturned in a hole in the ground, which was very rough and will need much levelling before the two planes can take off again.

Meanwhile, Flight Lieutenant Tommy Rose and the RAF pilot are making an enforced stay in the desert under a burning sun.

FLIGHT LIEUTENANT THOMAS 'TOMMY' ROSE DFC

To relieve their hardships arrangements have been made for cigarettes and beer to be sent from Luxor.

By mid-May Tommy Rose was back in the UK with the help of his RAF friend and he had started attending air displays again. The first meeting was at the Bucks and Oxon Aeroplane Club at Reading on Sunday, 21 June, where he was again the life and soul of the party and where he also won the obstacle race, which consisted of not flying but eating copious amounts of toffee apples, after which he gave an excellent display in an Avro Avian.

Flight for 17 July 1931, reported that Tommy Rose had attended the Blackpool Pageant in a Civilian Coupe Genet-Major, but he was unplaced as the engine cut out near Iver, Bucks, with the result being an argument with a horse and hedge, finishing with the machine on its back, luckily Tommy Rose was unhurt.

The following are a few more air races Tommy Rose attended.

The *Folkstone, Hythe, Sandgate and Cheriton Herald* for 25 July 1931 reported:

BAD WEATHER FOR FLYING MEN AT THE CINQUE PORTS FLYING CLUB
On Saturday numerous visitors arrived by air after the Ramsgate rally, among them were Captain Duncan Davis, of Brooklands and Captain Tommy Rose, late of the Midland Club.

On 29 July, Tommy Rose attended the Husbands Bosworth meeting at Cote Hill, near Rugby, 3,000 spectators arrived to watch the event, thirty-three aeroplanes registered, comprising of Puss Moths, Moths, Avians, the Comper Swift and the Blackburn Lincock. They all lined up in a display at the end of the aerodrome. Lunch was provided for the pilots and friends and took place in a large marquee on the grounds, provided by the Honourable Adrian Verney-Cave. Tommy Rose took part in the car-bombing competition, something he excelled in, and won first prize. Towards the end of the day it started to rain, out of eighteen machines that left for London, only four arrived. On the way home Tommy Rose, with several others, called into the Northampton School of Flying at Sywell.

The *Rugby Advertiser* for 28 July 1931 reported:

On 26 July the club sent four machines over to Cote Hill Aerodrome near Rugby, to assist at the Air Pageant held there, and in the evening a good number of machines paid a call at Sywell on their way home. Flight Lieutenant Armour, the Duke of Gloucester's pilot called on us, together with Mr Tommy Rose, the famous pilot, and many others.

The *Western Times* for 11 September 1931 reported:

AIR RALLY
The race was held in competition with the third annual air rally, organised by Mr W.R. Parkhouse, of the Agra Engineering Company, held at Haldon Aerodrome, near Teignmouth. Mr Parkhouse brought

together a splendid contingent of pilots and a large body of the general public, for what has become known as 'Devon's Air Day.'

The race for Teignmouth's hundred guineas trophy naturally aroused the greatest interest. There were ten competitors, who were sent off in two heats on a double circuit of the course from the aerodrome around Belvedere Tower on Great Haldon and on to Haytor Rocks and back, a distance of fifty-four miles. Handicapped according to engine power, weight etc. The machines took off at their handicap times which enabled the public to establish the winner at the conclusion of each heat.

The first heat provided a highly exciting finish, a second only separating the winner (E.C.T. Edwards) and the second (C.S. Napier), the tussle for third place was also keen, C.W.A. Scott crossing the line only three seconds ahead of K.E. Parker, and Tommy Rose came last.

Later that year Tommy Rose returned to Esna, with the help of his RAF friend, to recover 'High Test', which had been repaired, and the return trip was reported in the *Birmingham Daily Gazette*, 4 December 1931:

MIDLANDER'S FLIGHT
Tunis, Thursday
Mr Tommy Rose, the British airman who arrived in Tunis last night from Benghazi (Tripoli), is leaving today for London – British United Press.

Mr Rose is on the retired list of the RAF and is a former instructor of the Midland Aero Club. Earlier this year he crashed in Bechuanaland while attempting a record flight to the Cape and back.

Hull Daily Mail for Wednesday, 9 December stated that Tommy Rose had left Marignane aerodrome at 8.43 am for Lympne.

Birmingham Daily Gazette, Tuesday, 15 December reported:

*Mr Tommy Rose, the airman who was formerly instructor to the Midland Aero Club, arrived at Lympne, Kent, yesterday (*Monday, 14 December-SC*), at the conclusion of his return flight by easy stages from the Cape after his unsuccessful attempt to beat the record for the outward journey.*

He expects to visit Birmingham within the next ten days and may make another attempt on the Cape record in February.

On arrival back in the UK Tommy found that he was no longer employed by the Anglo-American Oil Company, for reasons that remain unclear due to lack of company archives.

He therefore was forced to move in with his in-laws with his wife and two-year-old daughter at the Mill House, Milford, near Salisbury. This was certainly a difficult decision to make, but with no income there was no alternative.

Chapter 8

1931 Tommy Rose's first attempt on the Cape Town record

'The engine is the heart of an airplane, but the pilot is the soul.'
– Walter Raleigh

1929: Anglo-American Oil Company Ltd

The first Aerial Service Station in Britain was installed by Pratts in May 1929 as previously mentioned but, after working as a flying instructor for the Midland Aero Club, Tommy Rose was enticed back by Anglo-American Oil Company's Aeronautical Division in June 1929, this time with an offer he couldn't refuse, that of Sales Manager for the whole of England. Primarily, his job appears to have been to fly the Company officials around the country to meetings and sales conventions, as well as to important European business meetings.

The Company leased Avro 616 Avian IVM, G-ABIE for this from R.A. Gardiner at Brooklands in January 1931, but prior to this Tommy Rose could fly any of the following aircraft already in use by Anglo-American Oil. These comprised a Widgeon 111A, G-AAFD 'Miss Ethyl' leased 25 March 1929, and sold in August 1931; DH 60X Moth G-AAKJ 'Sam' leased from 19 August 1929 and Avro Sports Avian IVM, G-ABDN, leased from August 1930 and sold in May 1932.

Pratts High Test was a new aviation fuel that had been developed by the Company in the late 1920s and at the Hull Air Pageant in 1929, Tommy Rose, flying in it, came in third. An advertisement in the *Daily Mail* for Saturday, 12 October 1929, claimed that all aircraft in the first four places flew on this new fuel.

In May 1930, Tommy Rose flew David S. Paul, the Chief of Research Department of Anglo-American Oil, to a sales convention in Ireland in 'Miss Ethyl,' in the hope of being able to introduce Pratt's Ethyl Spirit into Northern Ireland. The Company were looking for a 'high profile' sales initiative for their Pratt's *High Test* fuel, which was scheduled for maximum exposure to the public at the Olympia Stand No. 61 in the National Hall in 1932, and what better way to achieve this than a record-breaking speed attempt to Cape Town, whilst taking at the same time, urgent commercial despatches to South Africa.

In those days the only media available was the radio and newspapers, but with advertisements in the press, specialist magazines and stands in exhibitions, most of the potential users of a product such as *High Test* were buyers of motor cars and motorcycles,

1931 TOMMY ROSE'S FIRST ATTEMPT ON THE CAPE TOWN RECORD

The Avro 616 Avian IVM G-ABIE was hired by Anglo American Oil Company's Aeronautical Division on 30 January 1931. Tommy Rose is seen beside the aircraft, in his tropical clothing, with all the stops along the route painted on the fin. (*William Hale Collection*)

so were obviously aware of this new fuel. However, the only way to get noticed in the field of aviation was to have a highly visual, and successful, record-breaking attempt. This would hopefully, impress the users sufficiently for them to change over to the new high performing *High Test* fuel.

However, Tommy Rose, regardless of the sales initiative, was always ready for the next aviation challenge and the Lympne to Cape Town speed record was one he really wanted to achieve, plus the fact that he could really do with the prize money! The world would be looking and waiting for this record-breaking dash, and if it could also be claimed that *High Test* Ethyl Spirit played a significant part in the success of this trip, the future of this product was assured.

The name *High Test* had, however, been around for some time, having been used as a title for decorative road maps and motoring magazines, but the names of its manufacturers, Anglo-American Oil Company Ltd and Pratts was later changed to Esso.

This first attempt on the speed record for the return journey from Lympne to Cape Town coincided with a three-week business trip on behalf of Anglo-American Oil to South Africa. This was made in February 1931, and many newspapers reported Tommy Rose's first attempt of the Cape Town record.

However, one report of Tommy Rose's attempt appeared in *Down Africa's Skyways*, by Benjamin Bennett, published by Hutchinson in 1932, and this also revealed the existence of Tommy Rose's first wife and a child, as well as giving a brief outline of his career up to 1931. I had been unaware of this area of Tommy Rose's life, but I was able to confirm the Anglo-American Oil Company link that I had discussed with Tommy's nephew Mark Toogood at my father's funeral in 2014. This in turn led to finding articles in the British Newspaper Archive, which revealed some of his earlier achievements and previous employers and enabled me to ascertain just what he did after leaving the RAF in October 1926.

Benjamin Bennett (1904-1985) was a well-known South African crime writer who worked as a journalist with the *Cape Argus* from 1925 – 1975, and he wrote of meeting with Tommy Rose in Cape Town. This also gave me an account of the failed record attempt, plus insights into Tommy Rose's character at that time, his grit and determination to achieve the record, and what Tommy Rose had to endure during this arduous journey. The brief heading for Chapter 10 of his book was:

> 'No Panegyrics – Or Imperial "Tripe" – Hitting Palapye Road – Beer and Forget it – Daring Plant – To England in 4.5 days – High Test – At

FLIGHT LIEUTENANT THOMAS 'TOMMY' ROSE DFC

Full Moon – Another Dawn Patrol – Sailmaker's needle – Burn a Joss Stick – 1,200 Mile Hop – Misfortunes – Headwind – Stranded – Good-bye to Record – Shake on it.'

The story then continued:

No more unlucky man than Tommy Rose ever tackled the great Air Adventure of Africa. Rose's ill-luck, probably, has meant that you will have heard little of him, and seen no banner-headlined panegyrics of his flying. Yet for all this lack of fame let me tell you the story of Tommy Rose.

Flight Lieutenant Thomas Rose DFC was an airman by trade. A youth when the World War began, he won a fair amount of distinction by his work over the enemy lines. With peace he turned to civil aviation, and the post he occupied at the time of his flight was that of air representative of the Anglo-American Oil Company, a subsidiary of the gigantic Standard Oil Company of New Jersey. He was one of that small body, the Gosport A 1 instructors, a peerless cross-country pilot, and a stunt artist of outstanding ability. When I first met him, he had done 3,200 hours of flying. There are not a hundred men alive with that record. Indeed, Rose possibly had higher qualifications that any other pilot who had flown to the Cape.

But he remains in my mind as the most modest, too, among the big pilots. 'No fuss', was his watchword. 'Don't let anybody throw a long line of Imperial tripe about me,' he strongly phrased his aversion for publicity to me once.

Thus, it was in the Rose fashion that a single-seater Hermes Avian Sports sneaked away from Lympne aerodrome, Kent on February 11, 1931. Few people knew that its unflamboyant take-off spelt the beginning of still another attempt on the down-Africa record. Extraordinary precautions had been taken to prevent news of the arrangements for the flight getting into the London newspapers before the actual start. I had learnt before then that Rose was planning the flight; for a correspondent had cabled a week before giving brief news of it.

Soon, however, Rose was caught in the news-net. The ubiquitous **Reuter** *picked him up at Lympne just as he left on the lap to Rome. The press message relayed through London, revealed that his intention was to break the existing record – 'Caspar's' eight and a half days.*

He reached Rome at 4.35 pm that afternoon, slept the night, and left for Tripoli at 7 am next morning. Slight anxiety over the wires marked this hop, for at five o'clock in the afternoon he had not arrived, and watchers feared that he had come down in the Mediterranean. He told me, nearly two months later, that he had flown for hours over the sea in

1931 TOMMY ROSE'S FIRST ATTEMPT ON THE CAPE TOWN RECORD

driving mist and rain squalls, often only a score of feet above the lift of the storm swell.

'I flew in terror,' he confessed. 'I was really frightened. I don't think that I have ever suffered so much mentally in the whole of my career. My first dawn patrol was nothing beside those hours over the Mediterranean. I sang "Nearer, my God to Thee", 347 times on that crossing – I am not exaggerating'.

But he got through safely at 5.45 pm, and next morning he was off on a lap to Benghazi, Cairo, Khartoum and Juba – the romantic place names associated with other flights before him, tell the tale of his steady progress southwards. He landed at Khartoum at the sunset of Sunday, and at dawn on Tuesday he spurred Juba away from his undercarriage wheels and was off for Kisumu and Bulawayo.

All along the down-Africa line slight delays occurred to check his speed. Here it was difficult to find the fuel-supply man; there an odd job had to be done. By the time he reached Bulawayo, the capital of Southern Rhodesia, it was noon on Wednesday, February 19. He had been more than eight days on the flight. Caspareuthus had landed at Cape Town on the ninth. He had a bare chance of succeeding. But the joss of ill-luck won. With Bulawayo behind him at 2.30 pm, Rose hit Palapye Road just after five o'clock – and hit it hard. His landing wheels struck an anthill, one of those concrete-like mounds of sun-baked earth that crop up all over the veld landscape, and he narrowly escaped disaster. His plane careered on and smashed through a barbed-wire fence. He had to telegraph Bulawayo for a mechanic. Captain R. Smith, of the Rhodesian Aviation Company, set off with an engineer and spares in a plane the moment the telegram came through.

The damage, though, proved too serious to be put right on the veld. Rose dragged a weary way into Bulawayo, his hopes dashed, and cabled to England for a new undercarriage. That alone could enable him to see the flight through. For seven weeks he waited for that undercarriage. A mishap in Africa is no mere matter of moments. 'If my chance of breaking the record had still been more than a chance,' he told me, 'I should have been furious. But as it was, I just had a glass of beer and forgot about it'.

Poor Tommy Rose! He kicked his heels in Bulawayo longing to be in the air again but knowing that he had failed. Even the congenial company of the Rhodesians, ever ready to drink sundowners with a stranded stranger, failed to restore his happiness. Not that he let them know it. He was of the type that is always over-brimming with cheeriness.

Meanwhile, Lieutenant Commander George Pearson Glen Kidson, millionaire and sportsman, swooped down Africa in a flight that is still a sensation. He smashed the record by landing at Cape Town just six days and ten hours after he had left England. Tommy Rose was forgotten.

Kidson side-slipped his giant Lockhead-Vega monoplane down to the aerodrome at Bulawayo, then within reach of the record he coveted. Rose was one of those who met him there and renewed his old friendship. Kidson went on, and Tommy Rose remained. It is true that he had to wait but a little longer; Glen Kidson reached Cape Town on Monday, and on the Thursday of the same week Tommy Rose caught up with him.

One of a thrilled crowd, I stood at Maitland aerodrome as the sun sank over Table Bay and saw the triumph of Kidson. He was cheered wildly. The newspapers gave him streamer headlines. Sub-editors in St. Georges Street sat in vigil for the 'flash' message that they could 'full rate' to Fleet Street. Yes, Kidson had arrived.

On the Thursday afternoon I saw the landing of Rose. 'Keep an eye open for this fellow Rose', a news editor had said to me. 'I suppose we must say something about him'.

I drove out to Maitland that afternoon and turned in to the aerodrome for a minute or two. Climbing out of the car, I saw a dot on the blue silk that was the sky above the Hottentots Holland Mountains. It was Rose. Three other men were on the aerodrome – an officer of the South African Air Force, on duty over the planes that carried diamonds from Namaqualand; one businessman; and Mr Frank Solomon, a pioneer of flying in Africa, who had forsaken the air to run a service station at a seaside resort on the Cape coast.

A little red plane dropped out of the sky and ran along the sun-browned turf of the aerodrome. A man in shorts and sports jacket switched off the engine, clambered out of the solitary cockpit and twisted into a smile a mouth stiff with the cold of high altitudes. 'Hullo chaps,' said the mouth. Tommy Rose had arrived, though nobody seemed to care a great deal.

I had a word with Tommy Rose on his experiences flying down to Cape Town from Kimberley, the diamond city. He had nothing of interest to relate beyond the fact that he had been bumped up and down in one long aerial toboggan ride.

'What's a good pub to put up at?' Rose asked me. He had come friendless to a strange town. I suggested the Queen's Hotel, where Kidson was staying, and Rose drove off to there to soak in a stinging hot bath.

Next day he came into the city to drink tea with me. He still wore khaki shirt and slacks and a shabby sports coat. The liveried commissionaire at the café door looked askance at him as we joined a crowd of thin-voiced, pomaded youths who were sauntering in to hear the latest jazz inanity snarled by Africa's most blatant saxophone. Rose didn't give a damn.

Over that cup of tea evolved a daring plan, to fly back to England in four and a half days – 48 hours less than Kidson had taken on his dash out from Netheravon.

1931 TOMMY ROSE'S FIRST ATTEMPT ON THE CAPE TOWN RECORD

'I want to do something good on the way back', he declared. 'If I had broken the record to the Cape, I should have made £2,500. But rewards are not everything. My bus is called High Test, after the name of the spirit I am selling in Britain. I should like to see High Test get a bit of the credit for good work done. I fancy ... yes, I think ... I can get to England in four and a half days. With all the luck in the world, that is. I think I can take a chance on my luck this time. I am really lucky: at least, I always get away with it when misfortune happens along. Something goes wrong at the last trick, though. If I reached Rome on the fourth day on my way back and was just making the English coast by the fifth, a seagull would probably dash into my propeller and smash it.' Tommy Rose would be saved alright, but his record would be lost.

'I see no reason why I should not reach England in four and a half days. Kidson did it in six and a half, and he never flew at night. I shall have to fly by night. So keep an eye open when the full moon comes along. But meanwhile, mum's the word.'

So, it was announced that Rose was making tentative plans to lower the Duchess of Bedford's homebound record of ten days.

The full moon came and with it a word from Rose. My telephone rang at 5 pm on April 30th. 'Rose here', said a voice. 'I's shooting off at three o'clock tomorrow morning old chap. Coming to see me off?' That was all.

At his hotel that evening Rose showed me his maps and outlined his schedule. With me was a lawyer who insisted on telling Tommy Rose that he was bound to break his neck. Rose coolly bet a sovereign that he would get through safely. He planned to fly for 14 hours next day; a feat never before accomplished. I envied him rather, for a moment, because my lawyer friend and I were drawn into an interminable argument on India with a gentleman who introduced himself as a 'membah of the Empah Mahkhing Bohd'.

By the light of the full moon a few hours later I watched him leave on his flight, possibly the most daring African air adventure ever attempted. At 2.55 am the five men and three women who had gathered to see him off in the cold of the autumn night, grew a trifle flurried. 'Isn't he coming?' they asked. 'Where can he be?' But Tommy Rose slipped into the aerodrome quite unruffled at 3.am.

He looked at his plane, shook hands, and clambered into the cockpit. He was the calmest man there. 'Look after my kit Cathcart', he said. 'Right you are', said a slightly built man. This was Lieutenant O. Cathcart-Jones, Kidson's staff pilot, who came over in the millionaire's record-breaking Lockhead Vega. Cathcart-Jones was sailing for England in the Union Castle mail steamer next day and taking Tommy Rose's gear home with him.

Rose, in the cockpit of High Test, switched on his engine to hear the unfaltering roar of its cylinder explosions. The Hermes engine broke into

FLIGHT LIEUTENANT THOMAS 'TOMMY' ROSE DFC

life at the first swing of the propeller. Rose let it rev up for five minutes. 'After so many years – a dawn patrol again,' he said. 'Burn a joss-stick to the great god Luck for me'.

He taxied slowly to the far end of the aerodrome in the beam of a motor car's headlights. The car turned and raced across the aerodrome. High Test followed it. Then, a vague silver ghost in the fitful light, it braced its wings against the upward thrust of the air and swept into the sky.

Eight people on the aerodrome sighed with relief that he got safely off the ground. Only once before had a civil airman flown by night. That was when a Mr J. Williamson, engaged to fly an illuminated aeroplane over a tattoo by the Grenadier Guards, had crashed in thick mist and turned his bus over in a somersault.

Rose was attempting a feat far more hazardous than a solitary flight. I reflected on it as High Test wheeled up into the sky, crossed the face of the moon, and lost itself to sight in two minutes. The roaring of the engine came thinly from above for many minutes as Rose climbed higher and higher to cross the Hex River Mountains.

Flying alone, he was trying to smash a record set up by a monoplane that cost £6,300 – nine times as much as his. By the light of the full moon each night, he was to go on flying where, before him, all airmen had descended to sleep at jungle aerodromes.

Sleep was his chief enemy. To succeed he had to spend 78.5 hours in the air, with only 20.5 hours for rest, and ten more for five rigorous inspections of his engine. He was to keep himself awake by laving himself in eau-de-Cologne and breathing deeply of a smelling salts bottle. When the desires of the body drugged with sleeplessness demanded that he should doze, he was going to jab his thigh sharply with a sailmaker's needle.

The dangers of falling asleep in the air were undisguised. Wartime airmen will tell you stories of a patrol machine that glided down to land behind its own lines after the pilot, with the joystick still in his hand died of wounds. But Rose could not hope to land safely in his sleep where rivers and jungles and snow-capped peaks tore up the contours of the Central African no-mans-land. And if his engine failed – but he felt it could not fail.

'I am certain I can get through if my engine can; and my engine has never let me down', he had impressed upon me. 'I've been a pilot since 1916, and I've put in 3,200 flying hours. I have never once had an engine failure in the air.' I think I know the reason why. As Captain Ball, the war V.C. was reputed to do, Rose knew and loved, and doctored every nut in his engine himself.

Could Rose do it? He had given me his startling schedule to show his plans:

Friday 3 am leave Cape Town. Arrive Bulawayo, after flying 1,200 miles, 3 pm. Two hours for the engine; five for rest. Friday, 10 pm leave Bulawayo.

1931 TOMMY ROSE'S FIRST ATTEMPT ON THE CAPE TOWN RECORD

Saturday 10 am arrive Tabora (Tanganyika); refuel with 40 gallons of petrol, and straightaway fly on 400 miles to Kisumu. Arrive Kisumu 5.30 pm, Saturday. Engine two hours, rest 8.5 hours.

Sunday, 4 am, leave Kisumu; fly 1,250 miles over the Sudd to Khartoum; arrive Khartoum 4 pm. Engine two hours, rest six hours. Sunday, midnight, leave Khartoum; fly to Cairo, 1,086 miles; reach Cairo midday.

Monday. Engine two hours, rest two hours. Leave Cairo 4 pm. And then on by moonlight across the Mediterranean to Rome 1,400 miles with dangerous sea flying.

Arrive Rome Tuesday, 6 am; check over engine, rest an hour, and off on the last lap non-stop London.

If he were to reach London, according to plan, at 6 pm on Tuesday, May 5, Rose would have beaten Kidson's outward record by two days and the Duchess of Bedford's homeward record by six days. He would have flown 7,500 miles in 78.5 hours.

Kidson in a monoplane with a cruising speed of 150 miles an hour, had been only 56 hours in the air. But Rose's plane could only average 100 miles an hour. It was a fine plane for all that. Its sistership, the only other of the type built was 'Southern Cross Junior', Kingsford-Smith's record-breaking 'bus'. It had a range of 1,600 miles, possible by reason of an extra-large petrol tank holding 111 gallons. That was 200 miles more than the longest single hop he had planned for himself, the hazardous 1,400 miles across the Mediterranean from Cairo to Rome.

So Rose was speeding northwards while the sun rose and tipped the wings of High Test with a red glinting light. When Professor Piccard explored the upper air in a sealed cylinder in May 1931, he carried with him, besides an array of scientific instruments, brandy and sandwiches. When Tommy Rose dashed away from Maitland aerodrome, he carried dozens of caviar sandwiches, a flask of iced black coffee, another of orange juice and two hundred English cigarettes. Nibbling at his first caviar sandwich, he breakfasted on that May morning somewhere between the Hex River Mountains and Beaufort West. What did he think of when he made for inaccessible horizons, cramped in a few inches.?

Perhaps his engine, his two-year-old kiddie and wife in England, his work. Many a bearded unromantic farmer on the veld heard a drone of Rose's plane wax and wane, gazed from his work to the sky, and probably thought, 'another of these mad brained flying men'.

Rose raced on towards Bulawayo. That afternoon, when the hordes of coloured newsboys had broken loose on the streets of Cape Town yelling the news of the secret departure, I waited for tidings of High Test. They came. A telegram from Bulawayo, despatched at 4.17p.m. said 'Rose reached here.' Tommy Rose had not failed. He was one precious hour behind schedule, but he had created a record hop from the Cape to Bulawayo.

A phlegmatic sub-editor stood by me, waving another full-rate telegram from Bulawayo, 'Cancel previous message', it said. Some wandering Rhodesian plane, apparently, had flopped out of the blue on to the Bulawayo aerodrome, and an enthusiastic Pressman had sent the wire post-haste to Cape Town only to find that Rose was still somewhere down South – lost, crashed perhaps. Damn it. A brief paragraph announcing the arrival of Rose at the end of his first hop already stared blackly from isolation in a strip of white that was the late news column of the paper. That was that, anyhow. Perhaps we could hear later how the crash actually occurred.

The automatic telegraph tube suddenly shot out another message. Even as we were doubting, a message had been morsed from Bulawayo and flashed along a subterranean path from the Post Office to the newspaper offices. It was authentic news. Rose had made Bulawayo at 4.35 pm. Hop Number One up Africa was, after all, successfully accomplished.

For the next four days news filtered in, in dribs and drabs. In Bulawayo, we learnt, Rose immediately set to work on his engine. Volunteer mechanics busied themselves on a rapid overhaul. He snatched a few precious hours of sleep. Sleep. That was the real danger, not the jungles.

At 11.30 pm the second night, just after the huge moon had reared itself in the sky, Tommy Rose left for Tabora. This time it was real all-night flying. And a difficult job too, with nothing but a compass to guide him, and a speedometer to tell him the rate of progress. His start from Bulawayo was 90 minutes behind schedule, and he had not yet found the following winds he expected when approaching the Equator. A tiny crowd shivered in the cold as he streaked into the moonlit sky.

On Saturday Rose reached Tabora. He had intended to refuel with forty gallons of petrol and, without any sleep, soar off on the four hundred miles to Kisumu. But he arrived too late to assure his getting to Kisumu before nightfall. Instead, he slept again at Tabora, and tinkered with the engine.

Then away to Kisumu early on Sunday morning, May 3. Hours later a weary figure, wearing grey flannel trousers, a red woollen sweater, white canvas shoes but no socks, hatless and unshaven, clambered out of the cockpit of High Test at Kisumu.

There was little time to devote to the engine. There was less time for sleep. The sailmaker's needle would have been vigorously prodded. He left Kisumu at 11 am. He was seven precious hours behind schedule. His object was Khartoum over the impenetrable sudd of the Nile.

But more bad luck was in store for Tommy Rose. Winds continued against him and he had to break his flight at Juba. He could not go on that night either. There was some more sleep for him, not the sleep-

1931 TOMMY ROSE'S FIRST ATTEMPT ON THE CAPE TOWN RECORD

dispelling needle. Next morning, he departed for Kosti, on the White Nile, and Khartoum.

Great dust storms next checked him. 'Nearer my God to Thee', Tommy Rose may have hummed again, as his plane struggled heroically against the blast. It was swept back, nevertheless, and Juba saw them both once more. Two hours later Juba was behind a second time.

Rose remained at Kosti for nine hours and pushed on from there at 3.30 am on the morning of May 5. He hit Khartoum one and a half hours later. It seemed, at that stage, as though the record would evade his grasp by a few hours. To beat Glen Kidson's time he would have to be in Croydon the next day, Wednesday, May 6. But unless a strong flowing wind came to his aid ... well, he had passed the worst part of the up-country flight, and that was something to be thankful for.

Between Kisumu and Malakal, then left behind, was no place where he could have landed without serious results. The earth was a jumble of hills, rocks, sudd and thick scrub, without a level patch or bit of clear ground to afford a natural aerodrome.

This was the part that the late Air Commodore C.R. Samson, who led the annual RAF flight to the Cape and back in 1927, described as by far the worst of the whole route.

A mixture of good and bad luck had brought the lone flyer to Khartoum at dawn on May 5. He took to the air for Cairo at 5.30, having spent 30 minutes resting. After Cairo would come the hideous 1,400-mile night hop across the Mediterranean to Rome, and the last leg from Rome to Croydon.

He need not have troubled to work out the schedule. Flight Lieutenant Tommy Rose, tired, weary of the sport of misfortune, with nerves sorely frayed, was forced to land at Esna, 30 miles south of Luxor. Engine trouble developed and he was left stranded.

Thus ended the dash of an airman who had, with Lieutenant Pat Murdoch, the dubious consolation of knowing he was one of the unluckiest aviators ever to come down the African skyways. 'If I were just making the English coast on the fifth day', said Rose in Cape Town, 'a seagull would probably dash into my propeller and smash it.'

On the day of Rose's mishap, Lieutenant Commander Glen Kidson and Captain Gladstone hurtled to their death on the Mountain-of-the-Little-Teeth, in South Africa, and ironically enough, dynamited him once more out of the news, That day too Flight Lieutenant H.R.D. Waghorn, the twenty-six-year-old winner of the 1929 Anglo-Italian Schneider Trophy Race, was seriously injured in an aeroplane incident at Farnborough, England, and died later, He jumped from a machine which got out of control in a high wind and struck the ground with some force before his parachute had taken the burden. A black day for aviation.

FLIGHT LIEUTENANT THOMAS 'TOMMY' ROSE DFC

Help was sent to Rose from Cairo and he made his way back to England, taking with him letters still stamped 'Cape Town to London by air mail with Tommy Rose in the High Test in six days'.

That was the story of Tommy Rose and Pat Murdoch, who can shake on being the unluckiest pair of Africa's pioneers.

Meanwhile, the *Birmingham Gazette* for 2 February 1931 reported:

EX-MIDLAND FLYING INSTRUCTOR REACHES ROME. SUCCESSFUL FIRST 'HOP' IN BID TO BREAK RECORD TO SOUTH AFRICA

7,000-mile dash in light plane
Mr Tommy Rose, the ex-RAF officer and former instructor to the Midland Aero Club, who started from Lympne, Kent, at 5.30 yesterday morning on a surprise attempt to fly to Cape Town, South Africa reached Rome safely less than 11 hours later.

Mr Rose landed at the Rome Airport at 4 pm (Greenwich time). He intends to leave for Tunis, Algeria, on the second stage of the flight today.

MOONLIGHT START
Mr Rose, who is flying alone in an Avro Avian aeroplane, similar to the machines in which Mr Bert Hinkler and Squadron Leader Kingsford-Smith achieved record-breaking flights to Australia, hopes to lower the England - Cape Town record by at least 24 hours.

He kept his proposed flight a close secret and waited six days for favourable weather. The moon was shining when early yesterday morning he took off from Lympne in his little red plane. Before leaving Lympne Mr Rose said that his longest 'hop' would be the 1,200 miles between Bulawayo and Cape Town.

Everything has been sacrificed for speed, 'in order to keep down the weight, I am not carrying a parachute', said Mr Rose, 'and I am going the whole journey – about 7,000 miles – with only one change of clothes.'

NO WIRELESS
'I think the machine will stand anything. I am carrying 110 gallons of petrol, which is sufficient to give me 10 hours flying, so that all should be well. Naturally, I shall not be in wireless touch for I cannot afford the weight of the apparatus on this tiny bus.'

Mr Rose was with the Midland Aero Club as pilot instructor from February 1928 to May 1929, when he left to join the Anglo American Oil Company.

He trained a large number of the club members, and also represented the club in aerial pageants at Blackpool and Bristol. In October 1928, he entered for the King's Cup Air Race round Britain, piloting an SE5A machine, but unfortunately came to grief at Blackpool.

1931 TOMMY ROSE'S FIRST ATTEMPT ON THE CAPE TOWN RECORD

WAR SERVICE
Mr Rose saw service during the war and was afterwards employed as an instructor in the RAF at Netheravon. He was an Air Force Rugby player and appeared in most of the representative matches.

He is now pilot to the Anglo-American Oil Company's managers and it is understood that on his flight to South Africa he is carrying urgent commercial despatches.

The *Sheffield Independent* for Thursday, 12 February 1931 reported:

LONE FLIGHT IN PROGRESS ATTEMPT TO BREAK RECORDS FOR CAPE 'HOP'
Mr Tommy Rose the former RAF officer, who set out this morning in an Avro-Avian aeroplane from Lympne in an attempt to break the record for a flight from London to Cape Town arrived at the Liegorial Airport here at 4p.m. He will leave for Tunis tomorrow morning,

Mr Rose hopes to lower the record time by at least 24 hours. The flight has been undertaken to carry urgent commercial despatches.

Before leaving Lympne, Flight Lieutenant Rose said his longest 'hop' would be the 1,200 miles between Bulawayo and Cape Town.

Everything had been sacrificed for speed, 'I am not even carrying a parachute', he said.

'I am going the whole journey, about 7,000 miles, with only one change of clothing. Still, it is great sport and I am looking forward to it,'

The *Bath Chronicle and Herald* for 14 February 1931 reported:

BATH RUGBY FORWARD'S LONE FLIGHT TO CAPE
Flight Lieutenant Tommy Rose, flying alone in an Avro Avian Aeroplane to Cape Town, left Lympne on Wednesday morning and reached Rome at 4.35 the same afternoon. He took off again for Tripoli on Thursday morning, arriving there at 5.55 am the same night. Yesterday he left for Bengazi.

Tommy Rose is a former Bath and Somerset County Rugby footballer. A dashing forward, he will be well remembered by supporters of the Bath Football Club. He played for the Bath team and for the Royal Air Force representative teams, some six or seven years ago, whilst stationed at Netheravon. It was then that he used to play for Bath fairly regularly. He was in the County team in the year in which Somerset won the County Championship, and also played in the special representative teams of the Royal Air Force.

Rose is flying an Avro Avian, similar to the machine in which Herbert John Louis Hinkler AFC, DSM (8 December 1892 - 7 January 1933), better known as Bert Hinkler, was a pioneer Australian aviator (dubbed 'Australian Lone Eagle') and inventor. Rose and Squadron Leader

FLIGHT LIEUTENANT THOMAS 'TOMMY' ROSE DFC

Kingsford Smith put up record-breaking flights to Australia. He hopes to lower the record time by at least 24 hours.

A letter appeared in *Flight* 27 February 1931:

CIRRUS ACHIEVEMENT
Cirrus Aero Engineers, of Croydon, have received the following telegram from Bulawayo 'Britain to Bechuanaland in eight days. Hermes had behaved magnificently. Owing to contrary winds, she has been at full throttle two-thirds of the trip and is now better than ever. Every horse in her is fully thoroughbred.' Signed Tommy Rose.

The Yorkshire Post for Saturday, 2 May 1931 reported:

DASH FROM CAPE, NEW RECORD ATTEMPT BY TOMMY ROSE
Flight Lieutenant Tommy Rose has decided to take off from here (Bulawayo) at 11.30 pm for Tabora Tanganyika, on the second stage of his flight from Cape Town.

Rose left Cape Town at 3 am today for England. He hopes to accomplish the journey in four and a half days.

'I should like to show', he said before starting, 'that an all English light plane can do what Kidson's American machine did, and what the Duchess of Bedford's German machine did.'

Lieutenant Rose has worked out a timetable by which he will spend 78.5 hours in the air and 20.5 hours resting, and 10 hours in attending to and, if necessary, repairing his machine.

He is flying a small Avro Avian, and the longest hop of the flight will be the 1,400 miles across the Mediterranean, which he proposes to do by moonlight. He is carrying 111 gallons of petrol, which gives the machine a range of 1,600 miles. His personal luggage consists of a toothbrush and razor.

Flight Lieutenant Rose left Lympne Aerodrome on February 12, in an attempt to break the record of eight and a half days. Through meeting bad weather between Rome and Cairo all hope of beating the record had to be abandoned, and on February 20 he made a forced landing at Palapye Road, Bechuanaland and damaged the undercarriage of his aeroplane.

The *Shields Daily News* for Tuesday, 12 May 1931, reported from Cairo:

Flight Lieutenant Tommy Rose left Heliopolis aerodrome for Benghazi, Tripoli, en route for Tunis, whence he will attempt a non-stop flight to England.

1931 TOMMY ROSE'S FIRST ATTEMPT ON THE CAPE TOWN RECORD

> *Flight Lieutenant Rose set out from Cape Town on May 1 and hoped to reach England in four and a half days, but, as in his outward flight to Cape Town has been dogged by bad luck.*

Flight for 22 May 1931 reported:

> *We are glad to learn that the forced landing made by Flight Lieutenant Tommy Rose near Luxor, during his speedy flight home from Cape Town, was not so serious as some reports made out. According to a cable sent to Cirrus Hermes Engineering Co. Ltd., he flew blind for half an hour in a sandstorm, and when he landed he found the cowling full of sand and rear rockers seized. He remedied the trouble and is proceeding home by easy stages – at the time of writing he is held up in Benghazi.*

It would appear that Tommy Rose left the aircraft to be repaired and have a new engine fitted by Cirrus Hermes Engineering company Ltd and flew home, with his RAF friend who had come to pick him up, but unfortunately the name of this pilot is not known.

Tommy Rose returned to the UK and the next report, in *Flight,* for 26 June 1931, stated that he attended the Reading meeting, in another Avro Avian.

> *An old friend (Tommy Rose), who has for so long been, as he told us, 'eating very hot dust', is now with us again, and is, of course the life and soul of the party. Quite why he wanted to eat dust we cannot understand, since we have never yet seen him fail to cope with any liquid offered to him to assuage his thirst. We are referring to Mr Tommy Rose, and on this occasion, he distinguished himself by winning the obstacle race, which included no flying, but chiefly consisted in eating such things as toffee apples! Later he gave an excellent display in an Avro Avian.*

Tommy Rose had survived the First World War and the 'Roaring Twenties' but, after leaving the RAF it is hard to tell whether he was finding civilian life more difficult than he had envisaged. One thing for sure, it was more unpredictable.

What actually happened to Tommy Rose during 1931? Did the speed attempt give Tommy Rose time to reflect on his personal circumstances at home, and perhaps his employers, was his position with Anglo American Oil going to be changed into a high powered desk job in London, or were his employers disappointed with the poor performance of the *High Test* and the Avro Avian aircraft as, unfortunately, no records appear to have survived to confirm just what happened to him. However, as Benjamin Bennett says, '*Tommy Rose appears to have been a very focused, determined individual, prepared to put himself through great personal hardship, sleep deprivation etc to achieve his goals.*'

The disappointment he must have felt with the false starts, the lack of achieving a milestone of this magnitude must have been devastating for him, but he had survived intact. He successfully returned to collect the Avian and returned home in December full of resolve. However, this was to be one of the lowest points of his life, he had no job, even worse, very little money, a wife and small child to support.

No one knows what goes on in the personal lives of others, particularly between two very private people with different views on life, one a home maker, who managed the family finances, now with the added responsibilities of their daughter Elizabeth, the other a highly ambitious pioneer aviator, who was happiest competing in racing events and maybe with his eye on future records to South Africa and the 'Kings Cup Air Race'.

A notice appeared in *Flight* for 8 January 1932, reporting on Tommy Rose's replacement at Anglo American Oil Co:

> *Mr E.E. Soubry has been appointed General Sales manager of the Anglo-American Oil Co, who are the proprietors of Pratts High Test Petrol. Mr Soubry seems to be a very exceptional man, for he is probably one of the youngest to hold such a high executive position in the British Marketing field. He started his career as a junior in the Company's office at Queen Anne's Gate, Westminster, then served throughout the war in the Royal Fusiliers. After the armistice he returned again to the Company.*

Mr Soubry doesn't appear to have been an aviator, and Tommy Rose's flying position with the Company would seem to have been replaced by a young ambitious man, aged just thirty-five, who had been promoted from within Anglo American Oil to an office job at their London headquarters.

It was stated in *Flight* for 10 August 1933, that Emile E. Soubry had been elected as a director of Anglo-American Oil Co Ltd on 3 August 1933, being described as one of the younger London businessmen now coming prominently to the fore.

It was reported in *Flight* for 29 January 1934 that:

> **ETHYL NOW CHEAPER**
> *We are notified by the Anglo-American Oil Company that Pratt's Ethyl petrol, always hitherto marketed at a premium, is now reduced to the same price being operative as from Saturday, January 23. Arrangements are rapidly being completed for making Ethyl available at all points throughout the country. Pratts Ethyl petrol was used in the Schneider Trophy Contest.*

Although the publicity department and Tommy Rose would have liked to have seen that 'Pratts Ethyl petrol had been used to win the London to Cape Town record', alas it was not to be, and so Tommy's position was duly dispensed with and replaced with a new desk bound manager in London.

Chapter 9

Isle of Man Air Service
May 1932 – October 1932
Adventures with the Supermarine Air Yacht in 1933 and Isle of Man Air Racing 1936–1947

'Aeronautics was neither an industry nor a science. It was a miracle.'
– Igor Sikorsky

Tommy Rose's daughter, Elizabeth, was in her nineties when I found her and her son, by the strangest set of circumstances, to be described later, which was very fortuitous as she has since died. But she could not confirm, with any certainty, the details surrounding this period as Margaret, Tommy Rose's first wife, very seldom discussed matters of this nature in those early years. Margaret did, however, continue to avidly follow Tommy's blossoming competitive aviation career.

This chapter will try to reveal how Tommy Rose could have left the 'temporary' family home (with his in-laws) a month later (in April 1932) 'to go and try to find a job'. This he eventually managed to do, with another individual, in the Isle of Man, to fly an amphibious aircraft between the Isle of Man and Liverpool.

Tommy Rose's lifestyle would appear to have been rather nomadic, with Margaret following him around the country wherever possible to various seasonal air shows, pageants and races. This lifestyle must have taken its toll on her, particularly since she now also had a very small child. Tommy was a very private person, as indeed they both were, but his friends have stated in the past that you could never really get any idea of how he was thinking or feeling about any subject. He was always very sure and confident of his abilities, and had a fairly high self-esteem, he loved fair and honest relationships in every segment of his life and appreciated people who had the same outlook on life.

Tommy Rose loved the attention of the adoring crowds at air shows, but he could at times be unpredictable and, without any indication or reason, would suddenly retire and leave a social event. Yet he was a marvellous raconteur, always ready with advice, with a unique approach to any problem, giving others practical advice and solutions. It is without doubt he was liked by all those who employed him, as he also had an inventive, objective mind, which resulted in occasional flashes of genius to help with any problems.

FLIGHT LIEUTENANT THOMAS 'TOMMY' ROSE DFC

Margaret on the other hand came from a farming family (as did Tommy Rose) and, being an only child, she was very close to her parents. She was careful and prudent, good with managing the couple's finances, when there was an income and, like Tommy, she was independent and liked being in control, which possibly led to differences of opinion. There probably was not much of a home life with Tommy Rose who, whenever and wherever possible would be out undertaking competitive flying, trying to make a name for himself, and winning the couple some much needed extra cash. She possibly tried to be more assertive in the home, determined to make a success of the marriage, but was hampered by the time, the hours, and days, Tommy was away from home and particularly now with their daughter, maybe she hoped that one day, he would just settle down.

However, the job he found, quite how is uncertain, was in a partnership in the Isle of Man. His partner, who must have had the finances, was Captain Donald Campbell-Shaw who, in 1931, was trying to set up the Isle of Man Air Service. How they met is not known. Campbell-Shaw was previously personal pilot to Sir Sefton Brancker, the Director of Civil Aviation, who in those days was known to all the flying fraternity.

By January 1932 Tommy had entered into a partnership with Captain Campbell-Shaw, to lease a Saro Cutty Sark, G-AAIP, with Tommy as pilot, and by April 1932 he had made arrangements to leave his wife and daughter and move to the Isle of Man, covering his tracks on the way.

Donald Campbell-Shaw left the Royal Navy in 1924 to serve in the RAF, becoming a Pilot Officer on 17 July 1925 and he resigned his short service commission in 1928. He then joined the Civilian Aircraft Company, Burton-on-Trent, as personal pilot to Sir Sefton Brancker in 1928 but, following the death of his employer on 5 October 1930, he joined Civilian Aircraft Co Ltd as test pilot. The company established a factory on the southern perimeter of the Hull Municipal Airport at Hedon, but only produced one aircraft type, the Civilian Coupe, a two-seater light monoplane and after producing just six aircraft, the company was declared bankrupt, and the factory was closed in 1933. He then became manager of Fairchild Ltd, Montreal, Canada in 1930. He next started a new venture called Isle of Man Airways, in the Isle of Man and somehow arranged a lease on the Saro Cutty Sark, G-AAIP, an amphibious aircraft, for this operation, engaging Tommy Rose as pilot. He then sought permission to use the north shore at Douglas, which took several months, and it wasn't until July 1932, that an IoM-Liverpool service as Isle of Man Air Lines commenced in the summer of 1932, with Flight Lieutenant Tommy Rose as pilot.

The earliest information regarding the setting up of the Isle of Man Airlines was reported in newspaper articles as follows.

Isle of Man Examiner for Friday 18 September 1931:

> *An application for permission to utilise the North Shore for landing and taking off purposes on the occasion of his forthcoming visit to Ramsey had been received from Captain D. Campbell-Shaw, who has been giving aeroplane flights at Ronaldsway. The Commissioners decided to grant the required permission, subject to satisfactory arrangements being made between Captain Shaw and the Finance Committee.*

ISLE OF MAN AIR SERVICE

The Peel City Guardian (Isle of Man) for 17 October 1931:

MANX SEAPLANE SERVICES
Captain D. Campbell-Shaw has written to the Public Amusements Committee of the Douglas Town Council with respect to proposed seaplane services between the Isle of Man and different parts of Great Britain and Ireland and Captain Shaw also asked permission to use a small portable pier on the foreshore for the purpose of embarking and disembarking passengers when the machine is available for giving pleasure flights from Douglas Bay. The Committee have granted the necessary permission for the season 1932, in accordance with terms which they have laid down.

Mona's Herald for Tuesday, 20 October 1931:

SEAPLANE FLIGHTS FROM DOUGLAS BAY
Alderman R. Corlett asked for further information regarding the application made by Captain Campbell-Shaw for permission to use a small portable pier on the foreshore for embarking and disembarking passengers from seaplane.

Councillor Johnson replied that Captain Shaw, who had been responsible for passenger flights in the island, was hoping to establish seaplane transport services between the Isle of Man and Liverpool. That was going to cost him a considerable sum of money, not only for the planes, but also the staff at the booking agencies.

Isle of Man Times for Saturday, 28 November 1931:

It is common knowledge that Captain D. Campbell Shaw is endeavouring to arrange a seaplane service to the Isle of Man next year, with joy flights from the Douglas shore and Ramsey, when 'planes' are available. The Douglas Corporation stated their terms, and since that time Captain Shaw has asked for a reconsideration, as, in his opinion, the terms are rather high. Captain Shaw is still endeavouring to overcome existing difficulties and hopes to have his seaplane service operating as soon as necessary. For this traffic Captain Shaw has secured an amphibian aeroplane, which as its name indicates, is a flying boat which can land on the land. This Supermarine Sea Eagle machine is an all-British product, and one of its kind has been used on the Southampton-Channel Islands Imperial Airways service. It has accommodation for six people, and a speed of 100 mph. The engine is a Napier Lion. Captain Shaw's prowess as a pilot is well known. He was personal pilot to the late Sir Sefton Brancker, who lost his life in the R101 airship disaster, for a considerable time, and holds the highest testimonials from him.

FLIGHT LIEUTENANT THOMAS 'TOMMY' ROSE DFC

The prototype Saro Cutty Sark, G-AAIP, with two 105hp Cirrus engines was originally built as a flying boat and was first flown as such on 4 July 1929, but it was later modified into an amphibian with a retracting undercarriage and tail-skid.

This implies that Tommy leaving his wife and daughter was not done on a spur of the moment whim, but one which must have been well thought out and planned, but why he chose not to tell Margaret is not known. This must have been very upsetting for her when, or if, she found out what he had been planning.

Another new company was registered on 11 March 1932, and it was called British Amphibious Airlines Ltd, Blackpool, acquiring an agreement dated 4 February 1932 between the Borough of Blackpool of the one part, and R. Monk, J.E. Horseman and F. Booth of the other part, with regard to the use of the sea and foreshore at Blackpool for conducting flights in an amphibious flying boat.

Flight Lieutenant Monk was granted permission to use the foreshore at Blackpool and at Douglas and he was allowed to land in the Bay. His intention was to spend the day on pleasure trips over Blackpool and in the evening, he would make the return trip to Douglas when the bay was clear of sailing craft.

The service was advertised and the Saro Cutty Sark G-ABBC was purchased and named 'Progress' after the Blackpool motto. In 1932, its first year, it carried 348 passengers and in the second year working a three-day service it carried 130 passengers, this was not great news for Captain Campbell-Shaw and his Isle of Man Air Service.

On Thursday, 11 February 1932, Tommy Rose attended the Herts and Essex Aero Club Dinner, held at the Holborne Restaurant, Kingsway, London. *Flight* for 19 February 1932 reported on the event as follows:

> *The Herts and Essex Aero Club is one of the youngest but by no means the least important of our Light Aeroplane Clubs.*
>
> *After the usual toasts, Tommy Rose followed and proposed the health of the club as follows.*
>
> *He said this was an age of miracles, and if anyone had suggested two years ago that two people entirely new to flying, such as the brothers Frogley, could have established such a successful club as this one, he would not have believed them. The miracle had, however come about and he himself was one of the founder members. He deprecated an idea prevalent amongst certain people that the chief profits of the club were to be obtained from the bar. This was entirely the wrong idea, he said, for it was from the flying side that every club should endeavour to make its money. He drew attention to the fact that in no small measure the success of the club was due to the help received from Captain Duncan Davis and his assistants from the Brooklands School of Flying.*

Tommy Rose attended Sywell's Fifth Annual Display and *Flight* for 20 May 1932 reported on the event as follows:

> *At the dinner in the evening Miss Amy Johnson and Mr Mollison were the guests of honour, and both thanked Mr Shale, the chairman, in short*

but appropriate speeches. A dance followed the dinner, which was well attended, and though it lacked the exclusive aeronautical atmosphere of last year, it was good to see several old faces which have been missed for some time. Tommy Rose was there, but he did not, as in previous years, spend his time on the aerodrome 'knocking the necks off bottles'.

Meanwhile, in the Isle of Man it was reported by the *Isle of Man Times* for Saturday, 21 May 1932 that:

THE PROPOSED DOUGLAS TO LIVERPOOL SERVICE

The Air Service which has been arranged by Captain D. Campbell Shaw is to commence on 2 June with a regular morning and evening service between Douglas and Liverpool. A Saro amphibian aircraft, the 'Saro Cutty Sark', which carries six passengers has been purchased. At Douglas the amphibian will land in the bay, which has been licensed by the Air Ministry for the purpose, or if the sea is too stormy, at Ronaldsway. At Liverpool a landing will be made at the Liverpool Corporation aerodrome. The service will run during all weather conditions except thick fog.

The first mention of Tommy Rose's association with this enterprise was published in the *Isle of Man Examiner* for Friday, 10 June 1932:

LIVERPOOL-DOUGLAS AMPHIBIAN FORCED DOWN
SHORTAGE OF PETROL IN MID CHANNEL
PASSENGERS RESCUED BY '*TYRCONNEL*'

The Cutty Sark amphibian, which is maintaining a double daily air service between Liverpool and Douglas, had to make a forced landing in mid-channel on the way to Douglas. There were four passengers on board; Mr G. Kelly and his son of Breck Road, Anfield, Liverpool, Mr Y. Green, of Pinehurst Avenue, Liverpool, and Mrs Delaney, of Castlewood, Liverpool, the machine was piloted by Flight Lieutenant Tommy Rose. In a subsequent interview with a Press representative, Flight Lieutenant Rose said: 'After flying from Douglas to Liverpool aerodrome at Speke in the morning, I was making the return journey with the four passengers when about 50 or 60 miles out and in the middle of the Irish Channel a petrol pump failed and the engines stopped. I was flying just high enough to be able to turn the machine into the wind and make a successful forced landing. My passengers behaved splendidly, and there was no panic. We just had to wait there until we saw a ship and hailed her. It was 20 minutes before help came in sight. During this time, I was inspecting the engines and my passengers were terribly ill with seasickness'.

The rescue vessel was the cargo boat 'Tyreconnel', which formerly belonged to the Isle of Man Steam Packet Co She lowered a boat, took the passengers and pilot off, and towed the amphibian to Liverpool.

FLIGHT LIEUTENANT THOMAS 'TOMMY' ROSE DFC

Flying resumed yesterday, the Cutty Sark reaching Ronaldsway in the course of the morning.

An advertisement which appeared in the *Peel City Guardian* for Saturday, 11 June 1932:

LIVERPOOL TO DOUGLAS AIR SERVICE
A double daily air service was inaugurated on Wednesday by the Isle of Man Air Services, Flying Officer Captain Shaw and Flight Lieutenant Rose, being the pilots.

The service is scheduled to leave Douglas Bay at 7.30 am and 4.30 pm, arriving at the Liverpool Aerodrome at Speke, at 8.30 am and 5.30 pm respectively. The return services leave Speke Aerodrome at 8.45 am and 5.45 pm, arriving in Douglas Bay at 9.45 am and 6.45 pm, or if the weather is unfavourable for landing in the Bay, at Ronaldsway Derbyhaven.

The return fare is £3 10s, and seats can be booked with Mr W.H. Chapman, the local agent, 63, Athol Street, Douglas, Telephone 816. The Liverpool agents are Messrs Lewis's, Ranelagh Street.

Tommy Rose did not compete in the first Isle of Man Air Race, which took place on Saturday, 18 June 1932, due to his work schedule, but he competed in the balloon bursting competition, something he excelled at, and *The Aeroplane* for 22 June 1932 reported: *Balloon-bursting competition 1st Flight Lieutenant Tommy Rose, Avro Cadet; 2nd S. Hawley, Avro Avian.*

By July Captain Donald Campbell-Shaw was in the newspapers again, this time being fined:
Peel City Guardian IoM for Saturday, 30 July 1932 reported:

On Saturday, Captain Donald Campbell-Shaw, the airman associated with the air service between the Isle of Man and the mainland, appeared before High-Bailiff Cowley at Castle Rushden, Castletown, on a charge of unlawfully storing petrol in a field at Ronaldsway, he was fined £5, but his petrol and tins, which were subject to confiscation, were returned to him.

Isle of Man Examiner for Friday, 12 August 1932 reported:

THRILLING SCENE IN DOUGLAS BAY
AEROPLANE'S PASSENGERS RESCUED BY SPEED-BOAT
SERIOUS MISHAP TO 'CUTTY SARK' AMPHIBIAN
HULL TORN OPEN
Captain Campbell Shaw's amphibian 'Cutty Sark', which has been running between Liverpool and Ronaldsway and used for 'joy rides' from Douglas shore during the season, and Messers Hawley's speed boat

ISLE OF MAN AIR SERVICE

'I'm Alone', *figured in a thrilling incident which was watched by thousands of people on Sunday evening.*

The amphibian, which was being piloted by Flight Lieutenant T. Rose DFC, was engaged at the time giving short flights over the bay, and, about 6.50 pm, the machine was run into the water as usual with the following passengers on board: Mr Robert Radcliffe, Miss Jackson, Leo Nettleton and William Ahearn.

The machine was about a quarter of a mile from the shore, was skimming the bay preparing to take off, when, without any warning, there was a sudden rush of water into the hull, and pilot and passengers were soon almost immediately immersed. The machine sank until the wings were lapping the waters of the bay, and among the large crowd watching from the promenade there was great excitement.

Within a few minutes practically every rowing boat in the bay had been hired, and thousands of people were gazing with awe from the promenade towards the sinking machine, but there was really no occasion for undue alarm, because once the machine had sunk so far, there was sufficient buoyancy in the wings to have kept her afloat for hours.

The passengers, of course, were in the unfortunate position of being wet through, but luckily the "I'm Alone' *speed boat was close at hand on one of her runs from the Victoria Pier and the pilot immediately steered towards the 'Cutty Sark', whose passengers had by this time made their way through the emergency exit on to the wings.*

As a precautionary measure, an air float, lifebelt and lifeline were thrown out from the 'I'm Alone', *which then went alongside the amphibian, and took off the passengers who were rushed at top speed to the pier, and then motored to their respective hotels.*

THE MACHINE SALVAGED

Salvage operations were immediately commenced on the machine. Captain Shaw, who was on shore at the time of the accident, went out in Mr Swindlehurst's motorboat, which towed the waterlogged amphibian into shallow water. A rope was passed to the shore, and there was no shortage of volunteers for the attempts to pull the machine on to the beach, but twice the rope broke, and quite a few more adventurous volunteers, who had waded into the sea, got a severe ducking when the strain was so suddenly released. Then the motorboat attempted to move the machine further ashore, but without success, owing to the landing wheels having become embedded in the sand.

External help having got the machine so far, it was left to her own power to get her the rest of the way to safety. Flight Lieutenant Rose succeeded in starting both engines and the power created enabled him to guide the machine to the water's edge, where a rope was fastened to the nose of the hull, and, with a combination of engine and manual power, the 'Cutty Sark' was driven and hauled well up on the shore.

FLIGHT LIEUTENANT THOMAS 'TOMMY' ROSE DFC

As soon as the machine cleared the water it was seen there was a large hole about two feet square, in the bottom of the hull, through which the machine emptied itself as it ran over the sand.

Captain Shaw told our representative that the accident had been caused through a collision with a submerged object as the machine was about to take off. The hull is made of Duralium, and Captain Shaw explained that the machine would be doing about 45 miles per hour at the time of the collision, a stiff cardboard box would be sufficient to do the damage. Actually, it is not known what struck the machine, but Captain Shaw was merely pointing out the possible effect of a collision with the object named.

Flight Lieutenant Rose, who had stood by the machine until it was safely ashore, was soaked to the skin by the time he had saved the ship, but, after a change of clothing, he was back on the job again. Petrol supplies were taken on board, and at 9.15 pm Flight Lieutenant Rose made a perfect ascent from the shore and headed over the land to Ronaldsway Aerodrome, where the machine was to be repaired.

Things were going decidedly badly for the Isle of Man Air Service, when Captain Campbell-Shaw failed to realise that the obvious flaw was in trying to run an all-year-round air service. The seas around the Isle of Man would become unsuitable in stormy weather, with destructive waves hitting the shore, flying amphibians was only going to be possible from June to September.

Tommy Rose continued flying the aircraft until the season had finished at the end of September 1932 and he then flew G-AAIP to Saunders Roe at Cowes in the Isle of Wight in October. He had completed 250 hours in G-AAIP, but he decided to call into the Reading Aero Club on the way, as it will be seen in *Flight* for 6 October 1932, who reported: *Visitors this week included Flight Lieutenant Tommy Rose in the Cutty Sark G-AAIP.*

So, in early October 1932 Tommy Rose was again without a job, but he was soon approached to join the crew of G-AASE, the Supermarine Sea Yacht, as relief pilot to Captain Henri Charles Baird. The aircraft was furnished to a luxury standard and contained an individual cabin for its owner (complete with toilet, bath and bed), plus seating for five additional guests, a galley with full cooking facilities beneath the wing, deep pile carpets and settees, plus the luxury of electric lighting throughout. The crew were accommodated in an open cockpit in the upper nose of the aircraft.

When it first flew, in February 1930, it was found that its maximum speed and performance were well below specification. Initially powered by three Armstrong Siddeley Jaguar engines, these were later replaced by the more powerful Armstrong Siddeley Panther IIA's of 525hp. Performance, following the loss of one engine, remained marginal as the aircraft failed to maintain the necessary altitude for safe flight. This resulted in The Hon Arthur Ernest Guinness' decision not to proceed with his order, opting for the Saro Cloud instead.

So, in mid-October, Tommy joined the Air Yacht, which was at Cherbourg, France, en-route to Egypt and was, by then, owned by Mrs June Jewett James,

ISLE OF MAN AIR SERVICE

The Supermarine Air Yacht G-AASE on its beaching trolley at Cowes IoW, 1931. (*Nigel Gaudion collection*)

Romsey, Hants and named 'Windward III'. The Air Yacht was originally ordered by The Hon Arthur Ernest Guinness but not delivered. It was retained by Supermarine and its CofA was eventually issued on 22 December 1931. Registered on 8 October 1932 to Mrs June James, an eccentric American aviation and motorboat enthusiast, she came as a 'bit of a shock' to Supermarine, who were more used to dealing with pragmatic, long-winded negotiations with national governments. Mrs James could not understand why, after having seen the aircraft and decided to purchase it, she could not simply take it there and then. It took Chief Test Pilot Captain Henri Charles Baird to explain that the aircraft was being serviced, not only that, but the tide was out! Mrs James would have none of it and could not understand why the 12-ton aircraft could not be simply lifted by the Supermarine engineers and placed in the water. However, it was christened 'Windward III', its CofA was renewed on 11 October 1932, and it departed the same day on a Mediterranean cruise, piloted by H.C. Baird. However, he was taken ill and shortly after and was replaced by Tommy Rose. In November 1932. G-AASE suffered engine failure and was taxied into Port Navallo for repairs.

Flight for 20 October 1932 reported:

> *Mrs J. James of Kenya Park, Rownhams, Southampton, a keen motorboat and flying enthusiast has acquired the Supermarine 'luxury air yacht', G-AASE the three-engined mono-flying-boat (Armstrong Siddeley Panther), previously owned by the Honourable A.E. Guinness. On 11 October, the 'Winward III', as the air yacht is called, piloted by Captain Henri Charles Baird, and with Mrs James on board, left Southampton on a cruise 'somewhere' around the Mediterranean and North Africa. Later, bad weather forced them down off Cherbourg, where the aeroplane was moored to await better conditions, but these became worse, and on 14 October the party, who had remained on board, were taken off by tugs from Cherbourg which had answered their calls for help. As soon as conditions improve, they hope to continue the tour.*

FLIGHT LIEUTENANT THOMAS 'TOMMY' ROSE DFC

Tommy Rose takes over from Captain Henri Charles Baird.
This, the first 'cruise' was not a resounding success after landing at Cherbourg in worsening weather, and after spending three hours on a very rough mooring, Mrs James and her passengers were taken ashore.

Eventually reaching Naples, Mrs James proceeded to obtain audiences with both the Pope and Mussolini, Baird had to hand over the Air Yacht to Tommy Rose, the relief pilot, as Baird's stomach muscles, which had been torn in the Supermarine S.4 crash of 1926, now needed emergency surgery, in a hospital in Rome. The operation was performed by Mussolini's surgeon, under a local anaesthetic, owing to Baird's generally low condition, which Baird described as 'damned annoying'. The problems Baird suffered after his 1926 crash seem to suggest the Air Yacht was extremely heavy to handle.

The Air Yacht had an accident on 25 January 1933 when it stalled into the sea on take-off in the vicinity of Positano near Capri in the Gulf of Salerno, Italy. The owner suffered a broken leg, but otherwise there were no serious injuries sustained, but the aircraft was too badly damaged to be worth salvaging. The Air Yacht was impounded against payment of salvage claims under marine law and only parts of it, the engines, were shipped back to England, according to Supermarine employees still surviving. It was also reported that a wing was damaged in salvaging. G-AASE was towed to Castel del Mar and was later returned to Woolston, near Southampton, but it was not repaired. Tommy Rose had completed 150 hours in this flying boat.

Earnest (Fred) Smith was the flight engineer on this flight, Fred was from Supermarine, as was the pilot, Captain Henri Baird, and his account listed more occupants, including the owner's dog, all of which, except Fred and the relief pilot, Tommy Rose, left the sinking aircraft in the overloaded collapsible lifeboat and were eventually rescued by a local fisherman. Tommy Rose, Fred Smith and the rest of the party, continued their Grand Tour by conventional means.

Flight for 24 August 1933, reported that Tommy Rose was then back in the UK and had visited the Thames Valley Aero Club:

> *During the afternoon many visitors called in, including Captain Duncan Davis, who brought over Tommy Rose, now back in the country for some time.*

In September 1933, Tommy Rose was appointed Manager and Chief Flying Instructor at the Northampton Aero Club at Sywell, Northampton.

However, Tommy Rose continued to have a close association with the Isle of Man and the *Isle of Man Examiner* for 13 March 1936, reported on the occasion as follows:

OLD AIR COMRADES
FORMATION OF MANX BRANCH
A branch of the Comrades of the Royal Air Force Association was officially established in the Isle of Man last Saturday, the occasion

being celebrated by the inaugural supper at the Ridgeway Hotel, Douglas. Flight Lieutenant Tommy Rose, who has associations with the Island, and was, at the moment of his election on the last lap of his record-breaking flight from Cape Town to England, unanimously elected first President of the branch. The two Vice Presidents were Captain H. Pixton, winner of the Schneider Trophy for Britain in 1914, and Squadron Leader Sylvester Quine, who is at present in Egypt. Captain Pixton was one of the Company of fifty ex-servicemen who were at the supper.

The next mention of Tommy Rose was when the island was making arrangements for the forthcoming air race.

The *Isle of Man Examiner* for Friday, 20 March 1936 reported:

THE AIR RACE ARRANGEMENTS
DETAILS OF WHITSUNTIDE EVENTS
TOMMY ROSE A COMPETITOR?
Arrangements are now well in hand for the air races which are to be held at Whitsuntide under the auspices of the Amusements Sub-Committee of the June Effort and Seasons Extension Committee.

Following the Lancashire Aero Club's refusal to undertake the organisation, the Air Race Sub-Committee, acting on the advice of the Royal Aero Club, approached Captain Stocken, a professional organiser who after conferring with the committee, has submitted all details of organisation.

It is understood that Flight Lieutenant Tommy Rose, who recently set up new records from London to the Cape and back, will be one of the competitors, and it is also understood that the Director-General of Civil Aviation is to be invited to visit the island in connection with the races.

Tommy Rose confirmed that he intended competing in the Air Race, which was from London to the Isle of Man (Hanworth to Ronaldsway) and which was due to be held on 30 May 1936, and this time he would be flying the Miles Falcon Six.

The *Isle of Man Examiner* Friday, 22 May 1936 reported:

THE AIR RACES
EXCELLENT ENTRY RECEIVED
Entries at double fees for the air races close today, and at the time of writing, twenty entries have been received for the race from London, and fifteen for the Manx Air Derby. An additional entry does not specify in which race it is intended to compete. Two women are among those competing in the London-Douglas event.

However, Tommy Rose was back in 1937 for the London – IoM race, twenty-six entries were received for the start at Hanworth on 29 May 1937 of which twenty actually started. The handicappers placed the Taylor Cub of A.J. Walters in the front, starting at 10.50 am, and it was nearly two hours before 'scratch' man, Alex Henshaw, would be able to give chase. He was flying a new Percival P.6 Mew Gull powered by a 205hp DH Gipsy Six II engine, which gave the sleek monoplane a maximum speed of 235 mph, Tommy Rose flew a BA Eagle 2, but thick mist descended over the Maughold area, reducing visibility to between 300 and 400 yards, which caused complete chaos as competitors anxiously searched for check points. Both Tommy Rose and Herr Gerbrecht gave up and returned to Blackpool.

This resulted in a protest being lodged with the Stewards who held three meetings over the weekend to sort things out. It was not until Monday morning that they announced the final placings, declaring Major Seidemann in D-IOSA, the winner as he had been the only competitor to be recorded at Maughold Head. He was of course delighted to be taking the Challenge Cup back to Germany, claiming it was 'better to race in peace than in war'.

But the Manx Air Derby was the spectacle everyone was waiting for, with thirteen starters. Could one of the dark blue BFW 108s sporting the Swastika pull off another win? They would be away in front of Alex Henshaw's Mew Gull, which was giving fifty minutes start to the early starters over the three laps. The crowds at Ronaldsway were then treated to another hair-raising chase as they followed the machines round the turning point on the aerodrome. Lap 3 had started with the little red Comper Swift of S.T. Lowe doing well and he was able to hold off the challenge of the catching Messerschmitts, finishing just in front of Seidemann who was followed by Gerbrecht. Fifth; Flying Officer A.E. Clouston (Hawk Major) 65 min 17 sec (149 mph).

Tommy Rose, flying the Miles Falcon Six in Race No 9, was unplaced and with a handicap of 58 minutes 50 seconds, he finished in 131 minutes and 40 seconds, with an average speed of 133.5 mph. However, Tommy Rose did get to the evening dinner.

The race for 1938, then organised by the Royal Aero Club, was at Hatfield and, while the course remained unaltered, the finish was at Ronaldsway rather than Douglas.

When the entrants for the 1939 London - Isle of Man Race assembled at Hatfield on 27 May, the absence of Continental competitors was conspicuous, due no doubt to the increasingly tense international situation. There had been one Bf 108 entered by General Lieutenant Wenninger, who was anxious to support the races again. The machine was to have been flown by two of his London staff, but the entry was withdrawn when permission from Reichsmarschall Hermann Göring, Commander-in-Chief of the Luftwaffe, and Marshal of the Reich, had not been obtained. Geoffrey de Havilland was back with the T.K.2 G-ADNO, as was Alex Henshaw in his Mew Gull G-AEXF. He was joined by its designer, Captain E.W. Percival, in Mew Gull G-AFAA, while this time Tommy Rose was flying J-ACTE the Miles Hawk Speed Six. Regulations for the race had been altered so that there was no need for a compulsory stop at Speke and the course was changed whereby Blackpool became a turning point from where competitors could fly direct to a point in the north of Douglas Bay and thence to Ronaldsway. The total distance was now 256 miles of non-stop flying. The 64-mile sea crossing from Blackpool was patrolled by Douglas Lifeboat and naval vessels.

The race was blessed by fine weather though strong winds kept speeds down. The BBC broadcast commentaries from both Blackpool and Ronaldsway and listeners heard of the thrilling finish as Geoffrey de Havilland flashed over the line, hotly pursued by a rapidly gaining Alex Henshaw finishing just seconds behind him. The T.K.2 had taken 1 hour and 31 minutes to complete the distance averaging 168.25 mph, Alex Henshaw's faster Mew Gull had taken twenty minutes less and averaged 217 mph. Last to start was Captain Percival and he was under a minute behind in third place averaging 220 mph in his own Mew Gull. The Miles Hawk Speed Six, G-ADGP, flown by L. Fontes, came forth at 168.25 mph. The slower machines were well and truly outpaced this time. By far the oldest competitor in the race was Lord Londonderry, aged sixty-one, who completed the course flying a DH.87B Hornet Moth.

On 29 May 1939, the entry for the Tynwald Air Race Manx Air Derby was run with seven aircraft, all with engines of 120hp or less, but just four finished the course. The winner was Squadron Leader H.R.A. Edwards, accompanied by his wife, in the Sports Avian G-ABEE, at 106.5 mph, with Ranald Porteus coming second in the Chilton DW1 G-AFGH, and Squadron Leader Mole coming third in a Tipsy.

The Manx Air Derby, with nine starters, was also run on 29 May 1939, over a course of 156 miles, and was won by the Vega Gull, G-AFEA, at 167.5 mph flown by Albert Henshaw, with Alex as co-pilot. Alex Henshaw had withdrawn his Mew Gull after deciding to accompany his father, who had flown his Vega Gull to the island to take part in this event. The combination of father and son did the trick and the name Henshaw appeared on the magnificent trophy for the first time.

Tommy Rose averaged 186.7 mph with the Miles Hawk Speed Six G-ACTE, for second place and E.W. Percival flew at an average speed of 237 mph to come third with his Mew Gull G-AFAA.

The handicapping had been excellent with the first three finishing within the space of 46 seconds. The final results were as follows:

- 1st Albert Henshaw (Vega Gull) 58 min 0 sec. (167,5 mph)
- 2nd Tommy Rose (Miles Hawk Speed Six) 52 min 25 sec (183.75 mph)
- 3rd F.W. Percival (Mew Gull) 41 min 2 sec (237 mph)
- 4th T.W. Brookes-Smith (Miles Falcon) 60 min. 10 sec (161.5 mph)
- 5th G.R. de Havilland (T.K.2) 52 min 42 sec (184.5 mph)
- 6th J. Rush (Miles Sparrowhawk) 68 min 6 sec (168 mph)

There were no further races until after the war, when racing resumed in 1946, the year that Tommy Rose finally won the Manx Air Derby.

The first post war race meeting was held at Lympne on 31 August 1946 and was handicapped by Rowarth and Dancy. The race for the Folkestone Aero Trophy was revived, with heats being run on 31 August and the finals on 1 September. Among the many entrants was Tommy Rose, flying a Miles M.28 Mk.4, G-AGVX. Tommy Rose had retired from the position of Chief Test Pilot of Miles Aircraft Ltd in January 1946, but this didn't stop him from borrowing an aeroplane from Miles and getting back into air racing again!

Rowarth and Dancy were handicappers in the 1947 Isle of Man race held on 26 May 1947, at the revival of the Manx Air Derby. For this fifth event the pre-war London to Isle of Man Air Race was discontinued and Ronaldsway was to be the starting and finishing point for the three laps of 53.25 miles, which constituted the course for the Tynwald Air Race, which was open to all types of aircraft with a maximum of 120hp, for this race there was nineteen entries. The Manx Air Derby, for all types of British and foreign aircraft with a minimum total of 120hp had a total of thirteen entries.

The start was at 2.15 pm, and both events were run concurrently. Tommy Rose was flying the Hawk Speed Six G-ADGP, but the Tynwald Air Race for the Olley Challenge Trophy was won at 110.5 mph by Wing Commander A. McDowell in the Auster Autocrat G-AGXV, Tommy Rose, in the cream and crimson Hawk Speed Six G-ADGP came first in the Manx Air Derby at 181 mph.

The *Mona's Herald* for Tuesday, 27 May 1947 reported:

FIRST POST WAR AIR RALLY
MANX ENTRY SECOND IN TYNWALD RACE
TOMMY ROSE WINS THE AIR DERBY

Eighteen planes took part in the islands first post-war air races, the Manx Air Derby and the Tynwald Air Race yesterday, and the only Manx entry, an Auster piloted by V.H. Spencer, and entered by local company director Mr Harold Cash, gained second place in the latter race.

The main event, the Manx Air Derby, was won by Flight Lieutenant Tommy Rose in a Miles Hawk Speed Six, who completed the three circuits of the island at an average speed of 181 mph. Tommy Rose needs no introduction to Manx people as he was one of the early pioneers of air travel to the island. In pre-war years he held the England to Cape Town record.

Runner up in the Air Derby was Bruce Campbell, a de Havilland test pilot, in a Moth TK.2, whose speed was 179 mph, and John N. Somers AFC, in a Hornet Moth was third at a speed of 116 mph.

The Tynwald Air Race, which is for the baby machines under 120hp, was won by Wing Commander A. McDowall in an Auster Autocrat, at an average speed of 110 mph. V.W. Spencer (Autocrat) speed 101.5 mph was second and Group Captain Edward Mole (Benes Mraz Be.550 Bibi) speed 101 mph, third.

The planes started separately on a handicap time so that the first to cross the finishing line was the winner, and there was an interval of 35 minutes 45 seconds between the first machine away, an Autocrat, and the last was the American Beech D-17S, one of the few biplanes in the race. Tommy Rose in winning made up over half an hour on the first machine.

The start and finish were at Ronaldsway Airport and both races were over a distance of 159.75 miles, three times round a course from the airport to Douglas, Laxey, Maughold Head, Andreas, Peel Castle, St Johns and back to Ronaldsway.

All the machines completed the races except the Auster piloted by W.H. Leadbetter, of Birmingham, who retired at the end of the first circuit.

These air races were not only renowned for their exciting spectacle, speeds, and thrills, but they also gave the competitors a time to catch up with old friends, to keep abreast of the latest developments in aviation, and to enjoy the ambiance of the dinners after the races, which in many cases were lavish affairs.

A typical newspaper report of the races was given in the *Gloucester Citizen* for Tuesday, 27 May 1947:

TOMMY ROSE WINS MANX AIR DERBY
Tommy Rose, who in 1936 broke the England – Cape air record, won the Manx Air Derby yesterday in a Miles Hawk Speed Six. His speed was 181 mph for three circuits of the island (159.75 miles).

Tommy Rose was delighted, at the age of fifty-three, to win the Manx Air Derby, heading for retirement and the end of an incredible flying career, being able to bow out on a 'high'.

And finally…

The *Isle of Man Times* for Friday, 30 December 1960 reported in their *AT RANDOM* column by 'Islander':

HE WAS A PIONEER HERE
One of the men who pioneered regular air flights to the Isle of Man, has just been returned unopposed to another island parliament. He is Mr Tommy Rose, one of the three retiring members of the States of Alderney who return to their seats in the States for another three-year term.

Hampshire born Tommy Rose, was a flying ace of the First World War, when he shot down more than a dozen German planes and earned the DFC. His name was on everyone's lips, when, in 1935, he won the King's Cup Air Race and followed that up by beating Amy Mollison's London to Cape Town solo record in 1936.

And it was in the 1930s that Tommy Rose turned his attentions to the rapidly expanding field of commercial flying. He was one of the pioneers of regular air services to the island but did not remain here for long.

In the Second World War, he became Chief Test Pilot for Miles Aircraft Ltd and, since settling in Alderney in 1948, he has been a tenant of two hotels. Already a 'veteran' with six years' service in the States, 65-year-old Tommy Rose is also a member of the Inter-Island Advisory Council.

Chapter 10

Sywell September 1933 – December 1934

'You can fly well at Sywell.'

Tommy Rose attended the *first* Great Aerial Pageant at Sywell, which was held on 28 and 29 September 1928. The weather had been terrible for the previous twenty-four hours, including torrential rain, but it had cleared on the morning of the pageant just as the visitors and aircraft were arriving. Air Vice-Marshal Sir Sefton Brancker, the Director of Civil Aviation, flew in from a conference he had attended in Holland, to perform the opening ceremony and Tommy Rose flew in from the Midland Aero Club, Castle Bromwich in the club's recently acquired de Havilland Moth G-EBXT.

Upon arrival, Tommy Rose met up again with one of his students, Mr E.R. King, who he had taught to fly at the Midland club, he showed Tommy his Austin Whippet, G-EAPF, the second of only two ever built. This had been rebuilt for King by the Henderson School of Flying at Brooklands. King was one of the earliest members of the Northampton Flying Club and he was due to compete in the Great Aerial Pageant. Tommy Rose and Captain H. Broad participated in the flour bombing of a car, which Tommy nearly hit.

Tommy next attended the *second* Aerial Pageant at Sywell, which was held on 20 and 21 May 1929, and principal features of the first day were the number of memorable names attending, including Lady Bailey, Sir Alan Cobham, Sir Sefton Brancker, Miss Winifred Bown, G. and A. Linnell, and of course Tommy Rose. Many of these names were either famous at the time or were to achieve fame later. The landing competition in the morning, for private owners and club members, was won by Mr Jackaman in his Gipsy Moth G-AADX. This was followed by the official opening by the Club President, the Right Hon the Earl Spencer. Included in the grand parade that followed the grand opening were thirty-nine aircraft and Tommy Rose flew the de Havilland Moth G-EBXT again. Sir Alan Cobham took the Mayor and Mayoress of Northampton for their first flight, and also other dignitaries.

The third pageant at Sywell took place on 28 September 1929 and this was described as a 'Flying Meeting'. One of the events included Samuel Tyzack bombing a moving car with flour bags and an obstacle race where the lady passengers had to knock over beer bottles with a tennis ball, whilst the male pilots threaded a needle, after which each pair took off, flew around Sywell reservoir, landed and folded the wings of their aircraft. The winner of this event was Flight Lieutenant Tommy Rose, with Miss Maureen Harris, daughter of the Managing Director. There was also a balloon bursting competition, which allowed the competing pilot two minutes to burst two bunches of balloons. There was also the official opening of the clubhouse, now known as the Cirrus room.

SYWELL SEPTEMBER 1933 – DECEMBER 1934

The next event, 'Pack and Planes', was another first for Sywell. This unusual idea came from Geoffrey Linnell and Mr Noel Lloyd, Master of the Pipewell Foot Beagles, and took place on 30 November 1929. The meet of the Beagles on the aerodrome was supplemented by the arrival by air of supporters, Flight Lieutenant Tommy Rose, and the ubiquitous Sir Sefton Brancker, Director of Civil Aviation. There were mock air battles, and aerial acrobatics, plus various other aircraft of the club dressed in blue and white 'beagling' kit, plus assorted stuffed hounds and horses, some of which were later dropped from the air. In the evening at the dinner dance provided by the club, Mr Newton, Chairman of the club, expressed his pleasure at seeing so many people attending the club meeting, adding to the day's success. Mr Noel Lloyd, Flight Lieutenant Beathy from London, and Tommy Rose gave their return toasts to the club. and Tommy Rose gave high praise to the club's efforts.

In 1930 an important flying event took place, staged by the Northampton Aero Club at a private airfield near Peterborough owned by Mr K. Whittome. Nearly 6,000 spectators attended, including Tommy, this time flying the Moth G-AAKJ, by this time he was employed by the Anglo-American Oil Company (1929-1931) as their flying representative.

The early 1930s revealed a conflict between the Aero Club members learning to fly on the club aircraft, and the qualified pilots who had gone on to own their own aircraft. The root of this conflict was the belief that the 'private owners' did not adequately support the tuition sufficiently or financially.

On 5 October 1930, British civil aviation suffered loss of the airship R101, which crashed in France during its maiden voyage, killing forty-eight of the fifty-four people on board. Amongst those who lost their lives were Lord Thompson the Air Minister, Major Scott the captain of the airship and Air Vice-Marshal Sir Sefton Branker, the much loved and respected Director of Civil Aviation.

For much of the time the Northamptonshire Flying Club continued as before, but as 1931 progressed, the country entered a period of depression and slump, with all flying clubs up and down the country suffering, Sir Sefton Brancker was not there to represent their interests and promote the joy of flying. Club flying had to be run in a more business-like way, there were going to be problems in the future making ends meet.

At Sywell, 1931 started with a spell of bad weather which continued until the Spring. This affected nearly all the flying schools nationwide, with each school trying to stage events and displays when and where possible to bring in the public to increase revenue.

The Tatler, a prominent high society magazine, carried an advertisement providing the 'opportunity of a lifetime' for their readers to learn to fly at *The Tatler's* expense at one of twenty-three airfields nationwide. It was an exciting and unique idea, and one that had never been repeated on such a large scale nationally. The advertisement was first published on 18 April 1931 and explained the unusual promotion on 13 May 1931. The scheme closed with only eight flying clubs still having available places.

It was hoped it would stimulate the much-needed interest and resulting income for these flying clubs, who at the time were all seeing a downturn in their student numbers and resulting reduced income.

FLIGHT LIEUTENANT THOMAS 'TOMMY' ROSE DFC

Well-knowns in the flying world at the opening ceremony for the new clubhouse at Sywell. From left to right, Lord Willoughby de Broke, Major G.R.D. Shaw, Lady Willoughby de Broke, Flight Lieutenant Tommy Rose (formerly instructor at Sywell), Mrs Shaw, Mr C.M. Newton and Captain Duncan Davis. (*Flight*)

Another first for the Sywell Aerodrome was reported in the *Market Harborough Advertiser and Midland Mail* for Friday, 11 September 1931:

SYWELL MAKES AIR HISTORY
WORLD'S FIRST ALL-WOMEN FLYING MEETING
AMY A GUEST
The first flying meeting in the world to be organized by and confined to women will take place at the Northants Aero Club's headquarters, Sywell Aerodrome on Saturday, 19 September.

It will be attended by women pilots from various countries and some of the world's most famous aces are expected. Among those who so far have definitely promised is Miss Amy Johnson. On Friday, the Northants Aero Club received a telegram from her father to say that she will fly to Sywell on 19 September.

Another important visitor will be the Director of Civil Aviation, Colonel F.C. Shelmerdine and Mrs Shelmerdine.

SYWELL SEPTEMBER 1933 – DECEMBER 1934

On the face of it, it looked like Sywell aerodrome and the Northampton School of Flying should have been very successful, having hosted all these 'firsts' in the world of 1920s/1930s aviation, but at the end of 1931 the company suffered the loss of its Managing Director Bill Harris, and he was succeeded by Jack Linnell. A new flying committee was announced comprising of Jack and Geoffrey Linnell, Cyril Bayes, Perry Tyzack, and Bruce Olney, and the first action they took was to reduce flying charges. However, the experiment was not a success, as 1931 was the year of the great depression, few people were able to afford the expenditure on flying, or any other sports activity for that matter.

Flight for 20 May 1932 reported:

SYWELL'S FIFTH ANNUAL DISPLAY
All members of the Northamptonshire Aero Club are to be congratulated on their labours which resulted in the production of their fifth annual flying display on Whit Monday, 16 May last. Congratulations are, however, insufficient compensation for work like that, and nothing we can say as regards the excellence of their efforts can negate the disheartening effect of the bad weather, with the consequent smallness of the crowd.

The fact of the matter is that the Sywell displays have always been ahead of their time and have been too good. The local public are too air-minded; they are too used to really fine displays, and unless the weather is perfect, they will not turn out. This is all very hard lines on the club, who have probably put up a stouter show than any other flying club. They started at a time when they were told there was no chance of a subsidy, but nevertheless they made 'a do' of it and established their club on the soundest of lines. They have since been able to claim the subsidy, which has helped them to weather the difficult circumstances of the past year or so, but they are still dependent upon getting some money from such sources as a pageant, and this lack of support from the indigenous people of the countryside must have hit them severely.

Their private owner members are amongst the most active in the country, and the amount of flying they put in is a really wonderful tribute to the keen spirit which pervades the club, while few clubs have such organising talent, for getting up their displays, as have the Northamptonshire club, in the persons of the brothers Linnell; it is therefore all the more regrettable to see their display so little appreciated. This time they have the satisfaction in knowing that things might have been far worse, for even the rain did not keep everyone away, and although the public enclosures were not populated as they have been in past years, yet they contained quite a nice-sized crowd.

At the dinner in the evening Miss Amy Johnson and Mr Mollison were the guests of honour, and both thanked Mr Shale, the chairman, in short but appropriate speeches. A dance followed the dinner, which was well attended, and though it lacked the exclusive aeronautical atmosphere of last year, it was good to see several old faces which have been missed for some time. Tommy Rose was there, but he did not, as in previous years, spend his time on the aerodrome 'knocking the necks off bottles'!

Flight for 27 May 1932 reported:

> *It is with regret that we have heard the passing of the 'Sywell Windstocking'. It has been impossible to carry on the Journal of the Northampton Aero Club, as insufficient advertisement space has been taken to cover the cost of production. That yet another club journal should find the economic depression too much, for it is not surprising but it is to be deplored, for the maintenance of their own journal is a thing which inevitably tends to hold the members together. The 'Windstocking' has always been well run and certainly well worth reading, and we hope that it may be looked upon as merely dormant and thus likely to blossom again when watered with adequate finance in the not too distant future. We offer our sympathy to the Hon Editor Mr S.P. Tyzack, who has lately put in so much of his time and energy trying to keep it alive.*

It must also be remembered that Tommy Rose had walked out on his wife and daughter Elizabeth in April 1932, saying that he was going to look for a job. Having had a disastrous year trying to break the speed record to Cape Town, South Africa and also losing his job with Anglo American Oil Co Ltd in September, this must have been a great incentive for him to find another job as soon as possible,

However, by November of 1932, the flying school were considering calling in the liquidators.

The Birmingham Daily Gazette for Friday, 4 November 1932 reported:

> **FLYING CLUB FAILS**
> *At a meeting yesterday afternoon at Northampton of the creditors of the Northants Aero Club Ltd, which has been operating at Sywell, it was decided to appoint a liquidator. The chairman of the directors Mr I.J. Linnell stated he was in negotiation with a flying school with a view to aviation being continued at Sywell. If these negotiations were successful creditors would be paid in full.*

Then, in *Flight* for 10 November 1932 it was reported that:

> *The depression of the past year has caused a serious setback to the Northamptonshire Aero Club, and this as at present constituted will be wound up shortly. During the past year the club has organised some eleven flying meetings, but despite the success of these, the committee and directors have decided that they cannot continue any longer. Efforts are now being made to re-form the club which will be known as 'The Sywell Aero Club'. A new committee consisting of Lord Willoughby*

SYWELL SEPTEMBER 1933 – DECEMBER 1934

De Broke, Mr J. Joyes, Mr A.J. Linnell, Mr Shale, Mr E. Kew, Mr F. Twinning and Mr P. Hayward, having been formed for the purpose. Until further notice, inquiries and correspondence should be addressed to 53, St. Mathews Parade, Northampton.

A small article appeared in *Flight* 24 August 1933, which recorded Tommy Rose was back in England again:

A RETURN TO THE FOLD
Our old friend Tommy Rose, who has been out of the country for some considerable time, has now returned. He is at present disengaged, but by no means adverse to devoting his amazing energy to aviation in the way we remember him. He can be found for the present c/o Duncan Davis at Brooklands.

The Northampton Mercury for Friday, 22 September 1933 reported:

NEW ERA FOR CIVIL FLYING IN NORTHAMPTONSHIRE DEVELOPING SYWELL AS AN AIRPORT ACTIVITIES TO BE DIRECTED BY BROOKLANDS CLUB.
LARGER AERODROME
With the taking over of the Northamptonshire Flying Club by the Brooklands Flying Club, a serious bid is to be made to establish Sywell as one of the chief centres of civil aviation in the Midlands.

All the resources of the Brooklands Club are to be directed towards developing the valuable possibilities of Sywell as an airport, and extensive facilities will be provided for the accommodation, repair and refuelling of planes. In addition, services will be run for businessmen.

The club having leased a new and larger ground which will permit the landing of planes in any wind, already a licence for this ground has been secured from the Air Ministry.

The Brooklands Club have taken over the Northamptonshire Club at the suggestion of the Air Ministry. There are three sections to the old club, the Sywell Aero Club Company which owned the ground, the Social Club and the Flying Club. It was originally thought that the flying side of the club would receive adequate backing through the social side, but these hopes did not entirely materialize, and the club fell into financial difficulties. A new company was formed known as Sywell Aerodrome Limited. The Air Ministry then asked the Brooklands Club if they could help and as a result the Brooklands Club have taken over the scheme and will develop all activities in the future.

A defect in the old aerodrome was that the shape precluded taking off and landing, except in certain winds. This has a serious effect on instruction. The Brooklands Club have now leased from Sywell Aerodrome Ltd a much larger ground adjoining the present aerodrome.

FLIGHT LIEUTENANT THOMAS 'TOMMY' ROSE DFC

The site is now double the size of the old ground and will allow the taking off and landing of planes in any wind.

LICENCE GRANTED
The obtaining of a licence for this ground must almost establish a record for celerity. The club applied for a licence on Friday, September 8. Representations were made to the Ministry that the matter was urgent. On the following Monday Captain Campbell, of the Air Ministry, flew to Sywell and inspected the proposed site. On the Thursday a telegram was received stating that the ground had been approved, and on Friday a temporary licence arrived. Between the two grounds there stood a row of trees. Arrangements to demolish these were made last weekend, and by Monday they were all down.

On the social side the club intend to dispense with a large committee, and to substitute a small advisory committee. Already an attractive programme of entertainments have been arranged. On September 29 the club are holding a 'Tramps Party'. The idea is that members shall appear in clothing which will give them the nearest semblance to tramps, and great fun is promised. There will be a genuine coffee stall, a brazier and a barrel organ are being secured.

THE OFFICIALS
The chairman is Lord Willoughby de Broke, and Captain Geoffrey Shaw, of Whilton Lodge is the vice-chairman. Both possess planes of their own. Mrs Geoffrey Shaw qualified for her pilot's certificate at Sywell last week.

Captain Duncan Davis is the managing director of the Brooklands Flying Club. (During this time there had been changes at Brooklands. The School of Flying had grown until in 1933 it was managing flying training not only at Brooklands, but also at Sywell and Lympne – SC.)

Captain Davis was also director of Brooklands Aviation Ltd, Brooklands School of Flying, The Aeronautical Educational Trust, Brooklands Airways Ltd and the Cinque Ports Flying Club at Lympne.

Captain Davis has been engaged in aviation since 1910, when he started to fly with the late Colonel Cody, the famous air pioneer (becoming his assistant later – SC). *The Brooklands group of companies also had a fleet of twelve aircraft and several taxi machines in which they train pilots for their 'A' and 'B' licences.*

Duncan Davis had been one of Smith-Barry's instructors at the famous School of Special Flying at Gosport, from which in 1919 the Royal Air Force Central Flying School inherited its traditions of organized flying instruction, the Gosport method, by then recognized throughout the world as the supreme method of pilot tuition. Duncan Davis brought the Gosport method to Brooklands and when, in 1933, the Brooklands School of Flying took over the responsibility for flying instruction at Sywell, the Club and Sywell established the second link with the first and most famous of all military flying schools in the world.

A WAR ACE
Two machines are at present allocated to Sywell, and these are of the standard Gipsy Moth type. Tommy Rose – a noted personality in aviation circles – has been appointed manager and chief instructor. He brought down many German planes in his RFC career. He has already a record 6,000 hours flying and has flown down to the Gulf. An entirely new clubhouse will be erected in the new aerodrome. It will be of greater permanence than the present structure and will be built in stone.

It will comprise, on the ground floor, a dining room, a lady's lounge, a lounge bar, and a kitchen. Luncheons, tea and dinners will be served, and the dining room will also be utilized as a dancing hall. On the second storey will be the offices of the club and the control office and over this an observation platform from which a full view of the aerodrome will be secured. Along each side of the clubhouse will be erected the hangers.

There will be full-service facilities for repairs of all types of aircraft, and arrangements will be made for the staff to sleep on the premises.

An extensive motor park and swimming pool will be provided for the use of the members.

REGULAR SERVICES
Regular services will fly from Sywell to Heston in 40 minutes, to Brooklands in 50 minutes, or to Croydon in 50 minutes, or to Lympne and so to connect to all home and continental air services.

There will be a taxi service to Skegness during the summer months and Northampton will then be only 40 minutes from the seaside. In addition, the club will have a taxi service at 9d per mile laden anywhere anytime, the charge of 9d covering one or two passengers.

The question immediately arises as to what Northampton itself will do to encourage the new venture. There are those who object that Sywell is some distance from Northampton, but the journey can be made by car in 15 minutes and arrangements are in hand to provide a road service between the airport and the Borough, which will be available night and day.

Moreover, it is genuinely admitted that Sywell is the nearest possible aerodrome to Northampton. Careful observations have been made and the experts confirm that it is impossible to get a suitable site nearer to the town.

In view of the big changes impending the Town Council and other responsible bodies in Northampton would do well to reconsider their attitude towards civil aviation. The town has lost too many chances in the past.

Tommy Rose together with Captain Duncan Davis were now busy sorting out the facilities at the clubhouse.

FLIGHT LIEUTENANT THOMAS 'TOMMY' ROSE DFC

Flight 5 October 1933 reported:

> *At a General Meeting of the Committee and members of the Northampton Aero Club in the clubhouse on Wednesday, September 20, the reconstruction policy of the Club as obtained by Captain Duncan Davis, was unanimously adopted. Captain Davis and Mr T. Rose, who is now installed as manager and instructor, have devoted most of their time in rallying up members and improving conditions generally, assisted by two pupils, D. Smith and F.R. Wilson. The first task was to clear out the office and brighten up the clubhouse; the first of these tasks accomplished by the simple expedient of burning most of the papers. During the clearing up the party of four lived in the clubhouse, doing their own cooking. It was discovered that Captain Davis is quite adept at boiling eggs. Smith suffers from the delusion that they should be boiled for 25 minutes, and Mr Rose is quite impossible of frying them. While all this was going on, the instructional side was not neglected, and the daily sheets show an average of about five hours; also, Messrs E.T. Danson, P. Tyzack, J. Linnell and Captain G. Shaw have been flying solo. The Rally of members arranged for Sunday was a great success, Mr Thorn doing acrobatics on a Tiger Moth and a Gipsy Moth. On Thursday, 21 September, a day of low clouds, Mr Brian Allen, landed with Madame Marcelle as a passenger, the latter cooked an excellent lunch for those present, which was very much appreciated. It is hoped she will call again. Mr P. James has been putting in quite a number of flying hours duel and solo to renew his 'A' licence, Miss Pacey and Miss Hamilton are also working for 'A' licences.*

On 12 October 1933 *Flight* reported that:

> *Flying during the week has been somewhat restricted by bad visibility, the total being 17 hours 50 mins. Dennis Smith accomplished an excellent first solo, but his instructor's (Tommy's) hair is rapidly turning grey. Mr Frank Wilson finished his tests for an 'A' licence and has departed up north.*
>
> *The 'Tramps' party, which was held on Friday, October 6, was a great success, about 100 members and friends attending in most tramp-like attire, while a real coffee stall provided refreshment. On Friday, 13, there will be a 'When we were young party' when members will attend as children under the age of six. Visitors this week included Tom Campbell-Black, Roy Winn of Leicester, D. Winn of Tollerton, W. Sutcliffe of the Midland Club, and the Master of Brooklands with Mr Van Marken from Amsterdam. Among recent new members is Mr V.W.C. Jupp, the well-known England and Northants cricketer.*

SYWELL SEPTEMBER 1933 – DECEMBER 1934

The *Folkstone, Hythe, Sandgate and Cheriton Herald* for 14 October 1933 reported:

> *It is of particular interest to local members that Flight Lieutenant 'Tommy' Rose has been appointed Manager and Chief Instructor at Sywell. Many will remember the happy times spent with Flight Lieutenant Rose while he awaited weather conditions to embark on an attempt at the Cape record. An average of five hours flying per day has been the rule at the new aerodrome since it was taken over.*
>
> *September analysis: Hours flown, 174.45; first soloists 8; 'A' licences 5; 'B' licences nil.*

Flight for 2 November 1933 reported that:

> *As the weather has not been favorable for flying, the club has turned its attention to ground organization. It has been necessary to remove from the aerodrome, large quantities of mushrooms, not only for the sake of the aircraft landing, but also for the sake of Mr Harold Brown's cows; incidentally, these cows, which graze on the aerodrome from morning till night, have made Sywell a most exciting aerodrome on which to taxi. The site for the new clubhouse has been pegged out, and the Secretary of the Sywell Aerodrome Co. says it will be up by the New Year. (Members of the club want to know which New Year.) The annual dance will be held at the George Hotel, Kettering, on Friday, 3 November and already there has been a great demand for tickets.*

The Sywell Aerodrome Company was formed when the first meeting of the subscribers to the Memorandum of Association came together in January 1933. They appointed Lord Willoughby de Broke, Henry Duncan Davis, John Theophilis Percival Hayes, Arthur John Linnell and Charles Maurice Newton, as the first Directors of the Company.

At the subsequent meeting of the Directors in February, Lord Willoughby de Broke was elected Chairman, Charles Newton Secretary, Messrs Ray & Vials Solicitors, Mr T. Dutton Auditor, and Barclays, the Bankers. The first major change came in 1934, when Lord Willoughby de Broke resigned his position and was replaced by a director

From left to right: R.C. Soans, Faith Bennett, B. Sudborough, Flight Lieutenant Rose (chief flying instructor), and Billie Lott, taken at the Northants Aero Club Ball. (*Nigel Gaudion collection*)

and as Chairman of the Company by Captain G.R.D. Shaw. At the first annual general meeting of the Company on 18 May 1934, Mr W.E. Davis was elected a director.

The plan involved three immediate tasks, i) the enlargement of the aerodrome by eighty acres, ii) construction of a new clubhouse and permanent buildings, and iii) a new feature, removal of the old clubhouse to a new location, and its use as a headquarters for the Working Men's Flying Club, whose full and correct title was the Northamptonshire Aviation Club, also subsequently known as the East Midlands Flying Club.

After Tommy Rose joined Sywell in September 1933, confidence in the aero club improved, and Tommy's popularity certainly increased student and visitor numbers, social events became very popular, famous aviators visited the aerodrome and this, in turn, brought in spectators. New investors were appearing and, with the completion of the new clubhouse in April and the subsequent official opening in May 1934, Sywell was a star ascendant.

Finally, the clubhouse opened in 1934 during the time Tommy Rose was the Chief Flying Instructor, and on 8 June 1934, a Vickers Viastra of the King's Flight landed at Sywell with HRH Edward Prince of Wales on board on his way to the County Show at Kettering.

There were many other notable aviators who were regular visitors to Sywell at this time, all drawn to Tommy's magnetic, mischievous personality and more importantly the hospitable ambience of the clubhouse facilities. Charles Kingsford Smith ('Smithy')

Happiest Landing – Flight Lieutenant Tommy Rose, the great Cape Flier formerly instructor at Sywell, returns to Sywell to open Northants Aero Club new clubhouse. Left to right: G.R.D. Shaw (chairman of the club), Flt Lt Rose, Mr H. Deterding and Mrs Deterding. In the background is the Miles Falcon which Tommy Rose flew to the Cape. (*Mavis Parker*)

SYWELL SEPTEMBER 1933 – DECEMBER 1934

1897-1935 visited when he was in the country, and Flight Lieutenant Charles William Anderson Scott (1903-1946), who had known Tommy Rose from their time in the RAF together and the Schlesinger Race in 1936. Flight Lieutenant C.W.A. Scott was also a notable aerobatic display pilot and, together with Percy Phillips, they bought most of Sir Alan Cobhams company, National Aviation Displays Ltd, in December 1935.

Although Tommy Rose was still married to Margaret at this time, he was later to meet Beatrice (Billie) Lott (1899-1979) at Sywell. Billie was born in Hampleton Hill, London, one of eight children, and was apparently employed by Northampton Flying Club to manage the catering facilities in the clubhouse. Tommy appears to have fallen in love with her, perhaps it was an instant attraction, maybe he saw in her a kindred spirit but, in January 1934, an extract by Charles Bennett (see below), stated that Billie was known as Mrs. Rose, which she was certainly not at that time.

The following extract is the first reference to Billie Lott being associated with Tommy Rose:

Alfred Hitchcock's *Partner in Suspense*

The life of screenwriter Charles Bennett. By Charles Bennett.

Excerpt:

> In January 1934 Maggie and I decided to learn to fly. I met a young lady named Billie Rose at a party of the artist sculptor Jacob Epstein. We became friends and Billie persuaded us to drive up to Sywell, six miles outside Northampton – one of a trio of little flying clubs that embraced Brooklands and Lympne.
>
> We drove up and promptly fell in love with the flying club, with its little airfield and with her husband the ace First World War fighter pilot and the future King's Cup champion, Tommy Rose. He taught us to fly in a Gipsy Moth 1 biplane.
>
> But, getting back to Errol (Flynn): during our weekends in and out of the air at Sywell, Maggie and I, with Billie and Tommy Rose, would frequently spend a Saturday evening at the Northampton Theatre Royal, which was gallantly hosting a reparatory company. I say gallantly because by 1934 the going had to be tough, both for the theatre struggling to combat the talkie television and for the actors who had to learn, rehearse and perform a different play every week. The company was a good one, however, and I'm sure the audiences enjoyed seeing their local favourite appearing as debonair Charles Surface, one week and a young Sherlock Holmes the next. Among the acting troupe was a finely built hopeful named Flynn (Errol). I admired him and his work and when the company was invited out on a Sunday cocktail party at our flying club (Sywell) I met the young man in person. I think I knew even then he was destined for a great future… someplace.

FLIGHT LIEUTENANT THOMAS 'TOMMY' ROSE DFC

My flight instructor, Tommy Rose, had often taught as his second prime rule (the first never to land under stalling speed) to avoid flying blind through overcast. But being born stupid, I broke the second rule in June 1946. Only once!!

Tommy Rose also taught Faith Bennett (nee Riddick 1903-1969) to fly. In 1930, she married film writer Charles Bennett, and over the course of the 1930s starred in multiple British films. Faith took flying lessons alongside her acting career at Sywell, earning both a British Aviator's certificate and an American flying licence – the couple moved to the USA briefly while Charles worked for Universal Studios.

Writing this book has been a series of happy coincidences. As I was completing further editing of Tommy's biography another remarkable find surfaced, this time in the form of F.G. Miles's Autobiography (as yet unpublished). Contained within this autobiography is an interesting page that gives some insight into Tommy's character, and this is reproduced below:

Early in 1934, two major events cast their shadows before us. One was the King's Cup, the most important race of the flying year, and another announcement that an Australian millionaire proposed to give a ten thousand prize for a race from England to Australia. This aroused enormous interest and many new aeroplanes were schemed to fly in it.

Tommy Rose ordered a Hawk for the King's Cup (this was not strictly true as it was in fact, the prototype Miles M.2F Hawk Major G-ACTD, which was registered to Captain Geoffrey Reginald Devereux Shaw to be based at Sywell but flown by Tommy Rose – SC) *and I personally supervised its construction and finish. He was, and is, a remarkable man. At that time he was about thirty-eight years old and during the First World War had served in the RFC, and later in the RAF with great distinction.*

After he left the service he flew all over the world as a commercial pilot or on record flights. He had many adventures, including a gallant rescue of another pilot in the wilds of Africa. Later he became a club instructor at Nottingham (Sywell – SC) *and it was while he was working there that he decided to fly the Hawk. We designed and built a much improved model for him which we called the Miles Hawk Major, which became another great success. He flew it for the first time a few days before the race and for the second time in the race. He came in second and made the fastest time in the race. To hear the cheers you would have thought he was first by a mile.*

Tommy has always been one of the most popular people in the world. Anyone who has been with Tommy in difficult times – say, on a cold rainy morning waiting for a race or a record flight, after working all night, when frayed nerves and fretful tempers might well have been justified, had seen him on the top of his form, insulting his friends in that especial way that made them think they had just been awarded the VC, will know what I mean.

SYWELL SEPTEMBER 1933 – DECEMBER 1934

Flight for 19 July 1934 reported that:

> In spite of the fact that weather conditions have been by no means ideal for instruction, flying time for the week totalled 35 hours.
>
> On Saturday, July 7, the Miles Hawk M.2 Major G-ACTD, entered for the King's Cup by Captain G.R.D. Shaw, the chairman of the club, was christened at Sywell by Mrs Shaw, on 14 July 1934, piloted by Flight Lieutenant T. Rose, the chief instructor of the club, and worked through the field into second place at 183.75 mph – a magnificent effort.
>
> During the week Mr Charles Bennett, the well-known scenario writer, accomplished a first solo. The latter half has been very busy – partly owing to the enthusiasm of Mr A. Bear, who has put in more than eight hours in less than two days. On one morning he was receiving instruction at 9 o'clock, although an airline machine had been forced down here owing to bad visibility – the clouds then being at 300 feet.

The following appeared in the *Mercury and Herald* newspaper for 24 August 1934 under the heading:

FLYING TOPICS
CLUB ACTIVITY AT SYWELL

TAUGHT 200 TO FLY
The Aero club has taught nearly 200 members to fly – and there has never been an accident. At present it has about 300 members from all parts of the world.

The standard of instruction is the highest in the country. The chief instructor and manager is Flight Lieutenant Thomas Rose. Tommy Rose has been flying for nineteen years, and during the war he shot down twelve enemy aeroplanes and three kite balloons.

He has done 6,000 hours in the air, about 4,000 of which have been spent in teaching others to fly. Some idea of his capabilities in this direction may be gathered from the fact that, on the advice of the highest aeronautical authorities, people motor up from London and the south coast to receive instruction at his hands.

The aerodrome and clubhouse at Sywell are the finest in the provinces. The clubhouse, a modern building in 'snow-crete', can, on a fine day, be seen 50 miles away.

Tommy Rose getting out of Miles M.2F Hawk Major G-ACTD. (*Mavis Parker*)

FLIGHT LIEUTENANT THOMAS 'TOMMY' ROSE DFC

TEDDY AND KARL
Mrs G.R.D. Shaw, wife of Captain Shaw, chairman of Sywell Aerodrome Ltd., last week went solo in her husband's Miles Hawk monoplane – the plane in which Flight Lieutenant Rose flew to second place in the King's Cup race.

Mrs Shaw, who took her 'A' licence a year ago, has had a good deal of experience in Moths. In our photograph she is seen with Teddy, the black cat, and Karl, the Dachshund, after an evening in the Miles Hawk. Teddy and Karl, by the way, are the Club's mascots.

On Friday evening, Mrs Shaw lent the plane to Flight Lieutenant Rose to take 'Miss Northampton' over to Coventry for the Midlands section of the All-England beauty championship. He did the journey in a quarter of an hour!

Mr Rose, by the way, has a new assistant – Sid Jackson, the famous speedway star. Sid has quickly made himself popular, and both Mr Rose and he have recently had a busy time in instructional work during the fine weather.

To fully understand Tommy's impact in the two years he was involved with the flying club at Sywell, the newspaper article below explains in detail how the management team, and all those involved with Tommy Rose appreciated his outstanding contribution to the club.

The Northampton Mercury for 19 October 1934 reported:

Headlines: Flying Topics, New Appointment for Mr Tommy Rose, Success at Sywell
It is common news now that Flight Lieutenant Tommy Rose is severing his connection with Sywell Aerodrome and Brooklands Flying Club Ltd. He will leave Sywell early in December for a month's holiday and then on January 1, join Messers. Phillips and Powis, aircraft manufacturers, Reading, as sales manager.

Reading's gain will be Sywell's loss. The Aero Club has never had a more popular instructor and manager, and the famous boyish grin will be missed, not only by his hundreds of friends in Northamptonshire, but by the many pilots who made a point of calling at Sywell on their journeys to and from the north.

Mr Rose told me of his new appointment a month ago. He had just landed at Sywell in the Miles Hawk after a trip to Reading. He patted the monoplane with the same affection that Gordon Richards pats his mounts and said, 'I shall be selling these next year.' 'Don't break the news just yet', he added. We kept the secret for three weeks, but last week the news leaked out.

Hosts of Friends
Tommy Rose has been at Sywell for fifteen months. Under his guidance the popularity of the club has gone up in leaps and bounds. Sixty-six new

members have been enrolled during the last six months. He has made friends with everybody, and he has not a single enemy in the world.

His friendships are lasting. His daily post from all parts of the world proves it.

And he has never been known to lose his temper, which is remarkable when one thinks of the very raw material that goes through his hands for instruction.

Mr Rose has been flying for twenty years and it is due to his work that Sywell has gained a reputation for the highest standard of instruction in England. Many people have regularly motored up from London and the south coast every week to receive instruction at his hands.

His handling of the Miles Hawk in the King's Cup Race gained him additional prestige, and as demonstrator and sales manager for this type of machine he should have a very bright future.

Mr Rose's successor has not yet been appointed. Brooklands Flying Club will announce his name in due course, the annual ball, which will be held at the Salon, Northampton on November 16, will take the form of a farewell to Tommy. It will be preceded by a farewell dinner at the Grand Hotel.

Then, like the swallows, or should I say, 'the Hawk', Flight Lieutenant Thomas Rose DFC will migrate cross-country. The Sywell nest will be bare without him.

The *Northampton Mercury* for Friday, 30 November 1934 reported:

BRILLIANT WORK AT SYWELL, FLIGHT LIEUTENANT ROSE'S DEPARTURE, FAREWELL DINNER

A man with a lovable personality, and a marked individuality… an instructor, whose tuition methods should be patented…a pilot of outstanding ability…the man who has made Sywell the most popular country flying club in England.

These were some of the many glowing tributes paid to Flight Lieutenant Tommy Rose at the farewell dinner held in his honour by Northampton Aero Club at the Grand Hotel, Northampton, on Wednesday night. It was a dinner for men only. They had travelled from all parts of the country to honour the man who less than two years ago had come from the Isle of Capri to make Northamptonshire air minded.

Those present included Captain G.R.D. Shaw chairman, Northampton Aero Club, Captain Duncan Davis managing director, Brooklands School of Flying, Mr A.W. Weyman the new manager of Sywell, Mr E. Goldsmith the new instructor and Mr C.M. Newton, secretary of the Sywell Aerodrome Club.

'Our Guest' was proposed by Captain Geoffrey Shaw, supported by Mr Geoffrey Linnell representing private owners.

FLIGHT LIEUTENANT THOMAS 'TOMMY' ROSE DFC

After the speeches Flight Lieutenant Rose was presented with a silver cigarette case and a cheque from the Aero Club, and a cheque from the Aviation Club.

Captain Shaw described Flight Lieutenant Rose as a man of extraordinary individuality. He had a remarkable war record and wherever he had been flying people had gathered together.

'During the time he has been at Sywell,' he said, 'we have had more private owners than any other aerodrome. When he goes to Reading, they will have to enlarge the Woodley landing ground! He came to Sywell when it was in a low way, and now due to his magnificent work, he has made it one of the most popular country flying clubs in England.'

Mr Geoffrey Linnell spoke of Mr Rose's genial comradeship and his enthusiasm for flying. He hopes that the ranks of private owners would grow to enormous proportions, and that they would all have the sense to buy Hawks, if only for the sake of bringing Mr Rose back to Sywell as much as possible.

Mr C.F. Westley described Flight Lieutenant Rose as one of Britain's outstanding pilots. 'He has an extraordinarily successful method of instructing,' he said, 'and "A" licence pilots will not forget in a hurry. He has done brilliant work at Sywell, and I sincerely hope that his successor, Mr Goldsmith, will get similar support.'

Mr Alan Simpson said that Sywell's loss was Reading's gain. 'Phillips and Powis', he said, 'have captured one of the most charming and unassuming men that have ever handled an aeroplane. Tommy Rose has a marvellous philosophy, an extensive vocabulary, and the manner of a perfect host.'

Mr E.W. Twining described him as 'an affable man and a lovable one. He is no ordinary instructor,' he added.

Mr L.G. Brown thanked Flight Lieutenant Rose for all he had done for the Aviation Club. It was Tommy Rose who had helped them to become the pioneers of cheaper flying, and his wonderful help to the club would never be forgotten.

Flight Lieutenant Rose was given an exceptionally warm reception. He was accorded musical honours, and for some time he was unable to speak because of the cheering.

He warmly thanked his friends for the loyal help they had given him during his stay at Sywell. He was glad to see that at last the county was growing air minded. 'But it has been a hard struggle,' he said, 'it is a lovely county, but the town has disappointed me. If it is not careful. It will soon be a branch line of the air, just as it is a branch line of the railway. I shall frequently land at Sywell in the future, not because it is a good aerodrome, but because I have some extraordinarily good friends there.'

During the evening many telegrams of good wishes arrived from various parts of the country.

SYWELL SEPTEMBER 1933 – DECEMBER 1934

An extract taken from the *Aerodrome* journal entitled 'Recollections of Sywell' by Alex Henshaw in 2005, two years before he died, is reproduced below:

The late 1920s and 1930s was a period of deep hurtful depression and the agricultural community of Northants suffered in particular, Tommy Rose told Alex Henshaw MBE (Honorary President Sywell Aviation Museum and Friend of Sywell Aerodrome) that the proposed Airfield Flying Project almost failed before it started.

Apart from financial problems in establishing a sporting project – which had to be accepted – which was primarily aimed at the wealthier classes and those who could afford the luxury of a weekend amidst the delight of snow-white clouds against a background of azure blue sky. To be considered as well, this was a hunting county and horses and aeroplanes do not mix well.

The foundation of Sywell as an important social and flying establishment owes a great deal to Tommy Rose. Tommy Rose was a Flight Lieutenant in the RAF and on demobilisation continued the work he loved so much, as a flying instructor. Not only was Tommy Rose a fine instructor, he also had one of the most endearing and stimulating personalities of anyone I have ever known.

One has to appreciate that in those early years, class difference and divisional mode of living was accepted. To establish a flying club in a county where the aristocracy, prominent industrialists and wealthy landowners enjoyed a part-time shooting or racing to hounds over the lush green fields of their county, was bound to be a lost cause.

With trepidation and hesitancy, it was decided to work from the top downwards. Considerable time, money and expertise was spent in organizing a 'Banquet' and invitations were sent out to the most notable and affluent social set, the largest and most esteemed landowners and farmers coupled with industrialists and aviators or others who might stimulate a significant degree of interest in what the Sywell Flying Club was endeavouring to achieve.

I was later informed that the evening reception was very formal, somewhat 'starchy' and the portent of being a dull and boring event. After the meal, apparently the ladies gathered in one room and the men in another with small groups according to their 'pecking' order.

The story goes that later in the evening whilst the men were 'supping' their brandy or port there were some squeals of laughter from the adjoining room followed by hilarious 'giggles' as if some of the ladies were really enjoying themselves. Duncan Davis said that the carousing prompted the men to join the ladies to see 'what was going on'. He said he would not have believed it possible. Gone was the somewhat frigid conformity to social decorum. Each and every one of the ladies were bubbling with partially restrained exuberance as they listened to Tommy's enthralling and sometimes 'risqué' tales about an aviation world which

FLIGHT LIEUTENANT THOMAS 'TOMMY' ROSE DFC

they had never seen or heard of. As we all know Sywell Flying Club from then on became a premier social centre of the Midlands where all classes, young, and not so young, could enjoy the unique experience of watching in action a new science of the air and what is more, participate on a sporting or professional level.

On reflection, I think I must have made more friends at Sywell than at any other club in the U.K. This was brought home to me when Jeffrey Quill took me to the Polygon Hotel, just before I had a posting from Supermarine to Castle Bromwich at the outbreak of the Second World War. We came in from the 'black out' to be momentarily dazzled by the bright light, to be regaled by dozens of shouts from a large group of young men all in the uniform of the Fleet Air Arm, I saw immediately they were nearly all my old friends from Sywell. I have forgotten their names but two were farmers, one prominent in the Oil Industry, another a solicitor, there were two well-known 'film stars' and another the winner of the Grand National. The happiest time at Sywell was during the 1930s.

Captain Henry Duncan Davis became chief flying instructor at the Henderson School, took it over in 1928 and renamed it the Brooklands School of Flying. It was registered as a limited company on 12 October 1928, with Davis as managing director. Duncan later said that when he was offered the Henderson School, he had practically no money but several wealthy pupils and between them they raised enough to buy a typewriter and three 'Avros'. The profit for the first year was £7 10s! Duncan Davis had also operated flying clubs at Lympne, Shoreham, and Sywell Aerodromes in the 1930s.

The *Northampton Mercury* 12 June 1936 reported:

TOMMY ROSE WELCOMED AT SYWELL OPENING OF £2,500 CLUBHOUSE

Flying the Miles Falcon in which he recently made his great flight to the Cape and in which he won the 1935 King's Cup Race and wearing his old indelible smile, Flight Lieutenant 'Tommy' Rose swooped down on Sywell Aerodrome on Sunday, 7 June to open Northamptonshire Aero Club's £2,500 clubhouse.

The old clubhouse has now been taken over by the Royal Air Force Reserve training school at Sywell for use as an officers' mess. The new clubhouse has been built in a wing constructed at right angles to the old building.

Tommy Rose, who flew from Reading where he is now an instructor, got a great reception. Thirty plane loads of club members and well-wishers turned up, including a flight of six aeroplanes from the Leicestershire Aero Club. Hosts and guests came by car, while the general public packed the laneway passing the drome.

Major G.R.D. Shaw, chairman of the club, who presided at the opening ceremony, said Flight Lieutenant Rose did not need any introduction

SYWELL SEPTEMBER 1933 – DECEMBER 1934

from him, for he was well-known to everyone in Northamptonshire during the time he was instructor at Sywell. Flight Lieutenant Rose did not quite pull off the King's Cup while he was an instructor at Sywell, but all at Sywell were delighted when he pulled it off last year, and they were looking forward to him pulling it off again this year.

DISPLAY OF AIRCRAFT
Tommy Rose declared the new clubhouse open, observing 'I can honestly say that some of the happiest moments of my life have been spent in this place'. He hoped the club would go on 'forever'.

The speechmaking was soon over, and Tommy Rose was in the air again obliging admirers with 'hops' in his famous aircraft.

On the ground was a fine display of various types of civil aircraft, including the East Midlands Flying Club's Flying Flea and Drone. Major Shaw's and Lord Willoughby de Broke's Klemm Swallows, Mr D. Lloyd's Comper, Northamptonshire Aero Club's Gipsy Moth, Brookland's Aviation's Tiger Moth, Mr K. Waittome's and Mr J. Linnell's Gipsy III Moth's, Mr H. Detering's and Midland Airway's Fox Moth's, Mr G. Linnell's Hornet Moth, Mr S.P. Tyzack's Avro Cadet, Mr R. Shuttleworth's Dessouter, Mr E. Davis Leopard Moth, British Aircraft's Klemm Eagle, Mr H.R. Detering's Miles Falcon, Major Jack Shaw's Avro Commodore, and Mr W. Tomkins Gloster Gamecock.

The Flea did not go up, but great interest was taken in the £275 Drone, an ultra-light plane which flies sixty miles on two-shillings-worth of fuel.

Among those present during the afternoon and evening were Lord Willoughby de Broke, president of the club, who took the Drone up, Mr Vere Wayte Wood, High Sheriff of Northamptonshire, Sir Frederick and Lady Robinson, Sir Peter Grant-Lawson, Captain J.H. Drummond, Major Jack Shaw (who flew down from Kirkby Lonsdale, Westmorland), Mr Henry Detering, Captain H. Duncan Davis, Colonel Liddlem. Colonel Hodson, Colonel and Mrs G.H. Eunson and Mr J. Faulkner Strope.

The new clubhouse, which comprises of a spacious lounge, a cosy dining room, and a well-appointed bar panelled in walnut, was inspected by the company and won widespread approval.

Chapter 11

Phillips and Powis, 1 January 1935 – June 1936, Seagers Gin, July 1936 – August 1938
Sales Manager, Winning the King's Cup Race

'There is no money in record-breaking nowadays, and it is expensive for a hobby.'
– Flight Lieutenant Tommy Rose

Tommy Rose's career has not been easy to trace in chronological order, as some of the exact dates of his various employment changes have been easier to pinpoint than others.

However, after his RAF service career, Tommy Rose changed jobs irregularly, but as in those days, it was generally accepted that job security was paramount, particularly after the 1929 Stock Market crash, a good job was considered to be one for life.

For Tommy each new position seemed to be another chance to improve his personal circumstances, which was understandable, but each move also seemed to bring him greater opportunities. Perhaps he was just in the right place at the right time, and with his reputation growing, he sometimes received offers he really could not refuse.

However, although the numerous articles on his subsequent movements have been reported in the *Flight* magazine and the national newspapers have been of considerable help, discussing him with surviving members of his family and his godchildren and friends in Alderney have helped me enormously in trying to piece his later life together.

Tommy Rose then became Sales Manager for Phillips and Powis from 1 January 1935 until June 1936 (although it was reported, in the *Bystander* for 18 September 1935, that he was their chief test pilot in 1935), when he left to join Seager, Evans and Co Ltd, at the Deptford Distillery in July 1936, as their travelling (air) representative. This was marked by a report in *Flight for* 2 July 1936, where it was recorded that he was presented with a silver cigar box by Phillips and Powis Aircraft Ltd.

Seagers hired a Miles Falcon Six from Phillips and Powis Hire Department, at Hanworth Park, Middlesex, as and when required, as they never owned any aircraft. The Miles Falcon Six was usually G-ADLC, the aircraft in which Tommy Rose had won the King's Cup Race in 1935, and for his momentous record-breaking London to the Cape (and back) in February 1936.

Seagers were doubtless delighted to have such a very high-profile personality as their travelling representative, and they obviously hoped that it would increase their sales and market share as a result. Tommy had a reputation of being a marvellous raconteur, who could 'charm the birds out of the trees' (as one of his close friends eloquently said).

PHILLIPS AND POWIS, 1 JANUARY 1935 – JUNE 1936

He was well known by all in the aviation world. Seager's were pleased to have Tommy Rose in the company, as he clearly had all the required attributes needed to obtain future contracts, both via his contacts in the aviation world and beyond. This was a job opportunity he could not refuse, and he stayed with them until August 1938.

In September 1938, Tommy Rose left Seager's to join the Phillips & Powis owned Reading Aero Club at Woodley, as Chief Flying Instructor, Manager and Secretary. However, following the sudden and unexpected death of 'Bill' Skinner, Chief Test Pilot of Phillips & Powis Aircraft Ltd in November 1939, Tommy was invited to take over the vacant post of Chief Test Pilot for the company.

Tommy Rose stayed in that post until he retired in January 1946, following a wartime career of some six long and very busy years. This was the longest time he had ever stayed with an employer in the whole of his working life.

Tommy Rose liked the Reading area, having bought a house at Sonning, east of Reading, and settled down there.

He became an integral part of the aviation family of Phillips & Powis Aircraft, who really were true visionaries in the field of British aviation at that time.

Phillips & Powis Aircraft Ltd were based at Woodley Aerodrome, Reading, Berkshire and I feel that a brief history of the company should be included to show how it had evolved to that time.

Phillips & Powis Aircraft Ltd

The story started at Shoreham in Sussex in 1925, where, from very small beginnings, Mr F.G. Miles ('FG' or Miles to his friends and family), one of the sons of a laundry owner at nearby Portslade, decided that his future was to be in aviation, and he decided to design and build his own aeroplane – this he called the Gnat. It was built in the workshop of the laundry with the help of a few friends, including Don L. Brown, an engineer with a local gas company, but it was destined never to be flown.

Miles then decided that he ought to learn to fly, and he enlisted the aid of Cecil Pashley to teach him in his Avro 504K. Having then obtained his 'A' licence he lost no time in persuading Pashley to help him to operate a joy-riding business along the south coast.

Later, having acquired an Avro Baby, Miles modified and redesigned it into an aerobatic biplane, which was called the Southern Martlet (one of which survives to this day in flying condition at Old Warden with the Shuttleworth Trust). He then married one of his pupils, The Hon Mrs Inigo Freeman-Thomas, Viscountess Ratendone (or 'Blossom' as she preferred to be known), who was a very talented lady, who later helped him design a very small and highly aerobatic biplane, which they called the Satyr.

Miles was later to meet Charles Powis, a motor engineer from Reading, who became interested in aviation and founded Woodley Aerodrome. During the course of conversation they agreed that what was really needed was a cheap light aircraft for the private owner and aeroplane clubs. The outcome of this ultimately became the Miles M.2 Hawk, a low wing cantilever monoplane built of wood and the prototype made its first flight, from Woodley, on 29 March 1933.

Don Brown, who, in 1942, was to join Miles at Woodley, decided, in the late 1960s to write the story of the Miles enterprise in a book entitled '*Miles Aircraft since 1925*' which was published by Putnam's in 1970. Thurstan James wrote a review of it for *Aerospace* and I can do no better than reproduce this here:

> *No phenomenon of British aircraft construction deserves closer study than the outburst of the Miles efflorescence in twenty years between 1928 and 1948. In that time forty-seven different types of Miles aeroplane were flown and a total of 5,644 were built between 1929 and 1946. The story is told in this book. It tells how a young man (F.G. Miles) without training or money but blessed with unique talents and energy, coupled with those of his wife (Blossom), the aid of a gifted brother (George) and certain enthusiastic adherents (among whom the author of this book was one), revolutionised the look of British light aviation, grew big enough to go into partnership with Rolls-Royce and became a fully-fledged member of the SBAC.*
>
> *The protagonists learnt to fly before they learnt to design and test flew their own aircraft.*
>
> *It was a long time before Miles aircraft were built by a firm bearing that name. In the beginning was the great Gnat Aero Company. This grew into Southern Aircraft Ltd. For what was perhaps the firm's finest hour it was known as Phillips and Powis Aircraft of Reading – Charles Powis of that company played no small part in the Miles story, more than appears in this book. As one of Putnam's publications devised to give maximum data about aircraft types and projects, this volume succeeds in full measure. One of ninety separate types dealt with, half are projects – but what projects!*

It should now be mentioned that the name of the company, Phillips & Powis Aircraft Ltd, was changed on 5 October 1943 to Miles Aircraft Ltd, to reflect the fact that Charles Powis was no longer with it and it was now, to all intents and purposes, a family firm and the aeroplanes had always been better known as Miles aeroplanes anyway!

But nothing changed and things went on as normal, but what a company! Where indeed could you have found another company then – and certainly not now or ever more – whose Chairman & Managing Director and his wife, the Chief Designer and his assistant, could not only design and build a most remarkable range of very advanced, innovative and practical aircraft, but who were also approved, qualified, test pilots to fly and test them as well.

Now back to the biography of Tommy Rose. On Saturday, 16 May 1931, the new Reading Aero Club was officially opened and *The Chronicle*, for Friday, 22 May 1931 reported on the occasion thus:

NEW READING AERO CLUB.
OPENED BY DIRECTOR OF AVIATION.
MISS AMY JOHNSON TAKES PART.
Reading's new aero club at Woodley was opened on Saturday by the Director of Civil Aviation (Lieutenant Colonel F.C. Shelmerdine) in heavy

PHILLIPS AND POWIS, 1 JANUARY 1935 – JUNE 1936

rain. Lieutenant Colonel Shelmerdine, who flew with Mrs Shelmerdine from Heston, Middlesex, in a Puss Moth, made one of his first official public appearances. A large clubhouse has been erected by Messrs Phillips & Powis, and already the club has a good membership. Lieutenant Colonel and Mrs Shelmerdine were met by the president of the club, Lord Northesk, who was accompanied by Lady Northesk and the Mayor and Mayoress of Reading, Councillor and Mrs F.G. Sainsbury.

The Mayor of Reading (Councillor F.G. Sainsbury) drew attention to the fact that Reading was one of the first towns to foster the spirit of civil aviation by the opening of an aerodrome. He, personally, was proud of the fact that such foresight was being evidenced by that ceremony, and asked Lieutenant Colonel Shelmerdine to accept the key with which he was to open the clubhouse. The Deputy Mayor and Mayoress were present.

Phillip's and Powis 1 January 1935 – June 1936

It should be explained here that, although Miles designed all of the aeroplanes that were built by Phillips & Powis Aircraft Ltd, they were always known as Miles aeroplanes for obvious reasons.

The Berkshire Chronicle for Friday, 16 March 1934 reported:

A visit to Reading Aerodrome inspires the feeling that one has stepped into the future. At Woodley they have annihilated distance and mastered time and are working to make Reading the centre of a vast network of air lines extending throughout the country and linking-up with the whole world. Their vision is not an idle dream, for much work has already been done, and the Aerodrome is now firmly established as one of the leading centres of civil aviation in the south of England and is a growing aircraft factory already employing 160 men.

In the 1934 King's Cup Air Race, held on 13 and 14 July, the prototype Miles M.2F Hawk Major, G-ACTD, was flown by Tommy Rose into second place.

Also in 1934, Miles embarked upon the design of his first true cabin aircraft, a three-seater with the two passengers sitting side-by-side behind the centrally placed pilot. It was to be powered by a 130hp DH Gipsy Major I engine and was to retain the tried and proven wooden construction used on the Hawk, comprising spruce members covered with birch three-ply and in the tradition of the new breed of monoplanes, it was called the Miles M.3 Falcon.

Harold Leslie Brook of Harrogate became very interested in this aeroplane as he was considering entering the England to Australia MacRobertson Race. Although he came last in the race and didn't break any records, the contemporary issue of *The Aeroplane* gave a background history of Brook:

Brook departed on 20 October 1934 and finally arrived at Darwin, Australia, on 20 November 1934 and, having experienced problems en

FLIGHT LIEUTENANT THOMAS 'TOMMY' ROSE DFC

H.L. Brook being congratulated by Flight Lieutenant Tommy Rose on his arrival at Lympne, Kent, in his Miles Falcon, after his solo record from Australia to England. (*via Peter Amos*)

route, they arrived in Australia 26 days 20 hrs later. However, on the return flight, Brook arrived at Lympne, Kent, on 24 March 1935, after just 7 days 19 hrs 50 mins, to be welcomed back by Tommy Rose after his almost unheralded flight from Darwin, North Australia.

Brook had beaten the previous record set by Mr C.J. Melrose, by 13 hrs10 mins, and the officially recognised performance by Mr J.A. Mollison by 1 day 2 hr 25 min. The shortest time for the Australia-England trip is still the 6 days 16 hrs 10 mins of Cathcart Jones and Ken Waller set up in a 'Comet'.

In the spring of 1935, Miles designed and built a higher powered three seat version of the Falcon Major to be fitted with a 200hp Gipsy Six engine. The additional 70hp over the Gipsy Major was expected to give the new machine a maximum speed of about 160 mph and cruising speed of around 145 mph, The prototype was designated M.3B Falcon Six and the main noticeable difference between this and the Falcon Major, was that the bulkhead for the 6-cylinder engine was moved much closer to the windscreen to accommodate it. The pilot sat centrally with two passenger seats behind.

As the new Falcon Six prototype was being readied for its first flight, Tommy Rose looked at it and remarked 'it looks like Pregnant Percy', on account of its rather corpulent appearance brought about by the large cabin, and the name stuck. The Falcon Six was registered G-ADLC and was first flown by Miles on 20 July 1935 (not 27 July 1935 as often stated) and was entered by Lady Wakefield of Hythe in that year's King's Cup Air Race, to be held on 7 September 1935, to be flown by Tommy Rose.

In April 1935, Miles realised that if he could win the 1935 King's Cup Air Race, it would have a tremendous publicity impact on the company. He therefore decided to enter as many Miles aircraft as possible for the race, including a new single seat racing aeroplane for himself. He informed Blossom of his decision, and she asked Miles how on earth he thought a new aeroplane could be produced in time, he replied, '*The design of it is your problem and you had better get on with it straightaway!*'

Blossom realised that the only way of producing such a machine in the short time available would be to utilise a standard Hawk fuselage, delete the front cockpit, thereby shortening it by twelve inches, and reducing the wingspan by five feet by attaching the wings directly to the fuselage. Powered by a high-compression DH Gipsy Major engine, the result was the Miles M.5 Sparrowhawk, registered G-ADNL, and first flown by Miles on 19 August 1935, less than three weeks before the race.

However, in order to outwit the handicappers (who had handicapped the Falcon Six to do 157 mph), Tommy Rose decided to '*fib just a little*' over its performance! He could not blatantly lie as that would have prejudiced sales and put him in a difficult position, so he flew it all around the country and carried out many demonstrations, praising its handling and high cruising speed but complaining bitterly of its poor top speed. His first chance to 'bend the truth' came during the London to Newcastle race, in which he praised the Falcon Six's performance, saying it had a high cruising speed but felt disappointed with its top speed. It was about this time that it acquired the name 'Preggers'.

Of the thirteen Miles aeroplanes that were entered for the 1935 King's Cup Air Race, seven had been specially built for the race, including eleven Hawks of varying models and two Falcons. After qualifying 'at a gentlemanly speed', in the first day's qualifying race round England, Tommy Rose's complaints about the top speed of the Falcon Six proved to have been 'a tissue of lies', uttered in the hope the handicappers would take notice, particularly after he had been forced into second place with the Hawk Major the previous year, by a runaway winner who had totally out foxed the handicappers.

The first day's race was held on 6 September 1935, the course was from Hatfield to Scotland, across to Ireland and back to Hatfield, and the Sparrowhawk was fitted with long-range tanks to enable Miles to cover the distance with only one stop for refuelling.

While many of the competitors nursed their engines for the second day's race, Miles left the throttle wide open for the whole of the thousand miles and, thanks to the reliability of the Gipsy engine, he came in first at an average speed of over 170 mph.

The second day's race, on 7 September, was over a number of short laps and it soon became apparent that Tommy Rose in the Falcon Six would win the King's Cup, provided that his engine kept going. His course-keeping was as perfect as ever and an excited crowd saw him come around lap after lap, taking exactly the same time for each and maintaining a far higher speed than the handicappers had believed possible. Excitement increased when two Miles M.2P Hawk Trainers were seen lying in second

FLIGHT LIEUTENANT THOMAS 'TOMMY' ROSE DFC

Charles O. Powis (left) and Tommy Rose outside the Falcon Hotel at Woodley. (*via Peter Amos*)

and third places and it was fervently hoped that the three Gipsy engines would stand the pace, since they were all flying at full throttle.

Tommy Rose, in the Falcon G-ADLC streaked across the finishing line to win at the astonishing speed of 176.28 mph, with the two Hawk Trainers, G-ADLN flown by Flying Officer H.R.A. Edwards and G-ADLB flown by Owen Cathcart Jones, who had been flying almost neck and neck throughout the race, coming in second and third at 157.84 and 157.53 mph respectively. Another Falcon, G-ADLS, piloted by Samuel Harris and Laurence Lipton, came in fifth at about 147 mph to give Phillips & Powis their greatest success to date, taking four out of the first five places in the final! Miles in G-ADNL came in eleventh.

This was the first time that the first three aeroplanes to finish in a King's Cup Air Race had all been designed and built by the same manufacturer, and this unique feat has never been repeated by any other aeroplane manufacturer since.

After the race, Tommy Rose re-named the Falcon Six *'Preggers Primus'* (Primus being Latin for 'the first') and although it was duly christened as this, it was still usually known as *Preggers*.

With its success assured, the Falcon Six went on to be produced in several different models to suit individual tastes.

It was in late 1935 that Charles Powis and Tommy Rose made a 4,500-mile demonstration tour of non-European countries, flying the now famous Falcon Six, 1935 King's Cup Air Race Winner, G-ADLC and the M.5 Sparrowhawk G-ADNL.

Flight for 5 December 1935 reported that:

> *This year's race for the King's Cup served to attract attention to the qualities of the aeroplanes designed by Mr F.G. Miles and built by Phillips and Powis Aircraft Ltd, of Woodley Aerodrome, Reading, Berks. Three Miles machines secured first, second and third place, the race being won by Mr Tommy Rose in a Falcon Six, at an average speed of 178 mph.*

PHILLIPS AND POWIS, 1 JANUARY 1935 – JUNE 1936

> *All Miles designed Phillips and Powis aeroplanes so far produced have been all wood low-wing cantilever monoplanes with 'trousered' undercarriages. There is a strong family resemblance between the different models, so that it is usually easy to identify them wherever they are seen.*

On Wednesday, 18 September 1935, Tommy Rose took the winning Falcon to the official opening of Southend Airport, which was also the home of the Southend Flying Club, and the guests were welcomed to lunch in the newly erected large hanger. The Mayor of Southend, Councillor A.T. Edwards JP, spoke of the importance of Southend as a link between the UK and the Continent.

Sir Philip Sassoon stressed the value and future of internal air lines. He congratulated the borough on its wisdom and far-sightedness in the appeal on behalf of 'Playing Fields Day' made by the Duke of York at the Mansion House early in 1934. After the lunch all guests moved outside and watched Sir Phillip cut the tape to declare the airport open.

Tommy Rose took the Falcon to show people that a racing machine need not always travel quickly or be uncomfortable, ever the salesman.

On Saturday afternoon, 21 September 1935, while his son Campbell Black was setting off on another attempt on the England to Cape record, Alderman Milner Black, was opening the new South Coast Flying Club premises at Shoreham Airport. Speaking before the three Mayors of Brighton, Hove and Worthing, he outlined the origins of the airport.

Some sixty aircraft arrived during the afternoon for the inauguration of the new Club, which already had 159 members. The guests included F.G. Miles, Flight Lieutenants Tommy Rose, Cathcart Jones and Edwards. The party was greeted with a great ovation from the assembled guests and tea was held in the new hangers. A band of the Royal Sussex Regiment played for the guests, who were also shown around the luxurious clubhouse, the control tower, the boundary lights, floodlights, illuminated windsock, and the neon beacon, all of which could be activated from the control tower.

Tommy Rose had so far achieved his dream of winning the King's Cup Air Race and was making arrangements to take G-ADLC to South Africa but, in the meantime, for a little light relief, on 18 October 1935, he had borrowed G-AAKJ, a de Havilland DH.60X named *'Sam'*, formerly owned by his old employers, the Anglo-American Oil Company, but now with the London Air Park Flying Club Ltd, Hanworth Air Park, to take part in an event at the Associated Equipment Company Sports Ground at Southall, Middlesex. However, he crashed during the day on the sports ground, the aircraft was written of, luckily Tommy Rose was unharmed.

From the following articles it is possible that the accident may have been caused by high winds, which had also hindered the flying at the Reading Aero Club during the day. The fact that Tommy Rose had been unwell and suffering the effects of a bad cold, also may have contributed to the crash, but Tommy couldn't let anybody down.

FLIGHT LIEUTENANT THOMAS 'TOMMY' ROSE DFC

The *Portsmouth Evening News* for Monday, 21 October 1935, reported:

SICK MAN ATTENDS CHURCH BY AIR
WINNER OF THE KING'S CUP RACE
Flight Lieutenant Tommy Rose, this years' winner of the King's Cup Air Race, left his sick bed at his home at Woodley, Berkshire, and flew to Sywell aerodrome to attend the annual sportsmen service at Earls Barton (Northamptonshire) Parish Church to read the lesson.

He was still suffering from the effects of a bad cold and read the lesson in a husky voice.

Flight for 24 October 1935 reported that:

Flight Lieutenant and Mrs Tom Rose gave a house-warming last Saturday at their new residence, 'Falcon House', Sonning-on-Thames. This took the shape of a cocktail party. Amongst the guests were Mr and Mrs Charles Powis, Mr Luis Fontes, Miss Ruth Fontes, Mr Peter Godfrey, Miss Jean Forbes-Robertson, Mr and Mrs F.G. Miles, Mr C.A. Nepean Bishop, Mr J.J. Scholes, Mr and Mrs Payne Gallwey, Flight Lieutenant and Mrs R. Milne, Mrs Pleydel-Bouverie, Mrs Ellise Battye, and Mrs Wykeham-Barnes.

Mr Peter King and Mr P.G. James officiated behind the bar, and Fred Miles excelled himself as a cocktail maker and shaker. High winds have interfered somewhat with flying during the week, but whenever conditions have permitted the club and school machines have been busy. The new school Hawk Major is now being flown and four new pupils have arrived.

However, it should be mentioned that, although the report stated that Tommy and Mrs Tom Rose gave the house-warming, and although it was generally accepted that 'Billie' Rose was Tommy's wife, they were, in fact, not married at this time.

Tommy Rose next notable flight was to have been an attempt on the England-Cape Town record. A 75-gallon fuel tank was installed on G-ADLC and he duly left Lympne on 7 January 1936 but was forced to land at Abbeville in France shortly after due to icing. The Falcon was damaged in the forced landing and Tommy Rose was slightly injured, however, the machine was returned to Woodley and repaired. Tommy finally departed Lympne on 6 February on his second attempt on the record and arrived in Cape Town 3 days 17 hrs and 37 mins later.

Tommy established a new record for the distance and after the record-breaking flight, Tommy Rose sent a telegram to the firm which read *'Preggers definitely Primus'!* Tommy Rose also created a record for the return journey on 3 March 1936 by leaving Cape Town at 04.08 hrs (GMT), and arriving at Croydon on 9 March at 11.05 hrs, with five hours in hand. The Lord Mayor of London, Sir Percy Vincent, and his wife the Lady Mayoress, received him at the Mansion House at 13.30 hrs, where Tommy Rose presented the mayor with a letter from the Mayor of Cape Town.

PHILLIPS AND POWIS, 1 JANUARY 1935 – JUNE 1936

Flight for 5 December 1935 carried an article on British aircraft manufacturers and had this to say about Phillips and Powis:

PHILLIPS AND POWIS
This years' race for the King's Cup served to attract attention to the qualities of the aeroplanes designed by Mr F.G. Miles, and built by Phillips and Powis Aircraft Limited of Woodley Aerodrome, Reading, Berks. Three Miles machines secured first, second and third places, the race being won by Mr Tommy Rose in a Falcon Six, at an average speed of 178 mph.

Amy Johnson praised Tommy Rose's record in the *Dundee Courier* for 11 February 1936, thus:

AMY'S TRIBUTE TO TOMMY ROSE, BUT NOT TEMPTED TO BEAT RECORD.
Mrs Amy Mollison, referring at Leicester yesterday to the success of Flight Lieutenant Tommy Rose, who has broken her England to the Cape record stated, 'It was a wonderful achievement for a great pilot and a good machine, but it does not tempt me to have another shot for it.

'I believe that for now record-breaking must be left to rich amateurs or pilots employed by aircraft manufacturers for that purpose. At the moment firms have not the time or the money to think about stunt flying. They are too busy with RAF expansion work.'

But, barely two months later, the *Portsmouth Evening News* for 3 April 1936, reported Tommy Rose's response:

TOMMY ROSE THINKS AMY CAN DO IT IN TWO DAYS
'I see no reason why Amy should not get to the Cape in two days', said Flight Lieutenant Tommy Rose, holder of the record for both ways between here and South Africa, to an Evening News *representative at the South Parade Pier.*

'She is once again using the Western route across Africa, upon which she previously broke the record, and I used the all-red route, down the east of the continent. She has a much faster plane.

'If she does it, I suppose we shall have to find a British plane to beat it, and perhaps somebody will come along and ask me to beat Amy's record again'.

Flight Lieutenant Rose, who was appearing at the Pier with his travelogue 'My Life in the Air', later made a brief appearance at the Hippodrome stage; he has only been back in England about three weeks since beating the return record from the Cape.

Tommy Rose is still remembered well by country and farming people in the Petersfield district, for his father was bailiff and agent to Colonel W.G. Nicholson at Basing Park, and the famous airman spent all his

FLIGHT LIEUTENANT THOMAS 'TOMMY' ROSE DFC

The Mayor Councillor W.H. Bale presenting the casket to Flight Lieutenant Rose. (*Reading Standard*)

young days at his first school there, Churcher's College, which he left in 1911. Several of his old school fellows and others from Petersfield greeted him at the Pier last night.

The reputation that F.G. Miles had already earned, together with the logic of his arguments, so impressed Rolls-Royce that they decided to not only back him financially to build an advanced trainer to be powered by a Rolls-Royce Kestrel engine, but also to acquire a large financial interest in Phillips & Powis Aircraft Ltd. The Agreement was signed on 6 April 1936 and provided for Rolls-Royce to inject £125,000 by subscribing for 500,000 3.5% convertible preference shares, which gave Rolls-Royce the right to a 50% stake in the company and also to appoint two directors, A.F. Sidgreaves and A. Wormald, to the board. The latter died in December 1936 and was replaced by Lieutenant Colonel Maurice Darby OBE.

In May 1936, George Miles joined his brother at Woodley, having wound up Southern Aircraft Ltd and the Southern Aero Club at Shoreham. George had, in the interim, bought, flown and sold the Westland Widgeon G-EBRO, and replaced it with an Avro Avian IVM G-AAWH. He had also gained further valuable experience in flying, maintenance, and knowledge of aero engines, and it was about that time that Miles was getting interested in possibly producing the American Menasco engine in this country and so George was put in charge of that project.

On Wednesday, 13 May 1936, Tommy Rose was presented with a silver casket by the Mayor of Reading, after Tommy had given a lecture on his record flight to Cape Town. The *Reading Standard* for 15 May 1936 reported on the event:

FLIGHT LIEUTENANT ROSE HONOURED
Breezily skipping over the great difficulties and disappointment he experienced during his record flight to and from the Cape, Flight Lieutenant Tommy Rose made his audience laugh repeatedly when he gave a witty lecture on his achievement to a gathering of flying enthusiasts in the large Town Hall, on Wednesday evening.

The Mayor of Reading (Councillor W.H. Bale), who presided, presented Flight Lieutenant Rose, at the conclusion of the lecture, with a beautifully designed silver smoking casket cabinet surmounted by a silver scale model of the Miles Falcon machine with which he won the King's Cup and made the African flight. The model is affixed to a miniature globe on which the flyer's route is marked in red. The cabinet bears the inscription 'Presented to Flight Lieutenant Thomas Rose by the Mayor of Reading and other well-wishers in the Borough to commemorate his record flight to Cape Town and back by the east route in February and March 1936'.

A TOKEN OF APPRECIATION
In making the presentation the mayor said Flight Lieutenant Tommy Rose had made light of the difficulties he had encountered and went on to mention that the flyer covered the 2,300 miles to Cairo in fourteen hours, 'a remarkable achievement'. When asked to give a lecture on the flight, the airman agreed on the condition that the proceeds were given to the unemployed: that was typical of the man, and he also said he would be delighted to give four free flights. After Flight Lieutenant Rose had set up a new record it was suggested that his achievement should be recognised in a public manner, and he (the mayor) set on foot a fund with that object in view. The response had been gratifying, and they had been able, with the money subscribed, to provide that tobacco casket as a token of their appreciation. He hoped Flight Lieutenant and Mrs Rose would treasure it as a token from the citizens of Reading. 'We do regard Reading Aerodrome although it is just outside the borough boundary, as Reading,' the mayor proceeded, and the audience laughed at this allusion to a recent 'incident' commented on by a neighbouring rural district council. He added 'we are proud to recognise the aerodrome, and those who are connected with it, as part of the life of Reading and we think that the achievement of Flight Lieutenant Rose does add to the prestige of Reading. We do not lose sight of the fact, also, that the machine in which the flight was made to the Cape, was designed at the Reading Aerodrome by Mr Miles, and I know Tommy Rose would be the first to admit that part of the success of the flight was due to the designer of the aeroplane.' They were prepared to recognise that fact in a tangible form, the mayor announced, as a watercolour was being painted of the machine flying over Table Mountain. The artist had not yet completed the picture.

TRIBUTE TO THE DESIGNER
Flight Lieutenant Rose, accepting the gift, expressed his thanks and said no one recognised more than he how much was due to the man who designed the aeroplane. 'To my mind, and to the minds of a great many other people,' he said, 'he (Captain F.G. Miles) is the greatest designer of aeroplanes in this country, and possibly the world. And, secondly, I thank all the people in Reading who gave their last little bit to make sure that nothing fell off on the way. How well they did is history – nothing did fall off.' (Laughter). Flight Lieutenant Rose said he was very pleased that Mrs Mollison was doing so well on her return flight, adding, 'I only hope she gets back here without any mishap, because it will mean that sooner or later one of our Reading aeroplanes, if not flown by me, then by someone else, will have to go down that way and show them how to do these things.'

FLIGHT LIEUTENANT THOMAS 'TOMMY' ROSE DFC

There was an enthusiastic applause when the airman made the last remark. Earlier, however, in the course of his lecture he said, 'Everyone says are you ever going to do it again? The answer is, I don't think so for a minute. Because all sorts of people are going to do it, and if you get too many people flying past up and down Africa everyone will get dizzy and one won't know whether to turn to the right or left!'

The lecture was illustrated with slides and short films dealing with the King's Cup race, and the African flight was later shown.

Four lucky admission ticket holders won free flights offered by Flight Lieutenant Rose.

Berkshire Chronicle, Reading, for 15 May 1936 reported:

READING AERO CLUB NOTES

A landing competition was flown off on Sunday, and this resulted in a win for Mr E. Eugster. Machines had to land and try and pull up at a certain spot without further use of the engine or brakes. This means that the 'approach' and 'touch down' have to be very well judged, and Mr Eugster's win was a very good performance indeed with only some 29 hours flying to his credit.

Another of these competitions will be arranged for next month, and Flight Lieutenant Tommy Rose has very generously promised to present the club with a challenge trophy for the event. Needless to say, members are very grateful to Tom for his kind offer.

At the end of May 1936 an air tour for 'Amateurs & Others' was planned with Tommy Rose leading the owners of Miles Hawk Majors and Miles Falcons, from 23 May – 1 June.

Opening the Fete at Churchers College 1936 Tommy Rose's old boarding school.

On 25 June 1936, Tommy Rose was invited back to Churcher's College Petersfield, Hampshire, as guest of honour to open the Fete, and no doubt gave a brief talk about his exploits.

Flight for 2 July 1936 reported:

VIRTUE REWARDED

Tommy Rose, as Flight Lieutenant T. Rose is known throughout the world, was the recipient of an extremely handsome cigarette box last Wednesday. Mr C. Powis, as managing director of Phillips and Powis Aircraft Ltd, made a presentation on behalf of the directors of the firm. Speaking to a gathering of the senior staff and their friends, Mr Powis recalled the magnificent work Tommy Rose had done in winning the King's Cup Race last year and in breaking the Cape record early this year; both of these feats, he said, had done a great deal to assist the sales of Miles aircraft and he regretted that Tommy Rose had left the firm. After further apt remarks concerning the brand of gin which Tommy Rose will

PHILLIPS AND POWIS, 1 JANUARY 1935 – JUNE 1936

Mrs Powis presenting a silver cigarette box to Tommy Rose on behalf of the directors of Phillips and Powis, in recognition of his services to the company. The presentation took place outside the Reading Aero Club house. (*Reading Standard* 26 June 1936)

> *henceforth be selling, Mr Powis asked Mrs Powis to formally to make the presentation. Nothing official has been announced, but we do not think that, gin notwithstanding, there is any likelihood of Tommy Rose forsaking the air for many a year. As published entries show, he will be in the King's Cup Race again this year – and in one of Mr Miles' products, a Gipsy Six Hawk. Good luck to him!*

Tommy Rose left Phillips and Powis in June 1936 to join the Deptford distillery for Seager, Evans and Co Ltd, of gin and cocktail fame, as their travelling (air) representative.

Seager, Evans and Co Ltd July 1936 - September 1938

A small notice appeared in *The Scotsman* for 20 June 1936:

> *Seager, Evans & Co (Ltd), gin distillers announce that Flight Lieutenant Rose DFC has joined the House of Seager.*

In July 1936, Flight Lieutenant Tommy Rose took up an appointment with the old-established firm of distillers, Seager Evans and Co Ltd of London, to represent them and fly a Miles Falcon on their behalf. This moved C.G. Grey, the somewhat cynical editor of *The Aeroplane*, to observe of the company; *whose gin makes the 'World go around, but under complete control'*. And, of Rose: *His interest in aviation will not suffer as he will continue to make short work of long distances in flying competitions generally.*

No Miles Falcons were known to be registered to Seager and Evans, and it is thought they leased the now famous G-ADLC, as and when required.

Reading Evening Gazette for 11 June 1936 observed that Tommy Rose was severing his association with Reading Aerodrome thus:

> **TOMMY ROSE SEVERS HIS ASSOCIATION WITH THE READING AERODROME**
> **JOINS FAMOUS FIRM OF DISTILLERS BUT HE WILL OFTEN BE IN READING**
> *Flight Lieutenant Tommy Rose, winner of last year's race for the Kings Cup and former holder of the flight records to and from Cape Town, has severed his association with Reading aerodrome.*

This announcement comes at the same time as news that he will probably take part with C.W. Scott as co-pilot in the race from London to Johannesburg in September.

At the moment Flight Lieutenant Tommy Rose is at Ford Aerodrome, Yapton, Sussex, where he is spending the summer.

Although he is no longer at Reading he has not broken his connections with the district.

'I am coming back to Sonning in the Autumn,' he told me today, adding, 'I would not leave Sonning for anything. We are spending the Summer down here, but I shall often be at Reading.'

Tommy Rose has joined Seagers, the well-known firm of distillers, but for the present he is engaged on private air charter work.

For this purpose he is using his famous Falcon VI in which he won the Kings Cup and flew to South Africa.

'I am working in close association with Reading Aerodrome', he went on, 'and I shall be flying one of the Miles Hawk VI machines in next month's race for the King's Cup.'

He was reticent about plans for the forthcoming air race to Johannesburg.

'No definite arrangements have been made, and you will probably find that the announcement will be denied'. When I asked if he would be taking part in the race he added, 'you can take it from me that it is very probable.'

The machine that he and Scott will fly have not yet been decided upon, but it is rumoured, that they may fly one of the fast racing planes which competed in the Mildenhall-Melbourne race.

Mr A. Edwards, a wealthy Cape Town man, has agreed to finance the two airmen if a suitable machine can be obtained, while the prize money is being put up by Mr I. Schlesenger, the South African industrial magnate.

Mr C. Powis, managing director of Reading Aerodrome, by whom Tommy Rose has been employed since 1934, made a statement today.

'Flight Lieutenant Tommy Rose is starting on his own, using Reading as his base', he said. 'He is doing charter work and working in close association with us. Although he is not actually employed by this company, he has changed his status and he is a little more independent.'

Tommy Rose has become very popular in both Reading and Sonning.

As a memento of the eminence he brought to Reading's aviation industry, the people of the town recently subscribed for a silver casket, which was presented to him at a public lecture he gave at Reading Town Hall. The presentation was made by the mayor (Councillor W. Bale), who started the fund.

The Fifteenth King's Cup Air Race 10 and 11 July 1936

After the success of the 1935 King's Cup Air Race, Tommy Rose again competed in the 1936 race flown over two days, Friday, 10 and Saturday, 11 July. The weather was

PHILLIPS AND POWIS, 1 JANUARY 1935 – JUNE 1936

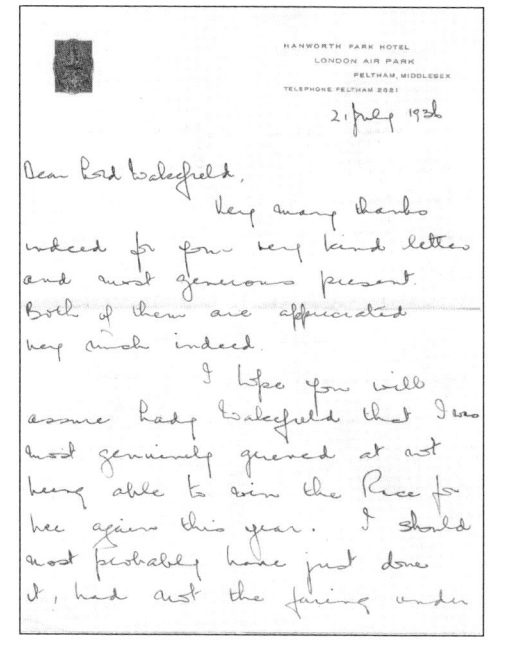

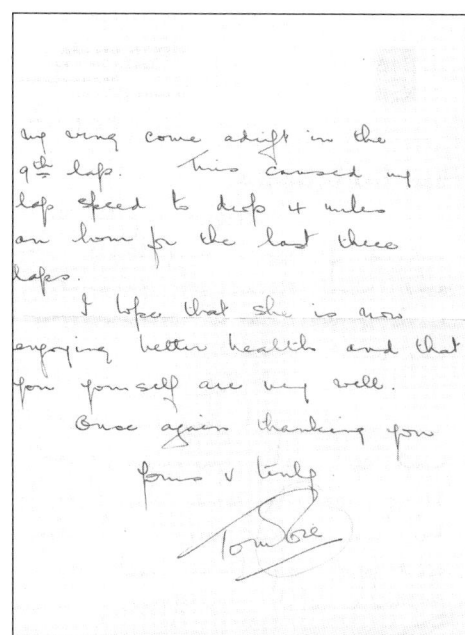

Tommy Rose wrote this letter to Lady Wakefield on 21 July 1936, which explained the fairing under the wing had come adrift in the ninth lap, causing him to reduce his lap speed by 4 mph for the last three laps. (*William Hale Collection*)

poor, cloud and rain all day on day one, day two started better, but then deteriorated over the course of the day, visibility was not as bad as it might have been, but there was an unpleasant bumpy wind.

Tommy Rose was in Lady Wakefield's Hawk Six G-ADOD, and was flying well, it was noticeable by the spectators that he put his mount's nose well down after each of the turns, which were at medium height. Tommy Rose was averaging 187 mph in most laps, which enabled him to pass the BA Double Eagle IV, flown by Flight Lieutenant J.B. Wilson, allowing Tommy Rose to climb from ninth to six place. Lap ten saw the Dragonfly still in second, with Tommy Rose in third place. The start of the twelfth and last lap seemed to promise a magnificent finish.

Tommy Rose received a warm welcome by a great cacophony of electric horns, which signalled he was in second place, and in true theatrical style swooped dramatically low when crossing the finishing line.

Flight for 23 July 1936 reported:

AVIATION 'SPIRIT' WITH A DIFFERENCE

Flight Lieutenant Tommy Rose is joining Britain's select little band of business representatives who use aeroplanes for work. He is not however, 'travelling in' anything so mundane as sparking plugs or oil, though it would be accurate to describe his new line as 'a popular brand of aviation spirit' marketed in bottles but so far unobtainable from the pump'.

FLIGHT LIEUTENANT THOMAS 'TOMMY' ROSE DFC

These facts were gleaned from Flight Lieutenant Rose when we cornered him at a cheery affair down Deptford way on Wednesday of last week, where Mrs Amy Mollison opened the brew warehouses of Seager, Evans and Co Ltd, of gin and cocktail fame. The distillery, actually, will be the source of the 'aviation spirit' which, with the aid of a Miles Falcon, Flight Lieutenant Rose will introduce to the clubs and other places where flying folk congregate.

On Saturday, 15 August 1936, Tommy Rose attended the Eastbourne Flying Club's Gala Day at Wilmington, Sussex. A crowd of 5,000 watched the thrilling demonstrations given by the following: the Duchess of Bedford in her Gipsy Moth Major, Tommy Rose flew in from Weston-super-Mare in a BA Swallow, Lord Patrick Crichton-Stuart of Cardiff also came over in his Hendy Hobo monoplane, and Prince Chiresaki flew his Hornet Moth from Heston.

By November Tommy Rose was back in Eastbourne attending the first annual dinner and dance of the Eastbourne Flying Club, held at the Grand Hotel on Friday, 27 November, included in the list of guests was Mrs Beryl Markham another aviation pioneer of 1936. Tommy's very good friend Tom Campbell Black had been Mrs Markham's flying instructor.

In December 1936, Tommy Rose attended the annual dinner of the Herts and Essex Aero Club and *Flight* for 10 December 1936, reported:

TEN TROPHIES
The annual dinner of the Herts and Essex Aero Club has, for some years, been notable for two features – the almost incredible mass of silverware presented to the club's star pilots, and the complete informality. This year the trophies numbered ten, apart from second and third place miniatures, and the speechmaking had, very sensibly, been cut down to a basic minimum.

Unfortunately, the most energetic supporter of the club functions, Sir Francis Shelmerdine, was unable to be present, confined as he was to his bed with a severe cold, and the trophies were duly presented by Flight Lieutenant Tommy Rose, who modestly alluded to himself as the 'misdirector of civil aviation'. This was his fourth H and E party, and it did not appear as if it was likely to be his last.

Captain F.A. Mason MVO, RE (Retired) was in the chair, and he replied, adequately and humourously, to the only toast, other than the loyal toast, of the evening – that of 'The Club', proposed by Mr W.J. Groome. Between the two speakers the visitors obtained a good idea of the club's vigour. As far as yearly hourage figure is concerned the Herts and Essex is third only to London and Brooklands, and in the last year this figure has already increased by a thousand hours.

In February 1937, as part of Tommy Rose's responsibilities as a flying representative, he was expected to fly the President of Seager, Evans and Company to attend various banquets and meetings, and he himself to be present at the openings of new licenced premises, such as the following examples:

Western Times for Friday, 5 February 1937 reported:

VICTUALLERS HOPE OF PROGRESS, NORTH DEVON SUMMER LICENSING HINT, LICENSEES BANQUET AT BARNSTAPLE.

The fact that last year the licensed trade contributed nearly one-eighth of a total of £100,000,000, turnover, was mentioned by Mr L.N. Nairn, of Messrs Seager, Evans and Company, President of the Association, presiding over the 57th annual banquet of Barnstable and North Devon Licensed Victuallers Association, held at the Imperial Hotel, Barnstaple, on Wednesday.

Appreciating the trade would have to find money for armaments, Mr Nairn held out no hope of reduction in taxation, but urged that the Government could take away some of the restrictions under which they suffered.

Flight Lieutenant Tommy Rose, the distinguished airman, was among the guests.

Proposing 'The President', Flight Lieutenant Rose expressed his pleasure at being in Devon, where many of his happiest days had been spent.

Tommy Rose attended the Blackpool and Fylde Aero Club dinner, which was reported on in the *Lancashire Evening Post* for 27 February 1937 as follows:

BLACKPOOL'S LEAD IN AVIATION

The possibility of Blackpool being a control point in the King's Cup Air Race on the second Saturday in September, was hinted by Major Alan Goodfellow of the Lancashire Aero Club at last night's dinner of the Blackpool and Fylde Aero Club, held at the Queen's Hydro Hotel, South Shore.

The President, Councillor W. Rostron Duckworth MP presided over a large company including Flight Lieutenant Tommy Rose.

Mrs Amy Mollison, who had promised to attend, was prevented owing to illness, and Mr Jim Mollison was unable to leave Paris by air owing to bad weather.

Tommy Rose was also still giving talks to aero clubs about his speed records and King's Cup win.

Staffordshire Advertiser for Saturday, 6 March 1937 reported:

Flight Lieutenant Tommy Rose, winner of the King's Cup Air Race in 1935, and former holder of the England – Cape Town record, paid a visit to Walsall (South Staffordshire) Aero Club on 25 February, and gave a

FLIGHT LIEUTENANT THOMAS 'TOMMY' ROSE DFC

delightful talk on his record-breaking flight. He was thanked by the club's vice chairman (Mr W.J. Minors) and the Secretary (Mr J. Hollier)

The *Middlesex County Times* for 6 March 1937, reported:

> *Hanwell's thirteenth public house, the 'White Hart' in Greenford Avenue, a house of Fuller, Smith and Turner Ltd, was opened on Tuesday evening. Among the visitors were three famous airmen, friends of Mr J.H. Bayley the licensee. They were Captain Neville Stack, Captain V.P.C. Baker, who taught the Duke of Windsor to fly, and Flight Lieutenant Tommy Rose.*

The Coronation of George VI and Elizabeth took place on 12 May 1937 at Westminster Abbey and was a big event of the BBC's early television service. It was their first true outside broadcast, using a mobile control van. However, very few families owned a television set in those days and relied on viewing news at local cinemas. The whole Coronation was filmed on three cine films, and it was copies of these sets of cine films that were given to the aviators to speed around the country.

The Midland Daily Telegraph for Friday, 7 May 1937, reported:

> **THEATRE PLANS FOR CORONATION COVENTRY PROGRAMMES, BROADCAST RELAYS, PROMPT SHOWING OF NEWS PICTURES**
> *Films by air:* The abridged versions of the Coronation films will be shown at the various cinemas. They are being carried from London to Castle Bromwich by air and transported from there to Coventry by road. In the case of the films to be shown at the Gaumont Palace, the film will be flown by the famous Tommy Rose.
>
> It is expected that the preliminary film will be at the Gaumont Palace by approximately 4.30 pm. Tommy Rose will be competing with a number of other pilots, in a sealed handicap race promoted by Gaumont-British.
>
> The King's broadcast will coincide with intervals in a play at the Opera House, and in the Hippodrome. Both will play it.

West Morning News for 12 May 1937, reported:

> **CORONATION FILMS FOR WEST COUNTRY FAMOUS PILOTS TO CARRY PICTURES**
> *Engaged in the task of conveying films and photographs of the Coronation events in London to the West Country today will be six of the foremost air pilots.*
>
> *They are Mrs Beryl Markham, Messrs C.W.A. Scott, H.L. Brook, David Llewellyn, Jim Mollison and Tommy Rose, all of whom are expected at Haldon, Teignmouth, during this afternoon at hourly intervals from 2.30 pm. Some of these famous pilots will also fly to Plymouth. Taking the west*

country as a whole, the Coronation decorations suffered little serious damage as a result of yesterday's heavy rain.

On 16 June 1937, *Eastbourne Gazette* reported:

FLYING CLUB'S COCKTAIL PARTY TOMMY ROSE WINS ARRIVAL COMPETITION
The Eastbourne Flying Club held a cocktail party on Saturday evening (12 June 1937 – SC). In addition, there was an arrival competition, in which fifteen aircraft took part, there being visitors from Portsmouth, Redhill, Southend, Southampton and Croydon, while three RAF Hawker Demons were flown from Hendon.

The competition was won by Flight Lieutenant Tommy Rose in a BA Eagle. Flight Lieutenant Blackwood in a Hawker received a second award.

Over seventy club members took part in the evening's proceedings. Awards won by club members were presented by 'Mrs' Rose (Billie – SC), *Mr Proctor for the cross-country competition and Captain Milward for the landing competition and cross-country event.*

In early July 1937, Tommy Rose entered the Newcastle Trophy Race in a BA Eagle but, sadly both Tommy Rose and R.P. Williams, also flying a BA Eagle, had to abandon the race after completing the first section from Newcastle to York and return, due to their engines, by coincidence, giving trouble after the stop at York.

The dinner-dance was held after the race at the Royal Station Hotel, Newcastle, where Tommy Rose responded to the toast of 'The Guests', by saying he had been flying for twenty-three years and unhesitatingly he would put the first three finishers of the race (C. Gardner, G. de Havilland and Alex Henshaw) as the best three amateur pilots in the country today – could Geoffrey de Havilland, an experienced test pilot really be considered as an 'amateur'?

On 17 July 1937, Tommy Rose attended the official opening of the new flying school and college mess at Witney (costing £2,500) which was officially opened by

Tommy's move also coincided with a very intensive advertising campaign Here is an example of the Seagers Gin advertisement from the *Flight* 1937.

FLIGHT LIEUTENANT THOMAS 'TOMMY' ROSE DFC

Lord Sherbourne together with the aerodrome manager Mr S.W. Saunders. The official opening was part of the Witney and Oxford Aero Club's Garden Party. Tommy Rose gave an aerial display, Herr Kronfield gave a gliding demonstration and Mr E.M. Slade of the Bristol and Wessex club gave a display. The RAF also gave a demonstration in an autogyro.

On Saturday, 23 July 1937, Tommy Rose had better luck in the Devon Air Race and with the Race No. 17, he piloted a BA Eagle and achieved an average speed of 130.25 mph. Everyone at the finish said that they had an uneventful trip, though Tommy Rose claimed he had 'heated up a brace of Eagles over Dartmoor', which everyone thought were more likely to be jailbirds! The race was won by Captain Phillips, second Miss Leathart and third was Flying Officer Leech.

On 30 July 1937, Tommy Rose competed in the Folkestone Trophy at the Cinque Ports Flying Club and despite dull weather, a representative entry of nineteen machines were divided into two heats. In heats one and two Tommy Rose was flying the BA Eagle, with the average speed of 131 mph to come first. In the final he came fourth, with Alex Henshaw coming first in his Mew Gull, second was A.J. Morris in his Hendy Hobo and third was K.K. Brown in his Tiger Moth.

On 10 August 1937, an article was published in the *Thanet Advertiser* stating that sixteen entries had been received for the forthcoming race, three Germans and one Latvian, the air race was to be flown from Ramsgate Airport on Saturday, 21 August. The handicap race was be flown over three laps of a triangular course, a total of seventy-five miles.

Tommy Rose was still looking for a 'mount', but he said that he would be at Ramsgate Airport in any event.

An interesting insight into Tommy Rose's relationship with the Henshaw family can be found in Alex Henshaw's book *The Flight of the Mew Gull* and can be found on page 83:

> *About this time I began to get bored with the air racing scene. I had become to realise that you were not really racing the other aircraft but trying to beat or fox the handicapper: they did their best with the information available, but if someone could secretly find a little more speed without them knowing it, or having to declare some minor alteration, he was on to a winner, and all the good flying by his opponents will be of no avail. My thoughts dwelled on Stan Halse's fantastic flight before he crashed near Salisbury.*
>
> *The opportunity came when dad and I were staying at Shoreham with Tommy and Billie Rose during the early part of August 1937. As I questioned Tommy on flying conditions in Africa, without any prompting he said seriously to dad, 'You know Pop, you ought to let Alex have a go at the Cape records in the Mew.' Dad said, 'I should think so, and bump himself off, like poor old Halse nearly did.' Tommy leaned across the table and said seriously, 'Pop, I really mean this; let Alex have a go, he could do it.' I didn't say a word, but my mind was made up.*

On page 168 this discussion went further:

> *I am not sure when I finally made up my mind. I do know that I had many mixed feelings. particularly when good friends like Arthur Clouston and Tommy Rose said, 'Use the Imperial Airways Route, it is the only safe way across Africa to the Cape'. I can honestly say this; when I said to my father, 'Dad I have decided to use the West route', and he replied, 'You should know what you're doing, if anyone does', I did not have one single misgiving nor did I feel I must change my mind.*
>
> *From now on everything I planned was related to overcoming the problems that lay ahead and to reducing the inherent dangers.*

Flight for 9 September 1937, published a small item on Tommy Rose, as follows:

> *Flight Lieutenant Tommy Rose (in the Miles Hawk Speed Six, Race No. 8), is perhaps the best known, and certainly one of the most popular, of our sporting pilots, Tommy Rose is a previous King's Cup winner – in 1936, flying a Miles Falcon – and was second last year in a Miles Hawk Speed Six. He has any number of other air-race and long-distance record successes to his credit, including a Cape Town flight last year in the Falcon, in 3 days 17 hours 38 minutes, with a return trip almost as fast. He was once instructor at Sywell, then sales demonstrator, and test pilot at Phillips and Powis, and now flying representative of the distillers of an 'aviation spirit' of high-octane value, Seagers Gin.*

Note, this is the first reference to Tommy Rose also being employed as a test pilot.

While employed by Seager, Evans & Co Ltd, Tommy Rose competed in the King's Cup Air Race for 1937, flying the Hawk Speed six G-ADGP.

10–11 September 1937. Hatfield.

The 1937 King's Cup Air Race was the sixteenth of the series and had been planned to cover the greater part of the British Isles in order to give the maximum number of people the opportunity to see the race at the control or turning points.

The race was again confined to British subjects and British aircraft and engines. Moreover, the aircraft must have been originally designed for use in civil flying. The only stipulation concerning the pilots was they must have had 100 hours experience of solo flying.

Competing aircraft were divided into two classes, Class A, for aircraft whose engines did not exceed 150hp total at the maximum permissible rpm, and Class B was for machines with engines exceeding 150hp.

The race itself was divided into two parts, the eliminating trial, to be flown on Friday, 10 September, with a start at Hatfield and finish at Baldonnell aerodrome, Dublin, and the final, from Dublin to Hatfield, to be flown on Saturday, 11 September. In the eliminating contest there were four controls at which landings were compulsory. At the turning points the machines were to pass within 500 feet of the mark, which was either a building, or a white cross, according to the locality, but they did not have to land. The four controls in the eliminating contest were: Woolsington Aerodrome, Newcastle, Dyce Aerodrome, Aberdeen, Renfrew Aerodrome, Glasgow, and Ards Aerodrome, Newtownards, in Northern Ireland.

Gusting winds between Newcastle, Aberdeen and Glasgow caused problems for the competitors in the eliminating trial on Friday, 10 September and the *Belfast Newsletter* for 11 September 1937, reported:

AT ARDS AIRPORT
BRUISED AND BLEEDING PILOTS,
THRILLING STORIES OF ROUGH PASSAGES
SHAKEN LIKE PEAS IN A POD

Bruised and shaken pilots, one of them with a handkerchief tied round his head, another with blood on his forehead and hands, stepped from their racing aeroplanes at the Ards Airport yesterday – the final control point before the finishing line of the elimination contest at Baldonnell, Dublin.

'Looks as though the bailiffs had been in', remarked two airport service men after viewing the tumbled interior of the four-engined Short Scion Senior which had tried to precipitate its pilot Mr Piper and his passenger through the roof, with painful results for them.

'Bumped to ...', said Flight Lieutenant Tommy Rose, briefly through his teeth.

Worst victim of all of the high wind – a northern with wicked gusts reaching 35 to 40 miles per hour – was Captain W.L. Hope, three times winner of the King's Cup race. He was the man with a handkerchief round his head. He said viciously, 'I've been punctured; I've lost half of my engine; I've been shaken about in the fuselage like a pea in a pod, and have nearly knocked myself out, and short of having a summons I've had a fine time'. And most bitter pill of all, he was the last man to arrive at Ards, and was last to leave.

OVER THE HILL AT 250 MPH

The wind laid the grass flat along the Ards Airport as the first aeroplane, a white and gold Percival Mew Gull, appeared in a gully between the hills to the north-east (almost every machine came over the same spot, making a deadline for Scrabo Hill, which could almost be seen from Portpatrick in the wonderful visibility) and streaked across the sky to the timing line at 250 mph.

Mr Henshaw, who came down in the North Channel last year, arrived in another Mew Gull and took care this time.

Flight Lieutenant Tommy Rose made a characteristically fine landing. His was one of the most beautiful craft racing. It was a Miles Hawk Speed VI, with a glistening black fuselage, white wings and undercarriage and a scarlet nose. It was so keenly streamlined that it was difficult to pick out in the sky until fairly close into Ards.

He refused refreshments, excusing himself because of the 'bumping' he had received, and said he was kept waiting two minutes at Renfrew while three Vega Gulls and a Sparrowhawk came in to land just as he was about to take off. He said that a bumpy trip was at its bumpiest on the other side, between Newcastle, Aberdeen and Glasgow.

On 17 September 1937, Tommy Rose was at the Eastbourne Flying Club's second 'At Home' at Wilmington Aerodrome. The pessimists said it was too late in the year and could not be successfully held as the pilots would have gone to earth, and it would rain again. However, the organiser, Captain E. Short, brought in seventy-two pilots. Tommy Rose gave a spectacular show of aerobatics in his black and white Hawk Speed Six G-ADGP, which was sunlit against an angry sky, arched by a rainbow.

On Saturday, 25 September, Tommy Rose and Billie were guests of honour at the South Coast Flying Club annual dinner.

The *Worthing Gazette* for 29 September 1937, reported:

PRAISE FOR THE AIRPORT TRIBUTE TO THREE TOWNS' ENTERPRISE
The view that three towns of Brighton, Hove and Worthing had shown great enterprise in providing an airport such as that at Shoreham and a clubhouse such as enjoyed by the South Coast Flying Club, was expressed by Flight Lieutenant Tommy Rose, the famous airman, at the annual dinner and dance of the South Coast Flying Club at the Grand Hotel, Brighton, on Saturday night. He had been to every aerodrome in the country, he said, and not one was better than the Shoreham Airport.

Flight Lieutenant Tommy Rose was accompanied by his 'wife' (Billie – SC) *and was responding to the toast of 'The Visitors', which had been proposed by the Flying Club's Chairman, Mr Francis Haddock, of Horsham, who presided, and who, in his speech, paid a very high tribute to the club's instructor, Mr Cecil Pashley.*

'The most cautious and safest instructor a Flying Club ever had', was how the Chairman described Mr Pashley.

Mr Haddock went on to refer to the establishment of the Royal Air Force Volunteer Reserve centre at the airport. Among the guests of over 200 were Captain Duncan Davis AFC, Managing Director of Brooklands Aviation, to which the South Coast Club is affiliated, and Mrs Davis, Mr Ken Waller, the record-breaking flier, and Alderman T.E. Hawkins and Mrs Hawkins of Worthing.

Tommy Rose was in great demand nationally and was asked to make a guest appearance on the radio on 5 October 1937.

FLIGHT LIEUTENANT THOMAS 'TOMMY' ROSE DFC

The *Berwickshire News and General Advertiser* for 28 September 1937, reported:

'FLYING HIGH' – THIRD EDITION.
Charles Brewer, BBC Assistant Director of Variety, has assembled another cast of ex-Air Force stage stars to take part in the broadcast on the National wavelength on 5 October. Among them will be Hugh Wakefield, Jack Warment, G.H. Elliott, Tod Slaughter, Gerald Nodin, and Frank Bellamy, at which it is hoped that Roy Royston will be able to make a brief appearance before the nightly performance in Leslie Henson's new theatre production 'Going Greek'. As a guest artist, listeners will hear Flight Lieutenant Tommy Rose DFC, hear of countless exploits both daring in the war, when he was a well-known scout pilot, and in search of records during recent years. He was one of the most popular pilots in this country, who set up a record for the flight to South Africa and back, in a Miles 'Hawk' machine (it was in a Miles Falcon – SC), *in February – March 1936. His participation in the broadcast will have a topical interest because he started as one of the favourites in the King's Cup Air Race on September 10-11. 'Flying High' will, as usual, consist of popular songs of the 1917-1918 vintage, and the humorous engine instruction sketch which listeners enjoyed so much on the occasion of the last broadcast, is to be followed this time by one on aerial navigation. Once more the audience will be drawn from Comrades of the RAFA and Old Comrades of the WRAF, and they will have the opportunity of joining in as lustily as they like in the chorus. The script for the production has been written by Alan Russell and Charles Brewer, both of whom were wartime pilots.*

After the flying season ended there were the many annual dinner dances to attend and, as Tommy Rose was such an eloquent raconteur, he would always be invited along to either give a speech, respond to toasts, or just be there to entertain his adoring 'fans'!

The *Sheffield Independent* for 20 November 1937, reported:

SEX APPEAL IN AIR RECORD PUBLICITY?
PRESS CRITICISED BY TOMMY ROSE
Criticism of the publicity given to record-breaking airmen was made by Flight Lieutenant Tommy Rose, when he spoke at the annual dinner and dance of the Sheffield Aero Club at the Grand Hotel Sheffield, last night.

Referring to the record by Flying Officer Clouston, who he said had flown to South Africa in the incredible time of 45 hours, he complained that this achievement received but half a column in the national papers of the country.

'Perhaps this is because he hasn't got sex appeal', he said. 'On the other hand, a very charming girl who flies to some other country received about three columns of publicity in the Press. People seem to forget that Charles Scott and Tom Black went to Australia in two and a quarter days.'

PHILLIPS AND POWIS, 1 JANUARY 1935 – JUNE 1936

Speaking afterwards to a 'Daily Independent' reporter, Tommy Rose said it was regrettable that Sheffield had no airport of its own. When he had been in this part of the country, he had been privileged to land at Firbeck, where he thought the Sheffield Aero Club were going to be lucky enough, through Mr Cyril Nicholson's permission, to have their new headquarters.

There was an 'airy' atmosphere about the gathering. Even the menu cards were written in aeronautical language, and balloons in the form of aeroplanes provided plenty of amusement.

A total of 300 guests and friends enjoyed the evening.

In 1937, Tommy Rose was asked to write an article for a book, *Flying*, on the benefits of air travel. Entitled, *'It's Quicker by Air'*, it appeared in the chapter entitled *'This Flying Business'* and it is reproduced below:

In these highly competitive days, speed is the essence of business. Speed and safety are all-important factors. That is why this is an age of air travel. SPEED is the life blood of air transport. If it wasn't for the fact that aircraft are considerably faster than land or sea transport it is possible that air transport wouldn't exist at all.

It costs more. It presents many more problems to the line operator. Very large sums of money have to be laid down before the hope of a profit can appear, and, not by any means least, a large amount of public inertia has to be conquered before the average traveller can be induced to fly at all. That they do fly – and in ever increasing numbers – proves the value of speed.

But even that big word speed has to be split up into several headings by the harassed airline operator. What is fast on one airline is slow on another. What was very fast a year or so ago is now regarded as slower than the snail.

To make matters worse, the average traveller steps in again. By now he has absorbed enough air knowledge to be able to put forward a good deal of criticism. Not much of it is constructive. He reads about airlines in the USA travelling at average speeds of 185 or 190 mph. He picks up on his travel statistics about European airlines. And he wants to know why his own airlines don't travel faster. He doesn't take into his argument at all the various problems that his own particular airline operator has to face.

Take an example. Airline travel is certainly fast at 100 miles an hour. But a machine that travels over the same route at 200 miles an hour is of more value to the traveller than the slower rival. He travels by air because he wants to get there quickly.

Therefore the 200 mph line should take all the traffic. But it isn't as simple as that. Suppose the high-speed line had a higher accident list, then the average traveller, by majority, would travel by the slow line.

FLIGHT LIEUTENANT THOMAS 'TOMMY' ROSE DFC

Suppose again that the 200 mph time was very uncomfortable compared to the 100 mph line. Once more our average traveller would go for the slow line.

But if the two lines offered equal safety and equal comfort – or nearly equal comfort – the fast line would win every time. This, to the traveller, sounds very simple. Why don't they do it? he asks.

One of the reasons is that it is very difficult to design and produce a high speed, comfortable airliner that will work at its high speed on a cost rate that produces profits. And it isn't much fun for the airline operator if he's got to run all his machines at a loss to himself. The line wouldn't last very long.

In the old days no commercial aircraft were comfortable. The travellers, mostly big businessmen, sacrificed a great deal for the sake of the speed that the aeroplane could offer them

Things have changed since then. Nowadays, every new commercial aircraft that is produced has a great degree of comfort – in some instances comparable to a Pullman train, and in other instances better than that.

Speeds on these comfortable new aircraft increase with the comfort. Passengers can find little to complain about. They can and do, find a great deal to complain about on some operational schedules. But even those are being speeded up, slowly but surely.

So, the passenger himself, who likes his speed and likes his comfort, is being well looked after. But what about those hundreds and thousands of passengers that are carried every day on every service of major international airlines?

I'm talking about the airmails. Those little white packets aren't being looked after as well as they might be. Take the present system. You post a letter to South Africa. The little fellow goes into the blue pillar box, or into the Post Office. He goes through the usual registration and then he's put in a van which takes him to Croydon Airport.

At Croydon Airport he's put into a bag with thousands of his fellows and piled into the mail compartment of the Imperial Airways liner which is due for the first leg of the South Africa service.

He follows the fortunes of the living passengers in that machine all the way. He arrives at Cape Town about a week after he leaves Croydon. Soon they'll cut that time down to four days, or they intend to.

But that little white envelope doesn't want the comfort and the cossetting that his living companions do. All it wants is to get to its destination as soon as possible.

That isn't an impossible request. There are aircraft nowadays quite capable of reaching the Cape in two days, perhaps less. They can carry a fairly large load of freight. But they can't offer the Pullman car comfort of their bigger and slower brothers. And it isn't too difficult to design a small economical, high-speed craft as it is to design a big one. Why not send the mails round the Empire and round the world on these smaller and faster machines? Important though it is to have the big machines, speed is the absolute life of air transport for the airmails. Those letters go by air because they are urgent, because they are first-class mail. They deserve to get to their destinations as quickly as it is humanly possible to send them.

That's where I think the real need lies. Give air speed by all means. It's essential. But segregate your speed. Provide speed plus comfort for the passenger, and speed plus speed for the international mails.

Send the passengers by the big, comfortable ships. Send the mails by the smaller, faster, but equally reliable mail planes. It is not a new idea, after all. It is done on some American lines. The French and Germans use the system over the South Atlantic Ocean. If you have a passenger machine with 200 miles an hour maximum you can get a smaller mail machine with a 250 mph or more maximum.

Then I think, everyone would be happy. The high speed which the airlines can and do give would be utilised down to the last possible mile.

And it's my opinion that the costs would be no higher, while the profits would rise. It is after all a proven fact that people pay for speed. You can all sell speed easier than anything else.

Why not sell it as much as possible? It's an attractive proposition.

In November 1937, Tommy Rose attended the Nottingham Flying Club dinner and dance at the Black Boy Hotel, Nottingham.

The *Nottingham Journal* for 26 November 1937, reported on the event as follows:

Tommy Rose, hero of the recent epic Cape flight, with which his name will always be associated, leaned carelessly against a radiator at the Black Boy Hotel, Nottingham last night and, in reply to a 'Journal' reporter's query as to whether he contemplated further flying achievements, said: 'Good heavens no! I'm travelling in gin.'

He added that he had definitely given up the idea of attempting any further hazardous adventures in the air, but others present at the annual dinner dance of the Nottingham Flying Club were of a different opinion.

'You will never tame Tommy Rose', said one member, 'he will make up his mind at the oddest of moments, and subsequent behaviour no-one could account for'. This was borne out by the nonchalant way in which he responded to the call made upon him to speak by Captain I.W. Hall (Chief Instructor at Tollerton).

He told a story against himself and Captain Cudemore (assistant instructor at Tollerton, with whom he served in the same squadron during the war), which evoked a roar of approbation from the hundred members of the club present. Captain Hall referred to 'the fine job he did in an ordinary plane'.

Tommy Rose replied, 'It is a far, far better thing to do than I have ever done, I am in the Gin trade!' He wished the Nottingham Flying Club every success in the future.

FLIGHT LIEUTENANT THOMAS 'TOMMY' ROSE DFC

In conversation to a 'Journal' reporter afterwards, he said he was disappointed by the reception that was given to Flying Officer Clouston and Mrs Betty Kirby-Green on their arrival at Croydon, after a record flight from the Cape on Saturday. 'Flying', he said, 'happened to be second best news, but the reception at the end of such a magnificent performance was terrible'. Amy Johnson was to have been present at the dinner but was prevented by a prior engagement.

In December 1937, Tommy Rose paid a visit to his old rugby club Bath whilst on a business trip for Seager's and was reported in the *Bath Weekly Chronicle and Herald* for 16 December 1937 as follows:

Mr Tommy Rose is used to hustling. In 1936 he hustled to the Cape said 'Hello' to South Africa, and was back in England, all in just six days.

On Thursday he hustled into Bath, said 'Hello' to some his old friends and hustled off again, all within 24 hours.

I cornered him for a few minutes by the City Club, and he was soon talking to me about his great love – flying. 'I might have another crack at the Cape next year,' he said. 'It all depends on whether I can get a machine. It is very doubtful though.'

Nowadays Tommy Rose is a businessman. He is a Director (I could find no evidence of this – SC) *of a firm of gin distillers, and it was this business which brought him to Bath, the first time he had been in the city to stay for fourteen years. He lost no time in meeting his old friends, but there were many others whom he could not see owing to lack of time. Among them was Eddie Simpkins, secretary of the Bath Rugby Club, who was also secretary in the days when Tommy Rose played for it. That was fourteen years ago. He was stationed at Netheravon and played for Bath for four seasons. He was in the Somerset side the year they won the county championship. He has been out of the RAF for ten years.*

Before he sets out on a record-breaking attempt, he cuts out drinking and gets as much rest as he can. Early to bed is his motto. According to him it isn't as much terrific strain as one might suppose. 'You get used to it and soon settle down', he said with a grin.

He still flies, but only in the summer. 'There isn't much pleasure in winter flying,' he told me. 'I live by the sea, near Bognor Regis, and there is an aerodrome close by, so I fly up to Town. It is much better and much quicker than motoring.'

Tommy Rose has a fine war record, and his peacetime record has been even finer. Beside the Cape record, since broken, of course, he won the King's Air Race in 1935, averaging a speed of 176 mph. He holds the DFC. High speeds mean nothing to him. As I said before, he is used to hustling.

Another social event to which Tommy Rose was invited by Mr Ian Peebles, was to a 'send-off' cocktail party at the Hungarian Restaurant for the Indian Expeditionary 'cricket force', and their skipper, Lord Tennyson. Lord Brabourne had just come home from India, where he was Governor of Bombay – India's cricket capital – was also getting ready to go out to be the Governor of Bengal.

Flight for 16 December 1937, reported:

NOT SO GRIM LECTURING

Flight Lieutenant Tommy Rose is nowadays in great demand as a lecturer, which in fact, if you have ever heard him lecture (though that is quite the wrong word) is understandable.

On Friday evening we had that pleasure when he gave a talk on his flying experiences before members of the Public Schools Business Society. His anecdotes, pruned off the Rose trimmings and without the Rose manner of delivery, quite defy reporting. One just listens to a tale of a violent forced landing, witnessed by only an aerodrome watchman in his night shirt (well, so I'm dead at last): of a low altitude search for Cairo in fog and darkness, with the ultimate sighting of an airport beacon, which turns out to be a cinema's neon sign advertising 'What Price Glory?'; of a deputy mayor in Africa who had the pleasure in welcoming 'Mr Tom Mollison, who has flown from England in 37 days 6 hours'; one just listened to these things.

Tommy Rose never forgot his old rugby team, Bath, and they remembered him fondly. The *Western Daily News* for Wednesday, 22 December 1937 reported:

Tommy Rose was in Bath last week. What a great forward this airman was – and what a fine sportsman! In his days Bath were a great side and provided no fewer than eleven out of the fifteen Somerset players. Last week Bath established another less than enviable record – they had only one player in the Somerset side.

Tommy Rose competed in the Isle of Man Air Races in May 1938, this time he entered a rare Hendy Heck, which failed to start due to engine problems.

On 20 July 1938, Tommy Rose was at the Cinque Ports Flying Club, revelling in brilliant sunshine, participating in the Folkestone Aero Trophy Race and the *Dover Express* for Friday, 5 August 1938 reported:

FOLKSTONE AERO TROPHY

The seventh race for the Folkstone Trophy was flown on Saturday over a triangular course of 60 miles, starting and finishing at Lympne Airport. The turns were at Capel Airshed and Folkstone gasholder.

The winner was Mr Hugh Buckingham of Hatfield flying a Hornet Moth, with an average speed of 125.25 mph, second was G. Samuelson in a Comper Swift with an average speed of 123.25 mph, and third was Geoffrey de Havilland in a T.K.2 with an average speed of 119.50 mph, Noel Coward presented Geoffrey with his £10 cheque. The fastest time was recorded by Tommy Rose, flying a Miles Hawk Speed Six at an average speed of 180 mph. A special prize of £10 and two pewter tankards were presented by Mrs W.E. Davis, managing director of the Cinque Ports Flying Club, for the fastest speed in a heat, which was won by Alex Henshaw, this year's King's Cup air race winner, whose Mew Gull covered the course at an average speed of 231 mph, a new record for the race.

The next Eastbourne Air Display was held on 20 August 1938, where Tommy Rose was one of the judges in the Concours D'Elegance, together with fellow judges Major C. Turner and Captain M. Deainant.

The 'foreword' to the programme, by E. Short Honorary Secretary stated:

To think of an aerodrome merely as a landing place for aircraft, is seriously under-estimating its potentialities. People are instinctively drawn to places where they know others will be. Men, women and children of all ages are quite content to sit along the edge watching aeroplanes landing and taking off, and manoeuvring gracefully in the air, which is infinitely more interesting.

In the new buildings, which are being opened today, we have concentrated on providing for the enjoyment of our members and for the general public, who are our future members, and we, the Eastbourne Flying Club, sincerely hope the new buildings and general developments will materially increase the membership. The new clubhouse, a fine modern building, contains lounges, bedrooms, fully licensed bar, tea-lounge and full-sized billiard room, all with a perfect view of the landing ground.

The days when flying was regarded as a dangerous novelty are passed, and the practical utility of aircraft as a means of commercial development and rapid communication is now an accepted fact.

The people of this country are air-minded and extensions which clubs are already contemplating to cope with the increase of new pilots, men and women of all ages, will spread through Great Britain, a vivid consciousness of the importance and possibilities of flying, apart from having thousands of capable pilots ready to answer any call the country may make.

Everyone must understand the necessity for Britain to lead in the progress of aeronautics. We here at Wilmington are doing our bit towards this end, and we want everybody's support.

Pilots started arriving from midday, with demonstrations by Flight Lieutenant R.A.C. Brie on the Autogiro. A demonstration by Alec Henshaw, 1938's King's Cup Winner, at an average speed of 236 mph, was showing the public a 300 mph dive. Squadron Drill by No. 79 (Fighter) Squadron RAF, with their Gloster Gauntlets from Biggin Hill, under the command of Squadron Leader G. Emms, who gave a running commentary on the display from a wireless in the air. A demonstration on the famous Tipsy Monoplane was also given.

The finale was a parachute descent by Gwynne Johns, holder of the world's record delayed drop, 22,400 ft, delaying to 18,000 ft, who had also completed forty-four successful parachute drops up to then.

Tommy Rose's next appointment was as Chief Flying Instructor of the Phillips & Powis School of Flying, which had been formed in 1929.

War was on the horizon and although the country was preparing for the next conflict, air shows and races were being cancelled, Tommy Rose's career was about to take a dramatic turn when, in November 1939 he was appointed Chief Test Pilot of Phillips & Powis Aircraft Ltd.

Chapter 12

Tommy Rose and the King's Cup Air Races

'The highest art form of all is a human being in control of himself and his aeroplane in flight, urging the spirit of machine to match his own.'
– Richard Bach, Author.

Tommy Rose and the King's Cup Race

There was no greater UK air race to raise the profile of any aspiring racing champion other than the prestigious King's Cup. If you wanted to be noticed and have a future in air racing this was the place to be seen.

It was in these early racing years, these pilots had to show their worth, expertise, prowess and showmanship. They had to catch the eye of a wealthy benefactor to sponsor them, who would win them the race, or second and third place, then hand over the not inconsiderable 'winnings' to the owners or sponsors of the aircraft.

Many of these pilots earned their living, as Tommy Rose did, after leaving the RAF, by taking up posts in the fledgling private flying schools as Chief Flying Instructors. Having a famous pilot in these flying schools provided not only very experienced pilots, but also the magnetic personalities of these fliers brought in future students all keen to learn to fly, and these included some very notable actors and writers from the performing arts, as well as members of the aristocracy and Royalty all wanting to try to gain their 'A' pilots licence.

This was a time of expansion in the private sector largely promoted by Tommy Rose, who was an advocate and pioneer of private aviation. At the same time these pilots were given access to aircraft to hone their skills with, take to demonstrations, shows and races, which in turn increased the reputation and publicised the various private aircraft manufacturers, the durability, speed and reliability of the fastest engines and the availability of the flying schools now expanding nationwide.

No bigger accolade could be afforded to these pilots/manufacturers/flying schools, than to 'win' in a prestigious Air Race, and the King's Cup Air Race was the most important and most notable in the country. Tommy Rose entered six King's Cup Air Races during his flying career, the first was in 1929, when he had to retire; he came sixth in 1930; second in 1934; first in 1935; second in 1936; tenth in 1937 and, in 1949, his last Kings Cup Race, he unfortunately failed to gain a place.

It was the original intention of the Royal Aero Club that the 1924 race for the King's Cup should be confined to seaplanes and amphibian types but at that time the number

TOMMY ROSE AND THE KING'S CUP AIR RACES

Tommy Rose's entry into the King's Cup Air Race 1929, G-EBTO, an S.E.5A, race number 1. (*Flight*)

of privately-owned seaplanes were very small and it was realised that it should be necessary to obtain the consent of the Air Council to let the manufacturers of military seaplanes enter these for the race, this the Air Council refused to do, so the Royal Aero Club opened the race to all entrants. The course, which had to be a circuit of the UK, had to have different starting and finishing places for the two categories of aircraft being entered. The aeroplanes started at Martlesham Heath, Suffolk, and the seaplanes from Felixstowe. The finishing lines for the two types were at Lee-on-Solent and Gosport. Needless to say, with such a course and such diversity of types of aircraft, the race was not a success. The machines were timed over the course but were not started off in the order of their handicaps, so that it was impossible to follow the progress of the race, and it was not until the last machine had returned that it was possible to know who the winner was. Handicaps were then re-introduced.

Tommy Rose's first entry was on 5 & 6 July 1929 at Heston, flying the S.E.5A G-EBTO, with Race No. 1, which was entered by W.L. Handley, but sadly he had to retire with engine trouble at Sittingbourne, Kent. Also in the race was Flight Lieutenant Anthony M. Kimmins, flying a DH 60G Gipsy Moth who, in later life, became an actor and film-maker. Kimmins was surprised by Eamonn Andrews to appear in '*This is your Life*' on 20 March 1961, and one of the guests on the programme was none other than Tommy Rose.

In the 1930 race Tommy Rose flew a streamlined Blackburn 'Bluebird' G-AACC, but was delayed due to engine cowling trouble, which Tommy fixed and carried on. His speed to Manchester was only 104.6 mph but his speed for the whole course was 109.8 mph, so he must have made up after fixing the cowling. He came sixth but, had it not

The Blackburn Bluebird G-AAGG (Hermes engine) in pre-race trim. Tommy Rose flew this in the 1930 King's Cup Air Race with Race No. 21, the exhaust stubs faired in, the passenger's side of the cockpit covered, the pilot's head rest fitted, and the lower wings faired into fuselage. (*via Peter Amos*)

been for the cowling, he would have probably done better and would likely have been in the first three.

Tommy Rose was unable to compete in the 1931, 1932 or 1933 races for various reasons, but he competed in 1934 flying the new Miles M.2F Hawk Major prototype, G-ACTD, with Race No. 42. Fitted with a 110hp Gipsy III engine, this was entered by Captain G. Shaw. In the second heat Tommy was declared as a 'dark horse'. His racing during Friday, had been in atrocious weather, and the speeds established were of no value as a guide to what the Hawk Major could do in good weather. Tommy was giving Edwards in his Southern Martlet (Gipsy I) a start of 16 minutes and giving away one minute to Parker in his de Havilland Leopard Moth (Gipsy Major). When the machines came in at the end of the first lap, Tommy Rose had moved up to sixth place, having overtaken the two 'Leopard Moths'. The wind, which was gradually veering to the North, seemed to have freshened, and the aeroplanes came across the aerodrome at speed. At the conclusion of the second lap Tommy had gained fourth place but, by the end of the third lap, Tommy was well in the lead and went on to finish second in the final, securing for Lord Wakefield a £100 prize. So close, and maybe next year he felt that he really could win the King's Cup Air Race.

However, in the 1935 race, Tommy was to finally achieve his goal by winning the King's Cup Air Race for the very first time, at a speed of 176.28 mph.

In 1935 an entirely new system was followed in the planning of the race regulations. Virtually the whole race consisted of two quite independent tests: a test of reliability and navigational skill on the first day, and a demonstration of sheer speed on the second,

Tommy Rose with his entry G-ACTD, a Miles M.2F Hawk Major prototype, for the 1934 King's Cup Air Race. (*via Peter Amos*)

something Tommy Rose excelled at. This change was an attempt to combine with the original idea of a circuit of Britain with the spectacle of many turns and a close finish.

The start was at Hatfield and during Friday, 6 September 1935, a circuit of Britain was flown by the competitors. The course took in England, Scotland, Northern Ireland and Wales and the total length was 953 miles. There was no handicapping, and the competitors could please themselves how fast they would fly, the only stipulation was that they had to round the official turning points correctly, and they must have their race card signed at the four official controls. The time spent on the ground counted as their flying time, in most cases the pilots taxied their machines up to the Royal Aero Club official, handed their race cards to the club officials for signature, and were off again.

Refuelling also counted as flying time, and the slickness of time spent refuelling counted a good deal. The more fuel-efficient machines who could do the entire circuit of 953 miles without refuelling did so but very few were able to do this and the control at Renfrew, Glasgow, was one of the most popular refuelling depots.

The finishing line at Hatfield was marked between two arrows on the airfield and the machines had to cross the line in the direction indicated by the arrows.

The race was held under the regulations of the Federation Aeronautique International and the Competition Rules of the Royal Aero Club. The King's Cup was awarded to the entrant of the aircraft which won the Handicap Race organised under the following conditions:

1. The entrants, pilots and passengers of competing aircraft had to be British subjects.
   The entrant must be an individual and not a Company.
2. Pilots who took part had to have flown solo for at least 100 hours prior to the start of the race. No change in personnel of the aircraft was allowed to be made during the race.
3. The race was open to any type of bona fide civil aircraft, provided that the aircraft, including the engine and its accessories, had been entirely constructed in the British Empire. For the purpose of this rule a bona fide civil aircraft was deemed to be one originally designed and constructed for use in civil aviation activities.

The first day's eliminating contest started at 08.00hrs on Friday, 6 September and flew over the following circuit:

Hatfield	Start	
Newcastle-upon-Tyne	Turning point	240 miles
Edinburgh	Turning point	90 miles
Glasgow Renfrew	Control	41 miles
Stranraer	Turning point	75 miles
Newtownards	Control	30 miles
Dalbeattie	Turning point	80 miles
Blackpool	Turning point	85 miles

FLIGHT LIEUTENANT THOMAS 'TOMMY' ROSE DFC

Woodford	Control	50 miles
Cardiff	Control	136 miles
Hatfield	Finish	126 miles
	Total distance approximately	**953 miles**

Competitors were expected to return to Hatfield from 16.00 hours onwards.

The competing aircraft were divided into two classes:

A Those with a total engine power not exceeding 150BHP.
B Those exceeding this power.

Tommy Rose was flying the Miles M.3B Falcon Six G-ADLC with its Gypsy Six engine, entered by Viscountess Wakefield of Hythe.

Ten machines in each of the two classes which completed the circuit in the shortest time passed into the final, no handicap allowances were being given for the eliminating contest.

All time spent on the ground, whether at the official control points or elsewhere all counted as flying time.

Any aircraft that failed to complete the course within the twelve hours from the official starting time was not able to enter the final.

The qualifying aircraft raced on estimated performance handicaps, the minimum handicap speed being 130 mph. Seven circuits of the following course were flown:

Hatfield - Broxbourne - Henlow- Hatfield.

The start took place at 15.00 hours on Saturday, 7 September 1935, and the winner was expected to cross the finishing line between 17.30 and 18.00 hrs.

Ten seconds before the time of starting, the official starter raised his green flag. The signal to start commenced with the lowering of the flag smartly to the ground.

The race numbers allocated to each competitor was painted on both sides of the rudder in black on a white background. In addition, each aircraft was to carry the Government registration on the wings and fuselage.

The Prizes were:	First	£500	£ 35,000	approx. worth 2019
	Second	£200	£14,000	"
	Third	£100	£ 7,000	"

Viscount Wakefield also presented the prize of £50 to the competitor in each of the classes A and B who accomplished the fasted time in the eliminating contest, together with £100 in prizes for other competitors who qualified for the final.

A prize of £150 was given to the competitor in each of the classes A and B who accomplished the fastest time between Hatfield and Cardiff, which was donated by the Cardiff Aeroplane Club.

TOMMY ROSE AND THE KING'S CUP AIR RACES

The 1935 King's Cup silver gilt trophy taken from the programme, made by Henry Hodson Plante in 1934, of twin-handled urn form, the domed top with flower bud finial over acanthus leaves in relief and stylised foliate border, the body of bellied form with wrythen branch handles and a frieze with thistle, rose and shamrock designs all over an anthemion stem on a stepped circular base, the front engraved 'Royal Aero Club, The King's Cup, 1935, presented by, King George V'.

At the conclusion of the race the King's Cup was presented to Tommy Rose DFC by The Right Honourable Sir Philip Cunliffe-Lister, GBE, MC, MP, Secretary of State for Air.

Flight for 12 September 1935 reported:

THE FOURTEENTH KING'S CUP RACE
A RUNAWAY WIN FOR THE MILES FALCON (GIPSY SIX) BY FLIGHT LIEUTENANT T. ROSE
TWO DAYS OF RACING DEMONSTRATE WONDERFUL RELIABILITY OF MODERN AIRCRAFT AND ENGINES

The fourteenth annual air race for the cup presented by His Majesty the King, flown last Friday and Saturday, resulted in the decisive victory for a Miles Falcon low wing cabin monoplane (Gipsy Six engine) entered by the Viscountess Wakefield and handled by Flight Lieutenant T. Rose, the makers test pilot. Completing Friday's 953-mile Eliminating Trial at an average speed of 154.5 mph., he won Saturday's handicap Final at an average speed of 176.28 mph., six minutes ahead of the next competitor. His flying time for the 350 miles of the Final was 2h. 3m. 8s., and his best lap of the fifty-miles course was at a speed of 178.206 mph.

FLIGHT LIEUTENANT THOMAS 'TOMMY' ROSE DFC

Tommy Rose proudly receiving the silver gilt King's Cup from Sir Philip Cunliffe Lister. (*Flight*)

The King's message
His Majesty the King sent a message of congratulations to Viscountess Wakefield. It conveyed in the following telegram, received by the secretary of the Royal Aero Club, from Balmoral Castle:

> 'Please convey the warm congratulations of the King to Viscountess Wakefield on winning this cup and also to the pilot.'

Second was a Miles Hawk Trainer entered by Mr R. Cornwall and piloted by Flight Lieutenant H.R.A. Edwards, who completed the Final at an average speed of 157.85 mph.

The third machine home was yet another product of the Reading factory of Phillips and Powis (Aircraft) Ltd – another Hawk Trainer, entered by Major G.W.G. Allen and flown by Mr O. Cathcart Jones, who, having averaged 157.52 mph., finished only 17secs after the second placed aircraft.

Fourth was Lord Wakefield's T.K.2 monoplane, built by the students of the De Havilland Technical School and flown by Captain Hubert Broad. The scratch machine, the Percival Mew Gull entered by H.R.H. the Duke of Kent was flown by Captain E.W. Percival and finished sixth, having averaged 208.91 mph. and made, as was expected, the fastest lap of the race in 14mins 41secs, equivalent to a speed of 211.178 mph.

Competitors and spectators were fortunate this year in the matter of weather, clear, bright conditions prevailing on both days. The 953 miles eliminating contest which took competitors over England, Scotland and Wales, and touched Northern Ireland, saw six of the twenty-nine starters retire through various causes, while one was excluded through an infringement of the turning-point regulations. Both the two women pilots were unlucky, neither reaching the final.

Except for a descent into the Irish Sea by Alex Henshaw, who was picked up by the Isle of Man passenger packet *Manx Queen which* fortunately happened to be passing nearby, there were no accidents,

TOMMY ROSE AND THE KING'S CUP AIR RACES

Written on the back of the photo: 'Victory in the King's Cup Air Races at Hatfield.' Rose piloted a 'Miles Falcon' to victory over a field of the Empire's outstanding fliers. (*Sarah Chambers*)

while in the Final the standards of mechanical reliability were high, not a single retirement taking place among the twenty starters. With the exception of the winner's runaway victory, the handicapping by Captain Darcy and Mr Rowarth secured a very close finish in the final, only 2 min. 51 sec. separating the second finisher from the ninth.

Public interest though was again comparatively meagre, but showed a distinct improvement as compared with previous King's Cup Races, especially at the controls and turning points in Friday's contest this was so.

The Bystander for Wednesday, 18 September 1935 reported by Charles Ward under the headline: *Air Race triumph for Designers*

THE KING'S CUP:
This year's race for the King's Cup was notable for the triumph of two designers, F.G. Miles, who produced the first three aircraft and Frank Halford the first three engines. A popular winner is always satisfactory at

Tommy Rose landing back at Hatfield after winning the 1935 King's Cup Air Race. The aircraft is a Miles M.3B Falcon VI, registration G-ADLC. *(Flight)*

a race meeting and no competitor could have deserved more than Tommy Rose, who piloted the Miles 'Falcon' to victory. He is the sales manager and chief test pilot at Woodley and has had considerable influence on the record sales of the Miles aircraft during the past year. It was estimated that his speed would be 157.5 mph, whereas he averaged 176 mph, compared with 166 mph by the pilot of other 'Falcon', competing fastest time of the day, and incidentally the fastest speed ever achieved in the King's Cup Race, was put up by Captain Edgar Percival, flying the 'Mew Gull' of his own design for the Duke of Kent.*

(Note, this is the first report of Tommy Rose being a Test Pilot.)

OVERHEARD ON THE TARMAC
All competitors in the final finished the course, twenty-seven minutes separating the winner from the last plane home. Every finalist but one used a Gipsy engine, and there were no cases of engine failure, which must have pleased Major Frank Halford considerably. The T.K.2 designed by the students at the De Havilland Technical School and flown by Captain Broad averaged nearly 160 mph, with 174 mph on the last lap. Its performance must be considered extremely good with a Gipsy Major of 130 horsepower. Both of the 'Hawk' trainers, taking second and third places, were most consistent with their speeds, each averaging 157 mph. and a fraction.

The Siddeley Trophy was won by Mr C.E. Gardner flying a 'Gull Six', at an average speed of 170 mph. He represented the Redhill Flying Club which is one of the youngest in point seniority but one of the most progressive clubs in the country. Quite a few of the entries used retractable undercarriages, but apart from this device few modern features were noted.

Tommy Rose wrote of his experience in the 1935 King's Cup in the September issue of the *Reading Review*:

For a number of years it has been my ambition to win the race for the Cup presented annually by His Majesty King George the Fifth, and this being the one year event, I was more anxious than ever to pull off this contest which is the Blue Riband of British Flying... the first day of the contest consisted of a circuit of Britain, the turning points being Newcastle, Edinburgh, Renfrew, Port Patrick, Belfast, Dalbeattie, Blackpool, Manchester and Cardiff. Compulsory stops were to be made at Renfrew, Belfast, Manchester and Cardiff, and the race started and finished at Hatfield. The machines were divided into two groups, one with engines up to 150hp, and those with engines over that power.

TOMMY ROSE AND THE KING'S CUP AIR RACES

We left Hatfield shortly after 8 am on Friday and reached Newcastle at 10 am. The weather was slightly hazy at first, but the further north we went, the better it became, until in Scotland we ran into brilliant sunshine, which with the exception of a shower of two in Ireland, remained, with us for the rest of the circuit. We arrived at Renfrew at 11 am and landed at Newtownards, Belfast, at 11.30 am. Here we refuelled and continued to Manchester. I have flown over Manchester hundreds of times, but never before have I seen the WHOLE of the town from the air in one piece. Cardiff was reached at 1.15 pm and we arrived back at Hatfield at 1.50 pm.

As the first ten machines in each class were eligible to compete in the final heat, and we knew the approximate speeds of our rivals, there was no need to go 'all out' during the circuit; but we nevertheless made an average over the course of 153 mph, including stops, which was not at all bad going. Actually, we started tenth and finished ninth.

The next day was quite a different affair, consisting of seven laps of a fifty-mile circuit round Broxbourne, Henlow and Hatfield. The weather was again ideal, with a slight breeze blowing from the north. Being one of the fastest machines in the race, we had the doubtful pleasure of seeing twelve other competitors get away before it came to our turn. However, we did not have to start thirteenth, as we were scheduled to go at the same moment as the other Falcon entered, and it got away just in front of us!

At the end of the first lap we had picked up two places and were lying eleventh, and by the end of the third circuit we had advanced to ninth. Fourth time round and we were third. At the end of this lap we had a brief moment of excitement, as there was a sudden noise and a jar from the front of the machine. I thought 'well that's that', but nothing else happened and we carried on as before. It afterwards transpired that the airscrew spinner, presumably having been hit by a bird, had come off, luckily without striking the machine.

By the end of the fifth lap, we were in the lead, and it was then just a matter of keeping going at full throttle and holding one's course. The Gipsy Six and the Falcon stood up to their respective reputations, and we eventually passed the post some minutes before the second man home, who incidentally was also flying a Miles machine.

The most dangerous part of the two days was then to come, for on landing I was seized and hauled out of the machine on the shoulders of men who had made it. They had come over from Reading in seven motor coaches to see their handiwork win. Lady Wakefield was most excited at seeing her machine come in first. She had not been in good health recently but said that my win had been as good as a tonic to her. I am very grateful indeed that she allowed me to be her doctor.

FLIGHT LIEUTENANT THOMAS 'TOMMY' ROSE DFC

In the *Aeroplane's* own flight-test shortly after the race:

> The winning pilot told us that he flew round the entire eliminating course with his feet off the rudder bar and for most of the way with his hands off the stick. And he said that in the final he flew feet off the rudder most of the time. When we heard this we were rather unconvinced, and put the statement down to the modesty of a great pilot. But we have taken the air in it ourselves, we agree that with a first-class navigator as passenger, the pilot might have crossed his legs and read the newspaper.
>
> Without minimising in any way the considerable personal skill of the very popular winner of the greatest British race of the year we can safely say that the performance and propensities of his Miles Falcon put it in a class by itself.
>
> With two aboard, tanks full, and the Gipsy Six awoken with one prod of the electric starter, we were airborne in less than ten seconds in the flat calm of last Friday. We demanded full speed ahead, and without increased din sundry needles went round till the airspeed stood at 180 mph. With the stick alone perfect turns were made both ways and then we went back to cruising speed. At 150-160 mph turns up to 60 degrees of bank were easy to begin, maintain or stop without a rudder. At what must have been about 40 mph the elevator and rudder bias levers on the floor under the dashboard could be set to keep the machine flying level and hands-off at about half a throttle, without any feeling of instability or insecurity. The lateral control was still quite sensitive enough to do reasonable turns either way and bumps left the trim unscathed.
>
> Side-slipping is unnecessary. Putting the nose down quite sharply made the descent still steeper without greatly affecting the airspeed. Landing was so easy that we felt there must be a catch in it. There wasn't. The only non-standard feature about this machine was the pilot, and the fact that such pilots cannot be drawn from stock every day of the week shows the foresight and good fortune of the designer-builders and entrant of the winning machine.

In 1936 Tommy flew the new Miles M.2U Hawk Speed Six, G-ADOD, with a Gipsy VI engine, which had been entered by Viscountess Wakefield with Race No. 4. Ominous grey clouds threatened the final, during lunch steady rain started and this continued throughout the race. Visibility was not too bad, but it was unpleasantly gusty. Tommy was averaging a lap speed of 187mph and had climbed from ninth to sixth place. On lap ten Tommy was in third place and on the twelfth lap a warm welcome signalled that Tommy had arrived in second place as he made a dramatically low crossing of the line, Tommy's average speed for the race was 160.5 mph.

In 1937 Tommy flew the Miles M.2L Hawk Speed Six, G-ADGP, with a Gipsy Six 1 engine and Race No. 8. Tommy was now aged forty-two, had won the King's Cup Air

Race in 1935 and beaten Amy Mollison's time to Cape Town and back, could he pull off another win in 1937?

Nineteen different types of aircraft were entered in the race and *Flight* for 9 September 1937 reported:

> *Perhaps the best known and certainly the most popular of our sporting pilots, Tommy Rose, is a previous King's Cup winner – in 1935, flying a Miles Falcon and was second last year in a Hawk Speed Six. Has any number of other air-race and long-distance record successes to his credit, including a Cape Town flight last year – in the Falcon – in 3 days 17 hours 38 minutes, with a return trip almost as fast. Was once instructor at Sywell, then sales demonstrator and test pilot at Phillips and Powis, and is now flying representative of the distillers of an 'aviation spirit' of high-octane value – Seagers's gin, is not in favour of the revised 1937 course.*

Chapter 13

World Air Speed Record UK to Cape Town and back January – May 1936

'It is as though we have grown wings, which thanks to providence we have learned to control.'
– Louis Blériot (1872-1936),
Atlantic Monoplanes of Tomorrow

Flying at this time featured many celebrities, heroes, risk takers, and of course the record breakers. It also has to be remembered the aircraft that these aviators and aviatrixes were flying were relatively primitive in design, compared to the aircraft we know today. They were mostly biplanes with open cockpits and very little instrumentation. By the 1930s there was an exponential growth in aircraft construction, with wood and fabric slowly giving way to metal stressed skin. Fully enclosed cockpits were being being introduced and some aircraft were being fitted with retractable undercarriages. It was also the age of the development of the airliners.

Many of the large aeroplane manufacturers were trying to develop commercially viable aircraft and the smaller aircraft designed for the flying clubs and private aviator were being entered into air races, mostly organised by the Royal Aero Club, but often hosted by the fledgling flying clubs opening up the length and breadth of the UK. These races were raising the profiles of not only the manufacturers but also of their pilots.

The Schlesinger Race, also known as the 'Rand Race', or the 'Portsmouth to Johannesburg race', or even more commonly the 'African Air Race', took place in September 1936. The Royal Aero Club announced it, on behalf of Isidore Schlesinger, who wanted to promote the Empire Exhibition in South Africa. Schlesinger also offered a total of £10,000 in prize money to be divided into two sections, a speed race and a handicap race. The two sections flown concurrently, but no competitor could have both prizes.

However, it was believed at the time that Schlesinger made a fundamental error by restricting the entries to British Empire crews and British machines only. This led to a smaller number of aircraft being entered and only one machine completing the course, many either failed, crashed, or just simply gave up. In September 1936 Tommy Rose flew in the Schlesinger race with Jack Bradshaw, a South African, in the BA Double Eagle IV G-AEIN, hoping his lucky streak would continue. Sadly, the Double Eagle suffered persistently from air locks in the fuel system, and Tommy Rose had already lost a good deal of time making special unscheduled landings. His run of bad luck continued when the undercarriage legs partially retracted while taxiing at Cairo. At the time it was thought something could be done about it, but not within the time period to secure him a place in the final.

Flight Lieutenant Thomas Rose DFC will be remembered not only for winning the King's Cup race on 7 September 1935 in the Miles Falcon G-ADLC, with its Gipsy Six 200hp engine, at the speed of 176 mph, but also for beating one of Amy Johnson's speed records to Cape Town, South Africa.

Amy Johnson set up one of these speed records to the Cape Town in November 1932, taking the shorter Western route (6,300 miles) in her Puss Moth G-ACAB in 4 days, 6 hours, 56 minutes, beating her husband's 1932 record of 4 days, 17 hours 22 mins by 10 hours 28 minutes. Tommy Rose subsequently broke this record by flying from England to the Cape in 3 days 17 hours 37 minutes, and then from the Cape to London in 6 days 7 hours, thereby breaking the record for both stages.

This record-breaking attempt was made in the same aircraft in which he won the King's Cup in 1935, in the Miles Falcon Six. The newspapers at the time all asked, *'Can Tommy set up a new record? Will Tommy achieve a double?'* The double was the speed record from Lympne airfield in Kent to Cape Town in South Africa and the return journey.

Tommy Rose initially told the press he was going to Cape Town on business on behalf of Phillips and Powis Aircraft Ltd., the builders of the Falcon Six. However, if you have got to go on business abroad, why not make the journey the fastest trip on record?

These early pioneering record flights involved monumental physical and mental stamina in order to endure sitting alone in a cabin for hours on end. Having the fuel stored correctly and sent out ahead to be made available at suitable safe landing areas, there were very few landing strips, just clearings in the landscape flat enough and sufficiently long enough to land safely, some major cities did have satisfactory airports to land at.

Tommy Rose, thankfully was already a very fit man, having played competitive Rugby and he also used his RAF contacts to help him get into mental and physical shape to focus for this monumental journey ahead of him.

In his article in *Popular Flying* magazine for May 1936, titled 'How to do that there 'ere', after his successful return from Cape Town, Tommy Rose, with his wry sense of humour, shared his views on the subject as follows:

> *Before one starts to attempt to fly to some place a long way away, quicker than anyone else has done before, it is necessary to do the following:*

- *Get hold of the world's best aeroplane and see it is fitted with the world's best engine.*
- *Arrange for supplies of fuel and oil at places one intends to stop at (and also at the places one does not!).*
- *Undergo a course of sitting absolutely still for long periods and lay in stock of lightning corn cure.*
- *Arrange that the weather shall be perfect the whole way, and that every wind shall be a following one.*

FLIGHT LIEUTENANT THOMAS 'TOMMY' ROSE DFC

Having assured every enquirer beforehand that the projected trip is purely a business one, it will be found that at every landing place one is besieged by newspaper reporters, who wish to know what the trip has been like so far. If one is able to assure them that it was absolutely uneventful, their faces drop, and they go away and invent some hair-raising episode which did not occur. If one tries to be kind to them and think of some little incident to brighten their lives, they will then go away and spend whole bags of gold cabling back to their respective newspapers exactly how the pilot looked death straight in the eye (and was very frightened).

It will be seen, therefore, that it was far better to say always that the flight was uneventful.

It is extremely unwise to eat or drink anything before one reaches one's destination, especially should this be in South Africa. One is treated to such a surfeit of food and drink by the hospitable people of this great country that it is difficult to hang out and one's only solace is in the fact that on the return trip one will be able to once again starve and get thirsty.

One should also avoid saying the following things, should one be fortunate enough to succeed:

- *'The engine and machine are wonderful'. Of course, they must be, otherwise a damn fool like oneself would never have got there as quickly.*
- *'Your women are the most wonderful in the world'. This is most dangerous. sooner or later one has to return home and deny having said it.*
- *'Of course, I will let you have a short article, old boy'. If you do, the editor invariably throws it in the wastepaper basket, writes one himself under your names and never speaks to you again.*
- *'I will be very glad to reply to the toast to the guests'. This is most awkward, because not only does one inevitably make a bad speech, owing to the amount of refreshment provided beforehand, but none of the other guests speak to you because they all think they should have been asked to do it.*

In conclusion, quite seriously I would urge all those private owners who can spare the time to go down across Africa and see Rhodesia and the Union of South Africa for themselves. Despite statements which have appeared to the contrary, I would say it is a grand country to fly in, its people are the most hospitable and kindly I have ever met and the climate is just too good to be true.

The flying club movement is just getting cracking along everywhere. For a number of years there have been two clubs operating at Johannesburg, and they have fourteen to sixteen aircraft in great demand all the time. The airports of the main towns are as near perfect as can be. The airport of Johannesburg, at Germiston, is one of the most efficiently run and certainly the most up-to-date aerodrome I have ever been on.

Contrary to general belief, if one's papers are in order and one does not carry a camera unsealed, there is no difficulty whatsoever in passing over Italian territory. It is necessary however to fly over it, to follow the route laid down and avoid prohibited areas and, finally, to return the courtesy of the Italian officials in a like manner.

Finally, in flying across Africa, at any rate between Khartoum and Salisbury, pin your faith in the old compass, as sometimes quite large mountains are marked on the map between 50 and 100 miles from the places they actually exist.

There is only one real way to ensure success, and that is to have the man who arranges weather conditions out to dinner every night before you leave, so that you can be assured of 100 miles visibility and 60 mph tail winds all the way.

And that's that.

The Outward Journey

The first of these events was when he first took off on his 'business' flight to the Cape from Lympne early on Tuesday, 7 January 1936. When he took off the weather was fine, but low clouds hung over the aerodrome, and a strong south-westerly wind blew in gusts. Owing to the heavy nature of the ground, the machine became stuck while taxiing to the starting point, and the engine stopped. The mechanics rushed across the aerodrome and were able to overcome the difficulty by pushing the plane as the engine raced. After twice circling the aerodrome the plane disappeared, but some minutes later it returned.

On Wednesday, 5 February 1936, the Miles Falcon was filled with approximately 116 gallons of fuel and with this the aircraft had a range of 1,000 miles. It was considered that with this range and the speed available, Tommy Rose would have a very good chance of breaking the journey south, even though he was going to use the longer East African route as opposed to Amy's West Coast Route.

The machine was repaired and Tommy departed from Lympne a second time on 6 February 1936. The weather reports were favourable as he left on his second attempt, but he was forced down two miles from Abbeville, France, owing to rain clouds increasing as he crossed the Channel.

Tommy Rose stressed at the time that he was just going on a business flight to sell aircraft, as he was the sales manager for Phillips and Powis, although, if at the same time he could break the record set by Amy Johnson, he would certainly like to do so. It was obvious from newspaper articles available at the time, that the public also hoped he would be successful.

FLIGHT LIEUTENANT THOMAS 'TOMMY' ROSE DFC

The Aeroplane for 12 February 1936 reported on the flight as follows:

Flight Lieutenant Tom Rose DFC, who won the race for the King's Cup on 7 September 1935 at 176 mph in the Miles Falcon (Gipsy 200hp) G-ADLC, started from Lympne on February 6 in the same machine, twenty-five minutes after midnight (GMT). He landed at Malta (1,260 miles) at 09.20 hrs (GMT) and left at 10.40 hrs. At 17.15 hrs (GMT) he landed at Almaza, Cairo (1,106 miles) and left at 22.10 hrs. He arrived at Khartoum (1,037 miles) at 12.00 hrs (GMT) on February 7 and left at 12.25 hrs.

On February 8 he reached Kisumu (1,088 miles) at 05.30 hrs (GMT) and left again at 06.55 hrs. He landed at dusk 80 miles south of Salisbury (Southern Rhodesia) after missing the town in a bad storm. He damaged the wheel fairings, which were repaired at Salisbury when he returned there in the morning. He left Salisbury (1,260 miles) at 06.00 hrs on February 9 (GMT) and landed at Cape Town (1,383 miles) at 18.03 hrs - (total 7,134 miles).

His route followed that of Imperial Airways and his time was 3 days, 17 hours and 37 minutes. He beat the previous best time made by Mrs Mollison, who flew the shorter Western route (6,300 miles) by 13 hrs 19 mins (her actual elapsed time being 4 days, 6 hours, 56 minutes). He was fresh when he arrived, though he had had but two hours' sleep and had not used the special tablets to prevent sleepiness, which he had carried with him.

One particular highlight in the trip was the very short time (14 hours) which he took to reach Cairo (2,366 miles). He had two mishaps. A petrol leak was caused by carelessly packing a suitcase against an ordinary metal petrol pipe. He was lucky it did not happen over the Mediterranean. This forced him back to Wadi Halfa for repairs. The second mishap was that he had to return to Salisbury to refuel after passing it in failing light during a bad patch of weather. Without these troubles he would certainly have clipped one whole day from the previous best flight to the Cape.

Flight Lieutenant Tom Rose had a distinguished war record in the RFC and RAF. He brought down more than a dozen enemy machines and earned the DFC (he actually destroyed nine enemy aircraft and shared in the destruction of another two). For some years he was chief instructor to the Midland Aero Club at Castle Bromwich. Then he went to the Anglo-American Oil Co Ltd (and while working for them in 1931, he made an attempt at the record to the Cape in the Avro Avian G-ABIE High Test but failed to reach it on the outward flight and then failed to break the record on the return flight). Thereafter he was chief instructor and manager at Sywell. And always and everywhere he was immensely popular. In 1934 he went as sales manager to Phillips & Powis Aircraft Ltd of Woodley Reading. Besides all that he earned four caps for RAF rugger against the Army and Navy in 1924-7 and he is one of the best all-round sportsmen and pilots whom we have the pleasure of knowing.

WORLD AIR SPEED RECORD UK TO CAPE TOWN AND BACK

After the record-breaking flight to the Cape, Tommy sent a telegram to the firm which read 'Preggers definitely Primus'!

On 3 March 1936 he left Cape Town on his return trip and *The Aeroplane* for 11 March 1936 reported:

> *Flight Lieutenant Tom Rose DFC left Cape Town on his return trip to London on March 3 at 04.08 hrs (GMT) in the same Miles Falcon (Gipsy Six) G-ADLC which won the King's Cup in 1935, and in which he made his recent record flight to the Cape in 3 days 17 hrs 38 mins. The previous best recorded time for the return journey was made in 1935 by David Llewellyn and Mrs Jill Wyndham, who flew the Hendy Heck home in*

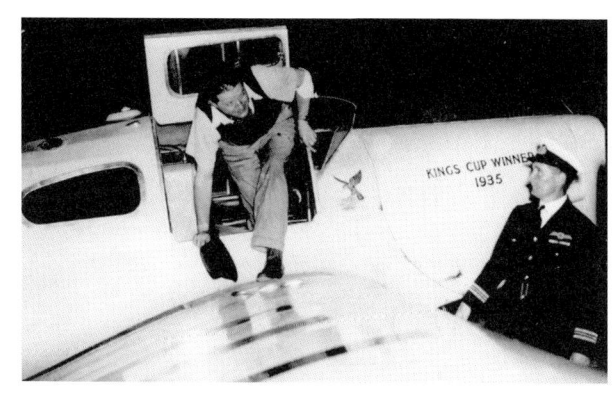

On 9 February 1936, Tommy Rose arrived at Cape Town, achieving his record time: 3 days, 17 hours and 37 minutes from Lympne, UK.
(*Nigel Gaudion collection*)

On the reverse of the photo: 'ARRIVAL OF BRITISH FLIER IN RECORD FLIGHT.

Flight Lieutenant Thomas Rose is lifted to the shoulders of admirers, upon arrival in Cape Town, South Africa, at the conclusion of his record-breaking flight from England. He clipped 13 hours off the previous record, negotiating the distance in 3 days, 17 hours, and 38 mins'. (*Nigel Gaudion Collection*)

FLIGHT LIEUTENANT THOMAS 'TOMMY' ROSE DFC

6 days 12 hrs 3 mins but were denied an official record for the flight because they failed to average more than 150 km per hr over the Great Circle course between the two places. Rose had waited two days for a break in the general bad weather.

He arrived in Bulawayo at 12.30 hrs and at Salisbury at 16.40 hrs. On March 4, after being twice forced back by low cloud and heavy rain, he left Salisbury at 10.45 hrs and reached Mbeya for the night. On March 5 he got to Kisumu, Lake Victoria, at 09.40 hrs, and took off for Juba at 11.30 hrs. On March 6 he arrived at Khartoum at 09.30 hrs and reached Cairo the same day at 20.07 hrs, thus fracturing all records between the Cape and Cairo.

Going out he had landed at Malta but he was forbidden to land there on the way back – perhaps the Admiralty feared lest the superior performance of the Falcon might dishearten the inhabitants. So, he was obliged to go by way of Tunis. On March 7 at 04.00 hrs he left Cairo and arrived at Benghazi, Tripoli, at 10.40 hrs. His chances of beating the record by more than 24 hrs began to look promising, but he was arrested by the Italians for flying over a prohibited area. He was detained during the rest of March 7 while the authorities conferred. A telegram to his wife, a telephone from her to Mr Harold Perrin, c/o Mr Lindsay Everard at Ratcliffe, and a cable from him to Marshal Balbo had immediate effect. The Falcon was de-gaoled to start next day.

On March 8 he left early, took off from Tunis at 14.26 hrs, and landed at Cannes at 16.30 hrs. On March 9, at daybreak, he left Cannes and arrived at Croydon at 11.05 hrs with five hours in hand. The Lord Mayor, Sir Percy Vincent, and the Lady Mayoress received him at the Mansion House at 13.00 hrs.

The total distance by the route he took is 7,863 miles. And considering that he lost a whole day in Tripoli, his time – 6 days 7 hrs – was very good going. The Great Circle Course is just on 6,000 miles, so his speed is not enough to be homologated as a record.

Less than a month later Tommy Rose began his homeward flight and this too, broke the existing time for the north bound route set up by Flying Officer David Llewellyn and

Tommy Rose inside the Miles Falcon, newly returned from his record-breaking flight, photo signed by him 'With best wishes, Tom Rose, 1936'. (*via Peter Amos*)

WORLD AIR SPEED RECORD UK TO CAPE TOWN AND BACK

Left: Croydon Airport, 1936, on Tommy Rose's arrival back in the UK. (*Nigel Gaudion collection*)

Above: Tommy Rose welcomed back at Croydon airport by Blossom and F.G. Miles. (*Nigel Gaudion collection*)

Mrs Jill Wyndham in November the previous year. Their time was 6 days 12 hours and 17minutes, their time was bettered by twenty minutes.

At forty-one, 'try again Tommy Rose' had the luck that had eluded him for five years.

Radio message from Cape Town

The Scotsman 4 August 1936.
It was reported later by the newspaper, that Tommy Rose was amused to be referred to by the Deputy Mayor of Cape Town from the recording studio as, '*Mr Tommy Mollison, who had just flown from England in 37 days 16 hours and 7 mins*'. One can imagine Tommy Rose chuckling away to himself.

Tommy was quoted as saying '*that he avoided boredom during a flight by peeling oranges and practicing blowing pips through the partially opened window.*'

Below is the transcript of that message:

>**Cape Town calling London**
>*Flight lieutenant Tommy Rose is going to tell you about his record-breaking flight to the Cape.*
>*Ladies and Gentlemen – Flight Lieutenant Rose.*
>*Good evening everybody. It seems weeks since I left England instead of just over four days. Sitting alone in the air for three days was very good for me because it makes one realise how utterly insignificant mere man is compared to the varied wonders of nature one passes over between England and the Cape.*

FLIGHT LIEUTENANT THOMAS 'TOMMY' ROSE DFC

Having no one to hold my hand on the trip, I found myself looking on the full moon as my friend on the night hop and the sun during the daytime. This probably sounds funny, but it is very comforting to make oneself believe that two such powerful things are on one's side.

As we are limited to time, I can only mention a few outstanding instances of the flight. First of all, the machine is the same one as I obtained from Lady Wakefield in this year's King's Cup Race, with such fortunate result. The first instance that stays in my mind was whilst looking down on Paris at 2am from a Cirrus cloud – it was incredibly beautiful. The next was the Mediterranean crossing as I flew over the sea from Malta to Mersah Matru. That was about 700 miles and took just over four hours.

As it was raining, I was at 50 feet most of the way as I've done many times before I said that if I can only get to land, I'll never do this again. After Wadi Halfar I had a very bad petrol leak in the cabin and a forced landing was an immediate necessity. It was just dawn and by sheer good fortune or luck, I was able to bring off a landing 50 miles from the nearest living person and more than 100 miles from water.

If anything had happened that time to the machine I should be there yet.

And then flying down across Rhodesia, after miles and miles and miles of bush, I suddenly came on a little farmhouse in a clearing. In front of this small farmhouse was a flagstaff and at the top of this flagstaff was a small Union Jack. It aroused my emotions most intensely and I was very proud I was under that flag.

On the way to the range, just south of Salisbury, I was forced onto the ground by a cloudburst. People think possibly in England that is impossible. If anyone had told me the same thing before I should have agreed that it was impossible that the machine, which had come through so well, could not stand against this unheard-of weight. Then, just at the critical moment, a clearing appeared in the bush and at full throttle, she landed without any damage whatsoever.

At Cape Town the welcome was indescribably boisterous, and I think was the most arduous part of the whole journey.

I would like to thank all my friends who were wishing me well during the trip. I am convinced that it was their thoughts that got things right, when everything seemed likely to go wrong during the last day and a half of really filthy weather.

The machine and engine were just perfect and that is poor praise, all I had to do was sit in and ever so slightly put everything in the right direction.

In case my friends at Reading Aerodrome are listening in, I can assure them that theirs was a job well done and I am grateful to every one of them for their help, and they can rest assured that no one realises more than I how much the success of the flight was due to them. If the weather improves, I shall have a go again coming back, but if it is still raining in Rhodesia, I shall be coming back on a bicycle!

Good night everyone and God Bless.

WORLD AIR SPEED RECORD UK TO CAPE TOWN AND BACK

Tommy Rose's account of the whole journey in his own words

Extracts from the *Reading Review* of April 1936:

'On the Mediterranean crossing, that is between Malta and the coast of Africa, I was not so lucky. The crossing was one of 700 miles and it was raining hard all the time. I had to fly at 50 feet most of the way, and as I have often done before (and probably shall again), I said to myself, 'If I can only get to land, I'll never do this again'. Sometime after leaving Cairo, I suddenly noticed a strong smell of petrol in the cabin, and on investigation found that a petrol pipe had been fractured owing to a suitcase vibrating against it, so a forced landing was an immediate necessity. It was just dawn and by sheer good luck I was able to pull off a landing in very wild country, 150 miles from the nearest living person, and 100 miles from water. I managed to repair the leak (at Wadi Halfa – SC) and took off again, arriving at Khartoum at noon, where the Falcon was refuelled. The next lap was to Kisumu, which I reached at 5.30 am on the morning of the eighth, and after an hour's rest I carried on to Salisbury. During this leg of the course, after flying across miles and miles of bush country, I suddenly came across a little farmhouse set in a small clearing. In front of this farm there was a flagstaff, and on top of this fluttered a small Union Jack. This sight aroused my emotions very intensely, and I felt very proud to think that I was flying under the same flag.

Just south of Salisbury, which I completely missed owing to bad visibility, I ran into a torrential cloudburst and was literally forced to the ground. This may seem strange to those used to flying in England, and if I had been told of it beforehand, I should not have believed it myself. However, the good old machine, which had come through so much could not stand this immense weight of water and was forced lower and lower. At the critical moment a clearing appeared ahead, and she landed at full throttle and without damage. In the morning I got off again and returned to Salisbury, where the tanks were refilled, and took off on the last lap to Cape Town, which was reached at about 6 pm just as dark was falling.

The next three weeks were spent in making business flights around the Union, and on the morning of March 3 I regretfully bade farewell to South Africa and took off at 4.08 am for England. The weather did not behave very kindly to me on the way back, as I had to contend with headwinds nearly all the way. At times these reached 60 mph and brought my cruising speed from 150 down to 90 mph. The flight back was done along the same route as the outgoing journey, with the exception that I had to cut out Malta owing to the aerodrome being prohibited for landplanes at the moment. I decided to land at

FLIGHT LIEUTENANT THOMAS 'TOMMY' ROSE DFC

Benghazi aerodrome in Tripoli. As I reached the 'drome the Italians fired every kind of rocket they could into the sky in order to bring me in to land. Down I came and was nearly arrested for flying over an Italian prohibited area! I said that I did not know it, but this did not help. However, when the authorities learned that I was trying to beat the record they were very helpful, and I was enabled to cable to England, where Commander Perrin of the Royal Aero Club at once sent a telegram to General Balbo, who is governor of Italian Tripoli, and on Sunday morning I was 'released'. I reached Cannes on Sunday night and left for Croydon early on Monday the ninth, arriving there at four minutes past eleven.'

Below is the report on Tommy Rose's return to the UK from the *Nottingham Evening Post* 9 March 1936.

The headline line read:

WINS THROUGH ON THIRD ATTEMPT

London to the Cape	Cape to London in
3 days 17½ hours	6 days 7 hours

POPULAR AIRMAN WITH BRILLIANT RECORD

Flight Lieutenant Tommy Rose landed at Croydon aerodrome at 11.50 a.m. today having broken the outward and inward Cape records. His time from the Cape was 6 days 6 hours 57 minutes.

A few seconds after the fawn-coloured machine was sighted, coming at good speed, it circled over the airport and landed at the centre of the aerodrome. A minute later Rose had taxied to the tarmac, where he was at once surrounded by friends.

Cars with movie cameras on their roofs circled round to take 'shots' of him as he emerged from the cockpit. He was wearing a soft felt hat and had a light scarf around his throat.

He was quite casual about his achievement. 'Well, well well'! was all he said as he shook the many hands stretched to greet him.

He had a slight mishap when, in response to photographers, he climbed back in to pose for a picture. His foot damaged part of the fabric near the cockpit. Then surrounded by cheering friends, he walked across towards the aerodrome.

At noon Rose left by car for the Mansion House. He had brought with him a letter from the Lord Mayor of Cape Town for the Lord Mayor of London, and his visit to the Mansion House was to deliver this letter and to stay to lunch with the Lord Mayor.

Prior to leaving Croydon, Rose said to the 'Post': *'I am glad to be back. I am very pleased to have broken the records both outward and inward'.*

WORLD AIR SPEED RECORD UK TO CAPE TOWN AND BACK

Asked how he was feeling he said, 'Oh! very fit. I could not wish to feel better'. Among those who welcomed the airman back at Croydon was Mr Fred Miles, the designer of the plane in which the records were achieved. With him was his wife – a daughter of Sir Johnstone Forbes-Robertson – who played a prominent part in the work of designing.

As Rose forced his way through the crowd towards a waiting motor car, he was asked what sort of a flight he had had on his way back. 'Oh! Headwinds all the way', he said.

'And the delay on Saturday at Benghazi on the Libyan coast? A matter of permits', he replied. Then he stepped into his car and drove away.

His flight has won for him the distinction of a record between London and Cape Town in both directions.

His outward flight at the beginning of February was accomplished in 3 days 17 hours 38 mins. By this feat he smashed Mrs Amy Mollison's solo flight record of 1932 by 13 hours 16 mins.

The Cape Town – London record was previously held by Flying Officer D. Llewelyn, who shortened the time of the journey to 6 days 12 hours 17 minutes last November.

Tommy left Cape Town at 4.08 a.m. (G.M.T.) on Tuesday. He said he was 'not going very fast'; when asked if he thought of attempting to break David Llewellyn's record.

TRIUMPH OVER PERSERVERENCE

'But', he added, 'I hope to be in London by Saturday'. His outward dash was a triumph over perseverance.

He had been attempting to 'bring it off' since 1930, but each time met with bad luck. On his first attempt he crashed in Africa after covering nearly 6,000 miles.

He tried again in January of this year, but was compelled to come down at Abbeville, France, by a heavy snowstorm.

But Tommy Rose never knows defeat and once more he set off on February 6 with the optimistic belief 'third time lucky'.

It nearly wasn't, for Tommy Rose had to come down just south of Salisbury, Southern Rhodesia. He landed in a desolate hump-backed country and made desperate attempts to reach the aerodrome 30 miles away.

He found it impossible at first but managed to take off again at dawn and reached Salisbury.

When he left there, he ran into tropical deluges and was driven off his course, but eventually landed at Mafeking and borrowed 12 gallons of petrol from an RAF pilot which enabled him to go on to Kimberley – and still achieve his great ambition.

Tommy Rose is one of the most popular men in British aviation and is regarded as one of the best pilots in the world.

FLIGHT LIEUTENANT THOMAS 'TOMMY' ROSE DFC

He began flying during the war, serving first in the RFC, and then in the RAF. He brought down a dozen (he actually destroyed nine enemy aircraft and shared the destruction of another two – SC) *German aeroplanes, and won the D.F.C.*

On one occasion he was shot down but succeeded in landing behind enemy lines. He stepped out of the cockpit and saw a car passing along the road. The passengers alighted, and walked over to the forlorn airman, standing by his wrecked machine. One of them sympathised with him. It was King George V. Last year Rose won the Kings Cup air race.

Details of Tommy Rose's flights to and from the Cape are as follows:

Outward Flight

6 February	*12.25 a.m., Left Lympne. Arrived Malta 9.20 a.m.*
	10.40 a.m. Left Malta. Arrived Cairo 5.15 p.m.
	10.10 p.m. Left Cairo.
7 February	*Arrived Khartoum 12 noon.*
	12.25 p.m. Left Khartoum.
8 February	*Arrived Kisumu Kenya 5.30 a.m.*
	6.55 a.m. Left Kisumu.
9 February	*Left Salisbury Southern Rhodesia 6 a.m.*
	Arrived Cape Town 6.03pm.

Return Flight

3 March	*4.08am Left Cape Town.*
	4.40p.m. Arrived Salisbury Southern Rhodesia, via Bulawayo.
4 March	*4.45 a.m. Left Salisbury.*
5 March	*9.10 a.m. Arrived Kisumu Kenya.*
	11.30 a.m. Left Kisumu Kenya.
6 March	*11.30 a.m. (local time) Arrived Khartoum via Juba.*
	8.0 p.m. Arrived Cairo via Wadi Halfa.
7 March	*4.00 a.m. Left Cairo.*
7 March	*10.40 a.m. Held up at Benghazi Tripoli.*
8 March	*4.30 p.m. Arrived at Cannes.*
9 March	*5.55 a.m. Left Cannes.*
	7.30 a.m. Arrived Lyons.
	7.51 a.m. Left Lyons.
	Arrived Croydon 11.5 a.m.

On his return to the UK Tommy Rose gave a talk on Southsea pier which was reported in the *Portsmouth Evening News* 3 April 1936. He spoke with great affection about his Miles Falcon, and the trip to Cape Town, stating on two occasions he had decided to drop by parachute in snow and in a raging storm, but was saved by freaks of fortune, of landing in a clearing, when the plane was forced down by torrential rain and on landing discovered the ammunition packed with his revolver did not fit. He also vowed never to fly over the Mediterranean after 4.5 hours of nothing but sea. He extolled the beauty of Paris by night, and of the splendour of Cape Town. I am sure he told a very compelling story to an enraptured audience.

After the 1935 Kings Cup Race Tommy Rose re-named the Falcon Six *'Preggers Primus'* (Primus being Latin for 'the first') and although it was duly christened thus, it was still usually known as *Preggers*.

Aberdeen Press and Journal 13 February 1936 reported:

TOMMY MEETS GENERAL HERTZOG
Intends to Endow Hospital Bed. Tommy, who broke the record for an England to the Cape flight, yesterday took tea with the Prime Minister, General Hertzog. He also saw General Smuts. A bed in the new Cape Town Hospital as a memorial to the lost airman, Sir Charles Kingsford-Smith, has been suggested by Tommy as a way of spending the proceeds of the exhibition of the record-breaking machine and of the sale of a souvenir brochure of the event.

Mr Rose also intends to endow a bed to the hospital himself.

However, the flight home was not without its problems and the *Yorkshire Post and Leeds Intelligencer* of Tuesday, 10 March 1936 reported:

THE HOLD UP
Rose's flight had not been without adventures. It was revealed yesterday how Marshal Balbo, Governor of Libya, intervened personally, when the airman was held up at Benghazi over (as Rose said on landing) 'a matter of permits.'

Commander Harold Perrin, secretary of the Royal Aero Club, said yesterday, 'On Saturday, about midnight, I received word in Leicestershire that Tommy was in difficulties with the authorities at Benghazi. I at once sent a telegram to Marshal Balbo and yesterday I received this reply sent by him immediately he had my wire': 'As soon as I got your telegram and heard of the arrival in Benghazi of Tommy, I immediately gave orders that he should be allowed to proceed, notwithstanding that he had not followed the prescribed route. Am always happy to show courtesy to English aviators,' Marshal Balbo.

The successful record-breaking attempt by Tommy resulted in the proliferation of advertising material below, all the companies involved in every part of aviation wanted Tommy Rose's endorsement of their products.

Tommy Rose was now in great demand, especially after the King's Cup win in 1935, and as they say, 'everybody loves a winner'. Tommy Rose had come a long way from

FLIGHT LIEUTENANT THOMAS 'TOMMY' ROSE DFC

Above left: An advertisement from *Flight*, 12 March 1936.

Above right: Photo taken in 1936. Tommy Rose used to sometimes fly Viscountess Wakefield's sponsored aircraft in major air races.

his failed attempt in 1931, now completely forgotten by his adoring followers, he had at last made his mark in aviation history, Tommy Rose had become a national hero.

On his return to the UK Tommy Rose was in great demand and commenced a series of talks about his African adventure commencing with a talk with cine film and slides at Southsea Pier theatre, which was completely sold out, such was Tommy Rose's popularity at the time.

The *Portsmouth Evening News* for 3 April 1936 reported:

TOMMY AT SOUTHSEA: HIS ADVENTURE STORY.
The long-distance and record-breaking flight is today a thing which appeals to the adventurous imagination of all ages, and a graphic description of such a flight, its perils, incidents and strokes of good and bad fortune is something which makes memorable hearing.

Last evening, and yesterday afternoon the famous Flight Lieutenant Tommy Rose DFC, whose early life at Petersfield makes him almost a local production, told audiences at the South Parade Pier of his great flight to South Africa and back, which finished with both records broken on March 8 last.

His 'plane', which he spoke of with much personal affection, was a Miles Falcon, equipped with a Gipsy VI engine, and their adventures before this journey was done. Tommy told a vivid tale of two occasions when he had decided to drop by parachute, in snow and in storm, but was saved by freaks of fortune; of landing in an isolated Rhodesian clearing, when the plane was forced down by rain, and when he found the ammunition packed with the revolver would not fit; of his vow never to fly over sea if possible after four and a half hours of the Mediterranean; of forced landings on hills and the many momentous decisions; of the beauty of Paris from the air by night, and of the splendour of Cape Town and Johannesburg, which he illustrated by slides; and finally his ambition to maintain the respect and friendship of the many friends in aviation and other spheres during his meteoric career.

His story was told in the amusingly and almost self-deprecatory tones of the typical RAF officer, but the wonderful tales of the modern 'Magic Carpet' which he told will long be remembered by his listeners, who gave him a warm ovation.

TOMMY THINKS AMY CAN DO IT IN TWO DAYS
'I see no reason why Amy should not get to the Cape in two days', said Flight Lieutenant Tommy Rose, holder of the record for both ways between here and South African to an Evening News *representative at the South Parade Pier.*

'She is once again using the Western route across Africa, upon which she previously broke the record, and I used the all-Red route, down to the East of the Continent. She has a much faster plane'.

'If she does it, I suppose we shall have to find a British plane to beat it, and perhaps somebody will come along and ask me to beat Amy's record again.'

Flight Lieutenant T. Rose, who is appearing at the Pier with his travelogue, 'Mr Life in the Air,' later made a brief appearance at the Hippodrome stage, has only been back in England about three weeks since beating the return record to the Cape.

Tommy is still remembered well by country and farming people in the Petersfield district, for his father was bailiff and agent to Colonel W.G. Nicholson at Basing Park, and the famous airman spent all his young years there, his first school being Churcher's College, which he left in 1911. Several of his old school fellows and others from Petersfield greeted him at the Pier last night.

By Monday, 4 May, Tommy Rose had another official booking to undertake, this time he had lost his voice, not wishing to disappoint anyone he appeared, but couldn't speak.
The Eastbourne Gazette Wednesday, 6 May 1936 reported:

TOMMY HAS LOST HIS VOICE
CAPE FLIGHT HERO AT NEW SHOWROOM
Acting against doctor's orders, Flight Lieutenant Tommy Rose, who recently made the record flight to the Cape, flew from Reading to Eastbourne on Monday to be present at the opening of the new showroom in Cornfield Road of Langney Motors.

Many guests attended the informal opening of the showroom in the morning, and at luncheon at the Clifton Hotel, including Lieutenant

FLIGHT LIEUTENANT THOMAS 'TOMMY' ROSE DFC

Colonel M. Grahame-White, Mr R. Cardwell, Mr H. Williott, Mrs Bovill and Mrs Short.

As Flight Lieutenant Rose was unable to speak, Mr D.H. Noble, publicity manager for Hillman Humber and Coventry, proposed success to Langney Motors, coupling with the toast the name of Mr B.F. Bovill. In apologising for Flight Lieutenant Rose, Mr Noble said that in his flight, he out-distanced sound and his voice had not got back yet. (Laughter)

The new showrooms featured Hillman, Humber and Talbot Cars.

An interesting insight into Tommy Rose's persona and his candid thoughts on long flights and record attempts were documented in the newspaper article written about a talk Tommy Rose gave to members of the Eastbourne Rotary Club in May 1936.

Eastbourne Gazette Wednesday, 6 May 1936 reported:

TOMMY ON LONG FLIGHTS SAYS RECORD ATTEMPTS ARE 'LARGELY BUNKHAM'.

This big flight business is bunkham! The authority for that picturesquely phrased piece of information is Flight Lieutenant Tommy Rose, and he should know, for he hit the headlines in all the national newspapers when he smashed all records for the flight from London to the Cape. In a talk to the Round Table at Stewart's Café on Monday, he summed up the whole business in those few words:

'All long-distance flights are largely bunkhum. The National Newspapers, if there is no other news at the time, whip up an interest in these flights, and if one gets there safely and breaks a record everyone thinks, "By gad, here's one of the twelve apostles come to life!" (Laughter). 'But I assure you there is nothing in it.

'The only things you have got to do to be successful are to get the best machine you can find, and practice sitting still for a long, long time'.

Reflections wise and witty on flying in general and his own flight in particular made Flight Lieutenant Rose's talk one of the most delightful and amusing to which Tablers have listened to for a long time. His visit was arranged by Tabler S.A. Perry and Captain E.I. Short.

His racy manner produced a laugh at almost every sentence, and a more unassuming world record breaker than this genial young man would be difficult to find.

There was one richly humorous story which is worth repeating. 'When I eventually got to the Cape, I had to broadcast to the Union,' he said. 'The announcer seemed very nervous and this is what he said: "Who do you think I have here in the studio? None other than Mr Tom Mollison, who flew from London to the Cape in 37 days 18 hours". I met General Hertzog a few days later and he said: "If it takes all that time to fly, don't you think you had better come by boat next time?" 'Flight Lieutenant Rose answered a number of questions and urged the need for municipalities laying down ground for aircraft.

Members of the Rotary Club and of other Round Tables were present, as guests, to hear the airman's talk.

On 12 June Tommy was welcomed back at Sywell for the official opening of the new clubhouse, where he got another great reception.

The *Bath Chronicle and Weekly Gazette* Saturday, 6 August 1936 reported:

TOMMY'S TALES.
Comedies of his record flight to South Africa
Some amusing stories were told by Flight Lieutenant T. Rose, the old Bath and Somerset Rugby football forward, to those attending the City of London Vacation Course in London on Monday, when he was the guest of honour at their luncheon.

After referring to his recent record flight to South Africa, Flight Lieutenant Rose told how he was announced by the Deputy Mayor of Cape Town from the studio there as 'Mr Tommy Rose Mollison who had just flown from England in 37 days 16 hours and 7 minutes'.

On his return journey he happened to hear the 'dulcet' tones of a news broadcast from Droitwich at Benghazi, where he was held up for a time by the Italians. The announcer read, 'Mr Tommy passed over Benghazi at nine o'clock this morning and is expected at Croydon at any moment'.

He added that his method of avoiding boredom during the flight was to peel oranges and practice blowing the pips through a partially opened window.

All records are set up to be beaten and after Tommy Rose's triumphant record-breaking attempt, the press was reporting the possibility of Amy Mollison's intention to beat Tommy Rose's new record.

Tommy Rose flew in the Eastbourne Gala Day on Saturday, 16 August. In September Tommy Rose was in training for the South Africa Race (the Schlesinger African Air Race), this time his 'mount' was to be the BA Double Eagle G-AEIN, starting on Tuesday, 29 September.

In the book, *MOLLISON The Flying Scotsman* by David Luff, there is an interesting insight into the reasoning behind Amy Mollison's attempt to beat Tommy Rose's world record flight from England to Cape Town. It can be found on pages 287-8:

Amy was planning to stage a 'come back' by attempting to recapture her old England to Cape record. It had recently fallen to the genial and popular Flight Lieutenant Tommy Rose in February of that year.

Amy was acutely aware she was no longer holding the media's attention as the Empire's favourite aviatrix

Amy Mollison did beat the record, by 1 day 14 hours 40 minutes, covering the 6,700 miles between Gravesend and Cape Town in 3 days 6 hours 20 minutes in a Percival Gull with a de Havilland Gipsy Six engine.

But that is the nature of competitive flying, once a record has been broken, there is always someone ready to improve on the time, or speed of any attempt. Tommy Rose arrived back in the UK on 9 March 1936 with the record, just two months later Amy Mollison regained the record which, probably, is one of the reasons why some of Tommy Rose's achievements have not received the lasting recognition that they truly deserve.

Chapter 14

1936 – The Schlesinger Race

'Mistakes are inevitable in aviation, especially when one is still learning new things. The trick is to not make the mistake that will kill you.'
– Stephen Coonts, American aviator
and suspense writer.

Tommy Rose's next big adventure was to be the Schlesinger Race. The first announcement of the offer by Mr I.W. Schlesinger, of prizes totalling £10,000 for an air race from England to Johannesburg was made by the Royal Aero Club of Great Britain in June 1936, when the club took over the organisation of this event. It was obvious that, if the race were to start on 15 September, as originally intended, which was also the day on which the Johannesburg Empire Exhibition opened, there would be no time for any aircraft manufacturer to build machines specifically for it.

However, in a remarkably short time, considering the difficulties, the racing committee of the club produced a set of regulations, and a formula. It was decided to divide the race into two classes, to be flown concurrently, one to be a handicap race, and the other a pure speed race, but it would probably have been more accurate to explain the regulations by saying the race was a handicap race with a very substantial prize for the fastest time.

After some discussion, it was decided to spread Mr Schlesinger's £10,000 prize (the equivalent of just over £1,121,000 today) into £4,000 for the entrant with the machine making the fastest time, and £3,000, £1,500, £1,000, and £500 for the handicap section. No entrant to be eligible for prizes in both speed and handicap, and an entrant with a 'double' win would have to renounce one of the prizes.

Portsmouth Aerodrome was chosen to be the starting point. This small aerodrome was sandwiched

Tommy exits from the red BA Double Eagle G-AEIN, called the 'Perfect Lady', at Portsmouth on 28 September 1936, the day before the start of the Schlesinger race. The aircraft was named after the winning cocktail at a Wine and Spirit exhibition in London. (*via Peter Amos*)

FLIGHT LIEUTENANT THOMAS 'TOMMY' ROSE DFC

G-AEIN taken before the race in 1936. (*via Peter Amos*)

between the Portsmouth-London railway line and the waters/marshes of Langstone Harbour off Portsea Island. The airport was constructed during 1931/1932 but it offered little scope for expansion. It is thought that Portsmouth was selected as the starting point for the Schlesinger Race because it would be easier to accommodate the large numbers of spectators that were expected for this unique event.

The competitors were given a free hand as to the routes they chose, but they had to pass over Belgrade Aerodrome low enough to be identified, as Belgrade was an official turning point. After Cairo the pilots were able to please themselves which stages and points for refuelling they took, and Imperial Airway's offered to illuminate their aerodromes throughout Africa at night during the race period. Tommy Rose's proposed route is described later in this chapter, but time spent while refuelling or repairing possible damage to the entrants' aircraft, would be counted as flying time, so that the competitors would naturally have to try and reduce the number of landings to a minimum.

Victor Smith, in his autobiography *Open Cockpit Over Africa*, gave a valuable insight into the personalities of some of the competitors in the race, and this extract is reproduced below:

> *I had felt strongly in those days that any pilot was a better pilot if he had spent a lot of time teaching others to fly, even though intercontinental flying is quite a different story.*
>
> *In this latter category we were fortunate to have some of the world's finest pilots in the Portsmouth to Johannesburg Race.*
>
> *Stan Halse and Tom Campbell-Black, while highly skilled and wide-ranging pilots, were both men of few words. Scott, that dour and rather unfriendly Australian had, with Campbell-Black, won the England to Australia Race in 1935. Tommy Rose and Major Miller were both friendly characters with outstanding personalities and impressive backgrounds, and Ken Waller and Arthur Clouston were RAF pilots of note.*

1936 – THE SCHLESINGER RACE

The race began with high hopes; 'The success of the International Air Race to Melbourne gives us good grounds for welcoming an Empire Air Race from London to Johannesburg, Mr I.W. Schlesinger, the South African Industrialist, is worthily following in the footsteps of Sir MacPherson Robertson KBE', the various national newspapers reported at the lead up to the race. Full of optimism, they hoped that, 'this race will enable businessmen of the Union to study the British Empire's landplanes, and judge for themselves which is the most suitable for the long internal stages, and which will be best for branch lines.'

However, Tommy Rose was having trouble with his aeroplane even before the race as the *Portsmouth Evening News* for Thursday, 3 September reported:

THRILL FOR ROSE
LANDS 'WHEEL-LESS' MONOPLANE
Tommy Rose, Johannesburg race entrant flying an Eagle monoplane at Hanworth airfield wound up his undercarriage when he took off, found that the mechanism had jammed.

He struggled with the winding apparatus, then swooped low and dropped a note, 'Undercarriage stuck. Trying to land'.

Watchers were anxious, but Tommy glided gently down, held his aeroplane a few feet off the ground until it stalled, and dropped it heavily on to its wing.

He climbed out unhurt from an aeroplane only slightly damaged.

In *Flight* for 24 September 1936 an article described Tommy's entry, the BA Double Eagle, G-AEIN, with Race No. 4, as follows:

With Tommy Rose as pilot and a distinguished King's Cup performance behind it, the Double Eagle is heavily fancied. A 1936 model of advanced design, it mounts a pair of Series I Gipsy Sixes, which drive fixed-pitch Fairey airscrews. With this combination and flown by Flight Lieutenant J.B. Wilson it secured third place in this year's King's Cup Race at the average speed of 181.13 mph. The maximum speed in its present form is about 200 mph.

Planned as a high-speed light transport or a luxurious private owner's machine the Double Eagle is characterised by an unusual wing arrangement, the inner portions of the wing sloping down from the top of the fuselage to the engine nacelles whence the main panels are run out with a dihedral angle.

The undercarriage is completely retractable into the nacelles.

Extra tankage has been installed in the cabin but no official figures for range or fuel capacity have been publicised by the manufacturers. In racing trim the Double Eagle has one seat in the cabin.

FLIGHT LIEUTENANT THOMAS 'TOMMY' ROSE DFC

Photograph taken from *Flight*, shows Tommy who had been in training for the Race under the supervision of the Arsenal trainer. Left to right: Tom Whittiker (trainer), Jack Crayston (later manager of Arsenal), Tommy Rose and Wilf Copping.

The preparation and route planning

To prepare for an endurance race such as the Schlesinger Race would take many months, not only to research the most effective route, but also to have the strength and stamina to be able to pilot an aircraft safely over its course.

Tommy was very fit and, having just flown to Cape Town and back earlier in the year, he knew the terrain, and what the conditions were. Also, having spent many years playing competitive rugby, he was a very focused and energetic individual. It was, therefore, probably some months after this successful event, included in which would have been a considerable number of functions, obligatory banquets and dinners, etc, that Tommy decided to start on a fitness programme!

Through his contacts in the rugby clubs he was able to call upon the Arsenal Football Club for help, who sent along their trainer Tom Whittiker and fellow team members to help. Many hours were spent returning Tommy to peak mental and physical fitness.

The suggested route of the race, by the organisers

As each pilot had a perfectly free hand in laying his course, providing he overflies or lands at Zemin Aerodrome, Belgarde, and lands at Cairo, it was not possible to give an accurate description of the route as every pilot had their favoured routes. The following general description, however, details the various types of country over which the competitors would have to fly.

Leaving Portsmouth, the pilots were to elect to take the long sea crossing over the Channel and pass over Le Havre and from there they were to take a direct course to Belgrade, which would have taken them over the Alps. There would probably be a slight change of course to avoid the highest mountain, then they would proceed to Vienna.

The river Danube, which flows through this country, and its tributaries, offered very visible 'fixes' for navigation purposes, but it is in this area the competitors were expected to meet fairly violent storms.

Vienna lies behind a long range of hills at a point where the Danube cuts through them, and navigation at these points was not going to cause any problems to the pilots.

1936 – THE SCHLESINGER RACE

On to Belgrade where the country tended to become rather flat and uninteresting, but here there was to be a turning point, competitors were to descend to 200 feet so their numbers could be checked by the ground control if they were to fly non-stop, otherwise they could descend and refuel at this point.

The course was over Skopje, on the way to Salonika, and onwards to Athens where many competitors would refuel prior to making the Mediterranean crossing.

From Athens the course was to be via Crete to Cairo, which was the one control all competitors had to land and report in to. The handicaps were adjusted so that the first man home at Germiston would be the winner of the handicap section of the race.

On that section of the route, pilots were to fly over the Libyan Desert until they could see the Nile and its accompanying green ribbon of cultivated fertile land. From the altitude at which they were to fly the Nile takes the form of a narrow green band winding away for hundreds of miles through the sand towards the south.

After Cairo, the next 1,770 miles consists of crossing and re-crossing the Nile no less than eight times, right down to the Equator.

The competitors were flying over what appeared to be a limitless desert, the Arabian Desert, the temperature there was almost unbearable at ground level, but at 10,000 feet it would have been just pleasant.

Luxor lay right in the heart of this desert and accurate navigation was necessary from Cairo, otherwise Luxor might have been missed and a forced landing in this part of the desert would have been extremely dangerous.

The modern is mixed with the ancient in a very marked manner in this district, pilots that had a very fast aircraft were due to fly right over the camel caravans with the Arabs in their heavy woollen blankets even in the suffocating heat. The competitors would have been able to marvel at the desert dawn, which they would have been able to appreciate the magnificence of more fully than those viewing it at ground level.

Tommy Rose and Captain S.S. Halse, taking the opportunity to advertise Seagers Gin before the Schlesinger race in front of the Double Eagle G-AEIN. (*Nigel Gaudion*)

FLIGHT LIEUTENANT THOMAS 'TOMMY' ROSE DFC

On the way over to Khartoum the machines would pass over the Nubian Desert, and it would be realised by the pilots that a forced landing here would mean days waiting for help, but there was no reason to suspect that any aircraft or engine would give any trouble over this section. It was hoped that the reliability of the British Aircraft in those days was absolute and would not let their pilot down.

After Malakal the journey and scenery became more interesting with the very fertile country and the deep red soil, however it was also known as a great breeding ground for the malarial mosquito.

From Juba, over Kisumu through Uganda and on to Lake Victoria, which was a splendid landmark, the course was difficult with large swamp areas in which it would have been impossible to make an emergency landing. The Nile was to be followed again and crossed over at intervals for 2,170 miles.

Nairobi as the next city on the route lying at the altitude of 5,000 feet above sea level, then on to Dodonia, Tanganyika, through wild and desolate country to Mbeya and Juba, over which large areas of scrub were passed, which were usually subjected to regular forest fires.

Broken Hill, Livingstone, not far from Victoria Falls and then on to Bulawayo. From here to Johannesburg was the final leg completing 7,000 miles of the most varied flying conditions that could be expected.

The task of the competitors was not easy, they would be very tired when they arrived at Gemiston, Johannesburg, but it was hoped that every person in the Empire would wish them all 'Good Luck' and hoped every competitor would claim their replicas of the trophy.

However, Tommy's preferred route for the race was described in *Flight* for 24 September 1936, in collaboration with Tommy Rose:

> **OVER THE ROUTE**
> *One of our best-known long-distance pilots explains some of the features and difficulties of the route to Johannesburg. As it will appear in the race.*
>
> Few pilots are better qualified to write about the East Coast Route to the Cape than is Flight Lieutenant Rose. Quite apart from his long experience, dating from the war years, of general flying and instruction, he made the penultimate out-and-home Cape records with a Miles Falcon, and therefore can see the Johannesburg race route and its difficulties from the point of view of the pilot who is covering the whole distance in four days or less.
>
> Tommy explained: 'First of all I must make it clear that what follows is merely a collection of notes consisting of personal suggestions and is not guaranteed to be entirely up to date. However, even if it is not of any great value to those of my fellow competitors who do not know the route, it may at least give the ordinary reader some idea of what people who do this sort of thing are letting themselves in for.
>
> 'The route across Europe to Belgrade is probably known to most readers better than to myself, for I have only been to that town once, and then not directly. Zemum aerodrome is easily recognisable and the

1936 – THE SCHLESINGER RACE

surface is good, moreover, the officials seem to do their best to help one. Most competitors should arrive here by noon the first day.

'*The flight to Almaza aerodrome Cairo, which is a control, will need a bit of thinking out.*

'*The direct course from Belgrade to Cairo measures 1,182 miles, and I think it would be extremely unwise to attempt this unless one has a safe range of 1,400 miles, although there is an aerodrome at Alexandria, about 150 miles NW of Cairo. With the possible exception of Mew Gulls, all machines will be making landfall on the North African Coast in darkness, and it is extremely easy, without wireless, to spend a long, long time finding the aerodrome one is looking for under these conditions; I have wasted a lot of time and peace of mind in this way. Those pilots who wish to make certain will probably make an intermediate landing to refuel at Athens and should have no difficulties put in their way there.*

'*Cairo, as most people know, is situated right at the south of the Nile Delta, and the one mainstream is recognisable by moonlight. The airport beacon can usually be seen from the town, and the floodlighting is good.*

'*The Egyptian officials are courteous and obliging, and for those who have time, the club bar is well stocked – but members always make it extremely difficult for visiting pilots to leave without a serious attack on the stock!*

'*The next leg is likely to be flown at night – at any rate by the faster machines. It is, therefore, going to be extremely boring. The Nile wiggles about a lot and on the direct course to Khartoum it is out of sight for most of the time. One can rest assured that whenever one sees a group of lights on the ground, it is a thousand to one that it is a village on the Nile's cultivation, and that the river itself is only a few yards away. The course to Khartoum, which is 176 degrees magnetic, leaves the Nile immediately one sets off from Almaza and crosses it again about thirty miles south of Assuit. The lights of the village of Sohag*

Tommy Rose with engineers and supporters before the Schlesinger race.

should easily be recognisable, as the river takes a decided kink to the NE here, about 250 miles from Cairo. The river having disappeared to the eastward, one crosses the railway to Kharga, which will probably not be visible from any height at night. The Nile is not crossed again until one has covered 500 miles and then it should be seen about 50 miles north of Wadi Halfa.

'The cultivation is very narrow, and rocky ground extends almost up to the riverbanks. There is no real landmark here, unless one decides to fly down the stream to Wadi, and to make certain of one's position.

'On again, one may go over ground which is a little higher and most inhospitable (I had to make a forced landing on this section last time) till one should meet our friend Mr Nile just north of the fourth cataract, about 770 miles north of Cairo. The river here is running almost NE and is left immediately. I myself shall alter course here a few degrees east, so as to ensure hitting the river some distance north of Khartoum. The town is easily recognisable, not only from its size and consequently the large number of lights, but because it is situated at the junction of the White and Blue streams.

'If it is night-time, care will have to be given in the approach to land, as there are a number of wires and other obstructions. The surface is reasonably good, but there are soft patches, which are sometimes cut up by heavy machines, there is no floodlighting, but the use of flares is usual. Those lucky devils with longer range may prefer to go on to Khosti, where a very good aerodrome now exists due east of the town and on the east bank of the river. I understand that the old landing ground here, which I have used (on the other bank), is no longer in action.

'Those who go direct from here to Kisumu or Entebbe are in for perhaps the most boring part of the journey, over very grim and hopeless country for a forced landing. There are several mountains over six thousand feet, which serve as some sort of check; but it has been my experience that these are frequently marked in the wrong place, and if there is any doubt about it, stick to the course the compass has given you.

'For those going to Kisumu, Mt Elgon should be visible for a very considerable distance, and one's course lies right over the top if one sticks strictly to it. I once saw Elgon from Kitgum, about two hundred miles away, but it is frequently obscured by clouds, which hang around it and are seen nowhere else. Those who have to go via Juba, will be well advised to stick very conscientiously to the compass after Malakal, for the river soon disappears into hundreds of small streams and a dreadful looking swamp known as the Sudd. This is a really shocking area, and several airmen who have been lost there have suffered a great deal of inconvenience, to put it mildly, and cost the Royal Air Force a lot of petrol and extra work looking for them. In fact, they were very lucky to have got away with it at all. Just north of Juba the Nile sorts itself out a bit, and the aerodrome is not difficult to find.

1936 – THE SCHLESINGER RACE

'From Kisumu onwards competitors will probably go various ways. I hope to go to M'Pika, refuel there, and then straight to Jo'burg, but this is supposing I have been able to stick to my schedule and get to Kisumu by noon on the second day. If I do not do this, then I certainly shall not attempt to find M'Pika after dark, but will go to M'Beya, take on some more fuel, and push off to Salisbury.

'Although it is not easy to find from the north, because of the hill (I missed it in daylight last time), they have a good aerodrome there as well as up-to-date floodlighting and a beacon. From Salisbury to Johannesburg is just over 600 miles, and if the weather is kind, this section should not be too bad at night – even without wireless.

'Some parts of the leg from Kisumu to Salisbury are supposed to be the worst of the whole trip, but personally I dislike the country between Khartoum and Kisumu far more. On this last leg but one – i.e. to Salisbury - the maps are far from infallible, but there is something growing on the ground and water to be seen, although they tell one that it is undrinkable and that the greenest areas spell tsetse fly.

'Coming south from Kisumu, one flies over fairly interesting country alongside Lake Victoria, leaving Tabora a few miles to the west, and after 600 miles one should pass between the end of Lake Rukwa and M'Beya. The mountain just north of the latter aerodrome is a good landmark, being about 8,000 ft high. Then, after about another hundred miles, one flies down the valley of the River Luangwa for over three hundred miles. It is almost 100 miles across in one or two places, and on the west side there is the Muchinga range, and on the east the mountains of Nyasaland. This is a very naughty bit of country, and, as it is said to be full of tsetse fly, not too good for a forced landing.

'The Luangwa eventually bearing off to the west, one's course is over high ground, some of it almost 5,000 feet, and then on to the Zambesi, which at all seasons is quite a large stream at this point. From the Zambesi the course can be exceedingly tricky, especially if the weather is bad and if one is getting tired. There is a good deal of high ground, and Salisbury is almost surrounded by hills. The aerodrome here is good and the officials exceedingly charming and helpful.

'From Salisbury on towards the finish there will be night flying for the faster machines. Umvuma should be seen after a hundred miles or so, and from there little will be seen until one hits the railway at Mylstroom, about 100 miles from journey's end. Then on over Pienaars River and Pretoria to the finish.

'It sounds ever so easy, but it is my opinion that the pilot of the aeroplane which gets there in under forty-eight hours will deserve just about the biggest bunch of bananas ever found.

'Having got lost myself many times down this route when flying without wireless, I fully expect to do so again, and the pilot in the race who can honestly say at the end that he was sure of his position, all the time, will either be very lucky, very clever, or have a queer idea of honesty. I have invariably found that whenever I thought that I should be somewhere, and wasn't, if I went on (once for over fifty miles) on the same course I got there. If I started to wander about, thinking I was off my course for some reason or another, I always got into trouble. The motto is obvious. There is sometimes a naughty grey mist on the Nile Delta. Last time I was down there I mistook a cinema sign of a fairly small town for the airport beacon.

'Unless one has a safe two hundred miles to spare, in range, on any leg across Africa, one is likely to be causing the nervous system a lot of trouble sooner or later. Mine has often been troubled, but not from this cause. Long sea crossings do it in my case.

'Taking a heavily laden machine off high altitude aerodromes is always a matter of extreme difficulty. When this has to be done with a full load in the middle of the day the pilot has to pedal (and pray) ever so much harder.

'After various hair-raising episodes, I have found that it is better not to try and pull the machine off until one can see the whites of the eyes of the ants on the far boundary fence. This saves Captain Lamplugh a lot of money.'

In addition to the prize monies, however, Mr I.W. Schlesinger will present a trophy to the winning pilot who reaches Johannesburg first and miniature replicas of this trophy to all pilots finishing the course.

The same aircraft may be entered for both sections of the race but no aircraft are eligible to win more than one prize.

The contest is restricted to British pilots and aircraft.

DATE: The contest will commence on Tuesday, 29 September at a time to be notified later. The organisers reserve the right to postpone the starting times or date in case of need or to cancel the contest entirely. The right of cancellations, however, will only be exercised in the event of war or national emergency.

ELIGIBILITY The race is open to any type of aircraft provided that the airframe and engine(s) have been entirely constructed in the British Empire. The restriction does not apply to airscrews, instruments or accessories.

The entrant and the pilot or pilots must be British subjects. The pilot in charge of each aircraft must have at least one hundred hours' experience of solo flying prior to the start of the race and must be prepared to produce evidence to this effect if called for.

CERTIFICATE OF AIRWORTHINESS. The following certificate must be produced to the Royal Aero Club not later than one clear week before the date of the contest.

1936 – THE SCHLESINGER RACE

An airworthiness certificate of either the normal or aerobatic category in respect of any one of the sub-division a-e inclusive. The aircraft must be equipped with an engine or engines classified as being to the normal category of engines.

INSTRUMENTS AND EQUIPMENT. The question of instruments and equipment will be left to the discretion of each entrant, subject to compliance with the Air Navigation and Airworthiness Regulations. No aircraft will be allowed to start in darkness unless properly equipped for night flying.

HANDICAP SECTION. The course for the handicap section will be identical with the course for the speed section, but the race will be decided on the fastest handicap time. 'Handicap time', means the actual elapsed time from start to finish, less the handicap allowance time. Nothing will be allowed for time spent on the ground.

PAYLOAD. The undermentioned items only will be recognised as payload:
- 200lb will be allowed for each person carried other than the pilot. This is inclusive of unsealed baggage.
- Sealed Packages. The actual weight of each package will be taken as payload provided it does not exceed 12lb per cubic foot. If this figure is exceeded the weight of the package for the purpose of determining 'L' formula will be assessed at the rate of 12lb per cubic foot, the volume of the package being taken as the product of its maximum dimensions in each plane. Packages containing fuel or oil will not be included as payload.

REPAIRS AND REPLACEMENTS. Repairs and replacements to the airframe and engine(s) may be made during the race, but neither may be changed as a whole. The airframe and engine(s) will be sealed at the starting point prior to the commencement of the contest and such seals must remain unbroken during the race on pain of disqualification.

PERSONNEL. Subject to compliance with C of A of the aircraft, there is no limit to the number of crew or passengers which may be carried. The entry form shall, however, specify one pilot as 'the pilot in charge' of the aircraft. Such pilot in charge must at all times be carried in the aircraft and shall be responsible as the agent of the entrant for compliance with all the rules and regulations and instructions of officials.

TIME LIMIT AND RETIREMENT. The time limit for both sections of the race is five days (120 hours) calculated from the time at which the starting signal is given to the competitor. Any competitor failing *to complete the course within this time limit will be automatically eliminated and will not be eligible to gain any prize unless the Stewards, in exceptional circumstances, and in their sole discretion, shall otherwise determine. Any competitor retiring before the completion of the course must notify the nearest aerodrome by speediest possible method. Failure to do so shall render the entrant and competitor liable for the cost of any search organisation instituted as the result.*

In the end, just fourteen entrants had arrived at Portsmouth for the start of the race, as follow:

Race Number	Registration	The list of the original entrants into the Schlesinger Race	Pilot	Aircraft
1	ZS-AHM	Len Oates	Capt. A.M. Miller	Percival Mew Gull
2	ZS-AHO	Capt. S.S. Halse	Capt. S.S. Halse	Percival Mew Gull
3	G-AELT	Victor Smith	Victor Smith	Miles Sparrow hawk
4	G-AEIN	Henry S. Home	Flt. Lt. T. Rose Bradshaw	BA4 Double Eagle
5	G-AEKD	Lt. Misri Chand	Lt. Misri Chand Lt. P. Randolph	Percival Vega Gull
6	G-AEKE	Sir Connop Guthrie	C.W.A. Scott Giles Guthrie	Percival Vega Gull
7	G-AEAB	D.W. Llewellyn	D.W. Llewellyn C.F. Hughesdon	Percival Vega Gull
8	G-ADOD	F/O A.E. Clouston F.E. Tasker	A.E. Clouston	Miles Hawk VI
9	G-AEMX	De Havilland Aircraft Co.	H. Buckingham	D.H.92 Dolphin
10	G-ADID	C.G.M. Alington	C.G.M. Alington Lt. P.H. Booth, RN	BA Eagle
11	G-AEDE	Bateman Scott	Flt. Lt. H.R.A. Edwards Sqdn. Ldr. B.S. Thynne	Miles Peregrine
12	VP-KCC	John E. Carberry	John E. Carberry	Percival Vega Gull

1936 – THE SCHLESINGER RACE

Race Number	Registration	The list of the original entrants into the Schlesinger Race	Pilot	Aircraft
13	G-AENA	Maxwell H. Findlay Kenneth Waller	Maxwell H. Findlay Kenneth Waller	Airspeed Envoy
14	G-AEKL	Air Publicity Ltd.	Tom Campbell Black	Percival Mew Gull

The Excitement Mounts

The Hampshire Telegraph for Friday, 25 September 1926 reported:

> Everything was in readiness yesterday for the arrival of the planes competing in the Schlesinger-Portsmouth-South Africa air race, which starts from the City Airport on Tuesday next.
>
> All the entries had to report to the Royal Aero Club officials at the airport by six o'clock last evening.
>
> Weather conditions are not favourable, as there was a mist, and Heston reported condition to be very thick this morning.
>
> The first plane to arrive landed on the airport and taxied up to the hangers at exactly 2 pm. It was the Miles Speed Hawk, entered by Flying Officer A.E. Clouston and Mr F.E. Tasker and flown by Flying Officer Clouston, who is a civil test pilot at Farnborough. His plane is a cream-coloured red lettered racer, built for Miss Ruth Fontes and raced by her in the 1934 Kings Cup and this year was flown into second place by Flight Lieutenant Tommy Rose.
>
> Next on the scene was the BA Eagle, which is being flown by a trio, two of whom are officers of the Royal Navy, were Mr C.G. Allington and Lieutenant P.A. Booth. Mr Allington is one of the youngest competitors in the race.
>
> **Tommy Rose's Machine**
> No sooner had these two pilots been greeted by the officials than Tommy Rose's red twin-engine Double Eagle was seen circling around the airport.
>
> The famous airman was greeted with much excitement by the crowd that had gathered. He was accompanied by Mr Jack Bradshaw, a South African, who is flying with him to Johannesburg.
>
> The Double Eagle was placed third in the summer's Kings Cup race, and with the Airspeed Envoy is the only twin engine machine in the race.

FLIGHT LIEUTENANT THOMAS 'TOMMY' ROSE DFC

Tommy Rose with Jack Bradshaw his co-pilot before the Schlesinger race.

Among those who were the first to greet Tommy Rose were Sir Charles Rose, and Mr Charles Clapham, of Clapham and Dyer.

Shortly after Flight Lieutenant Rose had arrived from Hanworth the Percival Vega Gull being flown by Messers C.W. Scott and Giles Guthrie landed. Mr Scotts co-pilot is a son of the owner, Sir Connop Guthrie, and is the youngest competitor in the race, having obtained special permission from Cambridge University to take part in the race on the condition he is back by 15 October.

The plane they are flying is this year's Kings Cup winner, having been flown then by Mr Charles Gardiner.

Lunch was provided before the race on Tuesday, 29 September 1936 for all those involved in what was thought was going to be a truly momentous race.

Flight for 1 October 1936 reported in their *'Here and There'* section:

A SEND OFF

At a luncheon on 29 September, given by the Portsmouth Airport authorities to the competitors of the race, speeches were made by the Lord Mayor of Portsmouth Alderman W.J. Avens, Major Miller, Flight Lieutenant Tommy Rose, Mr G.W. Klerck, Mr Harmel, Councellor J.E. Lane JP, Mr W. Lindsay-Evarard, MP, Councillor A.N. Blake and Sir Frances Shelmerdine. The importance of bringing the parts of the British Empire closer together was stressed by several of the speakers, and Sir Frances Shelmerdine reminded the gathering that everyone was hard at work expanding the RAF whose work it was to defend peace, and that without peace there could be no civil service.

The start of the Johannesburg race was also reported in the same issue of *Flight:*

As dawn broke at Portsmouth on Tuesday, cold and clear, nine aeroplanes in the £10,000 Schlesinger African Air race, took off from the City Airport on their 6,150-mile journey – an adventurous journey for some, a deadly monotonous one for others. That was only two days ago, yet by the time these words appear, the great adventure might well be over, with the winner being acclaimed in Johannesburg, en fete for its great Empire Exhibition.

Although the event was a formula handicap, the start was virtually a scratch one, allowances being adjusted at minute intervals.

The original entries numbered more than nine. Four machines did not come to the line. They were the new Miles Peregrine, not completed in time; Mr John E. Carberry's Vega Gull, put out of the running by the nose-over which terminated its Atlantic flight in the hands of Mrs Markham; and the Mew Gull, which would have been flown by poor Tom Campbell-Black.

There might have been low cloud and heavy rain over South-Eastern Europe, and all manner of meteorological horrors over Africa, but for the start of the race, no September morning's weather could have been better. Competitors, officials and the great mass of spectators motored, cycled or walked to the airport at 5 am under a cloudless night sky.

At the floodlight aerodrome the windsocks hung limply as the nine machines were wheeled by ghostly figures towards a preliminary starting line. However, with the rising of the sun a wind of some sort might have been expected, and even the low hills to the east of the airport were outlined against the dawn, the socks filled gently and swung away from their posts.

From 5.30 am onwards there were all the usual accompaniments of an approaching zero hour – made all the more impressive by the semi-darkness and reminiscent of the never-to-be-forgotten scene at Mildenhall, where engines were being warmed or run up, while exhaust smoke hung patterned in the floodlight beams and mechanics clambered around the vibrating machines.

Meanwhile, a dozen photographers from various papers and agencies had been carefully selected and carefully shepherded on to the sacred aerodrome-which was ordained out-of-bounds for all but those with the armlets and a multiplication of special badges obtained by devious means. But as these fortunate ones passed the barrier, a minor spectatorial leakage occurred; the trickle became an intermittent river, which could, nevertheless, have been easily dammed with a little polite firmness and a few more policemen.

At 6.15 am darkness still covered the face of the earth, and the competitors must have felt relieved that the start had been put back by a quarter of an hour. It was then that the organisers decided that the competitors should, as a special treat, be allowed to use the whole of the available run; the machines were moved back towards the airport buildings, and the vast number of gatecrashers moved back with them.

With a minute to go it did not seem possible that the race could be started until the crowd had been moved, but at 6.30 am the throttles of the big Envoy were gently pushed forward, while the more knowledgeable spectators prayed that the heavily loaded machine would not swing into humanity surging against its starboard wingtip. Slowly the machine gathered speed, the crowd *sighed with relief as the twinkling white navigation light lifted in the distance, and a moment later the Envoy was silhouetted against a grey-green sky. The crowd moved up one to brush against the wingtip of Halse's Mew Gull.*

Those who had not previously seen the Mew Gulls in action must have been astonished by Halse's full-load acceleration, take off and climb. Within ten seconds of dropping the flag the machine was airborne and climbing rapidly; there had not been a moment's anxiety.

The machines with fixed pitch airscrews showed up badly by contrast, though no one would have noticed the length of their full load runs if a comparison had not been possible. The Vega Gull's take-off was noticeably improved. On the other hand, overload C of A and all, Rose's Double Eagle, with normal airscrews, was prised loose in a surprisingly short time.

During the entire period of ten minutes, as machine after machine took off with clockwork precision, there were only three mildly bad moments. Miller's Mew Gull descended a slight dip just as the tail was properly in the air and the machine had reached, perhaps, 40 mph; it rocked and bounced, but five seconds later it was climbing towards the north.

The Victor Smith's metal airscrew was being abortively swung even while the flag dropped, evidently the mixture was too rich for a hot engine.

Finally, Scott's Vega required some heavy ruddering to avoid a peninsula of spectators at his port wingtip, and a few seconds passed before the machine was on a straight course. Meanwhile, the Sparrowhawk's engine had at last been started, but Smith had to wait until the Vega was well away, and he lost perhaps a minute and a quarter.

The crowd flowed over the airport. The race was on. Before some of the earliest departures had turned their cars out of the approach road, Halse's Mew Gull would be passing over the coast of France at operational height.

There were well over 500 spectators who turned up to see off the aircraft that cold morning. When Flying Officer A.E. Clouston set out to leave in his Miles Hawk Speed Six, the crowd were amused to see that a red 'L' had been displayed beneath the celluloid slide over the cockpit. It was a trick played on this youngest competitor by some of his fellow officers.

The Handicaps and the final nine contestants

Racing Number	Pilot	Aircraft and Engine	Handicap Allowance H m s	Formula Speed MPH
10	Alington and Booth	BA Eagle Gipsy Major	21 58 12	116.93
7	Llewellyn	Vega Gull Gipsy Six	13 27 36	139.52

1936 – THE SCHLESINGER RACE

Racing Number	Pilot	Aircraft and Engine	Handicap Allowance H m s	Formula Speed MPH
6	Scott	Vega Gull Gipsy Six	13 14 24	140.20
3	Smith	Sparrowhawk Gipsy Major	10 34 12	149.30
8	Clouston	Hawk Speed Six Gipsy Six	6 25 12	166.12
13	Findlay and Waller	Envoy 2 Cheetah IX	3 13 12	181.73
4	Rose	Double Eagle 2 Gipsy Six	3 06 36	182.34
1	Miller	Mew Gull Gipsy Six	0 01 12	200.73
2	Halse	Mew Gull Gipsy Six	Scratch	200.8

Sadly, Tommy's dream of completing the Schlesinger Race, was dashed when his aircraft was first forced down at Linz, Austria, by an airlock, but he continued on and lost valuable hours at Athens trying to remedy the problem.

It was obvious once Tommy had landed that he had been struggling with problems with airlocks in the fuel system.

They were forced to give up at Cairo when, upon landing, one leg of the retractable undercarriage gear collapsed, and one propeller was broken. Tommy and his co-pilot Jack Bagshaw were devastated.

Yorkshire Evening Post for Wednesday, 30 September 1936 reported:

TOMMY ROSE OUT, PLANE DAMAGED ON LANDING IN CAIRO

Men on a fire engine and an ambulance, which dashed out over the aerodrome here early today to a crumpled plane, found its chief pilot, Flight Lieutenant Tommy Rose, standing beside it in rueful contemplation.

Rose decided soon afterwards to retire from the race as a result of the damage to his plane.

The undercarriage retracted whilst taxiing and the propeller struck the ground and broke. A cameraman who raced 500 yards towards the plane to obtain a picture was chased by police, who collared him, his camera was broken in the scuffle.

The aeroplane remained at Cairo, but somehow, Tommy and Jack were able to continue their flight down to Johannesburg in an aircraft supplied by a sympathetic local firm.

FLIGHT LIEUTENANT THOMAS 'TOMMY' ROSE DFC

With the borrowed aircraft, Tommy and Jack Bagshaw's next stop was at Khartoum, where they met up with Victor Smith. Jack mentioned to Victor (as stated in Victor's book '*Open Cockpit over Africa*') that, when they came to land at Almaza, Tommy's seat in the BA Double Eagle slipped back so he was out of reach of the controls. Seated behind the pilot, Jack had been able to push the seat forward, and hold it there, to help Tommy land the plane. As it started to cool in the afternoon, they all walked to an ancient fortress on the northern edge of the field, where they were told the outside staircase with the landing at the top was where General Gordon had been killed.

They all slept under the wings of the aircraft that night on the soft sand covering the surface of Khartoum's airfield, before they continued on their way the following morning, after hearing that Halse, Clouston, Llewellyn, Findlay and Waller had all dropped out of the race.

Flight for 8 October 1936 reported:

> *The Double Eagle had suffered persistently from airlocks in the fuel system and Rose had already lost a good deal of time in making special landings at places which he certainly had not included in his schedule. His bad luck held to the bitter end when one of the undercarriage legs folded up while taxying in Cairo. At the time it seemed that something could be done about it, although hardly in the short period necessary to obtain a place but, who was to know that there would be just one finisher in the race?*

Tommy was out of the race, but he managed to complete the trip to Johannesburg, and was looking forward to seeing his fellow competitors at the Royal Aero Club banquet in Johannesburg at the end of the race.

Sadly, two lives were lost in the Envoy G-AENA during the course of the race, when both Captain Max Findlay and the radio officer A. Morgan were killed, although Ken Waller and the passenger Derek Peachey survived.

Flight's report continued:

> *The banquet which was to be given in their honour was cancelled when the sad news of the accident to the Envoy came through. When details were obtainable it was learned that after the machine had landed at Abercorn, Northern Rhodesia, in poor visibility, the wind changed round so that the only possible take-off was both up hill and towards some trees. If the Envoy had been flying in anything but a race Findlay and Waller would have waited for the wind to veer again – particularly as Abercorn is at an altitude of 6,000 feet, but they were naturally unwilling to delay to restart and probably considered that the run would be ample, despite the advice of a few people at the aerodrome. The Envoy struck the trees after take-off and both Captain Max Findlay and Mr A. Morgan, the radio operator, were so severely injured that they died almost at once. Mr Ken Waller, and the passenger Mr Derek Peachey, escaped with comparatively minor injuries.*
>
> *Immediately he had learnt of the tragedy, Mr Schlesinger wired to London to suggest that, if no other competitor arrived within the time*

1936 – THE SCHLESINGER RACE

limit, the balance of the prize money should be given to the dependants of those that had lost their lives.

On 19 September 1936, while preparing for the race, Tom Campbell Black was killed at the UK's Liverpool Speke Airport, in a ground collision with another aircraft. An RAF bomber that had landed ran into Black's Mew Gull as he taxied out for take-off. Black was reputed to have been looking down at his map at the time. The propeller of the large biplane tore through the side of Black's cockpit, striking and mortally wounding him in the chest and shoulder. He died on the way to hospital. He left a widow, the English actress Florence Desmond, whom he had married in 1935.

Although the Royal Aero Club's banquet and presentation of prizes was cancelled due to the fatalities and accidents, Viscount Swinton sent the following telegram to C.W.A. Scott:

I congratulate you and your fellow pilot most cordially. It is a great tribute to your airmanship and endurance that you have repeated your success in the Melbourne race of two years ago. The result is a striking justification also of the race in demonstrating the excellence of British aircraft design.

Mr Malcolm Macdonald, the Secretary of State for Dominion Affairs, also sent a telegram as follows:

Hearty congratulations to you both on your splendid flight. We are delighted to hear that the winner of the Air Race to Australia has repeated his success.

The Race in full

The post-race analysis run in numerous newspapers declared the race to be a 'farce', a 'complete fiasco', 'only one in nine finishes the Johannesburg race', the headlines of the daily newspapers painted a sorry picture of British aviation on a chilly morning in October 1936. The press of the British Empire echoed the news. The 6,500 miles Schlesinger Air Race from England to South Africa, conceived to focus attention on the opening of the 1936 Johannesburg Empire Exhibition had turned into a disaster. Like the ill-fated Pacific Air Race sponsored by the Hawaiian pineapple king James Dole almost a decade earlier, it was an aviation event that should never have taken place.

The race's sponsor, South African industrialist I.C. Schlesinger, most probably had in mind the lyrical headlines created in 1934 by the successful MacRobertson England-Australia Trophy when he donated £10,000 in prize money. Schlesinger did not know the race organisers would have trouble attracting entrants.

There were several reasons for the lack of interest from the aviation industry. In an effort to strengthen the tenuous link between the two countries, which were still strained by bitter memories of the Boer War, Schlesinger had limited his race to aircraft and pilots from Britain and its empire. This he hoped would give the British aircraft industry an edge in South Africa. Commercial aviation was expanding there, and fledgling South African Airways were operating a fleet of German Junkers aircraft.

FLIGHT LIEUTENANT THOMAS 'TOMMY' ROSE DFC

The other reason had nothing to do with the industrialists' apparent devotion to the British Empire. The lights of peace were dimming as power-hungry dictators cast the shadow of war across Europe and Africa. The forces of the Italian Dictator Benito Mussolini had crushed Ethiopia. General Francisco Franco and Bahamonde's Nationalist rebels were escalating the civil war in Spain, and Adolf Hitler's armies had occupied the Rhineland.

The actions of Europe's warmongers had produced a sudden expansion of the Royal Air Force, that resulted in the rush orders for military aircraft. There were even (illegal) sales to Spain's ill-equipped Republican forces. British aircraft manufacturers who had welcomed the MacRobertson affair two years earlier were not interested in Schlesinger's race. That prompted C.G. Grey, Editor of *The Aeroplane* magazine, to comment, 'What is a mere £4,000 prize, when compared with the profits on warcraft?'

The Schlesinger race was over. The press predictably composed blistering critiques, slamming the government and the aviation industry for a lack of interest and encouragement that had forced the racers to fall back on small and totally unsuitable aircraft. The headlines read: 'Tragedy Mars Race', 'Complete Fiasco', 'Whose Fault was the Johannesburg Race?'

The Aeroplane magazine admonished the airmen stating, 'Pilots generally showed an amazing lack of judgement in the flight and the African continent is strewn with wreckage of aircraft driven beyond their capabilities and over-revved, Bleary-eyed pilots are today trying to forget what they should have remembered: that they are only human and their machines are not beyond fallibility'.

Another British aviation writer, desperately searching for solace from the whole affair, suggested; 'But for the fact that the race cost valuable lives, one might have even said that the Schlesinger Race may have proved a blessing in disguise if it serves to shake us out of complacency, makes us see that next time Britain attempts any event of importance, she shall be fully and thoroughly prepared'.

It is interesting to note that no book covers this event in detail except a brief mention in *'Fifty Years Fly-past'*, by Geoffrey Dorman (Forbes Robertson, London, 1951). However, *Flight*, *The Aeroplane* and *Popular Flying* for November 1936, (who ran an article titled 'C.W.A. Scott's own story') are just a couple of the magazines that ran articles just after the race completion.

One very small article that almost escaped scrutiny, was found in *The Cornishman* for 22 October 1936 which reported:

> **OPERATION AT CAPE TOWN**
> Cape Town, Wednesday.
> *Flight Lieutenant Tommy Rose, the airman, was today taken to a Cape Town nursing home for an operation to his ear. His condition afterwards was stated as satisfactory. Flight Lieutenant Tommy Rose was competing in the Portsmouth to Johannesburg race, but suffered an undercarriage collapse at Cairo, which also damaged a propeller. He was forced to withdraw from the race, but afterwards he flew on to South Africa.*

Tommy Rose's family were unaware of any problems that Tommy had with his health at this time, but as he was very fit at the start of the race, one can only conclude it must have been caused by the incident at Cairo.

1936 – THE SCHLESINGER RACE

With Tommy back in England after the Schlesinger race, and always willing to help promote the proliferation of any new flying clubs, it was back to 'business as usual' attending flying events, races and pageants and, being one not to let anyone down, he continued to undertake his 'bookings' up to the time he returned to collect his repaired aircraft at Cairo and to return the borrowed aircraft.

Flight for 6 November 1936, reported:

> **EASTBOURNE'S FIRST**
> *Though its new President, Mr Hore-Belisha, was unable to be present, the Eastbourne Flying Club's first dinner and dance, was held at the Grand Hotel, Eastbourne, on Friday, and it was well graced with those (usually against their will), who are known as celebrities.*
>
> *For instance, the visitors were Mrs Markham and Squadron Leader Swain, and also Flight Lieutenant Tommy Rose and Mr Grahame-White, both of whom contributed to what used to be referred to as a few well-chosen words.*

Sometime in early December, Tommy returned to Cairo in the borrowed aircraft to collect the repaired BA Double Eagle and bring it back to England.

The Nottingham Evening Post for Friday, 13 November 1936, reported on his return journey thus:

> **'I WAS FROZEN TO DEATH', HE SAYS**
> **LEAVES FOR BELGRADE**
> *Flight Lieutenant Tommy Rose flying back to England from Cairo, left Athens today for Belgrade at 1.01 pm local time (11.10 GMT)*
>
> *It is understood that he is not attempting to break any records, but he is within his own scheduled time.*
>
> *Rose, who was looking tired when he reached Athens, told Reuter he had taken four hours to fly from Cairo. 'I was frozen to death', he said. He said his next stop would be Belgrade or Vienna, if he could 'make' it.*
>
> *Flight Lieutenant Rose is flying the BA Double Eagle in which he flew in the Johannesburg Air Race as far as Cairo, where he was compelled to drop out of the race.*
>
> *On this present return journey he flew from the UK to Cairo in the borrowed aeroplane, and there picked up his own machine.*

Only one out of the nine starters made it to Johannesburg, and two people were killed during the race. Scott and Guthrie were met with deafening silence on their return, and C.W.A. Scott said, 'The race was a piece of complete nonsense… I'm glad we didn't make the return journey in a packing case'. Their victory seemed a hollow one, and the unclaimed prize money, £6,000 out of the £10,000 total fund, went to the families of those who had died; £2,000 each to Mrs Max Findlay and Mrs A.H. Morgan, and £2,000 placed in trust for the child of Captain Findlay.

Chapter 15

Phillips and Powis Aircraft Ltd September 1938 – December 1939
Chief Instructor and Secretary of the Reading Aero Club (Phillips and Powis School of Flying), Air Racing and the Civil Air Guard

'I think it is a pity to lose the romantic side of flying and simply accept it as a common means of transport.'

– Amy Johnson

On 23 July 1938, Sir Kinsley Wood, Secretary of State for Air, announced the creation of the Civil Air Guard Scheme. Its intention was to provide pilots who could assist the Royal Air Force in a time of emergency. The scheme was civilian in nature and established in conjunction with local flying clubs, this also included Reading Aero Club, Woodley. The membership was open to any person between the ages of eighteen and fifty years. 'Blossom' Miles set up one of these schemes with Tommy Rose providing the extra training.

The Air Ministry already offered a grant of £25 to pilot members of flying clubs who obtained an 'A' type licence. As part of the new scheme, if they volunteered for the Civil Air Guard, the grant would be increased to £50 for those trained on standard types of aircraft or £30 for aircraft that are lighter than 1,200 pounds (544 kg). The renewal grant would be increased from £10 to £15. Members would receive flying training at subsidised rates of either 2s 6d or 5s an hour during the week, and 5s or 10s at weekends.

Tommy Rose left Seager's in August 1938 as he had found that the Reading Aero Club, were looking for someone to take over not only the running of the aero club, but they also required a Chief Flying Instructor and Secretary. So, in September 1938, Tommy Rose returned to his old friends at the Woodley Aerodrome.

Tommy Rose decided to buy Falcon House, Thames Street, Sonning, near Reading, where they lived until late 1949, as he was now fairly comfortably off, his nomadic years seemed to be over… for now!

An article on the Reading Aero Club and its facilities, and the Phillips and Powis School of Flying, was published in *Flight* for 19 February 1938:

> **THE READING AERO CLUB**
> *Saturday, 13 February, was very cheerful, not to say exuberant at times, for some eighty members of the Reading Aero Club. The occasion was*

This photograph shows George Miles, Blossom Miles and Tommy Rose in the back seat of a Miles Merlin, while F.G. Miles is the pilot and Charles Powis is sitting alongside him. (*via Peter Amos*)

one of the periodical dances arranged by this club and was, as all the functions at Reading, a thoroughly enjoyable one. The whole of the centre portion of the large clubhouse, which was incidentally designed and built by the En-Tout-Cas Co, of Syston, Leicester, has a most excellent dance floor, and, when the folding doors to the dining room are open, forms a very attractive ballroom. At the present moment there are quite a large number of people actually living in the clubhouse, and from personal experience, we can assure readers that the bedrooms and other facilities provided are excellent. Anyone who wishes to stay there over the weekend while putting in some flying time will be made thoroughly comfortable.

The club itself, which now has a membership of over 300, is actually run in conjunction with the Phillips and Powis School of Flying. It does not operate its own machines, and therefore does not claim the Government subsidy, although it is eligible for this. It chiefly looks after the social side of the aerodrome activities, and when any of its members wish to fly solo, the club hires machines from the school. This school is undoubtedly one of the successful ones in the country, and last year their number of flying hours was 2,194 hrs 20 mins, while forty-one men and three women gained their 'A' licences. Quite a large number of foreigners have come to this delightful country aerodrome to learn to fly, including an Afghan, a Dane, three Egyptians, two Indians and one Chinese, as well as a Greek, who is still under instruction.

Naturally, such an establishment as this also caters for the overhaul and repair, both of engines and aircraft. A tour of inspection of the shops immediately impresses one with the efficient manner in which everything is run. All manner of repairs can be undertaken, even to the complete re-covering and doping of the wings, for which, of course a special shop is set aside.

FLIGHT LIEUTENANT THOMAS 'TOMMY' ROSE DFC

One of the chief aims of the flying instructor at a school like this is to avoid their pupils developing any habits which may in emergency lead them into danger, for any sort of danger at all is the kind of thing that must be avoided, particularly at a club and school like that at Reading.

On Sunday morning we were the very happy witnesses of an occasion which showed to the full that the instruction the pupils received there is undoubtably of the highest quality. A private owner had just taken off, and when he was three quarters of the way across the aerodrome the engine cut out, but due to his good training, he held faithfully on, dead into wind, and brought off an excellent safe landing in a harrowed field beyond the aerodrome boundary. The dangers of turning back have in the past been all too forcibly impressed upon people, as several of our finest pilots have been killed by doing so, but even now it is not unknown for a comparatively inexperienced pupil to feel that he has room to do so, and it was therefore very gratifying to all of us who have the welfare of aviation at heart to see that this danger is one of those avoided at Reading.

Flight for 22 September 1938 reported:

Flight Lieutenant Tommy Rose has joined the club as chief instructor. Miss Joyce Adey made her first solo flight, and five new members joined the club.

The original Reading Aero Club clubhouse was built in 1932 but, by 1938, was becoming hemmed in by new factory buildings, a civil operated Reserve Training School, which had been built on the northern boundary. The Falcon Hotel was built in 1936 and this architecturally brilliant, art deco style building, which was officially opened in 1937, then became the Reading Aero Club's new home.

In October, Tommy Rose visited the South Coast Flying Club and *Flight* for 20 October 1938 reported:

The Reading Aero Club clubhouse, built in 1932, was becoming hemmed in by new factory buildings, and a civil reserve training school had been built on the northern boundary. However, the Falcon Hotel, which was built in 1936, became the Reading Aero Club's new home, a year later, in 1937, this architecturally brilliant art deco building was officially opened.

In October Tommy Rose visited the south coast. *Flight* for 20 October 1938 reported:

SOUTH COAST CELEBRATION
Over 200 members and friends turned up at the South Coast Flying Club's annual dinner and dance at the Grand Hotel, Brighton, last Saturday. Numbers alone are not always sufficient to ensure the success of such an affair, but those responsible saw to it that all the other necessary factors were present.

PHILLIPS AND POWIS AIRCRAFT LTD

In the approved modern manner, speeches were few and brief. The chairman, Mr Frances Haddock, reviewed the year's activities and proposed a toast to 'the Guests'.

Mrs F.G. Miles replied and made some interesting references to the progress of the Civil Air Guard (CAG) scheme, speaking in the light of her experience as one of the Commissioners. She then presented an impressive number of awards.

The guests included the Mayor of Brighton, the Mayor and Mayoress of Hove, Alderman Black (chairman of the Airport Committee and father of the late Tom Campbell Black), and Flight Lieutenant Tommy Rose. Needless to say, there was a large and hearty contingent from Brooklands, headed by Captain Duncan Davis.

In short it was a right sort of party to set the seal on a successful year and provide a fitting send-off for what looks like being an even better one.

The Reading Aero Club held their annual dinner and dance on Friday, 25 November 1938, and *Flight* for 1 December 1938 reported:

AT THE SIGN OF THE FALCON

The Reading Aero Club's annual dinner and dance last Friday was something in the nature of a conspiracy, if one is to believe Mr W. Eugster (and there is no reason why one should not). Mr Eugster, in an informal speech explained away the presence of steak and kidney pudding on the menu. Both he and that other 'technician', Flight Lieutenant Tommy Rose, had decided that the safety of the club members required the centre of gravity as low as possible, hence the pudding.

He then drew a pathetic figure of Reading with no club and all CAG (this with a furtive glance at Mrs 'Commissioner' Miles).

In reply, Chairman Tommy Rose was briefly flippant. He had a special word of praise for Mr and Mrs Prescott, the hosts of the Reading Aerodrome's own hotel, The Falcon.

Sportingly Miss Amy Johnson rose and pulled Tommy Rose's leg about some maps she had borrowed. Her difficulty in following the course that he had plotted on them was explained by the fact that the lines did not go from anywhere to anywhere.

After dinner, at which quite a few notables, including F.G. Miles, who had deferred the Paris show visit in order to be present, the party retired to the club lounge, while the floor was cleared for dancing. The dance attracted close on two hundred members, friends and guests, and it was a good party that finally disintegrated in the small hours of the morning in spite of a near hurricane that raged outside.

Sir Kingsley Wood, the Secretary of State for Air, officially opened the new extension to Reading Aerodrome on 27 January 1939, and the *Reading Mercury* for Saturday, 28 January 1939 reported:

FLIGHT LIEUTENANT THOMAS 'TOMMY' ROSE DFC

THE VISIT OF SIR KINGSLEY WOOD
OPENING OF READING AERODROME EXTENSION
DOING A VITAL WORK

Sir Kingsley Wood, the Secretary of State for Air, operated a switch at the aircraft factory of Phillips and Powis Aircraft Limited, at Reading Aerodrome yesterday (Friday), which set in motion all the machinery in the new £250,000 extension to the present factory, which will help to produce the fastest training aircraft in the world, the Miles Master, for which the Air Ministry has placed a record order for training aircraft.

In just five years, this company has produced eighteen different types of aircraft. The machines range from the two-seat Hawk, with a top speed of 116 mph, produced in 1933, to the new Miles Master, which, with its 500hp Rolls-Royce engine, is capable of a top speed of nearly 300 mph. Since 1933, when 243 aeroplanes were produced, the number of employees has increased by over 1,000 per cent, and with the new extensions, the area of the factory is forty times greater that it was last year.

The Miles Master is now the principal machine in production in the factory, and the first production model is expected to be ready in the middle of February.

An aerodrome dance was held on 27 January 1939 to celebrate Tommy Rose's forty-fourth birthday and the *Reading Mercury* for Saturday, 4 February 1939 reported:

The ball of the Reading Aerodrome Sports Club, held at Olympia, Reading, on Friday last week, was something in the nature of a celebration, for it was the birthday of Mr Tommy Rose the famous airman. Mr Rose was present with his wife, and the company numbered about 400. Those members of the club present had the novel experience of dancing to their own band, for music was played by the Night Hawks, a combination of members from the sports club.

On 28 February 1939, Tommy Rose attended, and gave evidence at the inquest, of George Hobbs, a member of Reading Aero Club who was employed at Phillips and Powis as a draughtsman, and Vernon Morris, a purser's clerk on the P&O steamship 'Cathay'. Both had died when the aircraft they were flying in was completely wrecked, and the *Reading Mercury* for Saturday, 4 February 1939 reported:

TWO MEN KILLED IN AIR CRASH
TRAGEDY NEAR EAST WOODHAY
READING PILOT INVOLVED

Two young men making a return flight from Yeovil to Reading Aerodrome, on Saturday morning, lost their lives when the machine, a two-seater Whitney Straight cabin monoplane (G-AEVH), crashed on Pilot Hill, a

900 feet ridge of the Hampshire Downs situated between the villages of East Woodhay and Faccombe.

They were the pilot, Mr George Richard Hobbs of Kingston, Yeovil, a member of the Reading Aero Club, and employed as a draughtsman by Messrs Phillips and Powis at Reading Aerodrome, and his passenger, Mr Vernon Claude Morris, a purser's clerk on the P and O steamship 'Cathay', both men were twenty-six years of age.

The aeroplane was completely wrecked; in fact, it was broken up into scores of pieces littered over an area of 50 yards long and 20 to 30 yards wide. The engine had dug its nose into the ground, the petrol tanks were crushed, wings splintered into bits, and the tail had broken away from the fuselage.

The inquest was held at the Plough Inn, Ashmansworth, on Wednesday morning, and was conducted by Colonel J.T.P. Clarke the Hampshire County coroner, with a jury. In attendance was Mr R.C. Hockey, Inspector of Accidents for the Air Ministry.

Dr N.F. Kendall, Highclere, said in both cases death had been due to multiple injuries. Both men had fractured skulls and both legs broken, death must have been instantaneous.

Flight Lieutenant Tommy Rose, the well-known airman, who is chief instructor at the Reading Aero Club, said Hobbs was one of their best 'A' licence members. He was fully qualified to fly either solo or with a passenger and had flown over 50 hours solo and altogether his flying time was over 100 hours. Hobbs had flown this machine frequently, and a witness said he did so himself on the morning before the accident, when it was thoroughly sound.

Questions were put to Flight Lieutenant Rose respecting the instruments for recording flying altitude, and he said this machine carried an altimeter actuated by barometric pressure, and he did not think variation in the barometric pressure would have altered the instrument to any extent or sufficient to have deceived the pilot. When flying at Reading on Saturday morning, a witness experienced a fall of snow at 1,500 feet and thought Hobbs' machine ran into a flurry of snow, in which case the natural instinct of the pilot would be to put the plane's nose down. Visibility must have been so bad that Hobbs could not have seen the ground until the last moment, if he saw it at all. Flight Lieutenant Rose said he himself flew over Pilot Hill on Saturday afternoon and had the greatest difficulty in detecting the snow-covered ground. 'I think the weather conditions were entirely responsible for this accident', he concluded.

Without retiring, the jury returned a verdict of 'Death by misadventure', and they and the coroner expressed deep sympathy with the relatives of both men.

FLIGHT LIEUTENANT THOMAS 'TOMMY' ROSE DFC

On 31 March 1939, Tommy Rose attended another inquest into the death of Paul Lailey Uphill, aged twenty-eight, a Berkshire police constable who was training at Reading for the Civil Air Guard, who lost his life on 29 March and the *Reading Mercury* for 1 April 1939 reported:

WOODLEY AERODROME TRAGEDY
BERKSHIRE POLICE OFFICER KILLED

A Berkshire police constable who was training at Reading for the Civil Air Guard lost his life in an aeroplane crash at Woodley. He was Paul Lailey Uphill, aged twenty-eight, who was attached to the Abingdon Division, and he was stationed at Didcot. He was flying a Hawk Major machine (G-AFKL) belonging to the Reading Aero Club, and apparently crashed when attempting a dive at speed, stated by eyewitnesses to be between 120 and 150 mph. Uphill was killed almost instantly, and his machine was completely wrecked.

At the inquest, which was conducted by Mr R.S. Payne, coroner at Sonning, yesterday (Friday), Uphill's father said, 'My son was hoping to make good use of his experience in flying. He recently received intimation that he was to be granted an interview concerning a short-service commission in the RAF, it must have given him tremendous pleasure. I think he was just working off his exuberance when he was killed.'

The coroner then proceeded to question Ranald Porteous, instructor at Reading Aero Club, who had given instruction to Uphill from the beginning of the year. Flight Lieutenant J.D.H. Slade, also an instructor at the flying school, saw the machine diving in an inverted position from 1,500 feet to 50 feet from the ground, it went into a left-hand inverted climbing turn and reached 400 feet. Uphill must have pulled the stick back, and the plane dived straight into the ground.

Flight Lieutenant Tommy Rose, chief flying instructor and secretary of the Reading Aero Club, said the Air Ministry had issued an 'A' licence to Uphill on 17 March this year.

The coroner said an official of the Air Ministry had intimated that he was satisfied that there was nothing wrong with the machine. Mr Payne added; 'This young man was rather too venturesome, and unfortunately attempted too much'.

Reading Mercury for Saturday, 13 May 1939 reported what was being planned for Empire Air Day:

EMPIRE AIR DAY AT READING
RAF AND CIVIL PILOTS IN FLYING DISPLAY

Low-level bombing, wing formation flying, individual aerobatics, and a fly-past of nine, 335 mph Hurricane monoplane fighters, are features of the Empire Air Day programme at Reading Aerodrome on Saturday, 20 May.

PHILLIPS AND POWIS AIRCRAFT LTD

Other events include formation flying by members of the RAF Volunteer Reserve stationed at Reading Flying Training School, flight aerobatics by four Gloster Gauntlet, 230 mph, single seater fighters, a fly-past of various types, including a 145 mph Magister, a 187 mph Hawker Hind day bomber, a Lysander, a 250 mph American Harvard, a Bristol Blenheim 285 mph twin engine bomber, a Hurricane and a 295 mph Master two seater, advanced trainer.

During the afternoon visitors will see pupils of the RAF Volunteer Reserve receiving training in the landings of six Hawk Trainers.

A broadcast description of the events will be given by Captain E.D. Ayre, and joy rides at 5 shillings will be available in a DH Dragon Rapide, an eight-seat, twin engined aircraft, from 2 pm until dusk. Lucky numbers for holders of tickets and programmes will be announced during the afternoon.

Reading is one of fifteen civil aerodromes which, in addition to fifty-two RAF stations, will give displays to the public on Empire Air Day.

Reading Mercury for Saturday, 20 May 1939 reported:

CIVIL AIR GUARD SPEED-UP FIFTY MEMBERS WITH 'A' LICENCE

Since the Civil Air Guard (CAG) scheme came into operation last October, over fifty members who have trained at Reading have passed their 'A' licence tests, but this year has seen a speeding-up in training. At the present moment there are still three hundred prospective pilots on the CAG waiting list.

The fleet of planes has been increased recently by two, and there have also been additions to the flying staff, making it possible for more members to undergo training at the same time.

Mr R.L. Porteous, who joined the Reading Aero Club as second instructor in September last year, has now left to join the instructors of No. 8 Elementary and Reserve Flying Training School at Woodley, previously known as the Reserve Training School. Flight Lieutenant Tommy Rose has been joined in the training of Civil Air Guard members by Mr Peter Dawson and Mr Maurice Thompson, both of whom have been with the RAF Volunteer Reserve and hold the rank of Sergeant Pilot. Mr Dawson was a member of the Reading Aero Club in 1933 and he later joined the RAF Volunteer Reserve, took an instructor's course, and started in his present position at the beginning of the month.

Tommy Rose competed in the fourth Manx Air Derby in May 1939 in the prototype Miles M.2E Hawk Speed Six G-ACTE, and came second at a speed of 183.75 mph.

On 23 May 1939, Tommy Rose was awarded the Master Flying Instructor's Diploma by the Guild of Pilots and Air Navigators of the British Empire (GAPAN). One of the prime reasons for founding the Guild in 1929, was the need for improvement in standards of piloting and instruction as it was apparent to the Guild that instruction should be properly organised and only carried out by qualified instructors. To this end a Panel of Examiners was to set up within the Guild, the members of which were authorised by the Air Ministry to carry out a flight test to endorse an instructor's license.

The signatures on the diploma were those of the Grand Master (George) The Duke of Kent, The Master Lord Londonderry (5th Marquess), and the clerk, Lawrence Wingfield. Tommy Rose had been tested by one of the panel who was authorised to instruct.

The qualifications for a Master Flying Instructor's Diploma were that they must be a British Subject (whether a member of the Guild or not), who on the 1 February 1939:

Group A

1. Holds the Guild's full instructor's certificate.
2. Had completed 2,500 instructional flying hours, or equivalent practical experience as a flying instructor.
3. Had been engaged as a flying instructor within the British Empire for approximately five years out of the eight preceding eight years.
4. Had a satisfactory pupil record.

Or alternatively:

Group B

Complied with the above conditions computed at any date subsequent to 1 February 1939, and in addition such further examination as the Guild required. Every application under Group B would be accompanied by a form signed by four Master Flying Instructors, of which Tommy Rose was now one.

In June 1939, the staff and Tommy Rose at Woodley provided aeroplanes, courtesy of Phillips and Powis, to play important parts in practice drills for National Service Displays at Hill Meadow, Reading, for the Reading National Service Committee and the group practiced a 'Village bombing', in front of the mayor (Councillor W.E. McIlroy), and other leaders of the borough.

An article published in the *Newcastle Evening Chronicle* for Wednesday, 28 June 1939, which undoubtedly caused a storm of protest from the ladies when it appeared, is reproduced below!

WOMEN TOO OLD TO FLY AT 30

'Once women reach the age of 30, they can never learn to fly', says Captain H.J.C. Gray, chief flying instructor of the Rand Flying Club, Johannesburg, South Africa.

'If a woman is young, healthy, keen and indulges in a fair amount of sport, and has some intelligence, there is a fair chance of making a pilot of her'. He added, 'But once they reach the age of 30 years it is hopeless'.

Flight Lieutenant Tommy Rose said, 'If you take fifty men and train them as pilots, forty of them will make good. But take fifty women and usually only one will pass. There are a few women instructresses who do well. But there again they are usually the ones-in-fifty who make reliable fliers.'

Miss Doreen Hooper, South Africa's leading woman flier and instructress, thinks Tommy Rose is exaggerating. 'You must not forget that women are just learning what men have known for years', she says. 'Aviation is like motor car driving. When a woman is good at it she usually beats the men. But when she is bad, she is very, very bad'.

Miss M. Byrd, Flight Commander in the South African Women's Civil Air Guard, says in a Johannesburg BUP message, that she was indignant when she heard of the men's statement.

'If women are as useless as all that why is Britain training her women into air guards and giving them equal rights with the men?' she demanded. 'Besides, women are very light on the controls and don't take the unnecessary risks that men take'.

Joan Parsons responded to the men's adverse comments about women pilots in the *Coventry Herald* for Saturday, 22 July 1939, as follows:

WOMEN AIR PILOTS TOO OLD AFTER 30?
JOAN PARSONS REPLIES TO MALE CRITICS

'Women over thirty make the best air pilots', declares Miss Joan Mary Parson, the well-known Leamington airwoman.

This is her answer to Captain H.J.C. Gray, a South African flying instructor, who recently said that if a woman is young, healthy, and keen and has indulged in a fair amount of sport, there was every opportunity of her becoming an air pilot, provided she has not yet reached the age of thirty. After thirty they could never hope to learn to fly.

Flight Lieutenant Tommy Rose has also put a damper on women who wish to become an air pilot by declaring that out of fifty men trained for the Air Force, forty of them usually make good, but, taking the same number of women for training, only one out of every fifty learns to become a reliable pilot.

But there is no need to be discouraged. Miss Parsons, who last year flew solo to the Cape, and who is a past pupil of Tommy Rose, thinks that their statements are utterly ridiculous.

In July, Reading's Civil Air Guard was inspected by Captain H.H. Balfour, the Parliamentary Under-Secretary of State for Air. The *Reading Mercury* for Saturday, 8 July 1939 reported:

A new air scheme under which members of the Civil Air Guard will assist in the delivery of aeroplanes from factory to service aerodromes all over the country was outlined by Captain H.H. Balfour, the Parliamentary Under-Secretary of State for Air, when he visited the Civil Air Guard at Woodley early on Saturday at the beginning of a tour of inspection of

FLIGHT LIEUTENANT THOMAS 'TOMMY' ROSE DFC

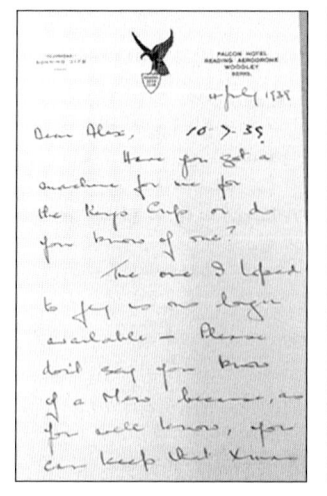

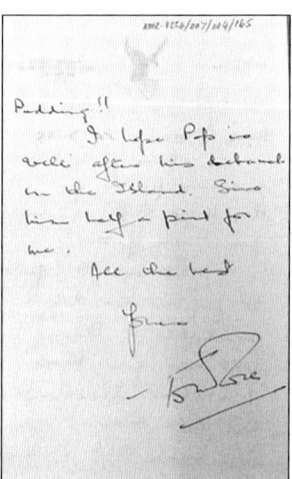

Letter sent by Tommy Rose to his good friend Alex Henshaw, regarding a possible entry for the 1939 King's Cup Air Race. Interesting to see Tommy Rose's opinion of the Mew Gull! In the end the race was cancelled due to the storm clouds that were gathering on the horizon.

various units throughout the country. Captain Balfour flew to Reading from Hendon, and despite the fact he arrived ten minutes before the scheduled time, and that they had only had short notice of the visit, fifteen members welcomed him and had their five machines all spick and span ready for him to inspect.

The purpose of Captain Balfour's visit was mainly to ascertain how the Civil Air Guard scheme was working, and he asked many questions of the members at Reading, who were under the charge of Flight Lieutenant Tommy Rose. He was informed that there were forty fully qualified members, whilst thirty-five were ongoing training, and there was a waiting list of 500.

During his visit Captain Balfour mentioned the scheme for forming a Civil Air Guards' Pilots Ferry Pool. Under this scheme experienced pilots will relieve RAF officers of the task of delivering new machines from the factories to the various service stations.

Before leaving Woodley for Shoreham, Captain Balfour congratulated the local unit in their efficiency and on the valuable work they were doing for their country. Captain Balfour was using a Vega Gull machine, which he flew himself, although having a pilot with him.

In July, Tommy Rose flew a Miles Magister over Wokingham, who were to stage a fire in Peach Street, where borough and rural ARP operatives combined in a special exercise. The personnel taking part included wardens, demolition squads, fire services and first aid workers, realism was given to the exercise by using high-explosive and incendiary bombs.

PHILLIPS AND POWIS AIRCRAFT LTD

On 5 August 1939, Tommy Rose attended the Cinque Ports meeting at Lympne, on what was to be the last major air race before the war. Tommy, flying a BA Eagle, had to be content with fifth place in the last heat of the Folkstone Trophy Race, which was won by The Hon A.W. Dalrymple, in a Chilton monoplane which he had co-designed.

The *Surrey Advertiser* for Saturday, 19 August 1939 reported on Tommy Rose's visit to Guilford:

> **FAMOUS AIRMAN VISITS GUILDFORD**
> **INTRODUCED TO ODEON AUDIENCE**
> *On Monday the audience at the Odeon Guildford, where Columbia's much heralded success* 'Q Planes', *is the main feature of the week, heard an ace flier's opinion of flying films. The airman who paid a visit to the Odeon stage on this appropriate occasion was Flight Lieutenant Rose.*
>
> *'I have seen most flying films', he said, 'and I think they are all lousy.* Hells Angels *is the best flying film I have seen but,' he added with a smile, 'I have yet to see this one.'*
>
> *If the experts' view coincided with that of the rest of the audience,* 'Q Planes' *provided the exception to his general opinion of flying films.*
>
> *Tommy Rose appeared on the stage just before* 'Q Planes' *was shown for the last time in Monday's performances, and he received a big ovation. He was introduced by Mr E. Rhodes, manager of the Odeon, who has known him for a considerable time. The Mayor and Mayoress of Guildford Alderman R.H. Tribe and Mrs R.H. Tribe, and Chief Constable Mr W. Oliver, were among the large audience.*

On 15 November 1939, 'Bill' Skinner, Chief Test Pilot of Phillips & Powis Aircraft Ltd, died suddenly at his home from a cerebral haemorrhage and his obituary, written by F.G. Miles, appeared in *Flight* for 23 November 1939:

> **AN APPRECIATION**
> *Mr Bill Skinner died from a cerebral haemorrhage on Wednesday, 15 November 1939. He was, as most flying people know, Chief Test Pilot to Phillips and Powis Aircraft Ltd. He joined us as an instructor in the Reading Training School, when it started in 1935, and transferred over to the testing job two years ago. He took a fierce interest and a constant delight in his work. I have never seen his desk except occupied by a technical book or report left marked and open, usually while he had been called away on his routine flight test.*
>
> *He really knew his job and until his death he was entering more and more into the life of the firm.*
>
> *In addition to the ordinary everyday test work, he contributed a great deal of knowledge towards the spinning of low-wing monoplanes. He was, I believe, the first man in England to recover from an uncontrollable spin*

by means of a tail parachute; certainly, nobody knew for certain that it would work and we did know the spin was uncontrollable.

His work made it possible to develop monoplanes which are absolutely safe in the spin. He probably tested more purely experimental wings, gadgets and aeroplanes than any other pilot over a similar period, and his reports were a model.

When he had a dangerous job, he did everything that common sense and knowledge could do to make it safe; if it was still dangerous he still did it.

We miss him very much and extend our deepest sympathy to his widow and two children.

Tommy Rose's Divorce 1939

As already mentioned earlier, Tommy Rose married his first wife Margaret Elizabeth Ashford on 16 July 1925 and from that marriage a daughter, Elizabeth, was born on 23 January 1929.

Margaret and Tommy appeared to have been reasonably happy, apart from his profligacy with money matters, but then Margaret felt that Tommy had little time for their married life and of supporting their daughter. It must have been very difficult for Margaret to cope with Tommy Rose's flying commitments, as in 1931 he was away for almost the whole year. Securing a career where he could earn an income to support his wife and family was difficult and up to this time it would appear the Rose family were living mostly in rented accommodation or hotels.

I am not making any excuses for what Tommy Rose did, but we can only imagine the pressure he was under after the failed 1931 attempt on the Cape record, having lost the chance to win £2,500 (just over £171,000 today), which could have bought the family security for the future, and a permanent place to live.

Margaret clearly loved Tommy and she must have been devastated by the way he apparently just abandoned her and their much-loved daughter. She could never understand why he did not keep her informed of his whereabouts, or his future intentions, and at first she was under the impression that Tommy had just left the house temporarily, so they could all continue to live together as a family. Margaret's parents had been very kind and accommodating in helping Tommy and Margaret, and at very short notice too. Margaret had always been very supportive of Tommy's flying aspirations and moved with him wherever he went, but this nomadic lifestyle must have been very difficult, especially with a small child to care for in rented accommodation.

Margaret was extremely anxious to find Tommy, as any wife would have been, she asked their various friends, where he had gone, and why, as it must have been traumatic for the whole family never knowing where he had disappeared to. One of Tommy's friends stated that he was taking a rich American on a round-the-world air cruise. This turned out later to be partly true, but it has been impossible to establish where he went during this time. Although Margaret was later to read about his exploits in the national newspapers and he did send sporadic payments for her and Elizabeth's welfare, Tommy contacted her in 1933 to arrange to see Elizabeth, but this came to nothing. Tommy later flew to Salisbury to see Margaret and while there he carried the delighted Elizabeth back to the house on his shoulders. Later, another meeting was arranged in London for Tommy to see his daughter when she was about ten or eleven years old, this was to be the last time he saw her.

By this time Margaret must have finally realised that their marriage was over.

However, it was not until 1936, when Margaret was reading the newspaper reports of Tommy Rose's triumphant return from the Cape, that he was being welcomed back in this country by a lady referred to as Mrs Rose. Only then did she realise that Tommy was involved with another woman. This must have come as a devastating blow for her. Margaret then, with the help of her parents, decided to employ a private detective, from the Strand, London, to investigate what was going on and to find out who this woman was, and was there enough evidence to be able to file for a divorce?

The private investigator proceeded to Falcon House, Sonning, where he confirmed that Tommy and the new 'Mrs Rose', in reality Beatrice (Billie) Barbara Lott, were in fact living together and neither Tommy Rose nor Billie contested the evidence made against them. Later, when interviewed in the London offices in 1941, Margaret was able to pursue her divorce from Tommy.

In the divorce petition (1939) Margaret stated they lived at the Sun Hotel, Hitchin, Herts, after Tommy Rose left the RAF in October 1926, and later at Shefford in Bedford. Tommy Rose clearly had responsibilities, including a young daughter who was only

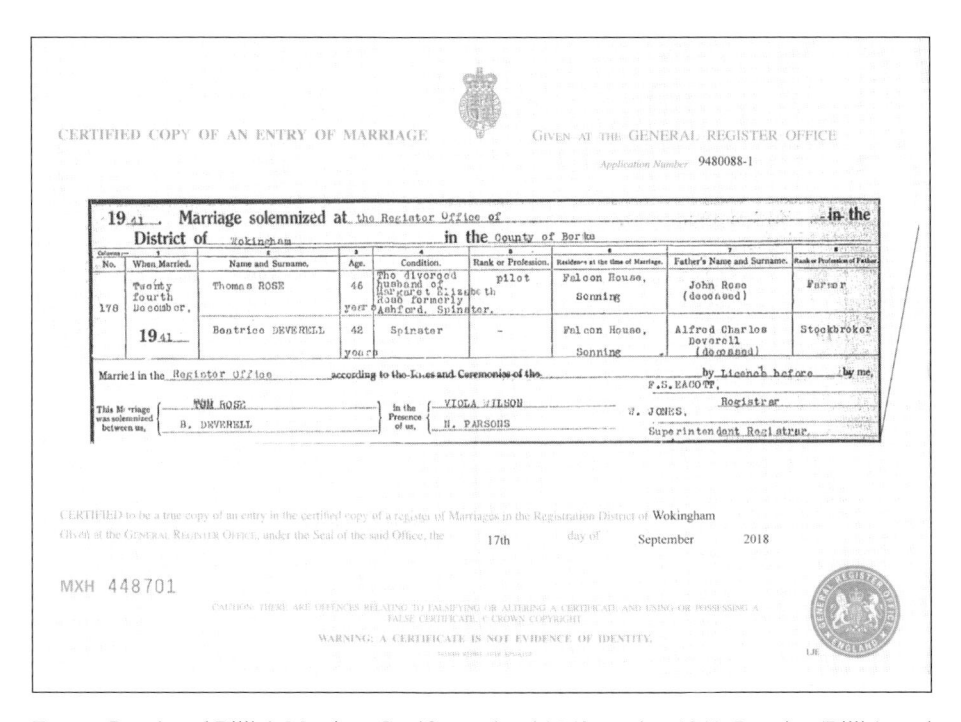

Tommy Rose's and Billie's Marriage Certificate, dated 24 December 1941. Beatrice (Billie) used two surnames one Lott and the other Deverell. Billies father was Alfred Charles Lott, Billies mothers maiden name was Deverell!

three years old, when he left. There was also the support of his young wife, who in those days was unable to work.

The Decree Absolute was dated 8 December 1941 and Tommy Rose actually married Billie on Christmas Eve 1941 at a very small ceremony at the Wokingham Registry Office. Everyone at Phillips & Powis Aircraft Ltd were unaware of their secret wedding, having assumed they were already married and had been so for some time.

In later years, after Tommy and Billie had retired to the Island of Alderney, stories about the reason for Margaret's divorce were being circulated to the effect that Margaret had been suffering from 'a mental illness' (a stock excuse for divorces at the time), but these were very defamatory and completely unfounded. Peter Amos also recalls this story as it was relayed to him by Mrs Loderer, who had also managed hotels on Sark and Guernsey while Tommy and Billie were staying there and had become great friends of theirs.

So, not unnaturally, Mrs Loderer believed it as it was told to her, 'in good faith', by Tommy.

Peter also had no reason not to have believed it either. However, this was long before the truth was finally revealed after I had met with Elizabeth, Tommy Rose's daughter.

FOOTNOTE
Ranald Porteous (of later Auster fame) wrote a story in *More Tails of the Fifties* (published by Cirrus Associates Ltd in 1998) of his flying experiences and his time as a flying instructor for the Reading Aero Club from 1938. In this he recalled that:

> *A chance arose to join the Miles organisation, starting as assistant to the famous, great and good (all three, in generous measure) Tommy Rose, who at that time ran the Reading Aero Club at Woodley. There was talk of occasional test-flying etc. within the firm, so brandishing my recently acquired instructor's licence, I bade fond farewell to Geoffrey* (Alington) *and Bunny* (Spratt) *(of the Gatwick-based Air Touring – PA). It had been a fun time but Woodley was a more serious challenge.*
>
> *Tommy Rose was beyond all praise. Bluff, jovial, kindly and extrovert, he was nevertheless shrewd in matters of human nature. His considerable fame and seniority rested lightly on his shoulders and to me, a relative whippersnapper, he combined the functions of benevolent boss, father-confessor and merry uncle. He had, to an exceptional degree, the rare gift of giving one a feeling of his real interest and genuine concern. He had lost none of this when I stayed with him many years later in Alderney.*

Chapter 16

Chief Test Pilot Phillips and Powis Aircraft Ltd, later Miles Aircraft Ltd
November 1939 – January 1946

> *Learn to test, test to learn*
> *– Empire Test Pilots' School Motto*

On 1 April 1937, Bill Skinner was appointed Chief Test Pilot of Phillips & Powis Aircraft Ltd, a post which he held until his untimely death from a cerebral haemorrhage while shaving in the bathroom at his home in Reading on 15 November 1939, at the early age of thirty-six years. This happened shortly after he had commenced test flying the Miles M.19 Master Mk.II prototype, N7422. It was, however, during the resolution of the spinning problems of the early Miles Magisters and the valuable contribution to the development of the Miles M.9 Master – the firm's first high-powered aircraft – that should really have made Bill Skinner famous. However, these achievements were never fully acknowledged outside the firm.

Flight Lieutenant Tommy Rose was then appointed Chief Test Pilot and, together with George Miles, they completed the trials of the new Bristol Mercury-engined Miles M.19 Master Mk.II prototype.

However, as the volume of flight testing increased, Tommy was joined by Flight Lieutenant Hugh Kennedy. From the Operational Record Book for RAF Woodley, comes the following record: 27.10.39 F/Lt. H.V. Kennedy transferred to Messrs. Phillips & Powis Aircraft Co. Ltd, as Test Pilot.

Shortly after the outbreak of the Second World War, with the formation of the Local Defence Volunteers (later to become the Home Guard), Tommy Rose joined the 6th Battalion, Berkshire Home Guard**,** Woodley, with the rank of Major. They were an armed militia; their role was mainly to act as a secondary defence force in case of an invasion.

Thankfully, their services were never needed, but in the December 1944 edition of the *Miles Magazine,* Tommy wrote:

> **To the Officers, and other ranks Aerodrome Company, 6**[th] **Battalion, Berks, Home Guard, from Major Rose,** *I would like to take this opportunity of saying 'Thank You' to all of you on the occasion of our official 'Stand-Down'. No one could have had more enthusiastic support and no Company Commander in the Home Guard could have had less to do or have done less, more successfully than I have.*

FLIGHT LIEUTENANT THOMAS 'TOMMY' ROSE DFC

Above left: Tommy Rose in his famous camel overcoat and cravat, posing for the photographer in the cockpit of an early Miles M.9 Mk 1 at Woodley. (*P&P via Peter Amos*)

Above right: Major Tommy Rose, of the 6th Battalion of the Berkshire Home Guard, Woodley. Note the RAF wings proudly worn on Tommy Rose's Home Guard uniform. This, surely, has to be unique in the annals of the Home Guard! (*via Peter Amos*)

> *The difficulties in a Factory Company are such that in the four years of our battle, 'Home Guard v Production', one has needed diplomatic rather than soldierly qualities to compete at all.*
>
> *As always, it was not those who shouted the loudest who did most of the work and, while appreciating everyone's efforts, I would especially single out those NCOs who have turned out without a murmur or word of thanks, for three or four nights a week throughout the whole time. To those few who made no effort to fulfil their obligations and did their best to influence others to their way of sabotage I bid 'Soldiers Farewell' and a loud one at that.*
>
> *I am more grateful to those who made an effort and turned out for our 'Stand Down' Parade at Bracknell. I feel certain that none of us will forget that for a long, long time.*
>
> *If at any time I can be of assistance to any of you, please do not hesitate to call on me. Once again Thank You and 'Fear Nothing'.*

Apart from the numerous aircraft produced by Phillips & Powis/Miles Aircraft, Tommy Rose also probably tested a number of Supermarine Spitfires at Woodley during the war as the firm also had a contract to overhaul and modify these aircraft.

Aircraft test flown by Tommy Rose

Before I list the various types he flew, however, I must relate a lovely story by Roy Morris, a 16-year-old very keen lad at the factory who often flew with Tommy Rose as 'ballast', in 1941, while he was waiting to join the RAF, as relayed to Peter Amos in a letter many years later:

> *Tommy usually carried out production test flights in the area just south of Reading, away from any built-up area, and they rarely lasted more than 40 to 45 minutes. They normally did not include any aerobatics and were usually between 2,500 and 5,000 feet altitude, depending on the weather.*
>
> *Roy's home was near the bottom of Southampton Street in Reading, not too far from where Tommy operated. His mother knew that he was flying with Tommy or Hugh Kennedy occasionally (as she had to sign a paper allowing him to do this, at their risk, of course), and every time she heard a plane overhead or in the distance she would rush out and wave in case he was in it. He told her it was unlikely because the test flight pilots were not allowed over the town.*
>
> *As he got to know Tommy very well after flying with him so many times, he resolved to wait for the right opportunity before taking off to ask him to 'shoot up' Southampton Street so that he could wave back to his mother. When the time came, he told his mother what he was about to do and when he next saw Tommy's car come round the corner of the Flight Shed, and as he seemed to be in a happy mood as he got out to go into the outside office, he sprinted over to ask him if he could go along as usual. He replied, 'Not today – the wind-speed is too high and you would be as sick as a dog in ten minutes'. Roy said that he'd never been even close to being airsick and when Tommy asked him how many passenger hours he had flown and of these, how many were in bad weather, Roy told him about 125 hours, including about 25 hours of bad weather. This wasn't true of course as Roy had only flown about 20-25 hours, and all in perfect flying weather.*
>
> *Tommy hesitated but replied, 'OK – sign the blood chit, get a parachute and hurry up!' That took him all of 20 seconds and as they walked over to the Master parked about 40 or 50 yards away, he asked Tommy whether he could 'shoot up' Southampton Street on the way there. Tommy laughed and said, 'Not a hope – I could get grounded for that.' As they climbed in he turned to Roy and asked if he was absolutely sure he wanted to go and pointed to the windsock, which was going up and down violently, Roy said that he was just fine and they took off.*
>
> *After they had reached an altitude of about 1,000 feet and although Roy was tightly strapped in it seemed like every projection in the cockpit, including even the nuts and bolts, made a beeline for his body. By the time they reached about 2,000 feet, Roy was feeling like 'a piece of meat in a meat-grinder'!*
>
> *Incidentally, while walking to the Master, Tommy had casually mentioned he had not had time to finish his lunch and after ten minutes flying, and feeling more and more sick all the time, Roy was hoping he was still feeling hungry and would return early!*

FLIGHT LIEUTENANT THOMAS 'TOMMY' ROSE DFC

Left: The Miles M.9 Master Mk.I in flight. (*via Peter Amos*)

Below left: A Miles Master Mk III being flown by Tommy Rose. (*via Peter Amos*)

Below right: Tommy Rose on the wing of the M.20 during 1940.

After a particularly nasty piece of turbulence hit, he turned around to Roy, with a huge grin on his face, and shouted, 'Isn't this fantastic!' Roy wasn't so sure though! But he nodded – and continued to pray for an early end to it!

Ten minutes or so later, after Tommy had completed the tests, he turned to Roy and shouted (the Masters were not fitted with intercom at that time), 'OK, let's shoot up Southampton Street.' Normally, Roy would have been ecstatic but anything to delay his return to solid terra-firma was definitely extremely negative. It was all Roy could do to stop himself from being violently airsick!

Roy kept dragging himself up to look over the side of the cockpit as they gradually lost height and built-up speed, but the turbulence near the ground was obviously worse. Tommy flew exceptionally low that day and Roy remembered looking up at the weathercock on the spire of St Giles Church near the bottom of Southampton Street! He never did see his house or his mother though.

CHIEF TEST PILOT PHILLIPS AND POWIS

They finally returned to Woodley and as they rolled to a stop Roy got out (fell out, more likely), and Tommy came up behind him and said, with a laugh, 'Well! How did you like that – good eh!' Roy replied, 'Fantastic!' Tommy then said, 'You know – you don't look so good – are you feeling alright?' Roy managed to say that he had loved every minute of it so Tommy then said, 'Good! Get in that Master over there while I go and sign for it – we'll do it again!' At that point Roy felt that he needed another flight like that like he needed a hole in his head! Roy made some excuse about getting the OK from his foreman and beat it to the nearest lavatory! Nothing could have persuaded him to leave the sanctity of that haven, until he heard Tommy start up that Master and taxi away.

The sequel to that flight came when Roy got home that night and asked his mother if she had seen him flying low about 3 pm, she replied she had not as she had been visiting a friend in Battle Hospital about that time. That just made Roy's perfect day!

Miles M.9B Master Mk.I, Miles M.9C Master Mk.IA and the Miles 'Peregrine' Fighter Project. This was an Advanced Trainer fitted with a Rolls-Royce Kestrel engine and was already in production when Tommy Rose was appointed Chief Test Pilot in November 1939. The first production Master Mk.1 was first flown by F.G. Miles on 31 March 1939, but production aircraft testing would certainly have kept Tommy Rose and Hugh Kennedy busy until early 1941.

Miles M.14 Magister and M.14A Magister. This was an Elementary Trainer, in which F.G. Miles had made the first flight on 20 March 1937. It was still in production when Tommy Rose joined, and production aircraft were also test flown by him.

Miles M.18 Mk.I, Mk.II, Mk.III and Mk.IV High Lift. An 'Improved Elementary Trainer'. Designed by Walter Gustav Kaeppeli who joined the team at Woodley as chief stress man. Kaeppeli, who was born in Zurich, Switzerland on 8 November 1913, had come to England in 1934. He was taught to fly by British Air Transport Ltd at Gatwick, in DH.60 Moths and qualified for his 'A' licence in June 1934. In June 1940 he was granted British nationality and he then changed his name to Capley. Soon after his arrival, however, Miles gave him the job of designing a replacement for the Magister and he was to become very well respected by Miles in later years. The prototype was first flown, by F.G. Miles, as U2 on 4 December 1938 and he noted that the M.18's controls were light, well-harmonised and effective. This was developed through three marks and served to test a multitude of requirements

Miles M.19 Master Mk.II, Miles M.19 Master GT Mk.II and the Miles 'Mercury Fighter'. This was an Advanced Trainer development of the Master Mk.I, but fitted with a Bristol Mercury air-cooled radial engine, as a result of a foreseen shortage of Rolls-Royce Kestrel engines. It was first flown in October 1939 by the Chief Test Pilot, 'Bill' Skinner. It was in this aircraft that Tommy Rose gained his first experience as the

FLIGHT LIEUTENANT THOMAS 'TOMMY' ROSE DFC

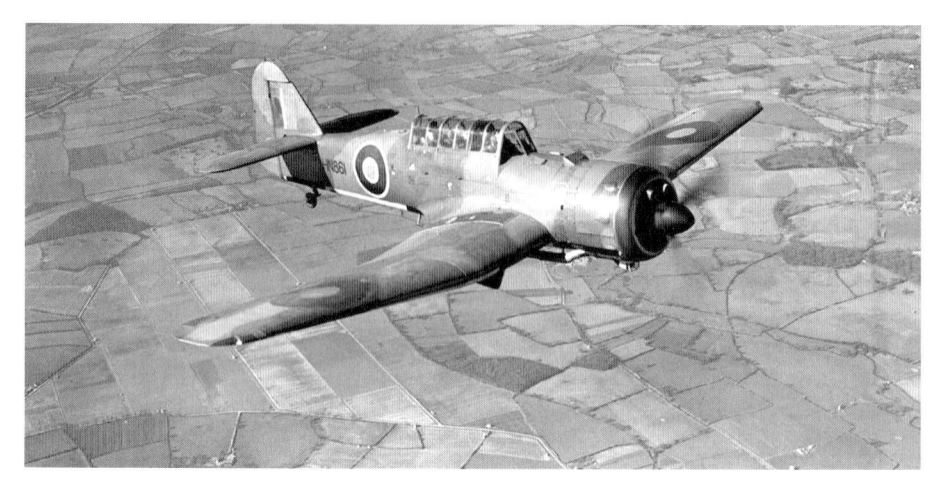

HN861, the first production Miles M.25 Martinet TT Mk.I target tug on a test flight. (*via Peter Amos*)

new Chief Test Pilot (following Bill Skinner's unfortunate demise), when he shared the test flying of it in November 1939 with George Miles. Some were also modified as glider tugs, 1,250 built at Woodley and 498 at South Marston.

Ken Waller, who had been the resident test pilot at South Marston, was then sent to South Africa with a working party from the factory to help with the introduction of the Master into the South African Air Force. SAAF records state that he had made his first test flight in a Master Mk.II by 13 January 1942, but he returned to the UK after a short period. While Ken was away the Masters were test flown, probably at weekends, by Hugh Kennedy from Woodley, whose logbooks confirm that he flew their completed Masters from 8 July 1941 to 25 July 1941 then, after a break when they were probably flown by Tommy Rose, again between 22 September 1941 to 16 October 1941, a total of forty-two new build aircraft. Ken Waller returned from South Africa in late 1941, so he would have then taken South Marston's production over again.

Miles P.V. 'Munich' Fighter, Miles M.20/2 P.V. Single-Seat Fighter to Spec. F.19/40, Miles M.20/3 P.V. Fighter Bomber, Miles M.20/4 P.V. Royal Navy Single-Seat Fighter to Spec. N.1/41 and the Miles M.20A Low Attack Fighter. In September 1938, at about the time of the Munich crisis, Miles decided that the RAF needed a fighter aircraft for defence, which would be cheap and easy to produce, to be of wooden construction, and to use the majority of Master metal components, however, the moment passed and nothing came of the project. Then, in June 1940, at about the onset of what we now know as the Battle of Britain, Miles resurrected the idea of a utility fighter aircraft with eight or twelve machine guns, for the medium and high altitude, day and night roles and commenced construction of a private venture prototype. This was to be made of wood and powered by a Rolls-Royce Merlin XX, twelve-cylinder, liquid-cooled engine fitted with a two-speed, single-stage supercharger, driving a three-blade, constant-speed Rotol airscrew.

The new fighter was designated M.20/2 and Miles approached the dynamic Minister of Aircraft production, Lord Beaverbrook, and showed him his proposals. Beaverbrook realised that if the Supermarine or Hawker works got bombed, then there would be a real need for the Miles fighter. Jeremy Miles recalls that Beaverbrook was apparently quite impressed with the idea and told Miles that if he could build it in three months, he would pay for it, but if he couldn't, then Miles would have to pay for it!

By then, construction of the prototype was under way and work proceeded at such a pace that the M.20/2 fighter was in fact designed, built and flown in the remarkably short space of just nine weeks and two days from its inception.

The prototype fighter, fitted with eight .303 Browning machine guns, was first flown, by Tommy Rose on 15 September 1940 (not the 14 September 1940 as stated in many reference works). Although it was confirmed that Tommy Rose's logbooks were lost during the course of several of his moves, it has still been possible to confirm the date of the first flight of the M.20/2 from the logbooks of Hugh Kennedy, the firm's assistant test pilot. Hugh Kennedy flew the Master Mk.II, N7447, on 15 September 1940, noting in his logbook: 'Guarding M.20 on its first flight'. A Hawker Hurricane Mk.I, L1788, and a Supermarine Spitfire Mk.IA, P9444, were loaned to Phillips & Powis by the RAE Farnborough, for comparative trials with the Miles M.20 Fighter. Both types would almost certainly have been flown by Tommy Rose and Hugh Kennedy.

However, to the great disappointment of the design and experimental team, the M.20 was not produced in quantity, with only the two prototypes being made, but it had made a good insurance policy in what had been the most difficult time for this country.

Flight trials progressed successfully and substantiated the fulfilment of all the design hopes at Miles. It was also demonstrated at Northolt Aerodrome, together with a typical Hurricane and Spitfire, in the presence of senior military personnel, and the Prime Minister, Winston Churchill.

Miles M.24 Master Fighter/Master six-gun Fighter Trainer. Immediately after Dunkirk, in June 1940, permission was given by the Air Ministry Development Branch, Harrogate, to convert twenty-five Master Mk.I's into Master Fighters, 'on the assembly line'. The Master Fighter was basically a single-seat version of the Master advanced trainer, fitted with 6 x .303 Browning machine guns in the wings and was intended as a reserve fighter should the need arise. The prototype, with a single-seat and fixed cockpit canopy, a reflector gunsight, bulletproof windscreen and plating added for the protection of the pilot and engine, was converted from Master Mk.I N7412. Twenty-five were actually completed as M.24 Master Fighters on the assembly line and these were delivered to the flying training schools between 20 June and 28 June 1940, but then, just two weeks after permission to convert the aircraft, Phillips & Powis were instructed to stop work on the project.

The Master Fighter had been designed and built with such speed that it was not allotted a type designation number and only after the Battle of Britain had been fought and won in September 1940, was it allotted the designation M.24, for record purposes, hence the Master Fighter's designation number being out of sequence.

FLIGHT LIEUTENANT THOMAS 'TOMMY' ROSE DFC

The firm's Ministry of Aircraft production approved Test Pilots in 1945, left to right: Hugh Kennedy, Assistant Test Pilot; Tommy Rose, Chief Test Pilot; George Miles, Technical Director and Test Pilot; Don Brown, George Miles' Personal Assistant and Test Pilot, with a Miles M.28 in the background. (*via Peter Amos*)

Miles M.25 Martinet TT Mk.I Target Tower to Spec. 12/41 and Miles M.25 Martinet Mk.II. Until 1941, target-towing duties had been performed by various obsolescent types of aircraft, which had originally been designed for other tasks. As supplies of these began to run short, Miles was asked by the Ministry whether he could design and put into rapid production a specialised target-tug based on the Master, using as many standard parts as possible but deleting the dual flying controls and substituting a winch and stowage for the targets. The first prototype Martinet was completed in a very short space of time, and was first flown, by Tommy Rose, on 24 April 1942.

This was followed, at regular intervals, by a succession of 'X' projects, ranging from passenger transports to heavy bombers, the last being the Miles M.27 Master Mk.III.

Miles M.27 Master Mk.III. This was an Advanced Trainer development of the Master Mk.I, but fitted with a Pratt & Whitney Twin Wasp Junior, air-cooled radial engine. It was produced as a result of an unforeseen shortage of Bristol Mercury engines and the prototype was first flown, by Flight Lieutenant Hugh Kennedy, on 17 December 1940. 602 built at South Marston.

Miles M.28 Training and Communications Aircraft. During 1939, George Miles started work on the design of a replacement aircraft for two very successful Miles aeroplanes; the Whitney Straight of 1936, and the Monarch, his first design, of 1938. However, on the outbreak of war in September 1939, the project had to be dropped. He resurrected the project in 1941 and the first of six variants was flown by George Miles on 11 July 1941.

CHIEF TEST PILOT PHILLIPS AND POWIS

Tommy Rose, standing in the cockpit after the first flight of the M.30 'X' Minor in February 1942 with, F.G. Miles, Blossom, and others listening to the verdict. (*via Peter Amos*)

Miles M.30 'X' Minor. The M.30 'X' Minor was first flown by Tommy Rose in February 1942. The principle of the Miles 'X' airliner project of 1936 was to have a broad, shallow fuselage of aerofoil section in the side elevation, blending gradually into the wing, with four buried engines driving propellers through gearboxes and extension shafts. F.G. Miles intended producing a full-size prototype passenger aircraft by 1938, yet the Air Ministry would only consider £25,000 for a development contract to include construction of a wooden mock-up of the 99ft wingspan design, which FG thought to be totally inadequate. The construction of the Miles M.30 'X' Minor was begun in 1941, and the design was based on a scaled-down version of the large Miles M.26 'X' airliner then being developed. The proposed Miles 'X' airliner designs, of which there were many, was to have the wing blended into the fuselage and was to be powered by six/eight engines, driving four sets of contra-rotating propellers. Seating was up to 100 depending on the routes to be flown and it would have had a range of 3,450 miles (5,550 km).

The small size of the 'X' Minor made it impossible to bury the limited range of engines available into the wings. The 'X' Minor was first flown in February 1942, by Tommy Rose, and was given the manufacturers 'B' mark U-0233, but the Miles 'X' airliner was ultimately rejected by the ministry.

Miles M.33 Monitor Target-Tower Mk.I and Mk.II to Spec. Q.9/42. The first design conference for an aircraft to meet the requirements of Specification No.Q.9/42, which, strangely enough, was not dated until 15 April 1943, was held under the direction of the Technical Director, George Miles, in October 1942. Specification No.Q.9/42 Twin Engined Target Tower, dated 15 April 1943, was issued to Phillips and Powis Aircraft Ltd on 27 April 1943. The Mk.I was to be for the RAF and the Mk.II for the RN. The prototype Monitor Mk.I, NF900, was an exceptionally clean, sleek and sharp looking aeroplane, which looked 'right' in every respect. It was first flown by Tommy Rose, with Assistant Test Pilot Flight Lieutenant Hugh V. Kennedy also on board, from Woodley, on 5 April 1944. The 35-minute flight confirmed that the new machine showed no swing on take-off, was docile and satisfactory to fly and gave no tendency to drop a wing at the stall.

During the subsequent flight testing which followed, it was found that the aircraft had a maximum speed of 360 mph and could cruise comfortably at 300 mph, and the firm considered that no major modifications to the basic design were necessary. This meant that the Monitor was, in effect, probably the fastest piston engined, non-operational aircraft in the world at that time.

The prototype Miles M.33 Monitor, NF900, was a high-speed, twin-engined, target tug, and was the largest aeroplane to be built by Miles Aircraft at the time. It was an exceptionally clean, sleek and sharp looking aeroplane, which looked 'right' in every respect.

However, a very interesting commentary on certain features of the Monitor was written by the Chief Test Pilot, Tommy Rose, after this event, on 28 April 1944. This has recently come to light amongst the papers of George Miles, and the last sentence suggests that certain problems needed urgent rectification before further flight testing was carried out!

To: Mr G.H. Miles

From: Major T. Rose   28 April 1944

PERSONAL AND CONFIDENTIAL.

As suggested, I am setting down for your consideration, a commentary on certain features of the Monitor. I have given a great deal of thought to the matter and I know you will make allowance for the fact that whilst my practical experience is considerable, my technical knowledge is not.

Rudder: This is very heavy at low speeds and gets progressively lighter as the speed increases. At 280 I.A.S. it was very light indeed and it seems likely that we shall run into very serious trouble when we go higher. There is a certain amount of stiffness in the control statically which might account for some of the heaviness at the lower range. Possibly the lightness at the other end is caused either by the servo tab being too large, (or over-geared), or by overbalancing, or both.

Trim: The fore and aft trim on the glide is unusual, inasmuch as with the C.G. in the forward position the aircraft is landed comfortably with the elevator trim tab central. With the C.G. extended aft, or even aft, it would seem that the approach will be made with the tab about halfway between central and fully forward.

The aircraft flies very starboard wing low with the control column free and requires practically full aileron tab to maintain level flight laterally. From experience on former types this is probably due to the warping of the ailerons although it may also be influenced by the rigging.

The throttles do require redesign. They should be completely rigid. At the moment they flex considerably and as they are also a little stiff in operation, they produce a stiffness and even bruising in the left hand of the pilot operating them.

Stability: You have received a confidential verbal report from Kennedy as to the instability, climbing, flaps and undercarriage fully down. As he had full fuel tanks the C.G. would be in approximately the midway position. Although I am of the opinion that the aircraft is stable in level flight at cruising boost with the C.G. forward, I have a hunch that this may not be so at the extended aft, or even aft position. I hope to goodness the hunch is a stumour, but I do think you will be well advised to take such steps as will put you in a position to remedy this in the shortest possible time should it turn out that way.

The undercarriage is such a headache to Miles and yourself that I will refrain from comment save to say that it seems to be so bloody-minded that it is not impossible that one day one leg will stick up and the other immovably down. Under this condition unless there was a very strong wind and ample time to use up all the fuel the pilot might decide to abandon the aircraft. Even if a landing was carried out the result would probably be a write off.

A copy of this will <u>not</u> be sent to Central Filing.

Signed
T Rose
CHIEF TEST PILOT

Miles M.35 Libellula. This was a tandem-wing experimental aircraft (and definitely NOT a canard, as some sources insist on calling George Miles' tandem wing projects!) that was designed in early 1942 by George Miles as a potential shipborne fighter. Such was George Miles' enthusiasm for the project that, with his courage and impetuosity, he decided that there was no time to start a programme of wind-tunnel tests, or to seek Ministry support, but to actually build a simple wooden flying mock-up as quickly as possible. This would give immediate full-scale data, although possibly at the expense of some risk to the pilot making the first flight! The rough 'flying mock-up' was actually designed, albeit unofficially and in secret, built and flown, within the incredibly short space of six weeks! By the end of April 1942, the M.35, as it was known, was complete. It was designed and built at Liverpool Road, Reading, home of the Experimental Department as, having decided not to notify the Ministry of Aircraft Production (MAP) of their intention to build it (the MAP would almost certainly not have given their authority to proceed with its construction as no work was supposed to be undertaken without their knowledge and authority during the war and failure to comply with this directive could have led to

FLIGHT LIEUTENANT THOMAS 'TOMMY' ROSE DFC

Tommy Rose at 50. (*via Peter Amos*)

the withdrawal of all materials and the consequent closure of the firm). However, although the MAP had a resident technical officer at Woodley, it was felt that if the aircraft were to suddenly arrive at Woodley it would have to be accepted as a *fait accompli*, and the firm might then just 'get away with it'!

The M.35 only had a 20ft span and was 20ft long, it was decided to tow it through the streets from Reading to Woodley early one morning before there were too many prying eyes, but the journey did cause considerable traffic problems and many of the employees arrived late for work at the factory!

When Tommy Rose first saw it assembled for the first time, he was purported to have been heard to say: 'Surely you don't expect me to fly *that*?' George Miles usually carried out the first flights of his new aeroplanes, but his flying logbooks for this period have been lost. However, assistant test pilot Flight Lieutenant Hugh Kennedy recorded 'Straights and taxiing' in the M.35 in his logbook for 29 April 1942. On 1 May 1942, George Miles, who was also a Ministry approved test pilot, then undertook the first fast taxiing trials, but during the course of these runs the M.35 showed no inclination to leave the ground, not even for the shortest hop. After two or three more attempts, he decided to risk opening the throttle again once the M.35 was airborne. This he did and to the surprise of the watchers below, he remained airborne – it had been an anxious moment – but all seemed well, so he continued straight ahead at a height of about 20ft and when some distance away, he started a gentle turn to port, continuing in a wide circuit but still at the same height. A few minutes later he appeared over the far boundary and proceeded to land. With the M.35, the first attempt to realise the expected benefits of the tandem wing was frustrated by an initial difficulty in obtaining take-off, and serious instability once in flight.

Although George found the M.35 extremely reluctant to take-off, it was later discovered that, if the throttle was closed sharply whilst at speed the aircraft would leap into the air. The initial flight had not been a success, with the aircraft almost uncontrollable due to its incorrect centre of gravity, but George managed to land it in one piece and later flights were more successful after the machine had been ballasted correctly. However, it is not known if Tommy Rose ever flew the M.35.

The design was developed into a tandem wing naval fighter project for the Admiralty as it took up less space in the hangar of an aircraft carrier, but it was not taken up. However, George was so encouraged by the tandem wing concept that he designed a twin-engined bomber based on it and submitted in July 1942 to meet the requirements of specification B.11/41, and started work on a $5/8^{th}$ scale version – the M.39B.

Miles M.38/28, Miles M.38/28 Ambulance, Miles M.38 Messenger AOP/Communications Mk. I aircraft to Spec. A.17/43 and Miles M.38 Mk. IIIB/M.48.
The Miles M.38 was designed primarily to meet the requirements for an AOP aeroplane. It is also adaptable to the following alternative uses:

a) Two to three-seater light communications aircraft.
b) Light ambulance aircraft carrying pilot, one stretcher case and one walking casualty or nurse.
c) Naval observation duties.
d) Light freight carrier.

The prototype was first flown by George Miles on 12 September 1942.

Miles M.38A Mariner. In 1943 with the war in the Atlantic becoming critical and the urgent need for an effective anti-submarine weapon, the following suggestion was advanced.

A number of ships in each convoy should be provided with a small aeroplane, or aeroplanes, designed primarily with the object of being able to fly at a very low speed and having exceptional visibility and reasonable load carrying capacity. Such an aeroplane could be rapidly developed from the Miles M.38 AOP aircraft. Such an aeroplane could be very easily launched by a variety of means, such as a simplified form of catapult, or by means of a rocket assisted take-off from a light wooden platform.

The landing apparatus would consist essentially of a sprung net arranged at an angle from the stern of the ship, together with a very simple form of arrester gear which had proved satisfactory on test.

The prototype Messenger was fitted with a light arrester hook and renamed the M.38A Mariner for the trials. These trials were to be carried out on the 60ft 'deck',

A charming photograph of Tommy Rose writing a report at his desk in 1945. (*via Peter Amos*)

which had by then been fitted with simple bungee cord arrester gear, and thanks to the excellent handling characteristics of the Mariner, no difficulty was found in engaging the arrester gear and landing within the confines of the small 'deck'. Finally, to prove that the aircraft would carry the weight of two depth-charges, Flight Lieutenant Hugh Kennedy carried out a 5 min 'Overload take-off' flight on 1 May 1943 with 'human ballast', which included George Miles, Don Brown and three others and Don recorded in his logbook '6 up, 2,580lb, t/o 8 secs!' Two light but powerful rockets, of the type used by the Royal Navy for rocket-assisted take-off, were then attached to the aircraft and these literally threw it into the air with a run of only a few yards. Flight Lieutenant Hugh Kennedy recorded a 10 min 'Take-off (Assisted)' flight on 10 June 1943 and this must have been the first time that rocket assistance was used. It is not known if Tommy Rose flew this aircraft, although I suspect that he would have done.

Miles M.39B Libellula 5/8th Flying Scale Model. George decided to build the M.39B, a single-seat, 5/8th scale flying model to prove the concept of the tandem winged aircraft and an undated artist's impression of this, entitled 'M.39B Developments (Engine Gipsy Major)' showed this with three fins and two rudders. The M.39B was first flown, by George Miles, on 22 July 1943 and it proved to have perfectly normal handling characteristics. It was found to have a slightly greater performance than that of a corresponding orthodox aircraft, and also to possess a remarkable C.G. range.

Miles M.50 Queen Martinet Pilotless Aircraft to Spec. Q.10/43. These were modified from the standard Miles M.25 Martinet to radio controlled target drone configuration. In 1943, Miles commenced work on the modification of the Martinet to Spec. Q.10/43. This called for a ground operated radio-controlled pilotless version of the M.25 Martinet TT Mk.I and this became known as the M.50 Queen Martinet.

Miles M.57 Aerovan Mk.I to Mk.6. During the spring of 1944, George Miles caught a chill and was away from his office at Liverpool Road for a week or so. When he returned to work, he had with him a sheaf of sketches and calculations, one of which was for a twin-engined low-powered cheap freighter, which could be used either for military or civil purposes, which would carry ten passengers, or a car with its four occupants, or equivalent loads, at 120 mph cruising speed and having a loaded weight of 5,200lb, to be powered by two Blackburn Cirrus Major engines. The prototype of the new aircraft, designated the Miles M.57 Aerovan, was designed and built by the Experimental Department at Liverpool Road, Reading, and was first flown by Tommy Rose on 26 January 1945. It proved an immediate success, being comfortable and easy to fly. Don Brown, who at that time had never flown a twin-engined aircraft, took off with no prior instruction and found no difficulty in piloting it. With full tanks the Aerovan could carry nearly a ton payload, a feat that had never before been achieved with an aircraft on this low power, and at this load, the run to unstick was only 600ft. Some fifty-seven were built and flown.

Without Tommy Rose's logbooks, and the wartime logbooks for Ken Waller, from 7 December 1940, which have also not survived, it has not been possible to determine the exact number of types and hours flown by Tommy Rose on production and experimental aircraft he flight tested, but fortunately, the logbooks for Flight Lieutenant Hugh Kennedy have survived and from these it has been possible to deduce a fairly accurate record of aircraft actually flown at Woodley by Tommy Rose.

There was one other test pilot at Woodley about whose test flying for Phillips & Powis is not known, and that was Brian Field, who came from Airspeed Ltd at Portsmouth. From reports, he was probably the test pilot for the Repair & Service Department at Woodley to test fly 'Repaired in Works' (RIW) aircraft. On 12 June 1943, the Master Mk.II, DM239, suffered a flying accident which necessitated it being returned to Woodley for an RIW, but while it was being test flown after repair by Brian Field on 26 August 1943, it was seen to dive into the ground, killing Brian Field.

Other service pilots that are known to have been seconded to the firm at various times included John Justin, a famous film actor who was also an RAF pilot and who it is believed was seconded to test fly the Spitfires which were being overhauled at Woodley, and Lieutenant Alan Peter Goodfellow RNVR (who had graduated from the second ETPS course). Alan Peter Goodfellow was seconded to Miles Aircraft Ltd from the FAA from 01 May 1945 to 28 July 1945, to assist with the test flying and evaluation of the Miles Monitor for the Royal Navy. Ex Air Transport Auxiliary, and later Fleet Air Arm test pilot Hugh Kendall joined the firm in September 1945 to be responsible for test flying the Miles Monitor from Tommy Rose when he retired in January 1946.

The Miles Aerovan prototype, U0248, was first flown by Tommy Rose on 26 January 1945. He can be seen at the controls with a flight test observer next to him. (*via Peter Amos*)

FLIGHT LIEUTENANT THOMAS 'TOMMY' ROSE DFC

After Tommy Rose retired, he was replaced by Ken Waller. However, while he was taxiing the M.20 from the experimental hanger across to the runway, he discovered a severe oscillation in the rubber disc shock absorbers on the main undercarriage gear, but, undaunted, the aircraft bounced off. Following a spectacular flight, the landing was very 'tricky', to say the least. Twenty-four hours later a pair of very effective dashpots, made by the nightshift workers of Sir George Godfrey, cured the oscillation.

On 5 October 1943, the name of the company was changed to Miles Aircraft Ltd as it was considered that the time had finally come to sever the link with the previous name, as by then, neither Phillips nor Powis retained any interest in the company and the aircraft had always been known as 'Miles' anyway. The company then virtually passed into the hands of the Miles family.

However, just prior to this change of name, the company had been honoured with election to full membership of the Society of British Aircraft Constructors.

The new directors made a happy combination; the practical but impetuous Miles, with his tremendous energy, enthusiasm, force of character and drive; George, with his clear, logical and incisive mind, while also sharing his brother's flair for design and mechanical ingenuity, and 'Blossom' Miles, F.G. Miles' wife, clear-thinking, calm and well-balanced – a perfect counterpart to her impulsive husband and shy brother-in-law. Meanwhile, Don Brown, who had managed to join the company in early 1942 from the A&AEE Boscombe Down, became George Miles' personal assistant.

The average flight time required for the initial flight test of a new aircraft was 40-50 minutes and the number of new Miles aircraft that were probably flown by Tommy Rose, the Chief Test Pilot, from November 1939 until January 1946 is approximated below:

Miles M.14A Magister, from 6 December 1939	**119**
Miles M.9 Master Mk.I, from August 1939	**302**
Miles M.19 Master Mk.II	**447**
Miles M.20 Fighter	**2** prototypes.
Miles M.25 Martinet	**866**
Miles M.28	**6** these were probably flown at various times by Tommy Rose, but he didn't make any of their first flights.
Miles M.30 'X' Minor	**1** scale model of 'X' airliner project.
Miles M.33 Monitor.	**2** Prototypes but possibly other production examples.
Miles M.38 Messenger Mk.I	**4** were possibly test flown by Tommy Rose.

Miles M.38 Messenger Mk.2A	Irish built aircraft probably not flown by Tommy Rose.
Miles M.50 Queen Martinet	**22** modified from M.25.
Miles M.57 Aerovan	**1** first prototype.
Miles M.65 Gemini Mk.1A	It is possible that Tommy Rose test flew some of these before he retired.
Approximate total of new build aircraft flown	**1772**

The total production of Miles Aircraft built was as follows:

Miles M.14A Magister Mk.I (including aircraft diverted to the air forces of Egypt and Eire)	1,225
Miles M.14B Magister Mk.II	5
Miles M.9B Master Mk.I (including aircraft converted to M.24 Master Fighter, and M.19 Master Mk.II and M.27 Master Mk.III prototypes)	500
Miles M.18 Elementary Trainer, which Tommy undoubedly would also have flown	4
Miles M.9C Master Mk.IA	400
Miles M.19 Master Mk.II (including M.19 GT Mk.II new build and conversions)	1,250
Miles M.25 Martinet Mk.I (including two prototypes and arcraft converted to M.50 Queen Martinet)	1,724
Miles M.28 (Mercury)	6
Miles M.33 Monitor Mk.I and Mk.II (including two prototypes)	22
Miles M.38 Messenger Mk.I (including one prototype)	11
Miles M.50 Queen Martinet	69
Miles M.57 Aerovan Mk.I	1
Total	**5,217**

The following aircraft production is added out of interest, as it is not known if Tommy Rose would have flown any of these, but for which he would have been ultimately responsible:

South Marston for the RAF	
Miles M.19 Master Mk.II (including 190 transferred from Doncaster)	**488**
Miles M.27 Master Mk.III	**602**
Total	**1,090**

FLIGHT LIEUTENANT THOMAS 'TOMMY' ROSE DFC

Built at Sheffield and Doncaster for the RAF	
Miles M.19 Master Mk.II (one assembled at Doncaster and nine sets of components to South Marston for assembly)	10
Total	10
Built at Banbridge and Newtownards, Northern Ireland for the RAF	
Miles M.38 Messenger Mk.I (five built at Banbridge and five at Newtownards)	10
Total	10
Grand total	6,327

The *Yorkshire Evening Post* for Saturday, 13 June 1942, reported on a flight made by a BBC commentator in a programme called '*Test Pilot*':

> *BBC Commentator Wynford Vaughan Thomas will broadcast on Tuesday from an aircraft travelling at over 300 mph* (in a Master – SC). *He will go for a trip with a famous test pilot – Major Tommy Rose DFC. The commentator, with microphone and air-to-air ground transmission, will give his listeners a realistic picture of a test pilot's job. Thomas hopes to tell listeners what it feels like to be in an aircraft diving at high speed, doing double rolls and looping the loop, if he doesn't get a blackout.*

Seven BBC Outside Broadcast programmes were made at Woodley Aerodrome between 1942 and 1948 and broadcast on the Home Service. The most popular were four '*Works Wonders*' lunchtime programmes, but there were also two editions of '*Workers Playtime*'. The first and most memorable radio broadcast, however, was called '*Test Pilot*' and the script and associated correspondence for this live, 15-minute programme now survives at the BBC Written Archives Centre.

Test Pilot was first broadcast on the Forces Programme at 6.30 pm on Tuesday, 16 June 1942. Wartime BBC radio commentators, Wynford Vaughan Thomas and Stuart Macpherson were both involved in the programme, which included an interview with F.G. and Blossom Miles, and Norman Parson, all standing beside the moving assembly line in the factory. A production test flight of a newly completed Master from the assembly line was also recorded in which Chief Test Pilot Tommy Rose took Wynford Vaughan Thomas for a flight, to enable him to broadcast a live commentary as the aircraft was being 'put through its paces' over RAF Watchfield.

The following extract from the script gives a vivid account of this flight:

> **Wynford Vaughan Thomas**: 'And while our test pilot flings our aircraft about the sky, I'll try to keep talking to let you know what aerobatics feel like at high speed – what a fighter pilot feels like, when he's diving full throttle to the tail of a Messerschmitt ... Now, I'm bracing myself firmly in my seat. I take a deep breath ready for the dive, but I'll keep on talking. OK Tommy!'

CHIEF TEST PILOT PHILLIPS AND POWIS

Tommy Rose: *'Here we go'.*

Wynford Vaughan Thomas: *'And the pilot puts the nose of the aircraft down – and down we plunge. We gather speed, 250 mph, 270, 300, 330 – we are racing down – 350! We are going all out, losing height. The earth is rushing up to me. I am bracing myself for the pull-out. We've got to pull out soon... we are at 2,000 feet, down to 1,500 ... 1,000! And suddenly we pull out. Up we go! My eyes have a thousand spots before them. I am being pressed down in my seat – my stomach contracts. The engine roar deafens me. And suddenly, the weight lifts off my shoulders, and I look out to find us straight and level again. Our aircraft has taken a dive!'*

In July, Tommy Rose became very ill with pneumonia and the *Nottingham Journal* for Saturday, 13 July 1943, reported:

TOMMY ROSE VERY ILL
Flight Lieutenant Tommy Rose, former King's Cup Air Race winner and one of our best-known test pilots, is ill with double pneumonia in his home at Sonning. He contracted a chill when captaining his works cricket team.

Tommy Rose, who is forty-eight, is within a few hours of logging his ten thousandth hour of flying. He transferred from the Navy to the RFC in the last war.

He was shot down three times in those days of no parachutes and was awarded the DFC for his work with the fighter squadron in which 'Billy' Bishop VC served.

He retired from the RAF with the rank of Flight Lieutenant and spent a period as an instructor and attempting long-distance records.

The *Evening Despatch* for 31 July 1943, reported on Tommy Rose's illness:

Tommy Rose is now well on the way to recovery. Flight Lieutenant Tommy Rose, the test pilot who had double pneumonia, was stated today at his home at Sonning Berkshire to have improved considerably and to be well on the way to recovery.

After service with the RAF, he retired with the rank of Flight Lieutenant, and became chief test pilot to the firm Phillips and Powis, and as well as testing machines he has flown many new and experimental models.

In 1943, a most impressive list of the firm's laurels was published, below:

1933 Miles Hawk was FIRST modern aircraft to sell for under £400.

1934 FIRST manufacturer to fit split flaps as standard.

FLIGHT LIEUTENANT THOMAS 'TOMMY' ROSE DFC

1935 FIRST, second and third in King's Cup Air Race.

1936 FIRST to introduce monoplane training in the RAF.

1937 Miles Kestrel trainer FASTEST in the world – 296 mph.

1938 Miles Master wins LARGEST contract ever placed for a trainer.

1940 Miles M.20 was FIRST and only modern fighter to be built in nine weeks.

1941 Miles M.28 was FIRST aeroplane to carry four people at 160 mph and over 20 mpg.

1942 Miles Libellula – MOST successful unorthodox aeroplane.

1943 We must not say, yet – but be assured that these are our laurels but – **MILES AIRCRAFT LTD ARE NOT SATISFIED TO REST ON THEM!**

However, the trials and tribulations of a test pilot are shown in the article in *Good Morning* for Friday, 7 July 1944:

> *Another ace flyer who made history just before the war, Tommy Rose, as a 'tester', has few equals – yet made the headlines when he narrowly escaped death. One afternoon, engaged on one of his usual 'death or glory trips', his oxygen failed when he was at a height of 18,000 feet – and Tommy did not recover consciousness until he was down to 7,000 feet. He found the throttle was closed, and probably owes his life to the fact that he must have shut it instinctively before 'passing out'.*

The *Miles Magazine News Supplement* for 17 October 1944, in their Postbag section, published Tommy Rose's amusing letter regarding 'Pregnant Percy' and this gives a great insight into Tommy Rose's sense of humour, and this is reproduced below:

> *Dear Editor*
> **APOLOGY DEMANDED**
> *I really must protest against the statement in your issue of 3 October. Under the heading 'Do you remember – in the News a year ago, you state that the prototype Falcon 6, was christened 'Pregnant Percy'.*
>
> *This is a foul libel on a very lovely young lady. Having been fortunate enough to spend a lot of time alone with her, on occasions a very long way from home, I feel that this statement is a reflection on me as well. A question of libel will not be pursued further provided that an ample apology appears in the next issue. For your information the lady in question 'rejoiced' in the name 'Preggers Primus'.*
>
> *Yours unfaithfully*
TOMMY ROSE

CHIEF TEST PILOT PHILLIPS AND POWIS

The following response was sent by Don Brown, equally tongue in cheek!

AND GIVEN (WE HOPE)
Dear Editor
I must apologise if we have unwittingly libelled Major Tommy Rose and the late lamented Preggers. I can only plead I am getting on in years and according to the Managing Director's theories, I am practically doddering. No doubt my memory is not as good as it was but nevertheless my recollection was that 'she' started life as 'Pregnant Percy', a title which was subsequently abbreviated into the more affectionate 'Preggers' or sometimes 'Preggers Primus' (Also see page 39 of the Miles Magazine of May 1939).

May I suggest that perhaps a mistake was initially made as to her sex, a mistake which would no doubt have been discovered by Major Rose who, on his own admission was on terms of considerable intimacy with the lady. I can only trust that he will accept the foregoing as 'amende deshonourable'.

D.L. Brown

The *Birmingham Mail* for Thursday, 7 December 1944 reported:

> *Major Tommy Rose DFC, a former instructor at the Midland Aero Club, Castle Bromwich, from February 1928 to May 1929, and holder of many long-distance records, will shortly celebrate his fiftieth birthday – and he is still operating as a test pilot, an exacting enough job for men young enough to be his sons.*
>
> *Only a day or so ago he joined the select few who have flown 10,000 hours and he still regards his work as a hobby, for it is 'the only outdoor sport at which one can sit down'.*
>
> *It was shortly after leaving Castle Bromwich that Major Rose began attempts on the London to the Cape solo record flight, but repeatedly he was thwarted by sheer bad luck until 1936 when he made the trip in 3 days 17 hours 38 minutes, beating the late Amy Mollison's time by over 13 hours, and then establishing another record for the return. In the previous year he had won the King's Cup race.*

An article was published in the news section of the *Miles Aircraft Works Magazine* for February 1946, announcing Tommy Rose's retirement and relevant extracts from this are reproduced below:

Tommy Rose relinquishes his title, at 51-years-old he has handed over the Chief Test Pilot's job to Ken Waller.
Major Rose has now handed the job of Chief Test Pilot over to Ken Waller. This does not mean we shall see no more of Tommy – far from it!

FLIGHT LIEUTENANT THOMAS 'TOMMY' ROSE DFC

We shall have the benefit of his help and companionship for many, many years. (Note, Major was the rank he was given while serving in the local Home Guard at Woodley).

Tommy Rose joined this firm eleven years ago. He had been Chief Sales Manager, then Chief Flying Instructor of the Civil School and a Chief Test Pilot since 1939. He was CO of our Home Guard unit and captain of our cricket team. When he joined us, he was already a veteran record pilot, and with us he won the King's Cup (1935), been second twice and broken the London – Cape Town and Cape Town – London record (1936).

During the war we all kept our noses to the grindstone, but there were certain occasions when surely one saw more than the ground crew on the playing field! We were watching Tommy do the first tests of, say, the Miles M.20 Fighter, or the Miles M.33 Monitor, waiting to give him a roaring cheer as he touched down after a successful flight. Half that cheer would be for his fine flying and the other half for him.

Tommy Rose is fifty-one. In fact, he is fifty-one and some days now, because his birthday was on 27 January.

With a most tremendous effort we managed to get a few words from him about his very early days. It is probably the nature of a journalistic 'scoop', and our own magazine has the honour of telling the story to its readers.

Here it is, in his own words:

'At school I had no difficulty in getting into the Rugger or Cricket sides, but it was a very different matter when it came into getting into the Civil Service! After several abject failures, my father bought me a frock coat, and I entered the service of the 'King's Bankers'. After nine months my release was arranged by Kaiser Wilhelm, and as far as I know, my frock coat is still hanging up in its lockers at number 440 Strand.

'At the beginning of the 1914-1918 war I was in the RN Armoured Cars and, with Commander Samson's assistance, I endeavoured to annoy the Huns in Belgium. Later, General Botha helped me clear the enemy out of South-West Africa, and later still, with the assistance of General Smuts, British East Africa. From then (1916) onwards, it has been flying; little ones and big ones, good ones and bad ones – both men and aeroplanes.

'My first solo was in a Shorthorn and was a memorable performance; my astonishment at survival was only excelled by that of my instructor. The RAF tolerated me until the end of 1926, and those ten years and the eleven I have been here, have been the happiest of my young life.

'There are some who look on fifty-one as being a great age, yet in most ways I feel no different than I did at forty. Of one thing I am certain; it is *that friends and friendliness make life worth living. To work for and with people who are one's friends is great good fortune'.*

Congratulations Flight Lieutenant Tommy Rose. Here's wishing you very many happy returns of the day.

Ken Waller

Kenneth Herbert Fraser Waller, who replaced Tommy Rose, was born on 7 April 1908 in Lambeth, London, and he learnt to fly with the Cinque Ports Flying Club at Lympne in 1930. He gained his Private Pilot's Licence, No.2557, dated 25 April 1930 and his Royal Aero Club Aviator's Certificate, No.9047, in May 1930. Ken Waller took the instructors' course at Brooklands in 1933 and became assistant flying instructor with the Cinque Ports Flying Club. In May 1935, he went to Brooklands Flying Club as their Chief Flying Instructor, with Captain Duncan Davis.

Ken Waller later became well known as a long-distance and air race pilot. Owen Cathcart Jones and Ken Waller entered the 1934 MacRobertson England to Australia Air Race in a de Havilland DH.88 Comet built specially for the race. They finished fourth. The same aeroplane was then used by Ken Waller and Maurice Franchomme to fly from Belgium to the Belgian Congo and return in record time in order to prove that an airmail route was possible. He was awarded the Segrave Trophy in 1934 for this feat.

Ken Waller and Max Findlay also competed in the Schlesinger Race to South Africa in 1936 – along with Tommy Rose and many others – in an Airspeed Envoy (No.13), but this crashed on take-off in Northern Rhodesia, killing Findlay and the radio operator, Ken was thrown out through a hole in the fuselage and badly hurt, but recovered from his injuries and returned to Brooklands at the end of November 1936.

On the outbreak of war, Ken was sent to Sywell with the school and given the rank of Flight Sergeant. In 1939, he joined Phillips & Powis Aircraft Ltd as a test pilot, starting work on 11 January 1940 at Woodley by test flying the Miles M.18 and a Miles M.16 Miles Mentor. He flew his first Master Mk.I on 17 January 1940 and thereafter it was a regular mix of M.18, Master Mk.I and Magister production test flying as newly built aircraft came off the assembly lines.

Phillips & Powis Aircraft's new 'Shadow Factory' at South Marston, near Swindon, Wiltshire, started full production from March 1941 and Ken then went there to test-fly the newly built Master Mk.II and Mk.III aircraft. After a short spell in South Africa in late 1941, to help with the introduction of the Miles Master Mk.II into service with the South African Air Force under the Joint Air Training Scheme/Plan, he returned to South Marston, where he carried on with flight testing the newly built Masters.

Upon becoming Chief Test Pilot at Woodley, Ken Waller flight tested the new Miles M.37 Martinet Trainer, the M.60 Marathon Airliner and the M.71 Merchantman.

The Miles M.60 Marathon was the first four-engined, all-metal, airliner to be built by Miles Aircraft, and this was first flown, by Ken Waller, on 19 May 1946. Ken also

FLIGHT LIEUTENANT THOMAS 'TOMMY' ROSE DFC

flew the Marathon on its first public appearance on 1 June 1946 at the Garden Party at Woodley, organised by the Reading Branch of the Royal Aeronautical Society.

To sum up, a concise history of Phillips & Powis Aircraft Ltd/Miles Aircraft Ltd was written by Thurston James in *Aerospace*, when he reviewed Don Brown's book *Miles Aircraft since 1925* (published by Putnam in 1970) and, as his views are very similar to those of Peter Amos, I therefore have much pleasure in reproducing this review below:

> *No phenomenon of British aircraft construction deserves closer study than the outburst of the Miles efflorescence in the twenty years between 1928 and 1948. In that time forty-seven different types of Miles aeroplane were flown and a total of 5,644 were built between 1929 and 1946. The story is told in this book. It tells how a young man (F.G. Miles) without training or money, but blessed with unique talents and energy, coupled with those of his wife (Blossom), the aid of a gifted brother (George) and certain enthusiastic adherents (among whom the author of this book was one) revolutionised the look of British light aviation, grew big enough to go into partnership with Rolls-Royce and became a fully-fledged member of the SBAC.*
>
> *The protagonists learnt to fly before they learnt to design. They test-flew their own aircraft.*
>
> *It was a long time before Miles aircraft were built by a firm bearing that name. In the beginning was the Gnat Aero Company. This grew into Southern Aircraft Ltd. For what was perhaps the firm's finest hour it was known as Phillips and Powis Aircraft of Reading – Charles Powis of that company played no small part in the Miles story, more than appears in this book. As one of Putnam's publications devised to give maximum data about aircraft types and projects, this volume succeeds in full measure. Out of ninety separate types dealt with, half are projects – but what projects!*
>
> *Outstanding was the Supersonic Project literally built round a Whittle turbine. Designed during the closing stages of World War II, it had been ordered by the Government with the object of attaining the hitherto unbelievable speed of 1,000 mph. After the war ended, chicken-hearted authority lost its nerve and cancelled the razor-winged projectile before completion so that the Americans, whom the same chicken authority enabled to study the design, got there first.*
>
> *Subsequent tests with the air-launched rocket-propelled models showed that the straight-winged Miles' design could have achieved its goal. Its success full-scale might have altered the whole pattern of Britain's post war aircraft progress.*
>
> *The essential rightness of Miles designs is shown by the fact that though Miles Aircraft were closed down in 1948, there were in 1969 still fifty-nine Miles designs on the British Register. It seems designers who can build and test-fly their own designs have a certain something!*

With regard to his last paragraph, where indeed could you have found another company then – and certainly none now – whose Chairman and Managing Director, their Chief Designer and his Personal Assistant, could not only all design very advanced, innovative and practical aircraft, but who could also fly them as approved and highly qualified test pilots as well – nowhere.

But, to return to Tommy Rose, upon his retirement in January 1946, he was given a very generous £18,000 by the company (equivalent in purchasing power today to about £803,000).

However, after his retirement, Tommy Rose apparently disappeared from the scene for some seventeen months, no doubt living off his retirement money but, in May 1947, he suddenly started work again, this time as General Manager of Universal Flying Services Ltd at Fairoaks.

Chapter 17

Universal Flying Services, Fairoaks – General Manager, May 1947 – February 1948
Boyes, Seagrave and Company – Charter Services, Consultancy, February 1948 – August 1948

Wings are the Wheels of today
– General Aviation

After Tommy Rose retired in January 1946, he apparently spent the next seventeen months in the wilderness, and it hasn't been possible to confirm exactly what he was doing during this time except for competing in various air races around the country.

F.G. Miles had given Tommy the use of the Hawk Speed Six G-ADGP and with this he could regularly be seen racing around a local closed-circuit in the evenings, in order 'to keep his hand in'. The 'markers' for his circuit being three conveniently spaced trees at Missen's Farm, near Chobham Church, which probably didn't go down too well with the local residents!

Tommy Rose flew G-ADGP, in Race No. 8, into second place, at 171.5 mph in his first post war air race, at Portsmouth, on 10 May 1947 and he flew it again, in Race No. 4, at Ronaldsway in the Isle of Man on 26 May 1947, where he won the Manx Air Derby at 181 mph.

This aircraft, which was extensively modified for the 1939 King's Cup Air Race, which was cancelled due to the outbreak of war, was restored again in 1987 and repainted to represent an earlier incarnation, by the late Ron Souch (I should point out that it was never flown by Tommy Rose in this condition), but now regularly flies with the Shuttleworth Collection at Old Warden Aerodrome, Biggleswade, Bedford.

Following the end of the war in Europe on 8 May 1945, the National Government, which was set up by Winston Churchill in 1940, came to a sudden and unexpected end, and a General Election was called for, and won, by the Labour Party.

Although the war on the Pacific had yet to be brought to a successful conclusion, Winston Churchill was unwilling to dissolve Parliament, but he had little choice when his coalition partners made clear their intentions to go to the country as soon as possible.

UNIVERSAL FLYING SERVICES, FAIROAKS – GENERAL MANAGER

The 1945 election was the first to be fought in Britain for ten years and during the war a new left-leaning consensus had gradually developed within Britain with the Beveridge report at its heart. The report, published in December 1942, recommended a comprehensive welfare state and National Health Service. Its proposals enjoyed widespread support throughout the country but received only lukewarm support from Churchill and the Conservative Party. The nation had undergone the horrors of war and expected to enjoy the fruits of victory, at least for a while.

Frank Bowles (1902-1970), who was the Labour candidate for Nuneaton in the 1945 General Election, was also a very good friend of Tommy Rose and, prior to the election, Tommy had attended several of Frank's fund-raising events. He also used his well-known status to canvas for his friend Frank in the run-up to the election during June 1945, when Frank won the Nuneaton seat with 30,587 votes, or 58.5 per cent of the voters.

Tommy Rose continued his friendship and support for Frank and the Labour party, and he was later reported to have attended, together with Douglas Bader, a lunch, hosted by Frank Bowles, at the House of Commons, in December 1946.

Tamworth Herald for Saturday, 30 June 1945, reported Tommy Rose's support of the Labour party thus:

> **LABOUR CANDIDATE**
>
> *Mr Frank Bowles, the Labour candidate and former member, is receiving active support from Flight Lieutenant Tommy Rose, one of Britains' most famous pilots, who was well known for his long-distance record-breaking flights. He won the King's Cup in 1935 and held the England-Cape and Cape-England record the following year. A chief test pilot during the war, he is one of the candidate's closest friends. Meetings in support of Mr Bowles were held at Atherstone and Warton on Monday, and the candidate was due at Polesworth yesterday (Thursday) evening. Lord Winster (former MP for the Division) is among the speakers announced at forthcoming meetings. 'Labour's case', says Mr Bowles, 'is scientific and scientifically right'.*

On 31 August 1946, Tommy Rose participated for the Folkstone Aero Trophy at Lympne, with the Miles M.28, G-AGVX, but was unplaced and *Flight* for 29 August 1946 reported on the races:

> **THE FOLKSTONE RACES**
>
> *Holidaymakers at Folkstone and Hythe should have a good view of the races to be organised by the Cinque Ports Flying Club, during the last weekend of this month.*
>
> *The heats for the Folkstone Trophy are being run off next Saturday, 31 August, starting at 2.30 pm, and the organisers ask that any aircraft attending the meeting will endeavour to land by midday, other aircraft are asked to keep well away from the circuit during the race. The public will not be admitted to the airfield on Saturday.*

> On Sunday, 1 September, the final will start at 3 pm, and the Lympne High-Speed Handicap race at 4 pm. Loudspeakers have been installed at the airfield, and a special relay has been organised to the promenade at Folkstone, for the benefit of those who will see the aircraft on the seaward leg.
>
> Although the main Lympne event may appear to be new to many, it will be, in fact, the ninth of the series. The last race, over an exactly similar course, was flown in the August prior to the outbreak of war.

Then, in *Flight* for 10 October 1946, it was reported that:

> The activities of Airtraining (Fairoaks), Limited, has been combined under the name of Universal Flying Services Limited, with Mr G. Goodhew as managing director. The companies are subsidiaries of General Aircraft Limited.

On 20 November 1946, Tommy Rose's stepmother, Charlotte Rose (nee Fairbrother, 1869-1946) died at the Carisbrooke Nursing Home, Goring Road, Steyning, Sussex, aged seventy-nine years, Tommy Rose had always kept in touch with Charlotte right up to the time she died and, being the eldest of five children, he organised the funeral arrangements. She had filled the void left after Annie died in 1911, at just forty-one years of age, by marrying their father in 1915.

It was announced in May 1947 that Tommy Rose had joined Universal Flying Services Ltd, Fairoaks Aerodrome, Chobham, Surrey, as their General Manager.

May 1947 Universal Flying Services, Fairoaks

In May 1947 the *Woking Review* published an article on the new appointment as follows:

> **MAJOR TOMMY ROSE – RECORD-BREAKING MAN OF SPEED**
> *Record-breaking, long-distance aero flights, rugby and cricket, have all been part of the adventurous career of 52-year-old Major Tommy Rose, the man with over 10,000 flying hours to his credit, who recently took over General Managership of Universal Flying Services, Fairoaks.*
>
> *Throughout the whole of his thirty-one years of flying, Tommy Rose has had an insatiable thirst for speed. He started flying during World War I, in single-seater scout planes and after the war with the Royal Air Force in India and the Middle East until 1926. In 1928 he became an Instructor with the Midland Aerodrome, which had one of the largest aero clubs in the country.*
>
> *His next job was as Aviation Manager* (flying representative – SC) *to the Anglo-American Oil Company, and afterwards became Chief*

UNIVERSAL FLYING SERVICES, FAIROAKS – GENERAL MANAGER

Instructor at the Northampton Aero Club. In 1935, he joined Phillips & Powis Aircraft Ltd. In November 1939 Tommy Rose became their Chief Test Pilot. In October 1943, the company changed its name to Miles Aircraft Ltd.

In 1935 he won the King's Cup, having secured second place the previous year. In 1936 he was second again. It was in this year, after having made a number of unsuccessful attempts, that he broke the long-distance record from England to the Cape and back again. He confesses the finest sight he has ever seen was Cape Town at night as he came into land at the end of his record flight.

He played rugby for Richmond, Bath and Somerset and rugger and cricket for the RAF. He modestly talks about 'playing about at Brooklands, and 'running around the houses in the Isle of Man'. It is interesting to note that Ken Waller, who was Chief Instructor at Brooklands in the pre-war days, was Tommy Rose's assistant test pilot at Phillips & Powis during the early part of the war and has since taken over the job of Chief Test Pilot.

Heavily built and genial, Tommy Rose is not content to sit behind a desk. He says he has another twenty years of flying yet and quotes a letter from a friend of his, aged seventy-three, who, while flying over Kenya at 3,000 feet, found his engine had cut out, made a good landing, and calmly walked away.

If there is a King's Cup Air Race this year, Major Tommy Rose will be one of the flyers.

His job at Fairoaks includes the control of the Flying School, Aero Club and Charter Services. He says that the club possesses greater amenities than any he has seen and forecasts a busy future at the aerodrome. Charter services have been booked throughout the season and the company are buying new aircraft as and when they become available.

Dundee Evening Telegraph for Friday, 9 May 1947 reported:

ROSE TO BLOOM AGAIN
Tommy Rose, King's Cup winner of 1935 and hero of many pre-war long-distance flights, is, at fifty-two, preparing for a comeback to sporting aviation.

He will be airing his cream-coloured plane at Fairoaks Aerodrome, Surrey, but it will fly in the race at Portsmouth's Air Display tomorrow, and in the Manx Air Derby at Whitsun.

Tommy Rose says he is finished with long-distance records – in 1936 he held that for the England - Cape trip – but intends to compete in air races for many years to come.

During the war he was a test pilot. He is now the General Manager of Universal Flying Services.

FLIGHT LIEUTENANT THOMAS 'TOMMY' ROSE DFC

Hampshire Telegraph for Friday, 9 May 1947 reported:

TOMMY ROSE IN AIR DISPLAY
One of the best-known figures in British flying, Tommy Rose, will be among the competitors in an air display at Portsmouth Airport on Saturday.

He will be flying his King's Cup plane in a race for light aircraft. Now fifty-three, he was educated at Churcher's College, Petersfield, and his exploits with the Royal Flying Corps in World War I gained him the Distinguished Flying Cross.

Subsequently he came into international prominence in the long-distance flying races to South Africa.

During World War II he was chief test pilot for Miles Aircraft at Reading.

Two Portsmouth competitors in the race on Saturday will be Squadron Leader H. Mitchell and Mr H.R. Gould, Chief Instructor and Secretary, respectively, of the Portsmouth Aero Club.

At the Portsmouth Air Display and Garden Party, Tommy Rose entered the light aeroplane race in a Miles Hawk Speed Six (171.5 mph), where he came second, first was H.E. Burke in a Tiger Moth.

Hampshire Telegraph for Friday, 16 May 1947 reported on the Portsmouth Air Display thus:

10,000 GATE AT AIR DISPLAY DAKOTA THRILL
Official estimate of the attendance at the display organised by the Air League of the British Empire at Portsmouth Airport on Saturday was over 10,000.

'We have to create airmindedness amongst the people of this country, and there is no finer way of doing it than by letting them see what is being done, and how it is being done', said Mr George Lindgren, MP (Parliamentary Secretary to the Ministry of Civil Aviation, who performed the opening ceremony). Mr Lindgren, who was deputising for Lord Nathan, the Minister of Civil Aviation, inspected a Guard of Honour of local Air Training Corps cadets.

Despite the withdrawal of Naval participation, and a large portion of the Royal Air Force originally promised, an 'interesting' programme, both on the ground and in the air, was carried through in perfect conditions.

JET AEROBATICS
An outstanding feature was an exhibition of aerobatics by Flying Officer Carter, in an RAF jet propelled Vampire. A fly-past of modern aircraft gave some idea of the sweeping advance of aviation, and a Dakota of the RAF Transport Command gave the crowd a thrill when it dived almost to the ground to snatch up a glider.

UNIVERSAL FLYING SERVICES, FAIROAKS – GENERAL MANAGER

Flying a Miles Hawk Speed Six, Tommy Rose, winner of the King's Cup in 1935, took second place in the light aeroplane race, which was won by Burke, flying a DH Tiger Moth. Commentator for this, the first of a series of displays being organised throughout the country by the Air League, was Stewart MacPherson. He was assisted by Humphrey Lestocq, otherwise known as 'Flying Officer Kite', who had a job 'he rather cared for', but no 'wizard prangs' to talk about.

Manx Air Races and Rally 26 May 1947

The Isle of Man Race was the first air race to be held after the Second World War and Tommy Rose entered, flying G-ADGP, the Miles Hawk Speed Six, his average speed for the three circuits of the island (156 miles) was 181 mph, second was Bruce Campbell in a de Havilland TK.2 (179 mph) and third was John Somers in a DH Hornet Moth (116 mph).

Flight for 29 May 1947 reported:

MANX AIR RACES AND RALLY
FIFTH ANNUAL COMPETITIONS FROM OLLEY AND AIR DERBY CHALLENGE TROPHIES

The first post-war Isle of Man Air Races were held over the Whitsun weekend and were the fifth in the series which had started in 1936, but which had been interrupted for seven years by the war. They were held under the competition rules of the Royal Aero Club and the regulations of the FAI.

As in previous years, the races were each over three laps of the island, with turning points at Port Carna (on the north-east coast, near Maughold Head), Bride Church, Peel Castle and Tynwald Hill. Each lap of the course was 53.25 miles and the starting and finishing point was at Ronaldsway Airport. It is regrettable that the air race from London to the Isle of Man, which was so popular before the war, could not be included this year, but it was felt that the present shortage of light aircraft and the considerable differences involved in organising such an event at the present time would have made it impracticable. However, the London to Isle of Man Race was replaced by an arrival competition, with prizes for the aircraft from anywhere in Great Britain, or the nearest Irish Free State, which touched down nearest to the sealed time. If conditions are favourable, it is hoped to reintroduce the London-Isle of Man race next year.

The organisation of the races was once again conducted by Wing Commander R.H. Stocken, and Messrs F.R. Rowarth, and W. Dancy undertook the handicapping of aircraft according to estimated performance. Mr J.M. Cubbon, who is a resident of the Isle of Man, again generously contributed £500 to be distributed as prize money.

FLIGHT LIEUTENANT THOMAS 'TOMMY' ROSE DFC

The Tynwald Air Race was open to all types of aircraft, both British and foreign, fitted with engines of 120hp and under, whilst the Manx Air Derby was for British and foreign aircraft of all types with engines exceeding a total of 120hp. In addition to £30 first prize and £10 each for second and third prizes given to aircraft from Britain in the arrival competition, similar prizes were offered to visitors from the Continent.

By four pm last Saturday all the competitors in the arrival competition had touched down at Ronaldsway, except Leadbetter's Auster, which had returned to Blackpool with engine trouble. The Essex Aero Vega Gull was scratched. Scott's Moth Minor was delayed at Speke but arrived later. After waiting at Speke to escort Scott's Minor over the Irish Sea it was touch and go whether the Rapide flown by Flight *would arrive in time. However, it was the last aircraft to arrive, with just thirty seconds to spare, and there was no need to drop the dinghy carried in case of emergency for the light aircraft.*

The first aircraft to arrive was Hugh Kendall's Miles Gemini, which touched down 1.75 minutes after three, winning the first prize. Second and third went to Hayman's Beechcraft and Esler's Messenger respectively. Late entrants not shown in the table were Temple-Harris in a Proctor and Spencer in an Autocrat.

On Sunday morning a few competitors flew the course for Monday's race. Others examined the turning points from a coach. These were marked by a bell tent and an orange cone. The weather was fine and made the polish on the cowlings shine brightly.

Monday morning broke, with damp cloud covering the island, but after breakfast bright patches began to show and there was heavy cloud on Snaefell only. Refuelling, engine runs, and more polishing occupied the time until lunch. After lunch we took the Rapide around the course and found patchy low cloud over the Douglas-Jurby stretch. The turning points were almost obscured, but the weather slowly improved, and by the time the race started the Jurby-Peel Castle leg was clear and the sun shone brilliantly. However, we found the air from Tynwald Hill very rough and had to fasten our straps. It was also rough flying through the dog-leg gap to Ronaldsway; but the weather was improving.

The two races (for the Olley and Manx Derby Trophies) were flown simultaneously and on the same handicap basis and a large crowd was present.

First machine away at 2.15 pm was Spencer's Auster, thirty-five minutes ahead of the scratch man. Hayman in his Beechcraft. The limit man was followed at short intervals by Hales in an Auster, Somers (Hornet Moth), McDowell (Autocraft), Scott (Moth Minor), and Mole (Bibi BE 550). The Bibi was the lowest-powered aircraft in the race, but it conceded 5.5 minutes start to the Auster. According to the programme Somer's Hornet

UNIVERSAL FLYING SERVICES, FAIROAKS – GENERAL MANAGER

Moth was competing in the Tynwald Race, but after flying very well and fast, and crossing the line an easy first, the light aircraft was declared above the 120hp limit, and so was placed third in the Derby (the Gipsy Major engine is normally rated at 118-122hp). Somers average speed was 116 mph.

The Tynwald Race winner was thus McDowell in the Auster Autocrat; second was Spencer in the Auster, and third Mole in the Bibi. Before the race there had been much discussion about the speed the TK.2 would achieve with the new high-compression Major X engine, and if Tommy Rose's Hawk Speed Six would prove faster. Some considered the Beechcraft biplane with retractable wheels a dark horse; others speculated about the new secret cream Gemini with coarse-pitch airscrews, or whether the experience, plus speed combination of Waller's Aerovan constituted a real danger to the others. The race developed into an exciting flight between the Hawk Speed Six and the TK.2, with Somers, Kendall, Waller and Temple-Harris all going well. Hayman made a great effort to make up his handicap and did well to finish sixth as fastest man, with a speed of 186 mph.

EXCITEMENT BUILDS UP

At the end of the second lap Somers increased his lead, McDowell's Aster was still in second place, and Waller moved up to third. Esler's Messenger held next place to the Aerovan in the Manx Derby, with Kendall's Gemini and Temple Harris's Proctor in close pursuit. Rose (Hawk Speed Six) and Campbell (TK.2) were catching up fast in eighth and ninth places.

Long before the winners were due, all eyes were on the hills to the north of the airport. Suddenly, flying very low, came Tommy Rose's cream Hawk Speed Six, to win at a very fast pace. His speed worked out at 181 mph, Campbell (TK 2) was only just behind, with a speed of 179 mph, Somers in the Hornet Moth arrived third, Kendall's Gemini fourth. Temple-Harris's green Proctor fifth. The Beechcraft succeeded in beating the Aerovan near the finishing line. It was a very good race.

Lord Londonderry arrived by air to watch the performance of his blue Gemini, but it was unfortunate that the wheels failed to retract, as did also those of the other Gemini over part of the first lap.

All competitors had very rough rides over the north and west legs of the island course. Leadbetter in the Auster turned his back and received a slight cut on his head. Scott (Moth Minor) finished at reduced speed, and several others were bruised, and Waller was aching after the Aerovan flight. Rose's engine momentarily cut on the last lap, owing to low fuel and the bumps. The breeze stiffened towards the end to make landings exciting for the ultra-light aircraft.

FLIGHT LIEUTENANT THOMAS 'TOMMY' ROSE DFC

> *His Excellency, the Lieutenant Governor, Air Vice-Marshal Bromet, attended the meeting and in the evening presented the prizes in the Palace ballroom at Douglas.*

Northampton Mercury for Friday, 30 May 1947 reported Tommy Rose's Manx Air Derby win thus:

> *I doubt if Northampton will ever forget Tommy Rose, once Flight Lieutenant Rose, Chief Flying Instructor at Sywell Aerodrome. The latest we hear of him is that at the age of fifty-three, and flying at an average speed of 131 mph, he has won the Manx Air Derby. He came first in the Miles Hawk Speed Six in a field of eighteen aircraft, all of which flew three times round the Isle of Man almost at chimney pot height, a total distance of 165 miles.*
>
> *Tommy Rose left Northampton in 1934, and went to Reading, but he had won such a place in our heart's during the two years he was manager of the Northampton Aero Club at Sywell, that we have faithfully followed his career ever since. And winning the King's Cup Air Race in 1935, and breaking Mrs Amy Mollison's Britain to the Cape inward and outward records.*

Meanwhile, Tommy's return to Fairoaks, with the Manx Cup caused *Flight* for 5 June 1947 to report:

> **FAIROAKS CELEBRATION**
> *Fairoaks Aero Club, at Chobham, Surrey, who are in the happy position of having a very pleasant premises in a country house near the airfield, had a special reason for holding their monthly dance, which took place on 31 May.*
>
> *Tommy Rose, with other members and guests, celebrated the capture of the imposing Manx Air Derby Challenge Trophy, which, with a small replica, now decorates the club bar.*
>
> *It was particularly pleasant on this fine evening to be able to extend the party on to the terrace, and the strains of RAF songs floated out over the lawns as the cup was filled with champagne, Guinness, and no doubt other ingredients as well.*

Civil flying commenced at Fairoaks in 1946 and one of the first operators was Universal Flying Services (UFS), with their Rapides on charter work, and the flying club at Fairoaks. The Midland Bank and London Passenger Transport Board flying clubs were also in residence and were soon in operation.

By 1947, Universal Flying Services (UFS) were also operating No. 18 Reserve Flying School for the Air Ministry and was developing a civil flying club.

Civilian Use
Universal Flying Services also operated the Fairoaks Aero Club, and the aerodrome was still extremely busy with De Havilland Dragon Rapides on charter work and with

UNIVERSAL FLYING SERVICES, FAIROAKS – GENERAL MANAGER

flying training. The aircraft used by the civilian clubs were Tiger Moths and Auster Autocrats, and the RAF also still used the ubiquitous Tiger Moth, but these were later replaced by DHC Chipmunks, they also had a few Avro Ansons.

The Light Plane for July 1947 reported on the Fairoaks Aero Club thus:

FAIROAKS AERO CLUB
The club fleet now consists of two Magisters, three Tigers, one Taylorcraft and a Proctor V is available for dual instruction. The club membership is now rapidly approaching 300. The tennis courts at the club are now ready for play. The grass court is quite famous, as it was the one used by Miss Helen Jacobs for practice for Wimbledon when she used to be a guest of the American Ambassador, Mr Bingham, when he was a tenant of what is now the clubhouse.

The monthly dances at the clubhouse are proving an ever-increasing success. At the next one, the success of the Chairman in the Isle of Man Aerial Derby will be celebrated. The club has had a number of aerial visitors, including a 'gaggle' of five aircraft, loaded with sixteen members of the Northants Aero Club at Sywell.

Tommy Rose next attended the official opening of Southend Airport on 9 August 1947, where he won the Southend Speed Cup (and £50) at 178 mph in G-ADGP and *The Aeroplane* for 15 August 1947 reported on the event:

SUNNY SOUTHEND
PERFECT WEATHER AND A WIDE SELECTION OF EVENTS MARKED SOUTHEND'S DISPLAY AND AIR RACES 9 AUGUST
Highlight of last Saturday's International Rally and Air Races at Southend Municipal Aerodrome, was No. 54 Squadron's four Vampire flight aerobatic demonstration.

Organised by the Municipality of Southend, under the chairmanship of Alderman W. Miles CBE, JP. Proceedings started with two Arrival competitions, one for aircraft arriving from anywhere in Great Britain, and one for those coming in from abroad. Mr Nat Somers, in his Hornet Moth, won the British section, and Mr Guy Fechyer, a Belgian, the continental.

Two races were included in the programme, one for the Southend Cup and one for the Shipside Cup. The first heat for the former was run off over the 22 mile, three lap course before lunch. Eleven aircraft took part, the first five of which Mr R.R. Paine, in a Miles Hawk Trainer, Lieutenant Commander Paul Godfrey in a BA Swallow, Mr Nat Somers in a Hornet Moth, Mr C.R. Jackson in a Miles Magister, and Mr Tommy Rose in his Hawk Speed Six, qualified for the finals.

Next on the programme was to have been the first heat for the Shipside Cup Race, but entries had been most disappointing. The heats were therefore scratched, and the four Austers competing did so at this stage.

FLIGHT LIEUTENANT THOMAS 'TOMMY' ROSE DFC

The race, three laps over a five mile course was won by Mr Hugo Parsons, Chief Flying Instructor of the Southend Flying School.

The Southend Cup was won by R.R. Paine in the Hornet, closely followed by the Swallow, the Hawk Speed Six and the TK.2 did not get a place, however Tommy Rose won the Southend Air Speed Cup prize for the fastest time, at a speed of 178 mph.

It was while Tommy Rose was working for Universal Flying Services (UFS) in 1947, that he first became acquainted with the charms of Alderney in the Channel Islands. UFS began operations in Guernsey carrying freight and passengers, which was also extended to Alderney, and Tommy stated some years later, 'I love this island and its people.'

On 20 October 1947, Tommy Rose accompanied two of the directors of Universal Flying Services, L. Peskin and F.F. Crocombe, to the second annual meeting of the British Air Charter Association, which came into existence on 1 August 1946, when they gave a reception and cocktail party at Londonderry House, Park Lane, Mayfair.

A very large number of leading personalities in the British air transport industry were at the party, which was hoped to become a regular feature of the aviation calendar.

Flight for 26 February 1948 reported:

UNIVERSAL FLYING SERVICES CEASE CHARTER WORK

The Board of Universal Flying Services Limited, have decided to discontinue charter operations. Mr T. Rose, former general manager of UFS Ltd, has joined Boyes, Segrave and Company of 69, Piccadilly, W1, where he is now dealing with aircraft sales and charters and is available in a consultative capacity on any matter connected with flying.

The Aeroplane for 5 March 1948 reported:

TOMMY ROSE

His many friends throughout the aircraft industry will be interested to hear that Tommy Rose is now associated with Boyes, Segrave and Co. of 69, Piccadilly, W1. He will deal with aircraft sales and charters of all sorts and will be available in a consultative capacity on any matter connected with flying. Until recently Tommy Rose was General Manager of Universal Flying Services.

Flight for 15 April 1948 reported:

DEATH OF JERRY BOYES

Captain G.E.F. Boyes, managing director of Boyes, Segrave and Company limited, died on 2 April after a short illness. Jerry Boyes will probably be remembered by many from the early flying-club movement, when he was associated with Colonel I. Edwards and Captain Guest in the formation of National Flying Services Ltd, who began work with a fleet of red and black Desoutter monoplanes at Hanworth.

UNIVERSAL FLYING SERVICES, FAIROAKS – GENERAL MANAGER

The last Miles aircraft that Tommy Rose flew – the Miles Gemini Mk.1A, G-AKKH.

On 31 March 1949, Tommy Rose attended a gathering of formers members of the RFC and RNAS held at Londonderry House, Park Lane, London, and this was reported by the press as follows.

The Aeroplane for 15 April 1949, carried a four-page article, with many photographs, under the heading *Celebrating an Anniversary* when some seven hundred former members of the RFC and RNAS met together at Londonderry House on 31 March 1949 in the first reunion of the sort which has taken place since the RFC and RNAS were merged to form the RAF, thirty-one years ago on April 1, 1918. Amongst the many attendees was Tommy Rose.

The last Miles Aircraft that Tommy Rose flew was the Miles Gemini Mk.1A, G-AKKH

On 18 July 1949, Tommy borrowed Gemini G-AKKH, from Group Captain 'Bush' Bandidt, an Australian who had been the Ministry of Aircraft Production Overseer at Miles Aircraft Ltd during the war, but had stayed on with Handley Page (Reading) Ltd, Woodley (after the orchestrated financial collapse of Miles Aircraft Ltd by its financial advisor in late 1947), for the King's Cup Air Race.

King's Cup Air Race Elmdon – 29-30 July 1949

The first of the National Air Races since 1938 was held at Elmdon, Birmingham, from 29 July 1949. The race for the King's Cup took place on 30 July. Tommy Rose, flying the Miles Gemini G-AKKH, was unplaced.

Thirty-six aircraft competed in this handicap event for the King's Cup and for prize money offered by the Royal Aero Club. Three heats (£25 for each winner) were flown on the Saturday afternoon and the final followed in the evening. After the first lap of Heat One, J. Somers in his Gipsy Major Gemini II came first with a speed of 165 mph, he was followed by A. Cole in the Comper Swift (128 mph), P. Fillingham in a Chipmunk (139.5 mph), and the scratch man, Ron Paine, flying the Hawk Speed Six (185 mph), qualified for the final, Tommy Rose, in a Gemini, came in eighth, but could not gain a place in the final.

FLIGHT LIEUTENANT THOMAS 'TOMMY' ROSE DFC

The final was won by J. Somers in a Gemini III (164.25 mph), second was Ron Paine in the Hawk Speed Six (164.25 mph), and third was A. Cole in a Comper Swift (126 mph).

The overall impression given by the organisers was that there were plenty of thrills as the aircraft turned steeply at low level, but there was a disappointingly small crowd of spectators. Among the spectators was Mr F.G. Miles, and his brother George, who watched the aeroplanes bearing their name take four of the five places in the King's Cup Air Race.

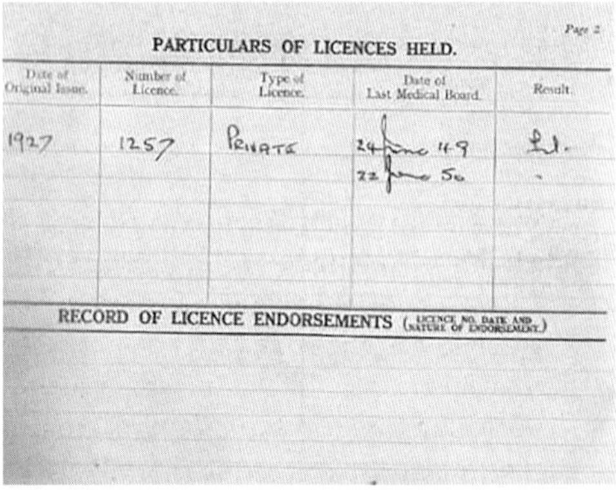

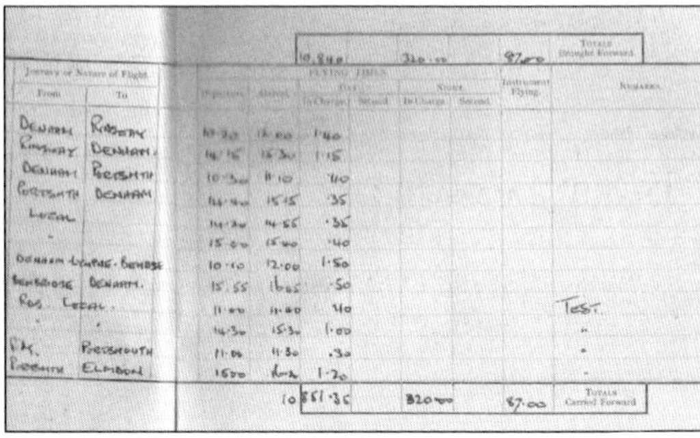

Many were disappointed that Tommy Rose failed to qualify in the final as he was the only former winner to take part, and Miss R.M. Sharpe was the only woman in the race.

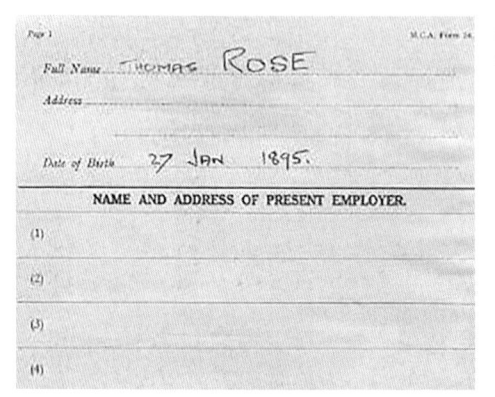

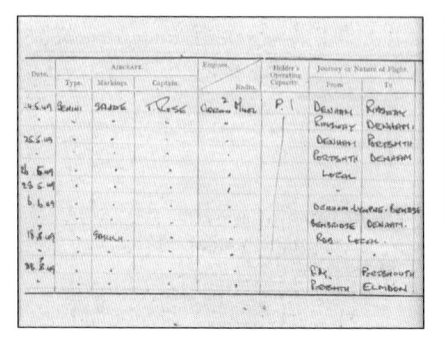

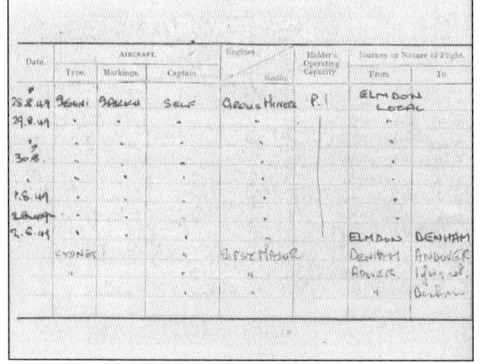

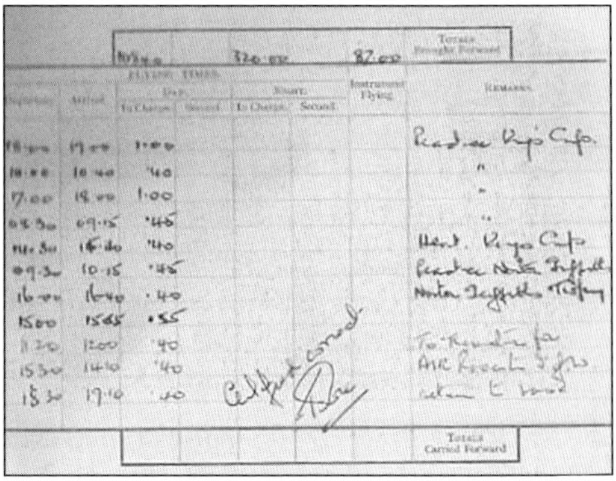

UNIVERSAL FLYING SERVICES, FAIROAKS – GENERAL MANAGER

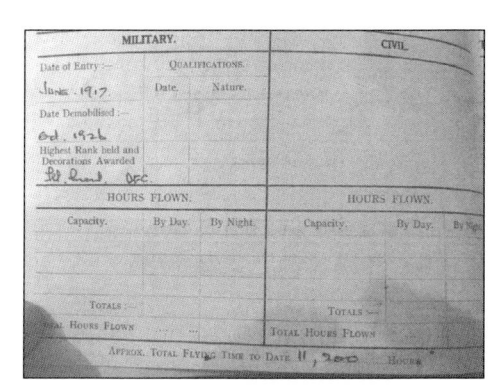

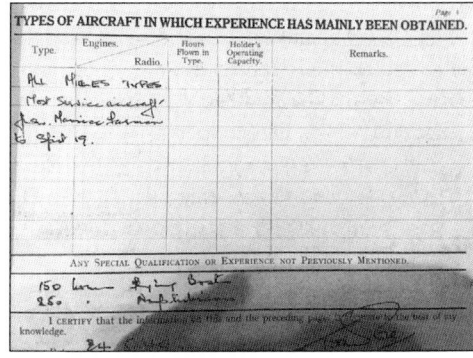

Pages from Tommy Rose's last pilot's logbook, the only one known to have survived.

Group Captain Peter Townsend, flying the Miles Whitney Straight, entered by Princess Margaret, also failed to get into the final.

However, on 1 August, Tommy Rose flew in the race for the Norton Griffiths Challenge Trophy in the Miles Gemini G-AKKH, but in a field of six starters, including Jim Mollison, he could do no better than finish in last place.

Although this had been Tommy Rose's last King's Cup Air Race, it was not to be his last competitive race. Tommy Rose was now aged fifty-four and he was possibly realising that perhaps this was time to consider retiring from flying altogether.

It will be seen from Tommy Rose's logbook, that he returned G-AKKH to Denham on 2 August 1949, but the reason for this is unclear.

Tommy Rose's last flight

Tommy Rose made his last flight, on 21 August 1949, not in a Miles aircraft, but in a GAL 42 Cygnet II, G-AGAU, which he borrowed from Denham Air Services Ltd, so

G-AGAU as flown by J.A. Mollison, who made a brief return to air racing in 1949 in the King's Cup Air Race, with the pale blue GAL 42 Cygnet II called 'Dumbo'. (*F.G. Swanborough*)

that he could compete in the Thruxton Air Races. He collected it from Denham and flew to Thruxton, Wiltshire, home of the Wiltshire Flying Club, who had organised Thruxton Air Races.

Flight for 25 August 1949 reported on the Thruxton Air Races, Tommy Rose's last race, thus:

> *A very lengthy programme was planned, including three different Auster Races (Mk.Is, Mk.Vs and Autocrats), around a good course visible at all times in each case. Four laps totalling twenty miles were flown in each case.*
>
> *The events would have been more interesting if flown concurrently, and the four, two and two entries respectively would not have caused dangerous congestion.*
>
> *The main race to Totland Bay on the Isle of Wight and back, a distance of seventy-five miles, for the Wiltshire School's Trophy, was a handicap event which received an excellent entry of twenty-three aircraft, including several King's Cup competitors. The winner was D. Jemmett of Wolverhampton in a Magister, Tommy Rose was a good second in the Cygnet and Flight Lieutenant Thompson in another Magister was third.*

So, on 21 August 1949, and with the Cygnet safely returned to Denham, Tommy Rose finally hung up his flying helmet and retired from flying, with a grand total of 11,252.85 hours.

The real reason that Tommy Rose gave up flying in 1949 is not known, as he had passed his aviation medical on 24 June 1949, and again on 22 June 1950, which was his last flying medical, so it couldn't have been on medical grounds, however, he was no longer a young man and quite possibly he was finding it difficult to find a sponsor or aircraft to borrow, also, he was probably disappointed with the lack of success in the 1949 flying season, and he then realised that his time had finally come to retire, confident he had done his best to promote flying to those who followed him. He had been flying continuously for over thirty-two years, which was a real achievement.

This was the end of Tommy Rose's illustrious flying career, the highlights of which was coming first in the King's Cup Air Race in 1935, and then beating the records to Cape Town, in both directions, in 1936. In 1947 he had also won the Manx Air Derby.

Tommy Rose's final move, in late 1949, was to be to Alderney, in the Channel Islands, where he and his wife, Billie, took over the tenancy of The Grand Hotel.

Alderney, an island of natural beauty, so recently reclaimed from the nightmare Nazi occupation, with all its attendant horrors, had now returned to its natural charm, sandy beaches, azure sea, and the most friendly people Tommy Rose had ever met. He, like many others, fell in love with the island of Alderney, just three miles long and one and a half miles wide.

Tommy and Billie wanted to be part of this new future, full of hope, so Tommy became hotel manager, with Billie helping in the kitchen and managing the domestic side of The Grand Hotel.

UNIVERSAL FLYING SERVICES, FAIROAKS – GENERAL MANAGER

Tommy Rose and Billie outside The Grand Hotel, Alderney, in the early 1950s.

Chapter 18

The Alderney Years 1949–1968
Hotel Manager, Member of the States of Alderney

'I feel we are all islands – in a common sea.'
— Anne Morrow Lindbergh

This is the last chapter in the life of Tommy Rose, but before I start, I must ask a few questions. Why did Tommy Rose and his wife choose Alderney to retire to, and why did he give up flying at the early age of fifty-four after his last competitive air race? These are questions I cannot answer despite much trying. Perhaps like many people, including myself, landing on Alderney for the first time, creates such an impression on you, that you can't help falling in love with the island.

Tommy Rose's arrival in Alderney coincided with that of Universal Flying Services (UFS), which had begun charter operations to Guernsey in 1947 carrying freight and passengers to Guernsey and Alderney. UFS also undertook a charter to the Channel Islands, on 22 July 1947, when an Alpha Romeo motor car (which weighed 18 cwt), was flown there in a Miles Aerovan, to take part in a hill-climb.

Meanwhile, between May and September 1947, the Grand Hotel had been extensively renovated by the British Government (at a cost of over £7,000), and then put up for sale by Monks at Bridgewater, Somerset. Staff were sought to help run the hotel and an advertisement was placed in the *Western Daily Press* for a company or individual to buy the hotel. A management company was set up on Alderney by the Grand Hotel

From left to right: Jim Mollison, R.H. Mcintosh and Tommy Rose. (*Guernsey Weekly Press*, 14 June 1950)

THE ALDERNEY YEARS 1949–1968

(Alderney) Limited, and it was this company that subsequently employed Tommy Rose and his wife.

Whilst in Guernsey, during one of his visits, Tommy Rose stayed at La Fregate Hotel at St Peters Port, then owned by Mr and Mrs George Hawes, who were very well placed to explain to Tommy Rose, in realistic terms, the full implications of taking on a licenced premises.

Working as their head chief was Karl Loderer, who, together with his wife Margaret, later became lifelong friends of Tommy Rose and Billie, and it was Karl and George Hawes, who first alerted Tommy to the possibility of becoming a tenant for the Grand Hotel (Alderney) Limited, who were looking for a manager to run the Hotel, that would become available towards the end of 1949. The Hawes' were able to give Tommy Rose and his wife Billie a reference and this, together with a couple of other references enabled Tommy Rose and Billie to take over the lease for the Grand Hotel.

The Grand Hotel was situated in a prominent position overlooking the harbour with one of the most delightful views, as well as providing some of the most outstanding sunsets.

The hotel boasted ample facilities, twenty-four bedrooms with modern facilities, most of which had verandas and lovely views. Some rooms had private bathrooms and showers, a great luxury in those days. There was also a ballroom, tennis courts, a billiard room, two beautifully appointed bars, and a 'silver service' restaurant, all set in just over three and a half acres. The hotel was all part of the island's concerted effort to encourage tourism and to improve its future prospects.

It would be a major step from flying and all things related to aviation, but with Billie, Tommy Rose felt this was their best option to ease into a 'quieter life'. He had, in the past, full experience of managing several flying clubs, and was familiar with the licensed trade from his time as the flying representative for Seagers Gin.

Advertisements began appearing in national newspapers to promote 'Alderney's bracing air, fishing, bathing, old world charm, and scenery'. The British public were keen to get back to normal, to start to look forward to a bright new future with family holidays, and Alderney, as well as Jersey and Guernsey, provided the idyllic destination. On the darker side, the tourists would also be able to see at first-hand what effects a German invasion might have had on England if it had ever been invaded.

The Grand Hotel was an unusual building, built like a fort and by no means an architectural masterpiece in its design, but in some ways that was its appeal. Once inside, its unattractive exterior gave way to a warm and sunny ambiance during the day, and a sunset that seemed to permeate the whole building, and an attractive and romantic candlelit charm at night.

The Grand Hotel provided good food and service, with well-chosen varied menus, locally grown vegetables, milk, cream and eggs from local farms, as well as two comfortable bars, well stocked with drinks and cigarettes at half the price paid in England. There was also two comfortable lounges and, in the 1950s, a television was added to one of the lounges.

The Grand Hotel had many memories for the Islanders and visitors alike and was lovingly remembered by all who knew it. However, it eventually became so run down and almost unusable towards the end of 1959/1960 and sadly, it was demolished after a devastating fire on 20 March 1981.

By mid-1949, the *Daily Mirror* was advertising Alderney as 'the Island of sunshine, the place for carefree holidays.' Day trips were made available from Weymouth and Torquay, which posed the question 'why not try a sample visit?' A brochure was made available from the 'Tourist and Publicity Committee' on Alderney.

Tommy said: 'I love this island, and its people. I think Alderney is the only place in which to live, and I hope to be able to spend the rest of my life here' – which, of course he did.

So, in late 1949, Tommy Rose and Billie took over the tenancy of the Grand Hotel, where they became extremely popular, and it was said of his personality that 'Tommy Rose likes everybody'.

The Grand Hotel, Alderney October 1949 – December 1954
Daily Herald for Wednesday, 19 April 1950 reported:

> **SEND OFF**
> *I have news of Tommy Rose, probably the greatest test pilot of all time. Tommy Rose, now fifty-five, retired from flying at the end of the war, after having clocked some 10,000 hours of actual test flying* (it was, in fact, approximately 11,200 hours total flying hours – SC), *the only test pilot in the world to have reached that total. Now he has taken over the Grand Hotel in Alderney, in the Channel Isles. He sends me his impressions of the island, which he describes as having 1,200 inhabitants and eleven pubs and there is one policeman, who comes over from Guernsey for a month's tour and is seen aboard the aircraft on his departure by the eleven licensees and the band of the Salvation Army,*

Bognor Regis Observer for Saturday, 16 October 1950 reported:

> *Frequent visitors to the village* (Yapton – SC) *were Tommy Rose and Billie Rose, the famous airman. At one time Tommy Rose held the record to South Africa. A friend recently on a tour in the Channel Isles, tells me the Roses are now proprietors of the Grand Hotel in Alderney.*

On 18 January 1952, Elizabeth Ann Rose, Tommy Rose's only child, married Rudolph Ivor Gordon Hale. Margaret Rose, Tommy Rose's first wife, chose not to attend the wedding, neither did Tommy Rose, which must have been very disappointing for Elizabeth.

Gordon and Elizabeth Ann Rose had two children, William and Anna (Tommy's grandchildren), but the marriage was dissolved in 1982.

On Monday 28 December 1953, the *Guernsey Evening Press* reported:

> **COCKTAIL PARTY**
> *Mr and Mrs Tommy Rose gave a cocktail party at the Grand Hotel to about sixty of their friends on Sunday. Among those present was Mr Peter Lee-Warner, fresh from his triumphant ride round the world on a bicycle,*

who was shortly going to join his fiancée in Australia. The President and Mrs S.P. Herivel were present and the newly elected States member, Mr C. Kay-Mouat.

Tommy Rose stood, for a third time, in 1954 to be elected a States Member.
The Guernsey Star for Thursday, 9 December 1954 reported the views of Tommy Rose:

PEN-PICTURES OF ALDERNEY ELECTION CANDIDATES
TOURISM IS IMPORTANT
Mr Tommy Rose is, or course, the well-known airman whose name is a household word in flying circles.

Joining the old Royal Flying Corps as a pilot in the First World War, Mr Rose was one of the first to win the DFC. He stayed in the Air Force for ten years after the war and then, later, became chief test pilot for Miles aircraft.

Piloting a Miles Falcon, Mr Rose won the King's Cup Air Race in 1935 and was second in the race in 1934 and 1936. In the latter year he broke the England-to-the-Cape and the return record in the same machine.

Mr Rose was a keen rugby football player. He played for Richmond and the RAF, and in the 1924-25 season captained Somerset against the All Blacks.

He came to Alderney nearly six years ago to take charge of the Grand Hotel, and remained in this position until quite recently, when the hotel was bought by the Guernsey Brewery.

Mr Rose said he had travelled very extensively and he thinks that Alderney is the only place in which to live, and he hopes to spend the rest of his life on the island. He went on: 'The tourist industry is one of the most important items in Alderney's economy, and it is most necessary to make supreme efforts to lengthen the tourist season. I think more publicity should be directed to this end.

'I think too, that having had thirty-seven years' experience of flying, I can give useful help in matters pertaining to the airport'.

Mr Rose stood for election unsuccessfully in 1951 and 1952.

The Marais Hall Hotel January 1955 – December 1959

Tommy Rose and his wife remained at the Grand Hotel until the end of December 1954 but, by 4 March 1955, the hotel changed hands from the holding company Grand Hotel (Alderney) Limited to The Guernsey Brewery Company (1920) Limited, of South Esplanade, St Peters Port, Guernsey. The brewery installed their own manager and Tommy Rose was forced to leave.

Tommy then applied for a Liquor Licence in January 1955 for the Marais Hall Hotel and signed the contract to take over the tenancy shortly afterwards. Maris Hall had

FLIGHT LIEUTENANT THOMAS 'TOMMY' ROSE DFC

Tommy Rose and Billie behind the bar of the Marais Hall Hotel in 1958. On the top shelf can be seen several of Tommy's cups and trophies from his flying days. Photograph taken by W. Tayleur. (*Courtesy John Tayleur*)

just been sold by The Marais Hall Limited, to Ronald William Randall, one of the directors of the company known as R.W. Randall Limited, whose registered office was in St Peters Port, Guernsey. It needed redecorating in places and, while this was being undertaken, by Tommy and Billie, they stayed in T.H. White's cottage (the famous author who wrote '*The Sword in the Stone*' that was later made into the film '*Camelot*').

They opened the bar in the evening until they were ready to move in and officially open as a hotel. Billie took over the catering and staff supervision at the Maris and looked after the eight letting rooms, while Tommy ran the bar and oversaw the management of the hotel, which he later admitted had ended in financial disaster.

In December 1955, Tommy Rose stood for election as a Member of the States of Alderney and was duly elected.

Tommy Rose – Member of the States of Alderney – January 1955–1963

Tommy Rose served on the following committees for the States of Alderney:

> Agriculture and Fisheries 1955–1963
> Transport and Harbour 1955–1963 and 1966–1967
> Publicity and Entertainments 1955 -1963 and 1966–1968
> Alderney Representative on States of Guernsey Elections and Deliberations 1957–1963
> Estates and Natural Beauties 1958 and 1966–1968
> Electricity and Water Board 1958, 1960–1961 and 1966–1967
> Potato Marketing 1958
> Mignot Memorial Hospital 1959–1963 and 1966
> Guernsey / Alderney Joint Council 1962–1963

THE ALDERNEY YEARS 1949–1968

Public Works 1962–1963
Air Advisory Council 1966

An article entitled *'Alderney: a Sojourn'* by Elizabeth McNamer, was published in the *Escape from America* Magazine for August 2006, which gave an insight into life inside the Marais Hall Hotel with Tommy and Billie Rose, and this is reproduced below:

August 2006
In the summer of 1956, I needed a job, I then read an advert for 'Waitress, chambermaid, and general help wanted at the Marais Hotel in Alderney; three pounds a week plus room and board; expenses from London will be paid. Contact Tommy Rose etc'. I looked up Alderney on the map and found that it was a small island, three and a half by one mile, just six miles off the French coast.

So, on 19 June 1956, I left London and flew from Heathrow to Guernsey (my first plane trip). Next morning, early, surrounded by screeching seagulls and the turquoise sea, I sailed the twenty miles across the English Channel to Alderney. Tommy Rose met me at the harbour in his ancient motorcar and drove me to his ancient hotel in St Anne's Square, where he installed me in an ancient room and told me to take a sleep. I was not tired but was told that was what everyone did on Alderney in the afternoon. The room was very small with an old four-poster bed and thick, thick walls. Not a sound could be heard from anywhere. I looked out the small window and saw the sunlight thrown on a whitewashed wall across the way, and a water trough, which had once been used to feed animals in the middle of the deserted square, and I fell in love with the scene.

Tommy Rose was a handsome man in his early sixties. I was soon to find out why he had to import help from England. His wife was an alcoholic and she was the cook and general supervisor, he ran the bar. They were constantly rowing with each other and she used to refer to him as 'that bloody fool'. She had obviously been a beautiful woman in her youth, but now drink and cigarettes had taken their toll. She wore her pearls every day and proudly told me that her husband had given them to her on her wedding day.

Two other persons worked at the hotel, a lovely young thing called Inez, who was a secretary in London and was taking the summer off 'to find herself', and a woman called Vera, who came in to do the washing up. Inez and I were the waitresses, chambermaids and general help. We got up at seven every morning and prepared the tea to take to the guests in bed. Some of the guests stayed in an annex, which was the other side of the vegetable garden. We served breakfast of bacon, egg, sausage, tomato and mushrooms, which Mrs Rose cooked while sipping her whiskey (it was gin, Billie never drank whiskey – SC) *and smoking her cigarettes, tipping over the milk and yelling at one of us!*

There seemed to be designated days for finding fault with each of us: Vera had got the water too hot, Inez whipped the cream too much, or

I had bruised the lettuce. Mrs Rose seemed only happy when she was scolding us.

Beds had to be made in the morning and the rooms swept and dusted, with the sheets being washed in a large old stone tub at the back of the hotel. We served morning coffee in the lounge at eleven, and then set the tables for lunch. Mrs Rose always checked to see that this was done properly and that the silver had been polished. A small plane flew in every week carrying the camembert cheese from France and this was the speciality of the house, served every day at lunch after the soup, entrée and dessert.

Such was the job description for waitress and chambermaid. General help involved weeding the garden, collecting the vegetables that were needed for the day and sometimes serving drinks in the bar when Tommy Rose was taking time off. We were given two hours off every afternoon to explore the island but had to be back to serve the usual tea and cake at four, to keep the wolf from the door until dinner at six, we worked seven days a week.

Tips were put in a glass jar and shared with Vera and Mrs Rose. I never saw Mrs Rose eat, but nonetheless she was an excellent cook, and the same people returned year after year to the hotel. Mr Rose seemed very pleased to have me working for him and used to call me 'Flora McDonald'. I had no idea who she was or why he called me that. Later I learnt that she had accompanied Bonnie Prince Charlie on his boat trip to the Isle of Skye and possibly saved his life. Perhaps Tommy Rose thought of me as a saviour.

During his periods of office in the States of Alderney, Tommy Rose also gave valuable advice on matters such as the work that needed to be done to enable Alderney Airport to take modern aircraft.

On 1 March 1957, Tommy Rose and Billie bought 2, Venelle des Gaudions, St Annes, Alderney, for £650, and this was to remain their home on Alderney for the rest of their lives.

As time went by at the Marais Hall, Billie's excessive drinking started to become a real problem, Tommy's consumption of alcohol had increased too, with 'lock in's', being common.

Tommy had the reputation of being extremely generous to his friends and visitors, many an evening during these sessions resulted in very little money being taken over the bar, which obviously impacted on the profits of the tenancy. Tommy started to have financial worries, together with the difficulties of Billie's alcohol consumption. Things were descending into an abyss, with no hope of escape and with the ever-diminishing income, the fabric of Marais Hall started to deteriorate through lack of maintenance. Added to this, the house they owned in Venelles was also being neglected and routine maintenance was postponed until the Hotel started to make a profit, which of course it never did.

In 1959, Tommy Rose gave up the tenancy for reasons unknown. His years as a licenced victualler and well loved 'mine host' had ended.

THE ALDERNEY YEARS 1949–1968

Tommy Rose talking to Captain Anthony Kimmins on 'This is Your Life', Monday, 20 March 1961.

This is Your Life

Tommy Rose appeared in the popular TV series, '*This is your Life*', on Monday, 20 March 1961, when the guest was Captain Anthony Kimmins OBE (1901-1964).

Captain Anthony Kimmins, actor and film maker, was surprised by Eamonn Andrews outside the BBC Television Theatre while working on a 'mock' film set.

Anthony became a film actor, playwright and screenwriter after serving as a naval officer during the First World War. He wrote and directed several films for British comedian George Formby in the 1930s. In the 1950s his work included the Sir Alec Guinness comedy *The Captains Paradise* and the children's Smiley series of films.

Tommy Rose met Anthony at the very first King's Cup Air Race, in which they both competed in 1929.

By 1963 Tommy Rose's domestic and financial circumstances had reached rock bottom. *The Sunday Express* for 22 December 1963, describes this in graphic detail:

> **GAVE LAVISH PARTIES… NOW HE CANNOT AFFORD TO LIVE.**
> **'I AM BROKE', SAYS PIONEER TOMMY ROSE**
> *Tommy Rose, the daring air ace who boosted Britain's aviation in pioneer long-distance flights, is living almost penniless on the Channel Island of Alderney.*
>
> *Once he ran the largest hotel on the island. But the gay parties he used to give with lavish hospitality almost nightly have ended.*
>
> *Tommy, at sixty-eight, is now living with his sixty-four-year-old wife Billie in a tiny house originally bought as extra quarters for the hotel staff.*
>
> *The house is in need of repair, but there is no money to put it right – not even to stop the roof leaking.*
>
> *And the house has been mortgaged to pay off some of Tommy's many debts. The dashing flyer who hit the headlines time and again with his*

FLIGHT LIEUTENANT THOMAS 'TOMMY' ROSE DFC

daring exploits is living like this because two hotel ventures on Alderney – first the Grand and later a smaller one – ended in financial disaster.

Now the Roses only income comes from dressmaking Billie does for their friends, and an occasional job for Tommy as a casual barman in one of the island's public houses during the summer season.

CREDIT STOPPED

Shopkeepers and publicans on the island have stopped all credit. But only once has a tradesman pressed for payment. Then, one of Tommy's many friends settled the account.

All his friends try to help tactfully, when they can. Despite hard times he is still an immensely popular personality.

Wearing his RAF blazer, with a spotted muffler round his neck, Tommy Rose told me: 'I made thousands of pounds from flying in the good days, but all the money has gone. Easy come easy go, that is the real answer. And it has always been like that. Now we don't even have a pension. We can't live comfortably. We exist.'

During the trail-blazing inter war years of aviation research the debonair Tommy Rose was a famous figure. He ranked as one of the romantic pilot heroes alongside his great friends Amy Johnson and Jim Mollison.

He won the DFC in the First World War after bringing down twelve enemy planes. In the late thirties he joined Phillips & Powis Aircraft Ltd (later Miles Aircraft Ltd), as Chief Test Pilot. And in 1935 he won the King's Cup Air Race.

In 1936, at his second attempt Tommy broke Amy Johnson's London to Cape Town record by 13 hours. On the return trip he broke another record.

10,000 hours

He stayed with Miles until the end of the last war. By then he had clocked up more than 10,000 flying hours – another record.

Tommy and his wife went to Alderney fourteen years ago to run the Grand Hotel. Their hospitality brought old friends flying into Alderney throughout the summer. Now their social life is reduced to an occasional sherry with one of their island friends.

Tommy, who has recently been in hospital for a stomach operation said: 'Things may not be easy but all that matters, is that we are living on Alderney. I would rather be managing like this than be well off and living somewhere else. I have no complaints. I do not get a state pension because we did not keep up our stamps. And I cannot expect anything from Miles. They were very generous to me always. When I retired from the test flying, they gave me a sort of compensation of around £18,000 (£18,000 in 1946 is equivalent in purchasing power to about £758,828.91 in 2020 – SC). That all went in a couple of years. Things did not work out, because, let's face it, I am not a businessman.'

DID NOT PAY

'We had to give up the hotel because it did not pay. All my old friends used to come over and stay in the Summer. They paid their way in the evenings; we had these huge parties in the bar. After a round or two of drinks, all the profits soon went.'

'But I don't regret one little bit. No talking of what might have been. Now Alderney is my only interest. I have got a host of friends and that makes everything worthwhile.'

Mr Charles Richards, an Island tradesman and vice president of the States said; 'One cannot stop being a friend of Tommy's. His trouble has been that he is too good-hearted.'

Mr Frederick Miles, who was chairman of Miles Aircraft and worked closely with Tommy throughout his record-breaking years, said yesterday: 'It is a shock to hear how things are with him. He has done a tremendous service to British Aviation. I shall have to think of something we old friends can do.'

Back on Alderney, another member of the States, Mr George Paultridge said; 'People have helped Tommy a lot. But I feel the world still owes him for all he has done.'

It was around this time that some close friends tried to help Tommy and Billie by sending unknown amounts of financial help to them. There is also hearsay from Tommy Rose's daughter's family that his ex-wife Margaret heard (or maybe read about it in the *Sunday Express* newspaper) of Tommy's plight, and sent some money to them to also help out, but it has not been possible to confirm details. A neighbour of theirs also provided lunch each day to ensure they both ate, and other islanders helped with spare produce.

Ray Parkin, the new owner of the Grand Hotel, was saddened to see and hear Tommy's plight and the financial and personal pressures he was under, including the difficult time he was having coping with Billie and it was around this time that Ray suggested to Tommy that he might like to become the driver of the VW people carrier, which was used to collect the new visitors to the hotel from the airport and return them at the end of their holidays. The other part of the job involved Tommy being 'mine host' in the bar in the evening, ensuring the residents had an enjoyable time, something he had a natural flair for.

Ray later said of Tommy that he was a gregarious, fun-loving individual with a warm personality, who possessed a rare skill of bringing together complete strangers and leaving them moments later as if they had known each other for years. So much so that the new visitors, by the time they had arrived at the hotel (barely a five-minute ride away), were chatting like long lost friends, and by the evening there was a real party atmosphere amongst the new arrivals.

In 1964, Sylvia Townsend Warner, an authoress, visited Tommy Rose to see if he could help her with her research into the life of Terence Hanbury 'Tim' White (29 May 1906 – 17 January 1964). 'Tim' White was an English author and historian, known for his autobiography and his other books, who had settled on Alderney in 1946. Tommy and Billie were good friends with 'Tim', as were many other Alderney residents.

Tim White lived to see his work adapted as the Broadway musical *Camelot* (1960) and the animated film *The Sword in the Stone* (1963), both based on *The Once and Future King*.

All Tim White's life he had remained a wonderful eccentric; in Alderney he used to surprise his guests when, wearing a scarlet towelling dressing-gown like a monk's habit, he welcomed them to his brightly red-painted kitchen or, when he entertained, he gave them a meal each day in a different room so as to leave the washing up behind, or when he told them he had only tinned milk in his tea because the dog did not like the milkman!

What was not so well known was that Tommy Rose had taught Tim White to fly while he was flying instructor at the Northampton School of Flying at Sywell in 1933-1934. The *Daily Express* had launched a scheme to encourage flying, following on from the *Tatler's* successful initiative in 1931. The scheme also paid for your flying expenses if your instructor reported you as his best pupil. The scheme was in operation at Sywell and Tim White had applied for instruction.

Tommy Rose gave the following interview to Sylvia Warner:

> *Our little club had over sixty applications and I was busy from early morning to dusk giving trial lessons. They were of all sorts, male and female, and it was obvious the decision would be a difficult one. The middle of this hectic period, I heard a vintage roar and a young man arrived in an old Bentley and came into the office.*
>
> *His opening remark was, 'I have come for a trial lesson for I have decided to learn to fly for nothing. I have to be back at the school by seven o'clock and my best time for the journey should be twenty minutes'. I pointed out that there were at least six people in front of him, and that it was now four-thirty, but he appeared not to hear. I tested three more and then young Mr White came up and said the others had 'volunteered' to let him do his test before them.*
>
> *Long before his half hour was up, I realised that here was the winner. He had the hands of a horseman; his reactions were perfect and his intelligence outstanding. He was named the victor and then the road between Stowe and Sywell was burned up by his Bentley every day.*

That is not the end of the story though, as Tim White moved into a three-storeyed house, 3, Connaught Square, St Anne's, in the centre of Alderney, with a cottage next to the house, two immense greenhouses, swimming pool and a small temple. He even had an arch dedicated to Julie Andrews, who played the part of Guinevere in *Camelot* when she visited Tim and participated in his plays.

In the last paragraph of a letter to L.J. Potts, his mentor at Cambridge, on 4 April 1955, he invited her whole family to go and stay with him for the Summer… *'BUT, at the moment, I have Tommy Rose and his wife in the cottage and I have no idea when they will go. They are decorating a house here, a slow job, and might not move into it before July.'*

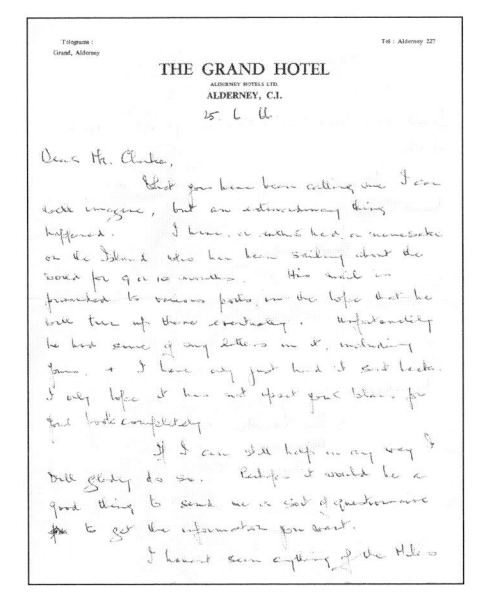

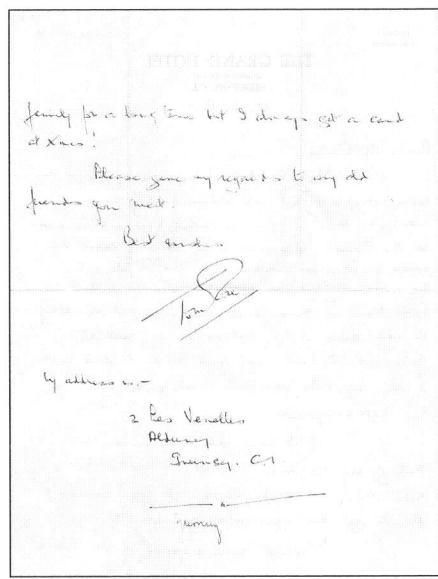

Bert was able to get Tommy Rose to talk briefly about himself while he was at Miles Aircraft, as this letter shows.

Bert Clarke, a great friend of Peter Amos, was the local Woodley aviation historian who had made an exhaustive study of the aerodrome and its personalities. He had also written to Tommy Rose in an attempt to get him to put his experiences of Woodley down on paper.

Although Bert Clarke sent a questionnaire (which was rather large), and further correspondence to Tommy, this remained unanswered, as Tommy Rose had, by then, become seriously ill.

In May 1968 Tommy Rose's health had deteriorated to such an extent, he decided to send a letter of resignation to the States of Alderney, giving up all his States commitments as well as his position within the States of Vice-President. This notification caused an immediate constitutional problem.

A special States meeting was convened, and this took place on 16 May 1968, as reported in the *Alderney Review* for May 1968:

SPECIAL STATES MEETING
A specially convened meeting of the States of Alderney took place on 16 May, consequent upon a letter of resignation as Vice President having been received from Mr Tommy Rose, owing to ill health.

In the absence of both the President and the Vice President, due to illness, the States, after a ballot, elected Mrs Eileen Hoskins to take the chair for the meeting.

Mrs Hoskins then asked for nominations for the Vice Presidency. These nominations were Mr Leslie Wells, who was Vice President last year and

FLIGHT LIEUTENANT THOMAS 'TOMMY' ROSE DFC

LES VENELLES,
ALDERNEY,
CHANNEL ISLANDS.
PHONE ALDERNEY 176.

July 25th 1966

Dear Mr Clarke,

On turning out my late husband's effects, I came across some letters of yours and that long questionaire – this latter I am afraid has not been answered, he had been very ill for the last 2 years. He many times said he would try to do it.

You may have now finished your book but if you haven't I am afraid I cannot help you very much (I only came into his life at the end of 1933 when we went to Northampton) except to tell you "Flight Lt." is correct and he was Major Rose, O.C. Aerodrome Company, 6th Batt. Royal Berks, which you will know started as "Home Guard". (during the last war)

I have a rotten memory for small things and was chiefly concerned with him getting down safely. I have tried to find his log books – but realised now that we haven't seen them during spring cleaning for many years, we have moved about so much since selling Foxen House. The only one I have is his latest one which only covers 1949 his last year in flying, at the end of that year we came over here.

I am sure he was very sorry not to be able to help you.

Would you like your questionaire back and "Introduction to Tommy"

Yours sincerely
Billie Rose
(widow of Tommy Rose)

(*Bert Clarke, via Peter Amos*)

Major C. Basham. After some discussion, a ballot was taken resulting in Mr Wells being elected (5 votes), with Major Basham obtaining three votes.

Tommy Rose died on 20 June 1968 and Billie died on 18 May 1979.

Tommy Rose's death

Tommy Rose died at 10.30 am on 20 June 1968 after a courageous fight with intestinal carcinoma. About fifty years ago, people with this type of cancer were typically operated on to remove their tumour, if possible, and surgery is still the mainstay of treatment today. But, in those days, little was known how best to use chemotherapy or radiotherapy for this condition.

Tommy Rose also suffered from myocardial degeneration, and this could have been picked up in Tommy Rose's last flying medical. This could have been the primary reason for him giving up flying completely on 21 August 1949. Tommy Rose's mother Annie died of cardiac failure in 1911 at the age of just forty-one years, which might indicate Tommy Rose had a predisposition to cardiac problems exacerbated by his (as the doctors would say today) lifestyle choices.

Harold Best-Devereux, an avid light aviation enthusiast and once chairman of the Popular Flying Association, said that *'Tommy Rose was a wonderful figure in aviation'*, and he went on to say:

> *He had a great liver and was a great liver – indeed he needed it to cope with all the booze he could put away. He was well known for the volume of alcohol he could imbibe in an evening, as were many of his contemporaries, it was a feature of the Edwardian era Tommy Rose grew up in, he, however, never appeared intoxicated – probably became immune to the effects as some people do. But this was added to by the cigarette consumption, Tommy Rose was a lifelong smoker, as many people of his generation were, again it was a sign of the times he grew up in. All in all, given everything Tommy Rose had faced during his life, he did very well to get to seventy-three.*

Tommy Rose was loved by all who met him, and no one in all my research had anything detrimental to say about him. He was particularly known as a good-hearted humourist, whose generosity was his downfall. Sometimes his judgement became rather blurred, as when he decided to leave his then wife Margaret and their 3-year-old daughter; in deciding not to go to Elizabeth's wedding in 1952, and never meeting his grandchildren Anna and William. He lived his life in the 'fast lane', a pioneer of early aviation, promotor of the early flying clubs, regular participant in air races, a Chief Test Pilot, true gentleman, raconteur, bon viveur and a man who achieved so much in his life from such humble roots, being born on a farm in Hampshire in the reign of Queen Victoria.

FLIGHT LIEUTENANT THOMAS 'TOMMY' ROSE DFC

The following extract was taken from the *Alderney Review*, Volume 2, No. 24, June 1968:

The Funeral
The funeral of Flight Lieutenant Tommy Rose DFC took place at St Anne's Church, Alderney, on Saturday, 22 June 1968 at 3.30pm.

Tommy Rose's widow, Mrs Billie Rose, headed the large congregation. Group Captain E.F. Odoire DFC, AFC, represented the Air Force Board and was therefore in uniform with decorations.

Mr C.J. Richards BEM, was at the organ and the St Anne's Church choir were in attendance. The service was taken by the Reverend John Trevithick, assisted by Captain C.H. Richards MBE (Lay Reader). Mr Trevithick was a Methodist minister who officiated in the absence of the Vicar, Reverend Kenneth Cadman, who was on holiday.

Mr Trevithick, in a moving tribute to Tommy Rose, said the keynote to his character and his whole life was his generous nature. 'It was his generous nature, with no thought for his own safety, which inspired his outstanding bravery as a pilot in World War I, earning him the decoration of the Distinguished Flying Cross. It was his generous nature that inspired his intrepid work as a Chief Test Pilot throughout World War II'.

The minister concluded: 'The Lord loves a cheerful giver. May all the trumpets sound for him on the other side!'

When Tommy Rose died, he was a serving member of the States of Alderney, and its immediate past Vice-President. The States and the Jurats were fully represented, together with representatives of Alderney's other official bodies and organisations.

Distinguished representatives from the mainland were also present. Great numbers of private mourners in the church were eloquent of Tommy's very wide circle of friends on the island.

The service of committal was brief, but very moving. Group Captain Odoire scattered earth on the coffin and then saluted, as the last tribute from the Service of which Tommy Rose was such a distinguished member.

The Royal Air Force ensign flanking the open grave, with a great bank of floral offerings a background, also ensured that fitting and final tribute was paid to the memory of Flight Lieutenant Tommy Rose, Distinguished Flying Cross.

The following are a selection of Obituaries from the National and local press at the time.

OBITUARIES
The Times Friday, 21 June 1968 reported:

FLIGHT LIEUTENANT TOMMY ROSE
WELL-KNOWN TEST PILOT
Flight Lieutenant Tommy Rose, DFC, formerly chief test pilot for Miles Aircraft Limited, and winner of the King's Cup Air Race in 1935, died

yesterday in Alderney at the age of seventy-three. He was for many years a well-known figure in flying circles.

The race of 1935 was a two-day event, and the final was a triumph for the designs of that pioneer of light aircraft F.G. Miles. Rose, in a Falcon Six, won at 176.28 mph, followed by two Hawk Trainers.

The following year in the same aircraft, he flew to the Cape in three days 17 hrs and 37 min, bettering Amy Mollison's solo time which had remained unapproached since 1932.

Rose was born 27 January 1895, at Chilbolton, Hampshire, served with distinction during the 1914-1918 War, first with the Royal Flying Corps and later with the RAF. He accounted for more than twelve enemy aircraft and won the DFC. After leaving the service he flew all over the world as a commercial pilot.

Flight International for 27 June 1968 reported:

TOMMY ROSE
We record with regret that Flight Lieutenant 'Tommy' Rose, DFC, who in 1935 won the King's Cup Air Race in a Miles Falcon Six and the following year set up a London – Cape Town solo record in the same aircraft, died last Thursday, 20 June, in Alderney, CI, at the age of seventy-three.

He served in the RFC and the RAF in the First World War, accounting for more than twelve enemy aircraft and winning the DFC; then after leaving the Service he flew all over the world as a commercial pilot. He had a long association with Phillips and Powis Aircraft, who built many of the F.G. Miles' designs, and later with Miles Aircraft. From 1947 to 1949 he was general manager of Universal Flying Services.

Reading Evening Post for 28 June 1968 reported:

THE ACE PILOT FOUND RECORD FLIGHTS BORING
Flight Lieutenant Tommy Rose – ace pilot holder of the Distinguished Flying Cross and man of mirth – did as much as anyone to put Reading on the air maps of the world.

When he died last weekend he left behind a personal legacy of courage, a legend of achievement – and hundreds of friends.

He was born on 27 January 1895 at Chilbolton, Hampshire, with a love of adventure, and flying was in his blood.

He served with distinction during the First World War, first with the Royal Flying Corps and later in the new-fangled Royal Air Force.

The young Tommy Rose spread his wings, and his flying prowess in the air accounted for twelve enemy aircraft in the 1914-1918 war. These feats gained him the DFC.

FLIGHT LIEUTENANT THOMAS 'TOMMY' ROSE DFC

When he left the RAF, he flew all over the world as a commercial pilot and had a long association with Phillips and Powis Aircraft Limited of Reading.

The Reading firm built many of the F.G. Miles designs, and Tommy Rose was later to join Miles Aircraft Limited to begin a career in which he tested large numbers of new training machines.

He became chief test pilot for Miles Aircraft in late 1939, but one of his greatest feats was wining the King's Cup race in 1935. This he accomplished in a Miles Falcon Six at an average speed of 176.28 mph.

The race was a two-day event and the final was a triumph for the Falcon Six's designer, F.G. Miles, as well as for the pilot. The following year, in the same aircraft, Rose flew to Cape Town and back by the eastward route and broke the then record. He covered the 2,380 miles to Cairo alone in 14 hours, which was a mammoth achievement in those early days. The whole flight took 3 days 17 hours 38 mins, and he was cheered by 3,000 people on return.

Even in 1948, at the age of fifty-eight, he was still one of the most active pilots in Britain. His appearances in the King's Cup alone up to that year totalled four (six actually – SC), *and he had joined the elite band of flyers who has clocked over 11,000 flying hours.*

His many friends in Berkshire knew him not only as a brilliant pilot but as a man of no mean sense of humour. He was the coolest of men on flight records. He once said he found them so boring that he took a bag of oranges with him to fill the time. 'I peel them and eat them slowly', he said, 'I reckon it takes me about ten minutes to deal with one orange – and then one can chew the pips'.

One of the anecdotes told around Sonning is the day he was shot down in the First World War. He clambered out of his plane and stood hands on hips gazing ruefully at the bullet-ridden fuselage.

A car pulled up on a nearby road to sympathise with him. The man taking pity turned out to be King George V.

He once said he chose flying as a profession and a hobby because it was 'the only outdoor sport at which one can sit down'.

It was not generally known that Rose had been in prison – in Italy. He came down during a long flight over Italian territory in North Africa. He had no permit, was arrested and thrown into prison. Urgent telegrams to the authorities produced special permission from Marshal Balbo for his release – and for fresh petrol he needed to continue home.

And he was a man of great personal charm. When hearing townspeople contributed to the cost of a commemorative casket to mark his historic Cape flight and honoured him with a special presentation at the town hall, he offered to give free flights to the holders of four lucky admission tickets.

In 1938 he joined the flying staff at the Aero Club in Reading and became one of the instructors training Civil Air Guard and club members.

THE ALDERNEY YEARS 1949–1968

He lived in Sonning and was nearly always near or at the aerodrome in his spare time.

He later moved to Alderney in the Channel Islands, and became a member of the States, the Island's government. It was in Alderney that he died last week aged seventy-three years.

Flight Lieutenant Tommy Rose is dead. But the legend of his life, his ways and his achievements will live on for as long as people admire courage.

With regard to Tommy Rose's missing logbooks Billie later said that, after leaving Falcon House in Sonning, they moved around and during this time these went missing but, for some reason, they kept the last one, see her letter to Bert Clarke on the subject, dated 25 July 1968.

Billie later confirmed that she only came into Tommy Rose's life at the Northampton School of Flying at Sywell in late 1933 and that Tommy Rose stopped flying in 1949. At the end of that year, they arrived on Alderney.

Beatrice (Billie) Rose died eleven years after Tommy, on the 18 May 1979.

Gone but not forgotten!

Aviation Exhibition

An extract from an article believed published in the *Alderney Journal* in 1985, gave the following details of an exhibition held in the Alderney Society's Museum:

A full-size figure of the late Tommy Rose dominates the Aviation Exhibition at the Alderney Society's Museum. This was the work of the Curator Kenneth Hempel as part of the celebrations to mark the 50th Anniversary of the Channel Islands first airport in Alderney.

The model wears the original helmet, goggles and overalls worn by the record-breaking aviator, whom Alderney came to consider as peculiarly her own. Tommy, who came to live in Alderney when he retired from flying, was a very popular figure, first as a hotelier and later on as a States member and eventually Vice President. It was in fact, a real 'trompe l'oeil' as one walked into the new extension (opened 1984 by Queen Elizabeth, the Queen Mother) to see his familiar figure standing guard over a showcase of personal memorabilia. In the case is a magnificent silver casket and press cutting books, which commemorated his record-breaking flight in 1936 from Lympne in Kent to Cape Town and back in 6 days 7hrs.

The people of Reading, where for many years Tommy was Sales Manager of the Aerodrome and later Chief Test Pilot, raised a public fund in order to present him with the casket. It was eventually bequeathed to the Alderney Museum by his wife, who also died in Alderney. There

FLIGHT LIEUTENANT THOMAS 'TOMMY' ROSE DFC

Caricature by Kenneth Aitkin appeared in *Aeroplane Monthly*, October 1991, together with a brief resume of Tommy Rose's life.

is also a silver cigarette box presented to him by Phillips and Powis Aircraft Ltd, and a signed copy of 'The One and Future King' *by 'Tim' White, who describes himself on the flyleaf as Tommy's 'spiritual and rather spirituous Godfather'.*

Sadly, the life size cut out of Tommy Rose cannot now be found.

The superb caricature by the aviation artist Kenneth Aitken, and the caption below, was published in the *Aeroplane Monthly* for October 1991:

One of the most popular pilots of his day was Major Tommy Rose DFC, born on 27 January 1895 and educated at King's College School (Churcher's College, Petersfield 1907-1911, he was at King's College for three terms only – SC). As a First World War RFC pilot, Rose shot down several German aircraft. He remained in the RAF until 1927, during which time he gained four rugby caps playing against the Army and Navy.

In February 1928 Rose became a flying instructor with the Midland Aero Club at Castle Bromwich. In 1929 he became the flying representative for the Anglo-American Oil Company and in that same year, took part in his first King's Cup race, flying the SE5A, G-EBTO. In the following year's event he raced a Blackburn Bluebird G-AACC into sixth place.

On 11 February 1931, Rose left Lympne on a 'business trip' in the Anglo-American Oil Company's Avro Sports Avian G-ABIE. This unsuccessful attempt to lower the Cape record was frustrated after an undercarriage failure in Bechuanaland. On his return flight Rose left the Cape on 1 May, but sand in the engine forced him down at Luxor.

Shortly afterwards Rose fell on hard times, but in September 1933 he became manager and CFI of the Northamptonshire Aero Club at Sywell and then took up a post of sales manager for Phillips and Powis, producers of Miles aircraft at Woodley.

In 1934, he raced the Miles M.2F Hawk Major, G-ACTD, into second place in the King's Cup and in the following year he came in first in the Miles M.3B Falcon Six G-ADLC.

In February 1936 Rose had another crack at the Cape record, departing the UK in G-ADLC and reaching the Cape on the ninth, having taken 3 days 17 hr 37 min following the Imperial Airways route. The return trip took 6 days 6 hr 57 min, knocking 5 hr 20 min off the record. That year Rose took second place in the King's Cup, flying Miles M.2U Hawk Speed Six, G-ADOD, at an average speed of 184.5 mph. In September 1936, he and South African Jack Bagshaw, took part in the ill-fated Schlesinger Race, departing Portsmouth for Johannesburg in the BA Double Eagle G-AEIN. They were forced to retire when an undercarriage leg failed at Cairo.

For the 1937 King's Cup Air Race, Rose flew the Miles M.2L Hawk Speed Six, G-ADGP.

In November 1939, Rose joined Phillips & Powis Aircraft as chief test pilot and made the first flights of the Miles M.20 Fighter, M.30 'X' Minor, M.25 Martinet, M.33 Monitor and M.57 Aerovan. After the war he returned to air racing and won the 1947 Manx Air Derby in G-ADGP. He died on the island of Alderney on 20 June 1968.

Tommy Rose will also be remembered each year on Alderney in the form of an air racing cup, a popular aviation event held in September each year, with the exception of 2020 and 2021 due to Covid.

It is competitive and great fun to watch. Organised by the Royal Aero Club Records, Racing and Rally Association, aircraft from around Britain compete in the 100+ mile races with Alderney's stunning rugged coastline spread out beneath. Alderney offers the perfect playground for private aviation, competitions and events, but also an ideal base for a weekend escape. The Cup, which has been commissioned by the Alderney Flying Club to recognise Tommy Rose and, as a former King's Cup winner, the Club felt it was appropriate to offer this new trophy to be awarded on the air race weekend in 2019. Over twenty aircraft from around the British Isles competed in the 100+ mile races, with the cup being awarded for 'The spirit of air racing'.

Both Alderney races involve six laps of a circuit following along the island's south coast, beyond Forts Raz and Albert and the Breakwater, around Burhou Island, the Casquets Lighthouse and due east, back to the airport.

I am sure Tommy Rose would have been delighted to be remembered in this way.

Epilogue

As this biography was being written, a remarkable discovery was made, by the most incredible of circumstances. George Burton, a friend of Peter Amos, was selling some surplus Miles Aircraft Magazines on Ebay and the buyer happened to mention in conversation that he was Tommy Rose's grandson! A family meeting was hastily arranged and I spent a very enjoyable weekend with William and his mother in 2019.

This meeting has added much valuable information, and memorabilia, to the unique story of Tommy Rose!

As I complete this biography, yet more information has come to light, this time from Nigel Gaudion, Tommy Rose's godson, who was given much of Tommy's memorabilia, photographs, scrap books and trophies that had once belonged to Tommy.

In December 2020, Tommy's daughter Elizabeth died, at the age of ninety-one, and was buried in the same graveyard as her mother and grandfather at the Church of St Peter, Britford, Wiltshire, in the village where she grew up.

What better way to complete Tommy Rose's Biography, other than with an autograph from Tommy Rose himself, wishing everyone *'Happy Landings'*.

Tommy Rose's daughter, Elizabeth, aged 91, and Tommy's grandson, William, in 2019. Elizabeth sadly died on 4 December 2020. (*Sarah Chambers*)

Bibliography

RAF Hendon the Birthplace of Aerial Power by Andrew Renwick
Crystal Palace Matters, the Journal of the Crystal Palace Foundation
British Armoured Car Operations in World War One by Bryan Perrett (Pen and Sword 2016)
The World War I Aviators pocket manual by Chris McNab (Casemate 2018)
No Parachute by Arthur Gould Lee (Jarrolds 1968)
The First World War in Africa by Hew Strachan (Oxford University Press 2004)
With Botha and Smuts in Africa by W. Whittall (Leonaur 2012)
Thesis by Robert M. Morley titled: *Earning their Wings, British Pilot training 1912-1918.*
Take to the Skies, Learning to fly 1916 style by Claude Grahame-White (The Macmillan Company New York 1916)
Samson and The Dunkirk Circus, 3 Squadron Royal Naval Air Service 1914-1915 by John Oliver (John Oliver 2017)
First World War in the Air by RAF Museum
The brief history of the Royal Flying Corps in World War I by Ralph Barker (Constable and Robinson Ltd 2002)
Combat Report by Bill Lambert DFC (William Kimber and Co Ltd/ Corgi 1973)
Dog Fight, Aerial Tactics of the Aces of the First World War by Norman Franks (Greenhill Books 2003)
SE5/5a Aces of World War I by Norman Franks (Osprey Publishing 2007)
Above the Trenches, The Complete record of the fighter aces and units of the British Empire Air Forces 1915-1920 by Christopher Shores, Norman Franks and Russell Guest (Grub Street 1990)
The Airman's War 1914-1918 by Peter H. Liddle (Blandford Press 1987)
Forgotten Aerodromes of World War I by Martyn Chorlton (Crecy 2014)
The History of Royal Air Force Rugby 1919-1999 by John Mace (The Royal Airforce Rugby Union 2000)
Thesis by Andrew Walters titled: *Inter war, Inter-Service friction on the North-West Frontier and its impact on the Development and application of Royal Airforce Doctrine.*
Operations in Waziristan 1919-1920 Compiled by the General Staff Army Headquarters (The Naval & Military Press Ltd 1923)
A Guide to Battles Decisive Conflicts in History by Richard Holmes and Martin Evans
The Great Government Aerodrome by Narborough Airfield Research Group (Author 2000)

FLIGHT LIEUTENANT THOMAS 'TOMMY' ROSE DFC

43 Squadron by J. Beedle (Beaumont Aviation Literature 1966)
50 Years Fly-past by Geoffrey Dorman (RAF)
Fifty Years of Brooklands by Charles Gardner (Heinemann 1956)
The RAF a Pictorial History by Bruce Robertson
Supermarine Aircraft since 1914 by C.F. Andrews and E.B. Morgan (Putnam 1981)
British Racing and Record-breaking Aircraft by Peter Lewis (Putnam 1970)
RAF Flying Training and Support Units since 1912 by Ray Sturtivant (Air-Britain 2007)
The Squadrons of the Royal Air Force & Commonwealth by James J. Halley (Air-Britain 1988)
Miles Aircraft since 1925 by Don L. Brown (Putnam 1970)
Wings over Woodley by Julian C. Temple (Aston Publications 1987)
Miles Aircraft: The Early Years 1925-1939 by Peter Amos (Air-Britain 2009)
Miles Aircraft: The Wartime Years 1939-1945 by Peter Amos (Air-Britain 2012)
Miles Aircraft: The Post-War Years 1945-1948 by Peter Amos (Air-Britain 2016)
Flight of the Mew Gull by Alex Henshaw
From Sea-Eagle to Flamingo by Neville Doyle (Neville Doyle 1991)
From Sea to Air – The Heritage of Sam Saunders by A.E. Tagg and R.L. Wheeler (Crossprint, Isle of Wight 1989)
Sywell, The story of an English Aerodrome 1928-1978 by Christopher Paul
T.H. White Letters to a Friend, the correspondence between T.H. White and L.J. Potts (Alan Sutton Publishing Ltd 1984)
Cecil Lewis an Autobiography All my Yesterdays (Element Books Ltd 1993)
Survivor's Story by Air Marshal Sir Gerald Gibbs (Hutchinson and Co Ltd 1956)
Down Africa Skyway by Benjamin Bennett
Hitchcock's Partner in Suspense by Charles Bennett
A brief history of Flying Clothing by Dr Graham Rood, paper number 2014/01.
Sigh for a Merlin by Alex Henshaw (Crecy Publishing 1996)
The *Aeroplane* and *Flight* archives (Malcolm Fillmore)
British Newspaper Archive
Surrey Airfields in the Second World War by Len Pilkington (Countryside Books 1997)
Fairoaks Airport: An Illustrated History: The First Seventy-Five Years by Michael G. Jones (Author 2013)
A History of Aviation in Alderney by Edward Pinnegar
Guernsey People by L. James Marr
Bader, The Man and his Men by Michael G. Burns (Arms and Armour 1990)

Index

Amos, Peter, vi, viii, xi, 44, 154, 156, 183–4, 200, 213–14, 235, 248, 250–52, 254, 256–7, 260–61, 263, 272, 302, 310, 312
Andrews, Eamonn, 183, 297
Anglo American Oil, ix, 66–9, 71, 80–3, 85, 87–9, 91, 93, 95–6, 99–102, 110–11, 113–14, 131, 134, 157, 198, 276, 292, 308
Ashford, Margaret, 60, 62, 72, 246
Ayr, 43

Baird, Charles Henri, 122–4
Battle of Cambrai, 43–5
Bennett, Benjamin Cape Argus, 101, 113, 312
Bennett, Charles, 141–2, 312
Bennett, Faith, 139, 142
Beverley, 42
Botha, General, 6, 10, 18–22, 270, 311
Bowles, Frank, 275
Boyes, Jerry, 284
Bradshaw, Jack, 194, 225–6
Bramham, Moor Tadcaster, 41
Brancker, Sir Sefton, 58, 66, 87–9, 93, 116–17, 130–31
British Air Charter Association, 284
British Amphibious Airlines, 118
Brook, Harold Leslie, 153
Brooklands, x, 65–70, 83–4, 89–90, 98, 100, 118, 130, 135–8, 141, 144–5, 148, 166, 173, 237, 271, 277, 312
Brown, Don, 151, 256, 262, 264, 269, 272
Brown, Winifred, 76, 91

Campbell, Bruce, 128, 279
Campbell-Black, Tom, 138, 166, 214, 225, 227, 231, 237
Campbell-Shaw, Captain Donald, 116, 120
Cazalet, R.G., 74–5, 78, 92
Churchill, Winston, 8, 255, 274
Clarke, Bert, vi, viii, 9, 37, 301
Cobham, Sir Alan, 130, 141
Colonel Cody, 4, 136
Cotton, Sidney, 33–4
Coutts Bank, viii, x, 5–8, 40
Crayston, Jack, 216

Davis, Captain Duncan, 98, 118, 124, 132, 136–8, 145, 173, 237, 271
de Havilland, Geoffrey, 126–7, 169, 179
Duchess of Bedford, 97, 105, 107, 112, 166
Dunkirk Circus, 13, 311

Everard, Lindsay, 95, 200

Farman, Maurice, x, 36–7, 43
French, Sir John, 14

Goodfellow, Lieutenant Alan 'Peter', 263
Grahame-White, Claude, 31, 36
Grosvenor Cup, 67, 73, 95
Guild of Air Pilots and Navigators, viii, 88–9, 241

Haddock, Francis, 173
Hale, Elizabeth (nee Rose), vii, 115, 134, 248, 303, 310

Hale, Rudolph Ivor Gordon, 292
Hale, William, vii, ix, 26, 64–5, 76, 93, 101, 165
Halse, Stan, 170, 214
Halton, 55, 59, 76, 79
Henderson School of Flying, 130, 148
Hendon, ix, 31, 36–7, 58–9, 65, 91, 169, 244, 311
Henshaw, Albert, 127
Henshaw, Alex, 126-7, 147, 169-70, 180, 188, 244, 312
High Test, 83, 97, 99-101, 105-108, 110, 113-14, 198
Hinkler, Herbert, 110
Home Guard, 6th Battalion of the, 249-50, 270

Isle of Man, v, 115-29, 179, 188, 274, 277, 279, 282, 283
Isle of Man Air Line, 116

James, June Jewett, 123
Johnson, Amy, 132-3, 152, 159, 178, 195, 197, 234, 237, 298
Jones, Cathcart, 105, 154, 156-7, 188, 271
Justin, John, 263

Kendall, Hugh, 263, 280
Kennedy, Hugh, Flight Lieutenant, 249, 256, 260, 262
Kimmins, Captain Anthony OBE, 297
Kings Cup Air Race, 114, 163–4, 182, 206–207, 225–6
Kingsford Smith, Charles, 140, 207
Kitchener, Lord, 14–16

Linnell, Geoffrey, 131, 133, 145–6
Linnell, Jack, 133
Llewellyn, David, 168, 199–200
Loderer, Karl, 29
Lord Thompson, 131
Lord Willoughby de Broke, 132, 136, 139, 149

Markham, Beryl, 166, 168
Marshal Balbo, 200, 207, 306
McNamer, Elizabeth, 295
Mianwali, 55
Midland Aero Club, 72–3, 75–81, 99–100, 110, 130, 198, 269, 308
Miles, Blossom, 134, 151–2, 155, 201, 234–5, 257, 264, 266, 272
Miles, F.G., 142, 151–2, 156–61, 189, 201, 235, 237, 245, 253, 257, 264, 272, 274, 286, 305–306
Miles, George, 160, 235, 249, 254, 256–62, 264
Mollison, Jim, 167–8, 287, 290, 298
Monk, Flight Lieutenant, 118, 290
Morris, Roy, 250

Nalder, Lieutenant Commander, 19, 23, 25, 27
Netheravon, 27, 55, 58–9, 61, 63, 104, 111
Newton, Charles Maurice, 131–2, 139, 145
Nicholson, William, 1, 24, 79, 159, 175, 209
No. 1 School of Aerial Flying, 43
No. 2 Aeroplane Supply Depot, 43
No. 2 School of Instruction Oxford, 31
No. 27 Squadron, 56, 58
No. 36 Squadron, 42
No. 43 Squadron, 64–5
No. 45 Squadron, 43
No. 64 Squadron, 43–6, 49
No. 68 Squadron, 41
Northampton Aero Club, 85, 124, 131, 134, 138, 145, 277, 282

Openshaw, L.P., 67

Parachutes, 35–6, 267
Parkin, Ray, vii, ix, 299
Pashley, Cecil, 151, 173
Percival, F.W., 127
Pierrepont, Claude, 71

INDEX

Powis, Charles, 151–2, 156, 158, 272
Pratts, 67–9, 81–5, 87, 94, 100–101, 114
Pregnant Percy, 45, 154, 268–9

RFC Denham, 30
Rose, Billie, 292, 295, 304, 307, 141, 158, 170
Rose, Constance, 1
Rose, Elizabeth Ann, 77, 114, 246, 292
Rose, John, 1–2, 4, 62, 78–9
Royal Aero Club, viii, ix, 40, 73, 84, 87, 125–6, 182–3, 185, 187–8, 194, 204, 207, 213, 222, 225, 230–1, 271, 279, 285, 309
Royal Naval Armoured Car Service, 6, 10, 25, 27
Rugby, ix, 29, 60–1, 66, 69, 98, 111, 178–9, 195, 211, 216, 276–7, 293, 308, 311

Samson, Charles Commander, x, 6, 8, 10, 12–14, 16–18, 109, 270, 311
Sassoon, Sir Philip, 157
Schlesinger Race, v, 141, 194, 211, 213–17, 219, 221–7, 229–33, 271, 309
Scott, C.W.A., 99, 141, 168, 224, 231–3
Seager Gin, v, 150, 164, 169, 171, 217, 291
Shelmerdine, Colonel F.C., 132, 152–3, 166, 226
Sidcot suit, 33–4
Skinner, Bill, xi, 151, 245, 249, 253–4
Slate, Captain Jimmy, 45
Smith, Victor, 214, 224, 228, 230
Smuts, General, x, 6, 10, 20, 23–7, 52, 207, 270, 311

Smythies, Major Bernard, 44
Soubry, Emile E., 114
South Carlton, 43
Supermarine, ix, 115, 122–4, 148, 250, 255, 312
Sywell, ix, v, 85, 86, 98, 118, 124, 130–49, 158, 171, 193, 198, 211, 271, 282–3, 300, 307, 309, 312

Tempest, Captain Edmund Roger, 45–6, 49–50
Townsend Warner, Sylvia, 299
Trenchard, Major H., 58, 65
Tyzack, Perry, 133
Tyzack, Samuel, 130

Universal Flying Services, 273–7, 282, 284
Upavon, 51, 58, 60
Uxbridge, 55, 58

Vaughn Thomas, Wynford, 266–7

Wakefield, C., 84, 155, 184, 186, 188
Wakefield, Lady, 155, 165, 191, 202
Wakefield, Viscountess, 186–8, 192, 208
Waller, Ken, 154, 173, 214, 225, 229–30, 254, 262, 264, 269, 271, 281
Waziristan, 52, 54–8, 311
White, Tim, 299–300, 308
Whittall, Lieutenant Commander, 18–21, 311
Whittiker, Tom, 216
Wood, Sir Kingsley, 237–8